Contents

Rainbow Cookies

Total Time Taken: 1 ¼ hours
Yield: 25 Servings

Ingredients:
- ¼ cup coconut oil, melted
- ¼ teaspoon salt
- ½ cup colourful sprinkles
- ½ cup butter, softened
- 1 ½ cups all-purpose flour
- 1 cup white sugar
- 1 egg
- 1 teaspoon baking powder
- 1 teaspoon vanilla extract

Directions:
1. Mix the butter, coconut oil and sugar in a container until fluffy and pale.
2. Stir in the egg and vanilla and mix thoroughly.
3. Fold in the flour, salt and baking powder then put in the sprinkles.
4. Drop spoonfuls of batter on a baking sheet coated with baking paper.
5. Pre-heat the oven and bake at 350F for about fifteen minutes or until a golden-brown colour is achieved on the edges.
6. *These cookies taste best chilled.*

Nutritional Content of One Serving:

Calories: 118 Fat: 6.3g Protein: 1.1g Carbohydrates: 14.8g

Raspberry Jam Cookies

Total Time Taken: 2 hours
Yield: 20 Servings

Ingredients:
- ¼ teaspoon salt
- ½ cup butter, softened
- ½ cup powdered sugar
- ½ cup seedless raspberry jam
- ½ teaspoon baking powder
- 1 ¼ cups all-purpose flour
- 1 cup almond flour
- 1 egg
- 2 tablespoons whole milk

Directions:
1. Mix the butter and sugar in a container until fluffy and creamy.
2. Stir in the egg and milk and mix thoroughly then fold in the flours, salt and baking powder.
3. Transfer the dough to a floured working surface and roll it into a slim sheet.
4. Cut 40 small cookies.
5. Preheat your oven and bake the cookies at 350F for about fifteen minutes.

6. When finished, chill the cookies and fill them two by two with raspberry jam.
7. *Serve immediately.*

Nutritional Content of One Serving:

Calories: 115 Fat: 5.7g Protein: 1.5g Carbohydrates: 14.9g

Rice Flour Cookies

Total Time Taken: 1 hour
Yield: 20 Servings
Ingredients:
- ½ cup butter, softened
- 1 teaspoon vanilla extract
- 1 egg
- ½ cup all-purpose flour
- ½ cup rice flour
- 1 teaspoon baking powder
- ¼ teaspoon cardamom powder
- ¼ teaspoon salt
- 1/3 cup white sugar

Directions:
1. Mix the butter, sugar and vanilla and stir until fluffy.
2. Put in the egg and mix thoroughly then fold in the remaining ingredients.
3. Drop spoonfuls of batter on a baking sheet coated with baking paper.
4. Preheat your oven and bake the cookies at 350F for about fifteen minutes or until a golden-brown colour is achieved on the edges.
5. *These cookies taste best chilled.*

Nutritional Content of One Serving:

Calories: 83 Fat: 4.9g Protein: 0.9g Carbohydrates: 9.1g

Rocky Road Cookies

Total Time Taken: 1 ¼ hours
Yield: 20 Servings

Ingredients:
- ¼ cup light brown sugar
- ½ cup dried cranberries
- ½ cup glace cherries, halved
- ½ cup mini marshmallows
- ½ cup walnuts, chopped
- 1 cup all-purpose flour
- 1 cup macadamia nuts, chopped
- 1/3 cup butter, softened
- 2 eggs

Directions:
1. Mix the butter and sugar in a container until creamy.

2. Put in the eggs, one at a time, then mix in the flour, followed by the remaining ingredients.
3. Drop spoonfuls of batter on a baking tray coated with baking paper.
4. Preheat your oven and bake the cookies at 350F for about fifteen minutes or until a golden-brown colour is achieved on the edges.
5. *These cookies taste best chilled.*

Nutritional Content of One Serving:

Calories: 139 Fat: 10.5g Protein: 2.6g Carbohydrates: 9.7g

Russian Tea Cookies

Total Time Taken: 1 hour
Yield: 30 Servings
Ingredients:
- ¼ teaspoon salt
- ½ cup powdered sugar
- 1 cup butter, softened
- 1 cup ground walnuts
- 1 cup powdered sugar
- 1 egg
- 1 teaspoon baking powder
- 1 teaspoon vanilla extract
- 2 cups all-purpose flour

Directions:
1. Mix the butter and sugar in a container until creamy and pale.
2. Put in the egg and vanilla and mix thoroughly then mix in the flour, walnuts, salt and baking powder.
3. Make small balls of dough and place them on a baking tray coated with baking paper.
4. Transfer the baked cookies in a container and dust them with plenty of powdered sugar.
5. *These cookies taste best chilled.*

Nutritional Content of One Serving:

Calories: 136 Fat: 8.8g Protein: 2.1g Carbohydrates: 12.9g

Salted Chocolate Cookies

Total Time Taken: 1 ½ hours
Yield: 30 Servings

Ingredients:
- ¼ cup cocoa powder
- ½ cup butter
- 1 ½ cups all-purpose flour
- 1 cup light brown sugar
- 1 teaspoon baking powder
- 1 teaspoon sea salt
- 2 cups dark chocolate chips
- 2 eggs

- 2 tablespoons coconut oil
- 2 tablespoons dark brown sugar

Directions:
1. Mix the chocolate and butter in a heatproof container over a hot water bath and melt them together until the desired smoothness is achieved.
2. Put in the coconut oil and mix thoroughly then mix in the sugars and eggs. Stir thoroughly to mix.
3. Fold in the remaining ingredients then drop spoonfuls of batter on a baking sheet coated with baking paper.
4. Preheat your oven and bake the cookies at 350F for fifteen minutes.
5. *These cookies taste best chilled.*

Nutritional Content of One Serving:

Calories: 122 Fat: 6.5g Protein: 1.7g Carbohydrates: 15.9g

Soft Baked Chocolate Cookies

Total Time Taken: 1 ½ hours
Yield: 30 Servings

Ingredients:
- ¼ cup light corn syrup
- ½ cup butter, softened
- ½ teaspoon baking soda
- ½ teaspoon salt
- 1 ¼ cups chocolate chips
- 1 cup dark brown sugar
- 1 teaspoon vanilla extract
- 2 ½ cups all-purpose flour
- 2 eggs

Directions:
1. Mix the butter and sugar in a container until pale and creamy.
2. Put in the corn syrup, eggs and vanilla and mix thoroughly.
3. Fold in the flour, salt and baking soda then put in the chocolate chips and mix thoroughly.
4. Drop spoonfuls of batter on baking trays coated with baking paper and preheat your oven and bake the cookies at 350F for about fifteen minutes or until a golden-brown colour is achieved and crisp on the edges.
5. *These cookies taste best chilled.*

Nutritional Content of One Serving:

Calories: 133 Fat: 5.5g Protein: 2.0g Carbohydrates: 18.9g

Soft Chocolate Chip Cookies

Total Time Taken: 1 ¼ hours
Yield: 20 Servings

Ingredients:
- ½ cup butter, softened

- ½ teaspoon salt
- 1 cup dark chocolate chips
- 1 cup light brown sugar
- 1 teaspoon baking powder
- 2 cups all-purpose flour
- 2 eggs

Directions:

1. Mix the butter and sugar in a container until fluffy and pale.
2. Put in the eggs, one at a time, stirring thoroughly after each addition.
3. Fold in the remaining ingredients then drop spoonfuls of batter on a baking sheet coated with baking paper.
4. Pre-heat the oven and bake at 350F for about fifteen minutes or until a golden-brown colour is achieved on the edges.
5. *These cookies taste best chilled.*

Nutritional Content of One Serving:

Calories: 148 Fat: 6.8g Protein: 2.3g Carbohydrates: 20.8g

Soft Ginger Cookies

Total Time Taken: 1 ¼ hours
Yield: 30 Servings

Ingredients:

- ¼ teaspoon salt
- ¾ cup butter, softened
- 1 cup white sugar
- 1 egg
- 1 teaspoon baking soda
- 1 teaspoon ground ginger
- 1 teaspoon vanilla extract
- 1/2 teaspoon cinnamon powder
- 2 cups all-purpose flour
- 3 tablespoons molasses

Directions:

1. Mix the flour, salt, baking soda and spices in a container.
2. In a separate container, mix the butter and sugar and mix thoroughly. Put in the egg and molasses and stir thoroughly until blended. Stir in the vanilla.
3. Fold in the flour mixture then drop spoonfuls of batter on baking trays coated with baking paper.
4. Preheat your oven and bake the cookies at 350F for about fifteen minutes or until it is aromatic and appears golden brown.
5. *These cookies taste best chilled.*

Nutritional Content of One Serving:

Calories: 105 Fat: 4.8g Protein: 1.1g Carbohydrates: 14.6g

Spiced Apple Cookies

Total Time Taken: 1 ¼ hours
Yield: 20 Servings

Ingredients:
- ¼ teaspoon salt
- ½ cup coconut oil, melted
- ½ cup light brown sugar
- ½ teaspoon cinnamon powder
- 1 ½ cups all-purpose flour
- 1 egg
- 1 teaspoon baking powder
- 2 red apples, cored and diced
- 2 tablespoons water

Directions:
1. Mix the oil, sugar and egg in a container until fluffy and light.
2. Put in the water and mix thoroughly then mix in the flour, salt, baking powder and cinnamon.
3. Put in the apples then drop spoonfuls of batter on a baking tray coated with baking paper.
4. Preheat your oven and bake the cookies at 350F for about fifteen minutes or until it is aromatic and appears golden brown.
5. *These cookies taste best chilled.*

Nutritional Content of One Serving:

Calories: 108 Fat: 5.8g Protein: 1.3g Carbohydrates: 13.4g

Spiced Chocolate Cookies

Total Time Taken: 1 ¼ hours
Yield: 20 Servings

Ingredients:
- ¼ cup cocoa powder
- ¼ teaspoon salt
- ½ cup butter, softened
- ½ cup dark brown sugar
- ½ teaspoon baking powder
- 1 ¼ cups all-purpose flour
- 1 egg
- 1 teaspoon all-spice powder
- 2 tablespoons honey

Directions:
1. Mix the butter, brown sugar and honey in a container until creamy and fluffy.
2. Put in the egg and mix thoroughly then fold in the flour, cocoa powder, salt, baking powder and all-spice powder.
3. Transfer the dough to a floured working surface and roll it into a slim sheet.
4. Cut the dough using a cookie cutter of your choices and move the cookies to a baking sheet coated with baking paper.

5. Pre-heat the oven and bake at 350F for about twelve minutes.
6. *These cookies taste best chilled.*

Nutritional Content of One Serving:

Calories: 95 Fat: 5.0g Protein: 1.4g Carbohydrates: 11.9g

Sugar Covered Cookies

Total Time Taken: 1 ½ hours
Yield: 30 Servings

Ingredients:
- ¼ teaspoon salt
- ½ cup rice flour
- ½ cup white sugar
- ½ teaspoon baking powder
- 1 cup butter, softened
- 1 cup powdered sugar
- 1 egg
- 1 teaspoon vanilla extract
- 2 cups all-purpose flour
- 2 egg yolks

Directions:
1. Mix the butter and sugar in a container until fluffy and pale.
2. Put in the egg and egg yolks, as well as the vanilla and mix thoroughly.
3. Stir in the rice flour, flour, salt and baking powder in a container.
4. Make small balls and place them on baking trays coated with baking paper.
5. Flatten the cookies then preheat you even and bake at350F for about fifteen minutes or until a golden-brown colour is achieved on the edges.
6. Move the cookies to a container and dust them with powdered sugar.
7. *These cookies taste best chilled.*

Nutritional Content of One Serving:

Calories: 128 Fat: 6.7g Protein: 1.4g Carbohydrates: 15.9g

Thin Coconut Cookies

Total Time Taken: 1 hour
Yield: 20 Servings
Ingredients:
- ¼ cup all-purpose flour
- ¼ teaspoon salt
- ½ cup butter, softened
- ½ cup white sugar
- 1 ¾ cups shredded coconut
- 2 egg whites

Directions:

1. Combine all the ingredients in a container until creamy. Put the dough in your refrigerator until firm.
2. Make small balls of dough and place them on baking trays coated with baking paper.
3. Flatten the cookies and preheat you even and bake at350F for about fifteen minutes or until a golden-brown colour is achieved and crisp on the edges.
4. *These cookies taste best chilled.*

Nutritional Content of One Serving:

Calories: 92 Fat: 7.0g Protein: 0.8g Carbohydrates: 7.3g

Toffee Apple Cookies

Total Time Taken: 1 ¼ hours
Yield: 20 Servings

Ingredients:
- ¼ teaspoon salt
- ½ cup almond flour
- ½ cup butter, softened
- ½ cup toffee bits
- ½ teaspoon baking soda
- 1 ½ cups all-purpose flour
- 1 cup light brown sugar
- 2 apples, peeled and cored
- 2 egg yolks

Directions:
1. Mix the butter and sugar in a container until fluffy and pale.
2. Put in the egg yolks and mix thoroughly then mix in the almond flour, flour, baking soda and salt in the container.
3. Put in the eggs and toffee bits then drop spoonfuls of batter on a baking tray coated with baking paper.
4. Preheat your oven and bake the cookies at 350F for about fifteen minutes or until a golden-brown colour is achieved on the edges.
5. *These cookies taste best chilled.*

Nutritional Content of One Serving:

Calories: 129 Fat: 5.8g Protein: 2.1g Carbohydrates: 17.8g

Toffee Chocolate Chip Cookies

Total Time Taken: 1 ¼ hours
Yield: 30 Servings

Ingredients:
- ¼ cup white sugar
- ½ cup dark chocolate chips
- ½ cup light brown sugar
- ½ teaspoon salt
- 1 cup butter, softened

- 1 cup chopped toffee pieces
- 1 teaspoon baking powder
- 2 ½ cups all-purpose flour
- 2 eggs

Directions:
1. Mix the flour, salt and baking powder in a container.
2. In a separate container, mix the butter and sugars and mix thoroughly. Put in the eggs and stir thoroughly until blended.
3. Put in the flour then fold in the toffee pieces and chocolate chips.
4. Drop spoonfuls of batter on a baking sheet coated with baking paper.
5. Preheat your oven and bake the cookies at 350F for about fifteen minutes or until a golden-brown colour is achieved on the edges.
6. *These cookies taste best chilled.*

Nutritional Content of One Serving:
Calories: 129 Fat: 7.3g Protein: 1.7g Carbohydrates: 14.5g

Triple Chocolate Cookies

Total Time Taken: 1 ¼ hours
Yield: 30 Servings

Ingredients:
- ¼ cup cocoa powder
- ¼ teaspoon baking soda
- ¼ teaspoon salt
- ½ cup dark chocolate chips
- ½ cup dark chocolate chips, melted
- 1 ½ teaspoons baking powder
- 1 cup butter, softened
- 1 cup light brown sugar
- 1 teaspoon vanilla extract
- 2 cups all-purpose flour
- 2 eggs
- 2 tablespoons whole milk

Directions:
1. Mix the butter and sugar in a container until fluffy and pale.
2. Put in the melted chocolate, eggs and vanilla, as well as the milk.
3. Fold in the flour, cocoa powder, baking powder, baking soda and salt then put in the chocolate chips.
4. Drop spoonfuls of batter on a baking sheet coated with baking paper.
5. Preheat your oven and bake the cookies at 350F for about fifteen minutes or until the cookies are golden-brown on the edges.
6. *These cookies taste best chilled.*

Nutritional Content of One Serving:
Calories: 129 Fat: 7.7g Protein: 1.7g Carbohydrates: 14.4g

Vanilla Malted Cookies

Total Time Taken: 1 ¼ hours

Yield: 30 Servings

Ingredients:

- ½ cup cream cheese
- ½ cup malted milk powder
- ½ cup white chocolate chips
- ½ teaspoon baking soda
- ½ teaspoon salt
- 1 cup butter, softened
- 1 cup white sugar
- 1 egg
- 1 teaspoon baking powder
- 1 teaspoon vanilla extract
- 2 ½ cups all-purpose flour

Directions:

1. Sift the flour, milk powder, baking powder, baking soda and salt.
2. Mix the butter, cream cheese and sugar in a container until creamy and fluffy.
3. Put in the vanilla and egg and mix thoroughly.
4. Fold in the flour mixture then put in the chocolate chips.
5. Drop spoonfuls of batter on a baking sheet coated with baking paper.
6. Preheat your oven and bake the cookies at 350F for about fifteen minutes or until a golden-brown colour is achieved on the edges.
   7. *These cookies taste best chilled.*

Nutritional Content of One Serving:

Calories: 161 Fat: 8.8g Protein: 2.1g Carbohydrates: 19.0g

Vanilla Sugared Cookies

Total Time Taken: 2 hours
Yield: 20 Servings
Ingredients:

- ¼ teaspoon baking powder
- ¼ teaspoon salt
- ½ cup butter, softened
- ½ cup powdered sugar
- 1 egg
- 1 tablespoon vanilla extract
- 2 cups all-purpose flour
- Powdered sugar for coating the cookies

Directions:

1. Mix the butter and sugar in a container until pale and light.
2. Put in the vanilla and egg and mix thoroughly.
3. Stir in the flour, salt and baking powder then transfer the dough on a plastic wrap and roll it into a log.
4. Wrap the dough and place it in the freezer for about half an hour.
5. When finished, cut the log of dough into thin slices.
6. Put the cookies in a baking tray covered with parchment paper and preheat your oven and bake at 350F for about ten minutes or until a golden-brown colour is achieved on the edges.
7. *These cookies taste best chilled.*

Nutritional Content of One Serving:

Calories: 103 Fat: 5.0g Protein: 1.6g Carbohydrates: 12.7g

Walnut Banana Cookies

Total Time Taken: 1 hour
Yield: 20 Servings
Ingredients:

- ¼ cup dark brown sugar
- ½ cup all-purpose flour
- ½ cup butter, softened
- ½ cup dark chocolate chips
- ½ cup walnuts, chopped
- ½ cup white sugar
- ½ teaspoon baking powder
- ½ teaspoon salt
- 1 banana, mashed
- 1 cup whole wheat flour
- 1 egg
- 1 teaspoon vanilla extract

Directions:

1. Mix the butter and sugars in a container until fluffy and pale.

2. Put in the egg, vanilla and banana and mix thoroughly.
3. Stir in the flours, salt and baking powder then fold in the chocolate chips and walnuts.
4. Drop spoonfuls of batter on a baking tray covered with parchment paper and preheat your oven and bake at 350F for about thirteen minutes or until a golden-brown colour is achieved and crisp on the edges.
5. *The cookies are best served chilled.*

Nutritional Content of One Serving:

Calories: 143 Fat: 7.6g Protein: 2.3g Carbohydrates: 17.7g

Walnut Crescent Cookies

Total Time Taken: 1 ¼ hours
Yield: 20 Servings

Ingredients:
- 1 teaspoon vanilla extract
- ½ teaspoon almond extract
- 1 egg
- 1 cup all-purpose flour
- 1 ½ cups ground walnuts
- ½ teaspoon salt
- ½ teaspoon baking powder
- 2/3 cup butter, softened
- 2/3 cup white sugar

Directions:
1. Mix the butter, sugar, vanilla and almond extract in a container until fluffy and creamy.
2. Put in the egg and mix thoroughly then fold in the flour, walnuts, salt and baking powder.
3. Take small pieces of dough and shape them into small logs.
4. Place them on a baking tray coated with baking paper and preheat your oven and bake at 350F for about fifteen minutes or until a golden-brown colour is achieved on the edges.
5. *These cookies taste best chilled.*

Nutritional Content of One Serving:

Calories: 164 Fat: 11.9g Protein: 3.2g Carbohydrates: 12.5g

White Chocolate Chunk Cookies

Total Time Taken: 1 ¼ hours
Yield: 30 Servings

Ingredients:
- ¼ cup white sugar
- ½ cup butter, softened
- ½ cup cocoa powder
- ½ teaspoon salt
- 1 cup light brown sugar
- 1 teaspoon baking soda
- 1 teaspoon vanilla extract

- 2 cups all-purpose flour
- 2 eggs
- 4 oz. white chocolate, chopped

Directions:
1. Mix the butter and sugars in a container until fluffy and pale.
2. Put in the vanilla and eggs and mix thoroughly.
3. Fold in the flour, cocoa powder, salt and baking soda.
4. Put in the white chocolate chips then drop spoonfuls of batter on baking trays coated with baking paper.
5. Preheat your oven and bake the cookies at 350F for about fifteen minutes or until risen.
6. *These cookies taste best chilled.*

Nutritional Content of One Serving:
Calories: 110 Fat: 4.8g Protein: 1.8g Carbohydrates: 15.8g

White Chocolate Cranberry Cookies

Total Time Taken: 1 ¼ hours
Yield: 30 Servings

Ingredients:
- ¼ cup coconut oil, melted
- ¼ teaspoon cinnamon powder
- ¼ teaspoon salt
- ½ cup butter, softened
- ½ cup dried cranberries
- ½ cup light brown sugar
- ½ cup white chocolate chips
- 1 ½ cups all-purpose flour
- 1 egg
- 1 tablespoon brandy
- 1 teaspoon baking powder

Directions:
1. Mix the butter, coconut oil and sugar in a container until fluffy and pale.
2. Put in the egg and brandy and mix thoroughly.
3. Fold in the remaining ingredients and mix using a spatula.
4. Drop spoonfuls of batter on a baking tray coated with baking paper.
5. Preheat your oven and bake the cookies at 350F for about fifteen minutes or until a golden-brown colour is achieved on the edges.
6. *These cookies taste best chilled.*

Nutritional Content of One Serving:
Calories: 95 Fat: 6.0g Protein: 1.0g Carbohydrates: 9.1g

White Chocolate Pistachio Cookies

Total Time Taken: 1 ¼ hours
Yield: 40 Servings

Ingredients:
- ¼ cup whole milk
- ½ cup light brown sugar
- ½ cup white chocolate chips
- ½ teaspoon baking powder
- ½ teaspoon salt
- 1 cup butter, softened
- 1 cup pistachio, chopped
- 1 cup white sugar
- 1 teaspoon baking soda
- 1 teaspoon vanilla extract
- 2 ½ cups all-purpose flour
- 2 eggs

Directions:
1. Mix the butter and sugars in a container until fluffy and pale.
2. Put in the eggs and mix thoroughly then mix in the vanilla.
3. Put in the rest of the ingredients and mix using a spatula.
4. Drop spoonfuls of batter on baking trays coated with baking paper.
5. Preheat your oven and bake the cookies at 350F for about fifteen minutes or until a golden-brown colour is achieved on the edges.
6. *These cookies taste best chilled.*

Nutritional Content of One Serving:

Calories: 119 Fat: 6.3g Protein: 1.6g Carbohydrates: 14.5g

Cakes hardly need an explanation. Just remember to sift the flour before using in a recipe as it aerates the flour before it is added to the batter. Also, the toothpick is one of the most popular methods to tell if a cake is cooked. Basically you insert a toothpick into the center of the cake, and if the toothpick comes out dry, your cake is done!

All righty then, let us jump straight into the recipes!

All Butter Cake

Total Time Taken: 1 ½ hours
Yield: 14 Servings
Ingredients:

Cake:
- ¼ teaspoon salt
- ½ cup whole milk
- 1 cup butter, softened
- 1 cup white sugar
- 1 teaspoon vanilla extract

- 2 cups all-purpose flour
- 2 teaspoons baking powder
- 4 eggs

Frosting:
- 1 cup butter, softened
- 1 teaspoon vanilla extract
- 2 cups powdered sugar

Directions:
1. To prepare the cake, combine the butter, sugar and vanilla in a container until fluffy and creamy.
2. Put in the eggs, one at a time then mix in the milk.
3. Fold in the flour, baking powder and salt then spoon the batter in a 9-inch round cake pan coated with baking paper.
4. Pre-heat the oven and bake at 350F for about forty minutes.
5. Let the cake cool in the pan then cut it in half along the length.
6. For the frosting, combine the butter, sugar and vanilla in a container until fluffy and pale.
7. Use half of the buttercream to fill the cake and the half that is left over to frost the cake.
8. *Serve the cake fresh or chilled.*

Nutritional Content of One Serving:
Calories: 443 Fat: 28.0g Protein: 4.0g Carbohydrates: 45.9g

Almond Apple Cake

Total Time Taken: 1 ¼ hours
Yield: 10 Servings

Ingredients:
- ¼ teaspoon salt
- ½ cup whole milk
- ¾ cup all-purpose flour
- ¾ cup butter, softened
- 1 cup almond flour
- 1 cup white sugar
- 1 teaspoon baking powder
- 1 teaspoon vanilla extract
- 2 red apples, cored and diced
- 3 eggs

Directions:
1. Mix the butter with sugar in a container until creamy.
2. Put in the vanilla and eggs and mix thoroughly then fold in the almond flour, flour, salt and baking powder.
3. Put in the milk and stir lightly then fold in the apples.
4. Spoon the batter in a 8-inch round cake pan coated with baking paper and preheat your oven and bake at 350F for forty minutes or until it rises significantly and seems golden.
5. Let the cake cool in the pan before you serve.

Nutritional Content of One Serving:

Calories: 294 Fat: 17.1g Protein: 3.9g Carbohydrates: 33.7g

Almond Butter Banana Cake

Total Time Taken: 1 ¼ hours
Yield: 12 Servings

Ingredients:
- ¼ cup canola oil
- ½ cup shredded coconut
- ½ teaspoon ground ginger
- ½ teaspoon salt
- 1 ½ cups white sugar
- 1 cup almond butter
- 1 teaspoon baking soda
- 1 teaspoon cinnamon powder
- 1 teaspoon vanilla extract
- 2 bananas, mashed
- 2 cups all-purpose flour
- 3 eggs

Directions:
1. Sift the flour, baking soda, salt, cinnamon and ginger. Combine it with the shredded coconut.
2. Mix the almond butter and sugar in a container until creamy.
3. Stir in the eggs, one at a time, then put in the vanilla, bananas and canola oil. Stir thoroughly to mix.
4. Fold in the flour mixture then pour the batter in a 9-inch round cake pan coated with baking paper.
5. Pre-heat the oven and bake at 350F for about forty-five minutes or until it rises significantly and starts to appear golden-brown.
6. Let the cake cool in the pan before you serve.

Nutritional Content of One Serving:
Calories: 388 Fat: 18.8g Protein: 8.3g Carbohydrates: 49.8g

Almond Date Cake

Total Time Taken: 1 hour
Yield: 8 Servings
Ingredients:

2 eggs
- ¼ cup cocoa powder
- ¼ cup rice flour
- ¼ teaspoon salt
- ½ cup white sugar
- ½ lemon, zested and juiced
- 1 ½ cups almond flour
- 1 cup dates, pitted
- 1 teaspoon baking soda
- 4 egg whites

Directions:

1. Mix the eggs, egg whites, lemon zest, lemon juice, sugar and dates in a food processor.
2. Put in the almond flour, rice flour, cocoa powder, baking soda and salt and stir lightly using a spatula.
3. Pour the batter in a 8-inch round cake pan coated with baking paper.
4. Pre-heat the oven and bake at 350F for around forty minutes.
5. Let the cake cool in the pan before you serve.

Nutritional Content of One Serving:

Calories: 188 Fat: 4.3g Protein: 5.6g Carbohydrates: 35.9g

Almond Fig Cake

Total Time Taken: 1 ¼ hours
Yield: 10 Servings

Ingredients:

- 2 eggs
- 4 egg whites
- 1 cup white sugar
- ½ cup butter, melted
- 1 cup all-purpose flour
- 1 teaspoon baking powder
- ¼ teaspoon salt
  - 1 cup ground almonds
- 6 figs, sliced

Directions:

1. Mix the eggs, egg whites and sugar in a container until creamy and volume increases to twice what it was.
2. Put in the melted butter, progressively, then fold in the flour, baking powder, salt and almonds.
3. Pour the batter in a 8-inch round cake pan coated with baking paper.
4. Top with figs and preheat your oven and bake at 350F for around forty minutes or until it rises significantly and starts to appear golden-brown.
5. Let the cake cool in the pan and serve, sliced.

Nutritional Content of One Serving:

Calories: 305 Fat: 15.1g Protein: 6.3g Carbohydrates: 39.3g

Almond Honey Cake

Total Time Taken: 1 ¼ hours
Yield: 10 Servings

Ingredients:

- ¼ cup light brown sugar
- ¼ teaspoon cinnamon powder
- ¼ teaspoon salt
- ½ cup ground almonds
- ½ cup honey

- ½ cup sliced almonds
- ¾ cup butter, softened
- 1 ½ cups all-purpose flour
- 1 teaspoon baking powder
- 3 eggs

Directions:

1. Mix the butter, honey and sugar in a container until creamy and pale.
2. Put in the eggs and mix thoroughly.
3. Fold in the flour, almonds, baking powder, salt and cinnamon powder.
4. Spoon the batter in a loaf cake pan coated with baking paper.
5. Top with sliced almonds and preheat your oven and bake at 350F for forty minutes or until a toothpick inserted into the center of the cake comes out clean.
6. The cake tastes best chilled.

Nutritional Content of One Serving:

Calories: 330 Fat: 20.1g Protein: 5.8g Carbohydrates: 34.2g

Almond Strawberry Cake

Total Time Taken: 1 ¼ hours
Yield: 8 Servings

Ingredients:

- ½ cup butter, softened
- ½ cup white sugar
- ½ cup whole milk
- ½ teaspoon salt
- 1 cup all-purpose flour
- 1 cup fresh strawberries, sliced
- 1 cup ground almonds
- 1 teaspoon baking soda
- 1 teaspoon vanilla extract
- 2 eggs

Directions:

1. Mix the butter and sugar in a container until creamy. Stir in the eggs, one at a time, then put in the milk and vanilla.
2. Fold in the flour, almonds, baking soda and salt and stir lightly.
3. Fold in the strawberries then spoon the batter in a round cake pan coated with baking paper.
4. Preheat your oven and bake the cake for about half an hour or until a golden-brown colour is achieved and it rises significantly.
5. Let the cake cool in the pan before you serve.

Nutritional Content of One Serving:

Calories: 306 Fat: 19.2g Protein: 6.2g Carbohydrates: 29.2g

Almond Strawberry Cake

Total Time Taken: 1 ¼ hours
Yield: 10 Servings

Ingredients:
- ½ cup plain yogurt
- 1 cup all-purpose flour
- 1 cup almond flour
- 1 cup butter, softened
- 1 cup white sugar
- 1 teaspoon baking soda
- 1 teaspoon vanilla
- 2 cups fresh strawberries
- 4 eggs

Directions:
1. Mix the butter with sugar and vanilla in a container until creamy.
2. Stir in the eggs, one at a time, then put in the yogurt and mix thoroughly.
3. Fold in the almond flour, all-purpose flour, baking soda and a pinch of salt and stir lightly using a spatula.
4. Pour the batter in a 9-inch round cake pan and top with strawberries.
5. Pre-heat the oven and bake at 350F for about forty-five minutes or until a toothpick comes out clean after being inserted into the center of the cake.
6. The cake tastes best chilled.

Nutritional Content of One Serving:

Calories: 344 Fat: 21.9g Protein: 5.2g Carbohydrates: 33.4g

Almond White Chocolate Cake

Total Time Taken: 1 ½ hours
Yield: 10 Servings

Ingredients:
- ½ cup dried cranberries
- ½ cup sliced almonds
- ½ cup sour cream
- ½ teaspoon salt
- 1 ½ teaspoons baking soda
- 1 cup all-purpose flour
- 1 cup butter, softened
- 1 cup ground almonds
- 1 cup light brown sugar
- 1 cup white chocolate chips
- 1 tablespoon orange zest
- 3 eggs

Directions:
1. Mix the butter and sugar in a container until creamy and fluffy.

2. Stir in the eggs, one at a time, then put in the orange zest and sour cream.
3. Fold in the flour, almonds, baking soda and salt then put in the cranberries and chocolate chips.
4. Spoon the batter in a 9-inch round cake pan and top with sliced almonds.
5. Pre-heat the oven and bake at 350F for about forty minutes or until it rises significantly and starts to appear golden-brown.
6. Let the cake cool in the pan and serve, sliced.

Nutritional Content of One Serving:

Calories: 485 Fat: 34.8g Protein: 7.5g Carbohydrates: 38.1g

Amaretto Almond Cake

Total Time Taken: 1 hour
Yield: 8 Servings
Ingredients:
- ¼ cup cocoa powder
- ¼ teaspoon salt
- ½ cup butter, softened
- ½ cup light brown sugar
- 1 ½ cups almond flour
- 1 teaspoon baking powder
- 1 teaspoon lemon zest
- 1 teaspoon orange zest
- 2 tablespoons Amaretto
- 3 eggs

Directions:
1. Mix the butter, sugar, orange zest and lemon zest in a container until fluffy and creamy.
2. Put in the eggs, one at a time, then mix in the almond flour, cocoa, salt and baking powder, preferably using a spatula.
3. Spoon the batter in a 8-inch round cake pan and preheat your oven and bake at 350F for 35 minutes or until a toothpick comes out clean after being inserted into the center of the cake.
4. Immediately after you take it out of the oven, sprinkle it with Amaretto.
5. Serve chilled.

Nutritional Content of One Serving:

Calories: 208 Fat: 16.1g Protein: 3.8g Carbohydrates: 12.0g

Apple and Pear Molasses Cake

Total Time Taken: 1 ¼ hours
Yield: 10 Servings

Ingredients:
- ¼ cup butter, softened
- ½ cup canola oil
- ½ cup light molasses
- ½ cup white sugar
- 1 egg

- ½ cup whole milk
- 1 pear, peeled, cored and diced
- 1 red apple, peeled, cored and diced
- 1 teaspoon baking powder
- 1 teaspoon baking soda
- 1 teaspoon cinnamon powder
- 1 teaspoon grated ginger
- 2 cups all-purpose flour

Directions:

1. Mix the canola oil, butter, molasses and sugar in a container until creamy. Put in the egg, ginger and cinnamon and mix thoroughly then mix in the milk.
2. Fold in the remaining ingredients then spoon the batter in a 9-inch round cake pan covered with parchment paper.
3. Pre-heat the oven and bake at 350F for about forty minutes or until a toothpick comes out clean after being inserted into the center of the cake.
4. Let cool in the pan then cut and serve.

Nutritional Content of One Serving:

Calories: 345 Fat: 16.7g Protein: 3.7g Carbohydrates: 46.9g

Apple Pound Cake

Total Time Taken: 1 ¼ hours
Yield: 10 Servings

Ingredients:

- ¼ teaspoon salt
- ½ cup cream cheese, softened
- ½ teaspoon baking soda
- ½ teaspoon cinnamon powder
- ¾ cup butter, softened
- 1 ½ cups all-purpose flour
- 1 cup white sugar
- 1 teaspoon baking powder
- 1 teaspoon vanilla extract
- 2 granny Smith apples, peeled, cored and diced
- 3 eggs

Directions:

1. Mix the butter, cream cheese and sugar in a container until creamy and fluffy.
2. Stir in the eggs and vanilla and mix thoroughly.
3. Fold in the flour, baking powder, baking soda, salt and cinnamon.
4. Put in the apple dices then spoon the batter in a loaf cake pan coated with baking paper.
5. Pre-heat the oven and bake at 350F for forty minutes or until a toothpick inserted into the center of the cake comes out clean.
6. *The cake tastes best chilled.*

Nutritional Content of One Serving:

Calories: 345 Fat: 19.4g Protein: 4.7g Carbohydrates: 40.0g

Apple Vanilla Loaf Cake

Total Time Taken: 1 ¼ hours
Yield: 10 Servings

Ingredients:
- ¼ teaspoon salt
- ½ cup butter, softened
- ½ cup canola oil
- ½ cup cornstarch
- ½ cup whole milk
- ¾ cup white sugar
- 1 cup all-purpose flour
- 1 tablespoon vanilla extract
- 1 teaspoon baking powder
- 2 red apples, cored and diced
- 3 eggs

Directions:
1. Mix the butter, oil and sugar in a container. Stir thoroughly to mix until creamy.
2. Put in the eggs, one at a time, then mix in the milk and vanilla.
3. Fold in the flour, cornstarch, baking powder and salt, then incorporate the apples.
4. Spoon the batter in a loaf cake pan coated with baking paper.
5. Pre-heat the oven and bake at 350F for around forty minutes or until a toothpick inserted into the center of the cake comes out clean.
6. The cake tastes best chilled.

Nutritional Content of One Serving:

Calories: 353 Fat: 22.0g Protein: 3.6g Carbohydrates: 36.5g

Applesauce Carrot Cake

Total Time Taken: 1 ½ hours
Yield: 12 Servings

Ingredients:
- ¼ cup dark brown sugar
- ½ cup canola oil
- ½ cup shredded coconut
- ½ teaspoon baking powder
- ½ teaspoon salt
- 1 cup applesauce
- 1 cup grated carrots
- 1 cup white sugar
- 1 egg white
- 1 teaspoon baking soda
- 1 teaspoon vanilla extract
- 2 ½ cups all-purpose flour

- 2 apples, peeled, cored and diced
- 3 eggs

Directions:
1. Mix the eggs, egg white, sugars and vanilla in a container until fluffy and pale.
2. Stir in the canola oil and applesauce and mix thoroughly then put in the carrots, coconut and apples, as well as the flour, baking soda, baking powder and salt.
3. Stir slowly until mixed using a spatula just until incorporated.
4. Pour the batter in a 9-inch round cake pan and preheat your oven and bake at 350F for about fifty minutes or until fragrant and a toothpick inserted into the center of the cake comes out clean.
5. Let the cake cool in the pan before you serve.

Nutritional Content of One Serving:
Calories: 307 Fat: 11.6g Protein: 4.7g Carbohydrates: 47.6g

Apricot Cake

Total Time Taken: 1 hour
Yield: 10 Servings
Ingredients:

6 eggs

- ½ cup canola oil
- ½ cup sour cream
- ½ teaspoon salt
- 1 ½ teaspoons baking powder
- 1 cup white sugar
- 1 tablespoon lemon zest
- 1 teaspoon vanilla extract
- 2 cups all-purpose flour
- 6 apricots, halved and sliced

Directions:
1. Mix the eggs with sugar, vanilla and lemon zest in a container until fluffy and creamy.
2. Put in the canola oil and sour cream and mix thoroughly.
3. Fold in the remaining ingredients then pour the batter in a 9- inch round cake pan coated with baking paper.
4. Pre-heat the oven and bake at 350F for about forty minutes or until a toothpick inserted in the center comes out clean.
5. Let the cake cool in the pan before you serve.

Nutritional Content of One Serving:
Calories: 337 Fat: 16.3g Protein: 6.5g Carbohydrates: 42.6g

Apricot Yogurt Loaf Cake

Total Time Taken: 1 ¼ hours
Yield: 10 Servings

Ingredients:

- ¼ cup sliced almonds
- ¼ teaspoon salt
- ½ cup butter, softened
- ¾ cup white sugar
- 1 ¼ cups all-purpose flour
- 1 cup plain yogurt
- 1 teaspoon baking powder
- 1 teaspoon vanilla extract
- 2 eggs
- 4 apricots, pitted and sliced

Directions:

1. Mix the butter and sugar in a container until fluffy and pale. Stir in the eggs, one at a time, then put in the yogurt and vanilla and mix thoroughly.
2. Fold in the flour, baking powder and salt.
3. Spoon the batter in a loaf cake pan coated with baking paper.
4. Top with apricots and drizzle with sliced almonds.
5. Pre-heat the oven and bake at 350F for around forty minutes or until it rises significantly and starts to appear golden-brown.
6. Let the cake cool in the pan before you serve.

Nutritional Content of One Serving:

Calories: 247 Fat: 11.8g Protein: 4.9g Carbohydrates: 31.1g

Banana Bundt Cake With Peanut Butter Frosting

Total Time Taken: 1 ¼ hours
Yield: 12 Servings
Ingredients:

Cake:

- ½ teaspoon salt
- 1 cup buttermilk
- 1 cup canola oil
- 1 cup white sugar
- 1 teaspoon vanilla extract
- 2 cups all-purpose flour
- 2 eggs
- 2 ripe bananas, mashed
- 2 teaspoons baking powder

Frosting:

- ½ cup cream cheese
- ½ cup peanut butter, softened
- ½ cup powdered sugar

Directions:

1. To prepare the cake, combine the oil and sugar in a container then mix in the eggs and vanilla. Stir thoroughly to mix then put in the buttermilk and bananas.
2. Fold in the flour, baking powder and salt then spoon the batter in a greased Bundt cake pan.
3. Pre-heat the oven and bake at 350F for about forty minutes or until a toothpick inserted into the center of the cake comes out clean.
4. Move the cake to a platter.
5. For the frosting, combine the ingredients in a container until creamy.
6. Cover the cake with peanut butter frosting and serve fresh.

Nutritional Content of One Serving:

Calories: 453 Fat: 28.1g Protein: 7.4g Carbohydrates: 45.9g

Banana Cake

Total Time Taken: 55 minutes
Yield: 8 Servings
Ingredients:

- ¼ cup butter, softened
- ¼ cup whole milk
- ¼ teaspoon salt
- ½ cup dark chocolate chips
- ½ cup white sugar
- 1 ½ cups all-purpose flour
- 1 teaspoon baking soda
- 2 eggs
- 2 ripe bananas, mashed
- 2 tablespoons dark brown sugar

Directions:

1. Sift the flour, baking soda and salt in a container.
2. Combine the butter, sugars and eggs in a container and stir thoroughly for five minutes.
3. Put in the mashed bananas and milk then fold in the flour, followed by the chocolate chips.
4. Spoon the batter in a round cake pan coated with baking paper and preheat your oven and bake at 350F for about half an hour or until a golden-brown colour is achieved and it rises significantly.
5. Let the cake cool in the pan and serve, sliced.

Nutritional Content of One Serving:

Calories: 273 Fat: 9.4g Protein: 4.9g Carbohydrates: 44.8g

Banana Chocolate Chip Cake

Total Time Taken: 1 ¼ hours
Yield: 12 Servings

Ingredients:
- ¼ teaspoon salt
- ½ cup butter, softened
- ½ cup dark chocolate chips
- ½ cup walnuts, chopped
- 1 ¾ cups all-purpose flour
- 1 cup white sugar
- 1 teaspoon baking soda
- 1 teaspoon vanilla extract
- 3 eggs
- 3 ripe bananas, mashed

Directions:
1. Sift the flour, baking soda and salt on a platter.
2. Mix the butter with sugar until creamy and fluffy.
3. Stir in the eggs, one at a time, then put in the vanilla and bananas.
4. Stir thoroughly to mix then fold in the flour, followed by the walnuts and chocolate chips.
5. Spoon the batter in a 9-inch round cake pan covered with parchment paper.
6. Pre-heat the oven and bake at 350F for about forty minutes or until a toothpick inserted into the center of the cake comes out clean.
7. Let the cake cool in the pan and serve, sliced.

Nutritional Content of One Serving:

Calories: 295 Fat: 13.4g Protein: 5.2g Carbohydrates: 41.3g

Banana Mars Bar Cake

Total Time Taken: 1 ¼ hours
Yield: 10 Servings

Ingredients:
- ½ cup butter, softened
- ½ cup light brown sugar
- ½ cup whole milk
- ½ teaspoon salt
- 2 bananas, mashed
- 2 cups all-purpose flour
- 2 eggs
- 2 Mars bars, chopped
- 2 tablespoons maple syrup
- 2 teaspoons baking powder

Directions:
1. Mix the butter, sugar and maple syrup in a container until fluffy and pale.
2. Put in the eggs and mix thoroughly then mix in the mashed bananas and milk.

3. Fold in the remaining ingredients then spoon the batter in a loaf cake pan coated with baking paper.
4. Pre-heat the oven and bake at 350F for about forty minutes or until a golden-brown colour is achieved and it rises significantly.
5. *The cake tastes best chilled.*

Nutritional Content of One Serving:

Calories: 299 Fat: 13.1g Protein: 5.3g Carbohydrates: 41.6g

Banana Peanut Butter Cake

Total Time Taken: 1 hour
Yield: 8 Servings
Ingredients:

- ¼ cup whole milk
- ½ cup smooth peanut butter
- ½ teaspoon salt
- 1 ½ cups all-purpose flour
- 1 teaspoon baking soda
- 1 teaspoon vanilla extract
- 2 eggs
- 2 ripe bananas, mashed
- 2/3 cup white sugar
- 4 tablespoons butter, softened

Directions:

1. Mix the butter with sugar until creamy and smooth.
2. Stir in the eggs one at a time, then mix in the vanilla and bananas, as well as milk.
3. Fold in the flour, baking soda and salt and mix thoroughly.
4. Spoon the batter in a 9pinch round cake pan coated with baking paper and preheat your oven and bake at 350F for about half an hour or until a golden-brown colour is achieved and it rises significantly.
5. Let the cake cool completely before you serve.

Nutritional Content of One Serving:

Calories: 342 Fat: 15.6g Protein: 8.5g Carbohydrates: 45.0g

Beetroot Carrot Cake

Total Time Taken: 1 ½ hours
Yield: 10 Servings

Ingredients:

- ¼ cup maple syrup
- ½ cup grated beetroots
- ½ cup light brown sugar
- 3 eggs
- ½ cup pecans, chopped
- ½ teaspoon ground cardamom
- ½ teaspoon ground ginger

- ½ teaspoon salt
- ¾ cup vegetable oil
- 1 ½ cups all-purpose flour
- 1 teaspoon baking powder
- 1 teaspoon cinnamon powder
- 1 teaspoon vanilla extract
- 2 cups grated carrots

Directions:
1. Mix the flour, salt, baking powder, cinnamon, ginger and cardamom in a container.
2. In a separate container, combine the oil, maple syrup, sugar, eggs and vanilla until fluffy.
3. Stir in the carrots and beetroots, as well as pecans then fold in the flour.
4. Spoon the batter in a 9-inch round cake pan coated with baking paper.
5. Pre-heat the oven and bake at 350F for about forty minutes or until a toothpick inserted into the center of the cake comes out clean.
6. The cake tastes best chilled.

Nutritional Content of One Serving:
Calories: 305 Fat: 18.9g Protein: 4.1g Carbohydrates: 30.4g

Beetroot Chocolate Fudge Cake

Total Time Taken: 1 ¼ hours
Yield: 10 Servings

Ingredients:
- ¼ cup canola oil
- ¼ teaspoon salt
- ½ cup almond flour
- ½ cup cocoa powder
- 1 ½ cups grated beetroot
- 1 cup all-purpose flour
- 1 cup light brown sugar
- 1 teaspoon baking soda
- 2 tablespoons honey
- 3 eggs

Directions:
1. Mix the eggs with sugar until fluffy and pale. Put in the oil and honey and mix thoroughly.
2. Fold in the flour, cocoa powder, baking soda, almond flour and salt.
3. Put in the beetroot and stir lightly using a spatula.
4. Pour the batter in a 9-inch round cake pan coated with baking paper.
5. Pre-heat the oven and bake at 350F for about half an hour.
6. Let the cake cool in the pan before you serve.

Nutritional Content of One Serving:
Calories: 209 Fat: 8.2g Protein: 4.5g Carbohydrates: 32.5g

Berry Lemon Cake

Total Time Taken: 1 ¼ hours
Yield: 10 Servings

Ingredients:
- ½ cup butter, softened
- ½ cup plain yogurt
- ½ teaspoon salt
- 1 ½ teaspoons baking powder
- 1 cup mixed berries
- 1 cup white sugar
- 1 tablespoon lemon zest
- 2 cups all-purpose flour
- 2 tablespoons lemon juice
- 3 eggs

Directions:
1. Mix the butter and sugar in a container until creamy and fluffy.
2. Stir in the eggs, one at a time, then put in the lemon zest and lemon juice, as well as the yogurt.
3. Fold in the flour, baking powder and salt then put in the berries.
4. Pour the batter in a 8-inch round cake pan and preheat your oven and bake at 350F for around forty minutes or until it rises significantly and starts to appear golden-brown.
5. Let the cake cool in the pan before you serve.

Nutritional Content of One Serving:

Calories: 285 Fat: 11.0g Protein: 5.2g Carbohydrates: 42.3g

Berry Meringue Cake

Total Time Taken: 2 ½ hours
Yield: 8 Servings

Ingredients:
- ½ teaspoon salt
- 1 ½ cups fresh berries
- 1 cup heavy cream, whipped
- 1 cup white sugar
- 1 teaspoon vanilla extract
- 2 tablespoons cornstarch
- 4 egg whites

Directions:
1. Mix the egg whites, salt and sugar in a container. Place over a hot water bath and keep over heat until the sugar is melted.
2. Turn off the heat and whip the egg whites until shiny and fluffy.
3. Fold in the cornstarch then spoon the meringue on a baking sheet coated with baking paper, shaping it into 2 rounds.
4. Pre-heat the oven and bake at 250F for about two hours.
5. Fill and cover the cake with whipped cream and fresh berries.

6. Serve immediately.

Nutritional Content of One Serving:

Calories: 178 Fat: 5.7g Protein: 2.3g Carbohydrates: 30.6g

Black Pepper Chocolate Cake

Total Time Taken: 1 ¼ hours
 Yield: 16 Servings

Ingredients:
- ½ teaspoon salt
- 1 ½ cups white sugar
- 1 ½ teaspoons baking powder
- 1 cup butter
- 1 cup sour cream
- 1 teaspoon ground black pepper
- 1 teaspoon lemon zest
- 2 cups all-purpose flour
- 4 eggs

Directions:
1. Mix the flour with baking powder and salt in a container.
2. In a separate container, combine the butter and sugar until fluffy and pale.
3. Stir in the black pepper, lemon zest and eggs and mix thoroughly.
4. Put in the sour cream and give it a good mix.
5. Fold in the flour, baking powder and salt then spoon the batter in a 9-inch round cake pan coated with baking paper.
6. Pre-heat the oven and bake at 350F for about forty minutes or until a toothpick inserted into the center of the cake comes out clean.
7. Let the cake cool in the pan before you serve.

Nutritional Content of One Serving:

Calories: 276 Fat: 15.8g Protein: 3.6g Carbohydrates: 31.7g

Blackberry Bundt Cake

Total Time Taken: 1 ¼ hours
 Yield: 10 Servings

Ingredients:
- ½ cup butter, softened
- ½ teaspoon ground cardamom
- ½ teaspoon salt
- 1 cup fresh blackberries
- 1 cup white sugar
- 1 cup whole milk
- 1 teaspoon vanilla extract
- 2 cups all-purpose flour
- 2 eggs

- 2 teaspoons baking powder

Directions:
1. Mix the butter with sugar until creamy, at least five minutes.
2. Put in the eggs and mix thoroughly then mix in the milk and vanilla.
3. Fold in the flour, baking powder, salt and cardamom then put in the blackberries.
4. Spoon the batter in a Bundt cake pan lined using butter.
5. Pre-heat the oven and bake at 350F for around forty minutes or until a toothpick inserted in the center comes out clean.
6. Let the cake cool in the pan for about ten minutes then flip it over on a platter.

Nutritional Content of One Serving:
Calories: 283 Fat: 11.2g Protein: 4.8g Carbohydrates: 42.2g

Blood Orange Cornmeal Cake

Total Time Taken: 1 ½ hours
Yield: 12 Servings

Ingredients:
- ½ teaspoon salt
- 1 cup all-purpose flour
- 1 cup butter, softened
- 1 cup cornmeal
- 1 cup fresh blood orange juice
- 1 cup white sugar
- 2 blood oranges, sliced
- 2 tablespoons blood orange zest
- 2 teaspoons baking powder

Directions:
1. Mix the butter, sugar and orange zest in a container until creamy and fluffy.
2. Mix the flour, cornmeal, baking powder and salt.
3. Stir the flour into the butter mixture, alternating it with the orange juice.
4. Position the orange slices at the bottom of a 9-inch round cake pan coated with baking paper.
5. Pour the batter over the orange slices and preheat your oven and bake at 350F for 45 minutes or until a toothpick inserted into the center of the cake comes out clean.
6. When finished, flip the cake upside down on a platter and serve it chilled.

Nutritional Content of One Serving:
Calories: 298 Fat: 15.9g Protein: 2.5g Carbohydrates: 38.8g

Blood Orange Olive Oil Cake

Total Time Taken: 1 ¼ hours
Yield: 12 Servings

Ingredients:
- ½ cup corn meal
- ½ cup light brown sugar

- ½ teaspoon baking soda
- ½ teaspoon salt
- ¾ cup olive oil
- 1 ½ cups all-purpose flour
- 1 ½ cups white sugar
- 1 cup buttermilk
- 1 teaspoon baking powder
- 2 eggs
- 3 blood oranges, sliced

Directions:
1. Position the blood orange slices in a 10-inch baking tray covered with parchment paper and drizzle them with brown sugar.
2. Mix the oil with eggs and sugar in a container until volume increases to twice what it was.
3. Stir in the flour, baking powder, cornmeal, baking soda and salt then put in the buttermilk and stir for a few seconds to mix.
4. Pour the batter over the orange slices and preheat your oven and bake at 350F for around forty minutes or until a golden-brown colour is achieved and it rises significantly.
5. The cake tastes best chilled, turned upside down on a platter.

Nutritional Content of One Serving:
Calories: 342 Fat: 13.9g Protein: 4.2g Carbohydrates: 54.0g

Blueberry Cake

Total Time Taken: 1 hour
Yield: 12 Servings
Ingredients:
- ½ teaspoon salt
- 1 cup butter, softened
- 1 cup buttermilk
- 1 cup fresh blueberries
- 1 cup white sugar
- 1/4 cup light brown sugar
- 2 tablespoons lemon juice
- 2 tablespoons lemon zest
- 2 teaspoons baking powder
- 3 ½ cups all-purpose flour
- 4 eggs

Directions:
1. Mix the butter and sugars in a container until creamy and fluffy.
2. Stir in the eggs, one at a time, then put in the lemon juice, buttermilk and lemon zest.
3. Fold in the flour, baking powder and salt, followed by the fresh blueberries.
4. Spoon the batter in a 10-inch round cake pan coated with baking paper.
5. Pre-heat the oven and bake at 350F for about forty minutes or until the cake is well risen and golden brown.
6. Let the cake cool in the pan and serve, sliced.

Nutritional Content of One Serving:

Calories: 380 Fat: 17.4g Protein: 6.6g Carbohydrates: 50.9g

Blueberry Streusel Cake

Total Time Taken: 1 ¼ hours
Yield: 10 Servings
Ingredients:

Cake:

- ½ cup sour cream
- ½ teaspoon salt
- ¾ cup butter, softened
- 1 ½ cups fresh blueberries
- 1 cup white sugar
- 1 tablespoon lemon zest
- 1 teaspoon baking soda
- 2 cups all-purpose flour
- 2 tablespoons lemon juice
- 4 eggs

Streusel:

- ¼ cup butter, chilled
- ½ cup all-purpose flour
- 1 pinch salt
- 2 tablespoons powdered sugar

Directions:

1. To prepare the cake, combine the butter, sugar, eggs and sour cream in a container for five minutes until creamy.
2. Put in the lemon zest, lemon juice, flour, baking soda and salt and mix using a spatula.
3. Fold in the fruits then spoon the batter in a 9-inch round cake pan.
4. For the streusel, combine all the ingredients in a container until grainy.
5. Spread the streusel over the cake and preheat your oven and bake at 350F for about forty minutes or until a toothpick inserted in the center comes out clean.
6. Let the cake cool in the pan before you serve.

Nutritional Content of One Serving:

Calories: 421 Fat: 23.0g Protein: 6.2g Carbohydrates: 49.4g

Boozy Chocolate Cake

Total Time Taken: 1 ¼ hours
Yield: 14 Servings
Ingredients:

Cake:

- ¼ cup brandy
- ½ cup canola oil
- ½ cup cocoa powder

- ½ cup hot coffee
- ½ teaspoon salt
- 1 cup buttermilk
- 1 teaspoon baking powder
- 1 teaspoon baking soda
- 2 cups all-purpose flour
- 2 eggs

Frosting:
- ¼ cup brandy
- 1 cup heavy cream
- 2 cups dark chocolate chips
- 2 tablespoons butter

Directions:
1. For the cake, combine the flour, cocoa powder, baking soda, baking powder and salt in a container.
2. Put in the rest of the ingredients and mix thoroughly.
3. Pour the batter in a 9-inch round cake pan , preheat your oven and bake at 330F for 50 minutes.
4. When finished, allow the cake to cool in the pan then move to a platter.
5. For the frosting, bring the cream to the boiling point in a saucepan. Turn off the heat and put in the chocolate. Stir thoroughly to mix until melted and smooth.
6. let the frosting cool down then cover the cake with it.
7. *Serve fresh or chilled.*

Nutritional Content of One Serving:
Calories: 281 Fat: 18.5g Protein: 5.1g Carbohydrates: 28.0g

Boozy Raisin Bundt Cake

Total Time Taken: 2 hours
Yield: 12 Servings
Ingredients:
- ½ cup brandy
- ½ cup whole milk
- ½ teaspoon salt
- 1 ½ cups white sugar
- 1 cup apricot jam
- 1 cup butter, softened
- 1 cup buttermilk
- 1 cup golden raisins
- 2 eggs
- 2 teaspoons baking powder
- 3 cups all-purpose flour

Directions:
1. Sift the flour, salt and baking powder.
2. Mix the butter, sugar and jam in a container until creamy and light.
3. Stir in the eggs, one at a time, then begin incorporating the flour mixture, alternating it with the buttermilk and milk.

4. Spoon the batter in a greased Bundt cake pan and preheat your oven and bake at 350F for about fifty minutes or until a toothpick inserted in the center comes out clean.
5. Let the cake cool in the pan before you serve.

Nutritional Content of One Serving:

Calories: 474 Fat: 17.0g Protein: 5.9g Carbohydrates: 77.5g

Brown Butter Walnut Cake

Total Time Taken: 1 ¼ hours
Yield: 12 Servings

Ingredients:
- ½ teaspoon salt
- 1 ½ cups all-purpose flour
- 1 ½ cups white sugar
- 1 cup butter
- 1 cup ground walnuts
- 1 cup sour cream
- 1 cup walnuts, chopped
- 1 teaspoon baking powder
- 1 teaspoon vanilla extract
- 2 eggs

Directions:
1. Place the butter in a saucepan and melt it. Keep on heat until mildly browned and caramelized. Let the butter cool then move it to a container.
2. Put in the sugar and mix thoroughly.
3. Stir in the eggs and mix thoroughly then put in the sour cream and vanilla.
4. Fold in the flour, baking powder, salt and ground walnuts.
5. Spoon the batter in a 9-inch round cake pan and top with chopped walnuts.
6. Pre-heat the oven and bake at 350F for about forty-five minutes or until a toothpick inserted into the center of the cake comes out clean.
7. *The cake tastes best chilled.*

Nutritional Content of One Serving:

Calories: 468 Fat: 32.5g Protein: 8.3g Carbohydrates: 40.1g

Brown Sugar Cake

Total Time Taken: 1 ¼ hours
Yield: 10 Servings

Ingredients:
- ½ cup dark brown sugar
- ½ teaspoon salt
- 1 cup butter, softened
- 1 cup light brown sugar
- 1 teaspoon vanilla extract
- 2 cups all-purpose flour

- 2 teaspoons baking powder
- 4 eggs
- ½ cup milk

Directions:
1. Sift the flour, baking powder and salt in a container.
2. In another container, combine the butter and sugars until creamy and light.
3. Stir in the eggs, one at a time, then put in the vanilla and milk.
4. Fold in the flour then spoon the batter in a 9-inch round cake pan covered with parchment paper.
5. Pre-heat the oven and bake at 350F for forty minutes or until it rises significantly and starts to appear golden-brown.
6. Let the cake cool in the pan and serve, sliced.

Nutritional Content of One Serving:
Calories: 370 Fat: 20.7g Protein: 5.4g Carbohydrates: 41.7g

Brown Sugar Pineapple Bundt Cake

Total Time Taken: 1 ¼ hours
Yield: 12 Servings

Ingredients:
- ½ cup buttermilk
- ½ cup cornstarch
- ½ cup light brown sugar
- ½ teaspoon salt
- ¾ cup butter, softened
- 1 cup white sugar
- 1 tablespoon lemon zest
- 1 teaspoon baking powder
- 1 teaspoon baking soda
- 1 teaspoon vanilla extract
- 2 cups all-purpose flour
- 3 eggs
- 4 pineapple slices, cubed

Directions:
1. Position the pineapple slices at the bottom of a greased Bundt cake pan and drizzle with brown sugar.
2. Sift the flour with cornstarch, baking soda, baking powder and salt.
3. Mix the butter with sugar in a container until light and creamy then mix in the eggs and vanilla, as well as the lemon zest and buttermilk.
4. Fold in the flour then pour the batter over the pineapple.
5. Pre-heat the oven and bake at 350F for about forty minutes or until it rises significantly and starts to appear golden-brown.
6. Let the cake cool in the pan for about ten minutes then flip it over on a platter.

Nutritional Content of One Serving:
Calories: 332 Fat: 13.0g Protein: 4.3g Carbohydrates: 51.5g

Butter Cake

Total Time Taken: 1 hour
Yield: 8 Servings
Ingredients:

- ¼ teaspoon salt
- ½ cup butter, softened
- ½ cup whole milk
- ¾ cup white sugar
- 1 cup all-purpose flour
- 1 teaspoon baking powder
- 1 teaspoon vanilla extract
- 2 eggs

Directions:

1. Mix the butter, sugar and vanilla in a container until fluffy and pale.
2. Stir in the eggs and mix thoroughly.
3. Fold in the flour, baking powder and salt, alternating it with milk. Begin and finish with flour.
4. Spoon the batter in a 6-inch round cake pan coated with baking paper.
5. Pre-heat the oven and bake at 350F for about half an hour or until a golden-brown colour is achieved.
6. Let the cake cool in the pan before you serve.

Nutritional Content of One Serving:

Calories: 256 Fat: 13.2g Protein: 3.6g Carbohydrates: 31.8g

Buttermilk Chocolate Cake

Total Time Taken: 50 minutes
Yield: 8 Servings
Ingredients:

- ½ cup butter, melted
- ½ cup cocoa powder
- ½ teaspoon salt
- 1 ½ cups all-purpose flour
- 1 cup buttermilk
- 1 cup sugar
- 1 teaspoon baking powder
- 1 teaspoon vanilla extract
- 2 eggs

Directions:

1. Mix the dry ingredients in a container and the wet ingredients in a separate container.
2. Pour the wet ingredients over the dry ones and stir for a few seconds to mix.
3. Pour the batter in a 9-inch cake pan coated with baking paper.
4. Pre-heat the oven and bake at 350F for about half an hour.
5. Let cool in the pan and serve, sliced.

Nutritional Content of One Serving:

Calories: 323 Fat: 13.8g Protein: 5.9g Carbohydrates: 47.8g

Buttermilk Chocolate Cake

Total Time Taken: 1 ¼ hours
 Yield: 10 Servings

Ingredients:
- ½ cup cocoa powder
- ½ teaspoon salt
- 1 ¼ cups buttermilk
- 1 cup butter, melted
- 1 cup white sugar
- 1 teaspoon vanilla extract
- 2 cups all-purpose flour
- 2 eggs
- 2 teaspoons baking powder

Directions:
1. Mix all the ingredients in a container.
2. Give it a quick stir until incorporated.
3. Pour the batter in a 9-inch round cake pan coated with baking paper.
4. Preheat your oven and bake the cake for about forty minutes or until the cake is well risen and it passes the toothpick test.
5. Let the cake cool in the pan then serve it chilled.

Nutritional Content of One Serving:
Calories: 365 Fat: 20.4g Protein: 5.7g Carbohydrates: 43.5g

Butterscotch Pecan Cake

Total Time Taken: 1 ½ hours
 Yield: 10 Servings

Ingredients:
- ¼ cup canola oil
- ¼ cup cocoa powder
- ¼ cup plain yogurt
- ¼ teaspoon salt
- ½ cup butter, softened
- ½ cup caramel sauce
- 1 ½ cups all-purpose flour
- 1 teaspoon baking powder
- 2 cups pecans
- 2 eggs

Directions:
1. Mix the butter, canola oil, eggs and yogurt in a container until fluffy.
2. Put in the flour, salt, baking powder and cocoa and stir lightly using a spatula.
3. Pour the batter in a 9-inch round cake pan and cover with half of the walnuts.

4. Mix the remaining pecans with caramel and set aside for later.
5. Preheat your oven and bake the cake for around forty minutes.
6. Let cool and then top with butterscotch pecans and serve fresh.

Nutritional Content of One Serving:

Calories: 281 Fat: 18.1g Protein: 4.4g Carbohydrates: 27.4g

Butterscotch Sweet Potato Cake

Total Time Taken: 1 ½ hours
Yield: 10 Servings
Ingredients:

Cake:

- ½ cup canola oil
- ½ cup coconut milk
- ½ cup dark brown sugar
- ½ cup white sugar
- ½ teaspoon salt
- 1 cup sweet potato puree
- 1 teaspoon baking powder
- 1 teaspoon baking soda
- 1 teaspoon cinnamon powder
- 2 cups all-purpose flour
- 3 eggs

Butterscotch sauce:

- ¼ cup butter
- ¼ cup heavy cream
- ¼ cup light corn syrup
- ¼ teaspoon salt
- ½ cup dark brown sugar

Directions:

1. To prepare the cake, combine the dry ingredients in a container and the wet ingredients in a separate container.
2. Combine the dry ingredients with the wet ingredients and give it a good mix.
3. Pour the batter in a 10-inch round cake pan coated with baking paper and preheat your oven and bake at 350F for around forty minutes.
4. Let the cake cool in the pan then move to a platter.
5. For the butterscotch sauce, combine all the ingredients in a saucepan and cook for about five to eight minutes until it becomes thick.
6. Let cool and then pour the sauce over each slice of cake before you serve.

Nutritional Content of One Serving:

Calories: 426 Fat: 21.1g Protein: 5.1g Carbohydrates: 56.2g

Buttery Orange Cake

Total Time Taken: 1 hour
Yield: 8 Servings
Ingredients:

- ¼ cup canola oil
- ½ cup butter, softened
- ½ teaspoon salt
- ¾ cup whole milk
- 1 cup white sugar Zest of
- 1 lemon
- 1 lemon Juice of
- 2 cups all-purpose flour
- 2 teaspoons baking powder
- 4 eggs

Directions:

1. Mix the flour with baking powder and salt.
2. Mix the butter and eggs in a container for five minutes until creamy then put in the eggs, one at a time, as well as lemon juice and zest.
3. Fold in the flour mixture, alternating it with milk. Begin with flour and finish with flour.
4. Spoon the batter in a 9-inch round cake pan coated with baking paper.
5. Pre-heat the oven and bake at 350F for around forty minutes or until a golden-brown colour is achieved and it rises significantly.
6. Let the cake cool in the pan and serve, sliced.

Nutritional Content of One Serving:

Calories: 417 Fat: 21.6g Protein: 6.9g Carbohydrates: 50.8g

Buttery Zucchini Cake

Total Time Taken: 1 ½ hours
Yield: 10 Servings

Ingredients:

- ½ cup dark brown sugar
- ½ cup dark chocolate chips
- ½ teaspoon salt
- 1 cup butter, softened
- 1 cup grated zucchinis
- 1 teaspoon baking powder
- 1 teaspoon baking soda
- 1/2 cup white sugar
- 2 cups all-purpose flour
- 4 eggs

Directions:

1. Mix the butter, brown sugar and white sugar in a container until creamy and firm.
2. Stir in the eggs, one at a time, then put in the zucchinis.

3. Fold in the remaining ingredients then pour the batter in a round cake pan coated with baking paper.
4. Preheat your oven and bake the cake for about forty minutes or until a toothpick inserted in the center comes out clean.
5. Let the cake cool in the pan then serve, sliced.

Nutritional Content of One Serving:

Calories: 374 Fat: 22.0g Protein: 5.5g Carbohydrates: 40.9g

Candied Ginger Applesauce Cake

Total Time Taken: 1 ¼ hours
Yield: 10 Servings

Ingredients:
- ¼ cup candied ginger, chopped
- ¼ teaspoon baking soda
- ½ cup butter, room temperature
- ½ cup golden raisins
- ½ teaspoon cinnamon powder
- ½ teaspoon ground star anise
- ½ teaspoon salt
- 1 ¼ cups applesauce
- 1 cup white sugar
- 1 teaspoon vanilla extract
- 2 cups all-purpose flour
- 2 eggs
- 2 tablespoons molasses
- 2 teaspoons baking powder

Directions:
1. Mix the flour, baking powder, baking soda, salt and spices in a container.
2. In a separate container, combine the butter, sugar and molasses until creamy and firm. Put in the eggs, one at a time, then the applesauce and vanilla and mix thoroughly.
3. Fold in the flour mixture then put in the raisins and ginger.
4. Spoon the batter in a 9-inch round cake pan coated with baking paper.
5. Pre-heat the oven and bake at 350F for about forty minutes or until a golden-brown colour is achieved and it rises significantly.
6. Let the cake cool in the pan and serve, sliced.

Nutritional Content of One Serving:

Calories: 310 Fat: 10.4g Protein: 4.1g Carbohydrates: 52.1g

Caramel Apple Cake

Total Time Taken: 1 ½ hours
Yield: 12 Servings
Ingredients:

Cake:
- ½ cup applesauce

- ½ teaspoon cinnamon powder
- ½ teaspoon ground ginger
- ½ teaspoon salt
- 1 ¼ cups white sugar
- 1 cup butter, softened
- 1 teaspoon baking soda
- 2 cups all-purpose flour
- 2 red apples, cored and diced
- 4 eggs

Glaze:
- ¼ teaspoon salt
- ½ cup heavy cream
- 1 cup white sugar

Directions:
1. For the cake, combine the sugar, butter and eggs in a container until creamy.
2. Stir in the applesauce then put in the flour, baking soda, salt and cinnamon, as well as ginger and apples.
3. Spoon the batter in a 9-inch round cake pan coated with baking paper.
4. Pre-heat the oven and bake at 350F for about forty-five minutes.
5. Let the cake cool in the pan then move to a platter.
6. For the glaze, melt the sugar in a heavy saucepan until it sppears amber in colour.
7. Put in the cream and salt and stir until melted and smooth.
8. let the glaze cool in the pan then sprinkle it over the cake.

Nutritional Content of One Serving:
Calories: 411 Fat: 18.9g Protein: 4.4g Carbohydrates: 59.1g

Caramel Banana Cake

Total Time Taken: 1 hour
Yield: 12 Servings
Ingredients:
- ¼ cup dark brown sugar
- ½ cup caramel sauce
- ½ teaspoon ground cardamom
- ½ teaspoon salt
- ¾ cup butter, softened
- 1 cup buttermilk
- 1 cup white sugar
- 1 teaspoon cinnamon powder
- 2 cups all-purpose flour
- 2 ripe bananas, mashed
- 2 teaspoons baking powder
- 4 eggs

Directions:

1. Mix the butter with sugars for five minutes until creamy. Put in the eggs, one at a time, then mix in the bananas.
2. Fold in the flour, spices, baking powder and salt, alternating it with buttermilk.
3. Pour the batter in a 9-inch round cake pan.
4. Sprinkle the batter with caramel sauce and preheat your oven and bake the cake at 350F for about forty-five minutes or until a toothpick inserted in the center comes out clean.
5. Let the cake cool in the pan and serve, sliced.

Nutritional Content of One Serving:

Calories: 334 Fat: 13.4g Protein: 5.2g Carbohydrates: 50.6g

Caramel Pineapple Upside Down Cake

Total Time Taken: 1 ½ hours
 Yield: 14 Servings

Ingredients:
- ¼ cup whole milk
- ¼ teaspoon salt
- ½ cup butter, softened
- ½ cup canola oil
- ½ cup cornstarch
- ½ cup light brown sugar
- ½ cup white sugar
- 1 cup all-purpose flour
- 1 cup shredded coconut
- 1 teaspoon baking soda
- 2 tablespoons butter
- 3 eggs
- 6 slices pineapple

Directions:
1. Melt the white sugar in a saucepan until it sppears amber in colour.
2. Sprinkle the melted sugar on the bottom of a 9-inch round cake pan coated with baking paper.
3. Top the caramelized sugar with butter and set aside for later.
4. For the batter, combine the butter, oil and brown sugar until fluffy and creamy.
5. Fold in the eggs and milk then put in the remaining ingredients and mix using a spatula.
6. Spoon the batter over the pineapple slices and preheat your oven and bake at 350F for about forty minutes or until a toothpick inserted in the center comes out clean.
7. Let the cake cool in the pan for about ten minutes then flip it over on a platter.
8. Serve chilled.

Nutritional Content of One Serving:

Calories: 309 Fat: 19.2g Protein: 2.9g Carbohydrates: 33.6g

Caramel Pumpkin Cake

Total Time Taken: 1 ½ hours
Yield: 12 Servings
Ingredients:

Cake:

- ¼ cup white sugar
- ¼ cup whole milk
- ½ cup coconut oil, melted
- 1 cup dark brown sugar
- 1 cup pumpkin puree
- 1 pinch salt
- 1 teaspoon baking powder
- 1 teaspoon baking soda
- 1 teaspoon cinnamon powder
- 1 teaspoon ground ginger
- 2 cups all-purpose flour
- 4 eggs

Caramel frosting:

1. 1 cup butter, softened
2. 2 cups powdered sugar
3. 1 pinch salt
4. ½ cup caramel sauce

Directions:

1. For the cake, combine the flour, baking powder, baking soda, spices and salt in a container.
2. In a separate container, mix the coconut oil, pumpkin puree, eggs, sugars and milk.
3. Pour this mixture over the dry ingredients and mix thoroughly.
4. Pour the batter in 2 circular cake pans coated with baking paper.
5. Preheat your oven and bake the cake at 350F for 35 minutes or until it rises completely and is aromatic.
6. Let the cakes cool in the pans then level them and set aside for later.
7. For the frosting, combine the butter, sugar and salt in a container for about five to seven minutes or until twofold in volume and firm.
8. Stir in the caramel sauce.
9. Use half of the frosting to fill the cake and the half that is left over to garnish the cake.
    10. Serve fresh.

Nutritional Content of One Serving:

Calories: 495 Fat: 26.4g Protein: 4.8g Carbohydrates: 63.2g

Caramel Spice Cake

Total Time Taken: 1 ¼ hours
Yield: 8 Servings
Ingredients:

Cake:

- ¼ teaspoon ground nutmeg
- ½ cup butter, softened
- ½ cup sour cream
- ½ teaspoon ground cardamom
- ½ teaspoon ground ginger
- ¾ cup light brown sugar
- 1 1/4 cups all-purpose flour
- 1 teaspoon baking soda
- 1 teaspoon cinnamon powder
- 3 eggs

Glaze:

- ½ cup heavy cream
- ½ teaspoon salt
- 1 cup white sugar

Directions:

1. For the cake, sift the flour, baking soda, spices and salt in a container.
2. In a separate container, combine the butter and sugar until creamy. Stir in the eggs and mix thoroughly then put in the sour cream and mix thoroughly.
3. Fold in the flour mixture then pour the batter in a 9-inch round cake pan covered with parchment paper.
4. Pre-heat the oven and bake at 350F for around forty minutes or until a toothpick inserted in the center comes out clean.
5. Let the cake cool in the pan.
6. For the glaze, melt the sugar in a heavy saucepan until it sppears amber in colour.
7. Stir in the cream and salt and mix thoroughly. Keep over low heat until the desired smoothness is achieved.
8. Let the glaze cool down then sprinkle it over the cake just before you serve.

Nutritional Content of One Serving:

Calories: 400 Fat: 19.2g Protein: 4.9g Carbohydrates: 54.4g

Cardamom Carrot Cake

Total Time Taken: 1 ¼ hours
Yield: 16 Servings
Ingredients:

Cake:

- ¼ cup dark brown sugar
- ½ teaspoon baking powder
- ½ teaspoon salt

- 1 cup crushed pineapple
- 1 cup pecans, chopped
- 1 cup shredded coconut
- 1 cup vegetable oil
- 1 cup white sugar
- 1 teaspoon baking soda
- 1 teaspoon ground cardamom
- 1 teaspoon vanilla extract
- 2 cups all-purpose flour
- 2 cups grated carrots
- 4 eggs

Frosting:
- ½ cup butter, softened
- 1 cup cream cheese
- 1 cup powdered sugar
- 1 teaspoon vanilla extract

Directions:
1. For the cake, sift the flour, baking soda, baking powder, salt and cardamom in a container.
2. In a separate container, combine the eggs and sugars until creamy and fluffy.
3. Put in the vanilla, carrots, pineapple, coconut and pecans and mix thoroughly.
4. Fold in the dry ingredients then pour the batter into a 10- inch round cake pan coated with baking paper.
5. Preheat your oven and bake the cake for about fifty minutes or until it rises completely and is aromatic.
6. For the frosting, combine all the ingredients in a container for minimum five minutes.
7. Frost the chilled cake with the cream cheese buttercream and serve fresh or place in your refrigerator.

Nutritional Content of One Serving:
Calories: 416 Fat: 28.0g Protein: 4.6g Carbohydrates: 38.4g

Chai Spiced Cake

Total Time Taken: 1 ½ hours
Yield: 10 Servings
Ingredients:

Cake:
- ¼ teaspoon ground cloves
- ½ teaspoon ground ginger
- ½ teaspoon salt
- ½ teaspoon turmeric
- 1 ½ cups white sugar
- 1 cup butter, softened
- 1 teaspoon cinnamon powder
- 1 teaspoon vanilla extract
- 2 cups all-purpose flour

- 2 teaspoons baking powder
- 6 eggs

Frosting:
- ¼ cup light brown sugar
- ½ cup butter, softened
- 1 cup cream cheese
- 1 teaspoon grated ginger
- 2 cups powdered sugar

Directions:
1. For the cake, sift the flour with baking powder, salt and spices on a platter.
2. Mix the butter and sugar in a container until pale and thick.
3. Put in the eggs, one at a time, then mix in the dry ingredients, mixing gently using a spatula.
4. Spoon the batter in a 9-inch round cake pan coated with baking paper.
5. For the frosting, combine the cream cheese, butter and brown sugar in a container for minimum five minutes.
6. Put in the rest of the ingredients and mix thoroughly. Cover the cake with buttercream and serve fresh.

Nutritional Content of One Serving:
Calories: 484 Fat: 27.6g Protein: 5.7g Carbohydrates: 55.8g

Chai Spiced Streusel Cake

Total Time Taken: 1 hour
Yield: 10 Servings
Ingredients:

Streusel:
- ¼ cup all-purpose flour
- ¼ cup butter, melted
- ¼ cup light brown sugar
- ½ teaspoon cardamom powder
- ½ teaspoon cinnamon powder
- ½ teaspoon ground cloves
- ½ teaspoon star anise
- 1 cup pecans, chopped

Cake:
- ¼ cup butter, melted
- ¼ cup whole milk
- ½ cup white sugar
- 1 ¼ cups all-purpose flour
- 1 pinch salt
- 1 teaspoon baking powder
- 6 eggs, room temperature

Directions:

1. Mix the eggs, sugar and salt for minimum five minutes until its volume increases to almost three times it was.
2. Put in the milk then fold in the flour and baking powder.
3. Progressively mix in the melted butter then pour the batter in a 9-inch cake pan coated with baking paper.
4. For the streusel, combine all the ingredients in a container and stir thoroughly until grainy.
5. Spread the streusel over the cake and preheat your oven and bake at 350F for about forty minutes or until a golden-brown colour is achieved and fragrant.
6. Let cool in the pan and serve, sliced.

Nutritional Content of One Serving:

Calories: 254 Fat: 13.3g Protein: 5.7g Carbohydrates: 29.0g

Cherry Brownie Cake

Total Time Taken: 1 hour
Yield: 8 Servings
Ingredients:

- ¼ teaspoon salt
- ¾ cup butter
- ¾ cup light brown sugar
- 1 cup all-purpose flour
- 1 cup cherries, pitted
- 1 cup dark chocolate chips
- 1 teaspoon vanilla extract
- 3 eggs

Directions:

1. Mix the butter and chocolate chips in a heatproof container. Place over a hot water bath and melt them until the desired smoothness is achieved.
2. Turn off the heat and mix in the eggs, vanilla and sugar.
3. Fold in the flour and salt then pour the batter in a 8-inch round cake pan coated with baking paper.
4. Top with cherries and preheat your oven and bake at 350F for 20 minutes.
5. *The cake tastes best chilled.*

Nutritional Content of One Serving:

Calories: 367 Fat: 23.1g Protein: 4.9g Carbohydrates: 38.1g

Cherry Chocolate Cake

Total Time Taken: 1 ¼ hours
Yield: 10 Servings

Ingredients:

- ¼ teaspoon salt
- ½ cup butter, melted
- ½ cup milk
- ½ cup pine nuts, ground
- 1 ½ cups all-purpose flour

- 1 cup white sugar
- 1 teaspoon baking powder
- 1 teaspoon vanilla extract
- 2 cups cherries, pitted
- 3 eggs

Directions:
1. Mix the eggs and sugar in a container until volume increases to twice what it was.
2. Stir in the milk then progressively pour in the butter, stirring thoroughly.
3. Put in the vanilla then fold in the flour, baking powder and salt.
4. Put in the ground pine nuts then fold in the cherries.
5. Pour the batter in a 9-inch round cake pan coated with baking paper.
6. Pre-heat the oven and bake at 350F for about forty minutes or until a toothpick inserted into the center of the cake comes out clean.
7. Let the cake cool in the pan before you serve.

Nutritional Content of One Serving:
Calories: 314 Fat: 15.6g Protein: 5.1g Carbohydrates: 40.3g

Cherry Liqueur Soaked Cake

Total Time Taken: 1 ¼ hours
Yield: 8 Servings

Ingredients:
- ¼ cup cherry liqueurs
- ¼ cup dark brown sugar
- ¼ teaspoon salt
- ½ cup all-purpose flour
- ½ cup butter, melted
- ½ cup hot coffee
- ½ cup white sugar
- ½ teaspoon baking powder
- 1 ½ cups dark chocolate chips
- 1 cup almond flour
- 2 eggs

Directions:
1. Mix the coffee and chocolate in a container. Stir until melted and smooth.
2. Stir in the sugars, butter and eggs then fold in the almond flour, all-purpose flour, salt and baking powder.
3. Pour the batter in a 8-inch round cake pan coated with baking paper.
4. Pre-heat the oven and bake at 350F for a little more than half an hour.
5. Let the cake cool down then move to a platter.
6. Brush the cherry liqueur over the cake.
7. *The cake tastes best chilled.*

Nutritional Content of One Serving:
Calories: 343 Fat: 20.8g Protein: 4.6g Carbohydrates: 39.7g

Chestnut Puree Chocolate Cake

Total Time Taken: 1 ¼ hours
Yield: 10 Servings

Ingredients:

- ¼ cup butter
- ¼ teaspoon salt
- ½ cup canola oil
- ½ cup cocoa powder
- ½ cup ground almonds
- 1 cup all-purpose flour
- 1 cup chestnut puree
- 1 cup dark chocolate chips
- 1 cup white sugar
- 1 teaspoon baking powder

Directions:

1. Mix the canola oil, butter and chocolate chips in a heatproof container. Place over heatproof container and melt them together.
2. Turn off the heat and mix in the sugar and chestnut puree.
3. Fold in the cocoa powder, flour, almonds, salt and baking powder.
4. Spoon the batter in a 9-inch round cake pan coated with baking paper.
5. Pre-heat the oven and bake at 350F for around forty minutes or until a toothpick inserted into the center of the cake comes out clean.
6. The cake tastes best chilled.

Nutritional Content of One Serving:

Calories: 354 Fat: 21.8g Protein: 3.9g Carbohydrates: 41.6g

Chia Seed Chocolate Cake

Total Time Taken: 1 ¼ hours
Yield: 10 Servings

Ingredients:

- ¼ cup cocoa powder
- ¼ teaspoon salt
- ½ cup butter
- ½ cup dark chocolate chips
- 1 ½ cups all-purpose flour
- 1 cup canola oil
- 1 cup white sugar
- 1 tablespoon orange zest
- 1 teaspoon baking powder
- 2 tablespoons chia seeds
- 3 eggs

Directions:

1. Melt the chocolate and butter in a container until the desired smoothness is achieved.

2. Turn off the heat and mix in the eggs, orange zest, sugar and canola oil.
3. Fold in the cocoa powder, chia seeds, flour, baking powder and salt then pour the batter in a 9-inch round cake pan coated with baking paper.
4. Pre-heat the oven and bake at 350F for around forty minutes or until a toothpick inserted into the center of the cake comes out clean.
5. *The cake tastes best chilled.*

Nutritional Content of One Serving:

Calories: 470 Fat: 34.4g Protein: 4.5g Carbohydrates: 40.0g

Chocolate Biscuit Cake

Total Time Taken: 3 hours
Yield: 10 Servings
Ingredients:
- ¼ cup cocoa powder
- ¼ cup dried cranberries
- ½ cup butter
- ½ cup dark chocolate chips
- ½ cup golden syrup
- ½ cup milk chocolate chips
- ½ cup pecans, chopped
- 1 cup golden raisins
- 1 cup heavy cream
- 1 cup milk
- 10 oz. digestive biscuits, chopped

Directions:
1. Melt the chocolate chips and butter in a heatproof container over a hot water bath.
2. Mix the cream, milk and cocoa powder and place over low heat. Bring to a boil and cook just until slightly thickened. Turn off the heat and mix in the chocolate mixture.
3. Mix this mixture with the remaining ingredients in a container then transfer in a 8-inch cake pan coated with plastic wrap.
4. Place in your refrigerator to set for about two hours then serve, sliced.

Nutritional Content of One Serving:

Calories: 408 Fat: 24.0g Protein: 4.3g Carbohydrates: 49.1g

Chocolate Bundt Cake

Total Time Taken: 1 ¼ hours
Yield: 10 Servings

Ingredients:
- ½ cup butter, softened
- ½ cup cocoa powder
- ½ cup dark chocolate chips
- ½ teaspoon baking soda
- ½ teaspoon salt

- 1 ½ cups all-purpose flour
- 1 cup white sugar
- 1 teaspoon baking powder
- 1 teaspoon vanilla extract
- 2 tablespoons canola oil
- 3 eggs

Directions:

1. Mix the butter, canola oil and sugar in a container until light and pale.
2. Stir in the eggs and vanilla and mix thoroughly.
3. Fold in the flour, cocoa powder, baking powder, baking soda and salt.
4. Put in the chocolate chips then spoon the batter in a greased Bundt cake pan.
5. Pre-heat the oven and bake at 350F for about forty minutes or until well risen and it passes the toothpick test.
6. Let the cake cool in the pan and serve, sliced.

Nutritional Content of One Serving:

Calories: 308 Fat: 15.7g Protein: 4.9g Carbohydrates: 41.1g

Chocolate Chip Blackberry Cake

Total Time Taken: 1 ¼ hours
Yield: 10 Servings

Ingredients:

- ¼ cup canola oil
- ¼ cup cornstarch
- ¼ teaspoon salt
- ½ cup butter, softened
- ½ cup dark chocolate chips
- ½ cup plain yogurt
- 1 ½ cups all-purpose flour
- 1 cup fresh blackberries
- 1 cup white sugar
- 1 teaspoon baking powder
- 3 eggs

Directions:

1. Mix the butter, oil and sugar in a container until creamy and fluffy.
2. Put in the eggs and yogurt and mix thoroughly.
3. Fold in the flour, cornstarch, baking powder and salt and mix using a spatula.
4. Put in the chocolate chips and blackberries then spoon the batter in a 9-inch round cake pan coated with baking paper.
5. Preheat your oven and bake the cake for about forty minutes or until it rises significantly and starts to appear golden-brown.
6. Let the cake cool in the pan before you serve.

Nutritional Content of One Serving:

Calories: 347 Fat: 18.0 Protein: 5.0g Carbohydrates: 43.8g

Chocolate Chip Bundt Cake

Total Time Taken: 1 ¼ hours
Yield: 12 Servings

Ingredients:
- ½ teaspoon salt
- ¾ cup dark chocolate chips
- 1 cup butter, softened
- 1 cup plain yogurt
- 1 cup white sugar
- 1 teaspoon vanilla extract
- 2 cups all-purpose flour
- 2 teaspoons baking powder
- 3 eggs

Directions:
1. Mix the flour with baking powder and salt.
2. Mix the butter with sugar until creamy. Put in the eggs, one at a time, then mix in the vanilla and mix thoroughly.
3. Put in the yogurt and mix thoroughly then fold in the flour, followed by the chocolate chips.
4. Spoon the batter in a greased Bundt cake pan.
5. Pre-heat the oven and bake at 350F for about forty minutes or until a toothpick inserted in the cake comes out clean.

Nutritional Content of One Serving:

Calories: 341 Fat: 18.9g Protein: 5.3g Carbohydrates: 39.5g

Chocolate Chip Pumpkin Bundt Cake

Total Time Taken: 1 ¼ hours
Yield: 12 Servings

Ingredients:
- ½ teaspoon salt
- 1 ½ cups white sugar
- 1 ½ teaspoons baking powder
- 1 cup butter, softened
- 1 cup dark chocolate chips
- 1 cup pumpkin puree
- 1 teaspoon vanilla extract
- 2 cups all-purpose flour
- 2 eggs
- 2 tablespoons molasses

Directions:
1. Mix the butter, sugar and molasses in a container until creamy and light.
2. Stir in the vanilla and eggs, as well as the pumpkin puree.
3. Fold in the remaining ingredients and stir lightly.

4. Spoon the batter in a greased Bundt cake pan. Pre-heat the oven and bake at 350F for about forty-five minutes or until a toothpick inserted into the center of the cake comes out clean.
5. Let the cake cool in the pan before you serve.

Nutritional Content of One Serving:

Calories: 381 Fat: 19.0g Protein: 4.1g Carbohydrates: 52.1g

Chocolate Coconut Cake

Total Time Taken: 1 ¼ hours
Yield: 10 Servings

Ingredients:
- ¼ cup cocoa powder
- ¼ teaspoon salt
- ½ cup butter
- ¾ cup milk
- 1 ½ cups all-purpose flour
- 1 cup shredded coconut
- 1 cup white sugar
- 1 teaspoon baking powder
- 2 eggs
- 2 tablespoons canola oil

Directions:
1. Mix the butter, oil and sugar in a container until fluffy and creamy.
2. Put in the eggs, one at a time, then mix in the milk.
3. Put in the dry ingredients and stir lightly using a spatula.
4. Spoon the batter in a 8-inch round cake pan coated with baking paper.
5. Pre-heat the oven and bake at 350F for around forty minutes or until a toothpick inserted into the center of the cake comes out clean.
6. *The cake tastes best chilled.*

Nutritional Content of One Serving:

Calories: 305 Fat: 16.4g Protein: 4.4g Carbohydrates: 37.9g

Chocolate Coffee Cake

Total Time Taken: 1 hour
Yield: 12 Servings
Ingredients:

Cake:
- ½ cup canola oil
- ½ teaspoon salt
- 1 cup buttermilk
- 1 cup hot coffee
- 1 cup white sugar
- 2 cups all-purpose flour
- 2 teaspoons baking powder

- 2 teaspoons instant coffee
- 3 eggs

Frosting:
- 1 cup heavy cream
- 2 cups dark chocolate chips
- 2 teaspoons instant coffee

Directions:
1. For the cake, combine the buttermilk, canola oil, hot coffee and eggs in a container.
2. Stir in the dry ingredients and mix thoroughly.
3. Pour the batter in a 9-inch round cake pan coated with baking paper.
4. Pre-heat the oven and bake at 350F for about fifty minutes.
5. When finished, transfer the chilled cake on a platter.
6. For the frosting, bring the cream to the boiling point in a saucepan. Put in the chocolate and stir until it melts completely. Stir in the coffee.
7. Cover the cake with chocolate coffee frosting and serve it fresh.

Nutritional Content of One Serving:

Calories: 371 Fat: 19.6g Protein: 5.8g Carbohydrates: 47.6g

Chocolate Dulce De Leche Cake

Total Time Taken: 1 ¼ hours
Yield: 12 Servings

Ingredients:
- ½ cup butter, softened
- ½ cup canola oil
- ½ cup dulce de leche
- ½ cup sour cream
- ½ teaspoon salt
- 1 ¾ cups all-purpose flour
- 1 cup dark chocolate chips
- 1 cup white sugar
- 2 teaspoons baking powder
- 3 eggs

Directions:
1. Mix the butter and oil in a container. Put in the sugar and stir thoroughly until creamy.
2. Put in the eggs and sour cream and mix thoroughly.
3. Fold in the flour, baking powder and salt then put in the chocolate chips. Pour the batter in a 9-inch round cake pan coated with baking paper.
4. Drop spoonfuls of dulce de leche over the batter and preheat your oven and bake at 350F for about forty minutes or until a toothpick inserted into the center of the cake comes out clean.
5. *The cake tastes best chilled.*

Nutritional Content of One Serving:

Calories: 397 Fat: 23.2g Protein: 5.0g Carbohydrates: 45.8g

Chocolate Fudge Cake

Total Time Taken: 1 ½ hours
Yield: 12 Servings
Ingredients:

Cake:
- ¼ cup cocoa powder
- ¼ teaspoon salt
- ½ cup dark chocolate chips
- 1 cup hot water
- ½ cup sour cream
- ½ teaspoon baking soda
- ¾ cup butter, softened
- 1 ½ teaspoons baking powder
- 1 ¾ cups all-purpose flour
- 1 cup dark brown sugar
- 2 eggs
- 2 tablespoons vegetable oil
- 1 teaspoon vanilla extract

Frosting:
- ½ cup cocoa powder
- 1 pinch salt
- 1 cup butter, softened
- 2 cups powdered sugar
- 2 tablespoons whole milk

Directions:

1. To prepare the cake, combine the chocolate chips, hot water and cocoa powder in a container.
2. In a separate container, combine the butter and sugar until creamy and pale. Stir in the eggs, one at a time, then put in the sour cream, vanilla and oil.
3. Mix the flour with baking powder, baking soda and salt then mix it with the butter mixture alternating it with the chocolate mixture. Begin and finish with flour.
4. Split the batter between two 9-inch circular cake pans covered with parchment paper.
5. Pre-heat the oven and bake at 350F for about half an hour.
6. Let cool and then take the cakes out of the pans and let them sit on the side you perform the next few steps.
7. For the frosting: combine the butter and powdered sugar for minimum five minutes until creamy and fluffy.
8. Put in the cocoa powder, salt and milk and stir thoroughly for another five minutes.
9. Use half of the frosting to fill the cake then garnish it with the half that is left over.
    10. Serve immediately or place in your fridge until it is time to serve.

Nutritional Content of One Serving:

Calories: 517 Fat: 34.2g Protein: 4.8g Carbohydrates: 52.9g

Chocolate Hazelnut Cake

Total Time Taken: 1 ¼ hours
Yield: 10 Servings
Ingredients:

Cake:
- ½ cup cocoa powder
- ½ teaspoon baking powder
- ½ teaspoon salt
- 1 cup all-purpose flour
- 1 cup ground hazelnuts
- 1 cup white sugar
- 6 eggs

Glaze:
- ½ cup heavy cream
- 1 cup dark chocolate chips

Directions:

1. To prepare the cake, combine the eggs with sugar until fluffy, minimum volume increases to twice what it was.
2. Fold in the flour, cocoa powder, baking powder, salt and hazelnuts then pour the batter in a 9-inch round cake pan coated with baking paper.
3. Preheat your oven and bake the cake for forty minutes or until a toothpick inserted in the center comes out clean.
4. Let the cake cool in the pan then move to a platter.
5. For the glaze, bring the cream to the boiling point then put in the chocolate and mix thoroughly.
6. Pour the warm glaze over the cake. Serve immediately or place in your refrigerator.

Nutritional Content of One Serving:

Calories: 292 Fat: 13.3g Protein: 7.4g Carbohydrates: 41.6g

Chocolate Hazelnut Cake

Total Time Taken: 1 ¼ hours
Yield: 10 Servings

Ingredients:
- ¼ cup heavy cream
- ½ cup cherry jam
- ½ cup cocoa powder
- ½ cup white sugar
- ½ teaspoon baking soda
- ½ teaspoon salt
- 1 cup all-purpose flour
- 1 cup ground hazelnuts
- 1 teaspoon baking powder
- 2 whole eggs
- 6 egg yolks

Directions:

1. Mix the hazelnuts, flour, baking powder, baking soda and salt in a container. Put in the cocoa powder as well.
2. Mix the eggs, egg yolks and sugar in a container until thickened and fluffy. Stir in the cream and cherry jam.
3. Fold in the flour then spoon the cake in a 8-inch round cake pan coated with baking paper.
4. Pre-heat the oven and bake at 350F for around forty minutes or until a toothpick inserted into the center of the cake comes out clean.
5. The cake tastes best chilled.

Nutritional Content of One Serving:

Calories: 240 Fat: 9.9g Protein: 6.0g Carbohydrates: 34.9g

Chocolate Mousse Cake

Total Time Taken: 1 ½ hours
Yield: 10 Servings
Ingredients:

Cake:

- ¼ cup cocoa powder
- ¼ cup heavy cream
- ¼ teaspoon salt
- ½ cup dark chocolate chips
- 1 cup all-purpose flour
- 1 cup buttermilk
- 1 egg
- 1 teaspoon baking powder

Chocolate mousse:

- ½ cup heavy cream, heated
- 1 cup dark chocolate chips
- 1 cup heavy cream, whipped

Directions:

1. For the cake, melt the cream and chocolate together in a heatproof container.
2. Stir in the remaining ingredients and stir for a few seconds to mix.
3. Pour the batter in a 9-inch round cake pan coated with baking paper.
4. Pre-heat the oven and bake at 350F for around forty minutes or until well risen and fragrant.
5. When finished, move the cake to a cake ring and place it on a platter.
6. For the chocolate mousse, combine the cream and chocolate chips in a container. Stir until melted and smooth. Let cool down.
7. Fold in the whipped cream then pour the mousse over the cake.
8. *Chill the cake before you serve.*

Nutritional Content of One Serving:

Calories: 223 Fat: 13.6g Protein: 4.7g Carbohydrates: 24.7g

Chocolate Nutella Cake

Total Time Taken: 1 ½ hours
Yield: 10 Servings

Ingredients:
- ½ cup brewed coffee
- ½ cup canola oil
- ½ teaspoon salt
- 1 cup ground hazelnuts
- 1 cup Nutella
- 1 cup whole milk
- 1 teaspoon vanilla extract
- 2 cups all-purpose flour
- 2 eggs
- 2 tablespoons Kahlua
- 2 teaspoons baking powder

Directions:
1. Mix the ground hazelnuts, flour, baking powder and salt in a container.
2. Mix the eggs, milk, canola oil, Kahlua, vanilla and coffee in a separate container. Stir in the flour mixture then spoon the batter in a 9-inch round cake pan coated with baking paper.
3. Drop spoonfuls of Nutella over the batter and preheat your oven and bake at 350F for about forty minutes or until a toothpick inserted into the center of the cake comes out clean.
4. *The cake tastes best chilled.*

Nutritional Content of One Serving:

Calories: 295 Fat: 18.5g Protein: 5.8g Carbohydrates: 25.4g

Chocolate Olive Oil Cake

Total Time Taken: 1 ¼ hours
Yield: 10 Servings

Ingredients:
- ¼ cup whole milk
- ¼ teaspoon salt
- ½ cup cocoa powder
- 1 cup all-purpose flour
- 1 cup white sugar
- 1 teaspoon baking powder
- 1 teaspoon orange zest
- 1 teaspoon vanilla extract
- 2 eggs
- 2/3 cup olive oil

Directions:
1. Mix the eggs with sugar until fluffy and pale. Stir in the vanilla and orange zest and mix thoroughly.
2. Put in the olive oil and milk then fold in the cocoa powder, flour, salt and baking powder.
3. Pour the batter in a 8-inch round cake pan coated with baking paper.

4. Pre-heat the oven and bake at 350F for forty minutes or until a toothpick inserted in the center comes out clean.
5. *The cake tastes best chilled.*

Nutritional Content of One Serving:

Calories: 263 Fat: 15.2g Protein: 3.4g Carbohydrates: 32.6g

Chocolate Peanut Butter Bundt Cake

Total Time Taken: 1 ¼ hours
Yield: 10 Servings

Ingredients:
- ¼ cup whole milk
- ½ cup cocoa powder
- ½ teaspoon salt
- 1 ½ cups all-purpose flour
- 1 cup butter, softened
- 1 cup light brown sugar
- 1 cup sour cream
- 1 teaspoon baking powder
- 1 teaspoon baking soda
- 1 teaspoon vanilla extract
- 2/3 cup smooth peanut butter
- 3 eggs

Directions:
1. Mix the butter, sugar and vanilla in a container until fluffy and creamy.
2. Put in the eggs, one at a time, then mix in the sour cream and milk.
3. Fold in the flour, cocoa powder, baking powder, baking soda and salt.
4. Spoon half of the batter in a greased Bundt cake pan. Top with spoonfuls of peanut butter then cover with the rest of the batter.
5. Pre-heat the oven and bake at 350F for about forty minutes or until a toothpick inserted into the center of the cake comes out clean.
6. *The cake tastes best chilled.*

Nutritional Content of One Serving:

Calories: 470 Fat: 34.1g Protein: 9.8g Carbohydrates: 35.9g

Chocolate Peppermint Cake

Total Time Taken: 1 ½ hours
Yield: 8 Servings
Ingredients:

Cake:
- ¼ teaspoon salt
- ½ cup butter, cubed
- ½ cup light brown sugar
- 1 cup all-purpose flour

- 1 cup dark chocolate chips
- 1 teaspoon baking powder
- 2 eggs
- 2 tablespoons cocoa powder

Glaze:
- ¼ cup heavy cream
- ¼ cup whole milk
- 1 pinch salt
- 3 tablespoons cocoa powder

Directions:
1. For the cake, combine the chocolate chips and butter in a heatproof container and place over a hot water bath. Melt them together until the desired smoothness is achieved.
2. Put in the sugar and eggs and mix thoroughly.
3. Stir in the flour, cocoa powder, baking powder and salt. Pour the batter in a 8-inch round cake pan coated with baking paper.
4. Pre-heat the oven and bake at 350F for about half an hour.
5. For the glaze, combine all the ingredients in a saucepan and place over low heat. Cook until it becomes thick.
6. Sprinkle the glaze over the cake and serve chilled.

Nutritional Content of One Serving:
Calories: 304 Fat: 18.8g Protein: 5.1g Carbohydrates: 33.5g

Chocolate Pumpkin Cake

Total Time Taken: 1 hour
Yield: 10 Servings
Ingredients:
- ½ cup buttermilk
- ½ cup cocoa powder
- ½ cup sour cream
- ½ teaspoon ground star anise
- ½ teaspoon salt
- 1 cup butter, softened
- 1 cup light brown sugar
- 1 cup pumpkin puree
- 1 teaspoon baking powder
- 1 teaspoon baking soda
- 1 teaspoon ground cinnamon
- 1 teaspoon ground ginger
- 1 teaspoon vanilla extract
- 2 cups all-purpose flour
- 4 eggs

Directions:
1. Mix the butter and sugar in a container until fluffy and creamy.

2. Stir in the eggs, one at a time, then put in the vanilla, pumpkin puree, sour cream and buttermilk and mix thoroughly.
3. Fold in the dry ingredients then spoon the batter in a 10-inch round cake pan coated with baking paper.
4. Preheat your oven and bake the cake for about fifty minutes or until a toothpick inserted in the center comes out clean.
5. Let the cake cool in the pan and serve, sliced.

Nutritional Content of One Serving:

Calories: 385 Fat: 23.6g Protein: 6.9g Carbohydrates: 39.6g

Cinnamon Chocolate Cake

Total Time Taken: 1 hour
Yield: 10 Servings
Ingredients:
- ½ cup buttermilk
- ½ cup cocoa powder
- ½ teaspoon salt
- 1 ½ cups white sugar
- 1 cup butter, softened
- 1 cup hot coffee
- 1 teaspoon cinnamon powder
- 1 teaspoon vanilla extract
- 2 cups all-purpose flour
- 2 teaspoons baking powder
- 3 eggs

Directions:
1. Mix the butter, sugar and cocoa powder in a container until creamy.
2. Stir in the eggs and vanilla and mix thoroughly.
3. Fold in the flour, baking powder and salt then put in the cinnamon, coffee and buttermilk and stir lightly.
4. Pour the batter in a 9-inch round cake pan coated with baking paper and bake for around forty minutes or until well risen and fragrant.
5. Let the cake cool in the pan before you serve.

Nutritional Content of One Serving:

Calories: 402 Fat: 20.6g Protein: 5.7g Carbohydrates: 52.7g

Cinnamon Frosted Banana Cake

Total Time Taken: 1 ½ hours
Yield: 16 Servings
Ingredients:

Cake:
- ½ cup dark chocolate chips
- ½ teaspoon salt

- 1 cup canola oil
- 1 cup light brown sugar
- 1 cup sour cream
- 2 cups all-purpose flour
- 2 eggs
- 2 teaspoons baking powder
- 3 bananas, mashed

Cinnamon cream:
- ½ cup butter, softened
- 1 cup cream cheese
- 1 cup powdered sugar

Directions:
1. For the cake, combine the flour, baking powder and salt in a container.
2. In a separate container, combine the oil, sugar and eggs until fluffy and pale. Put in the bananas and sour cream and mix thoroughly then fold in the flour. Put in the chocolate chips too.
3. Spoon the batter in a 9-inch round cake pan and preheat your oven and bake at 350F for around forty minutes.
4. Let the cake cool in the pan then move to a platter.
5. For the frosting, combine the butter, cream cheese and sugar in a container for 5
6. minutes.
7. Cover the cake in frosting and serve it fresh.

Nutritional Content of One Serving:
Calories: 419 Fat: 29.2g Protein: 4.4g Carbohydrates: 37.2g

Cinnamon Maple Pumpkin Cake

Total Time Taken: 1 ¼ hours
Yield: 10 Servings

Ingredients:
- ¼ teaspoon salt
- ½ cup canola oil
- ½ cup maple syrup
- ½ cup whole milk
- ½ teaspoon baking soda
- 1 ½ cups pumpkin puree
- 1 tablespoon cinnamon powder
- 1 teaspoon vanilla extract
- 2 ½ cups all-purpose flour
- 2 eggs
- 2 teaspoons baking powder
- 3/4 cup white sugar

Directions:
1. Mix the flour, baking powder, salt, baking soda and cinnamon in a container.
2. Mix the oil and sugar in a container for 2 minutes. Put in the eggs and mix thoroughly.
3. Stir in the pumpkin puree, vanilla and milk and mix thoroughly.

4. Fold in the flour mixture and mix using a spatula. Pour the batter in a 9-inch round cake pan coated with baking paper.
5. Pre-heat the oven and bake at 350F for about forty-five minutes or until a toothpick inserted into the center of the cake comes out clean.
6. *The cake tastes best chilled.*

Nutritional Content of One Serving:

Calories: 342 Fat: 12.6g Protein: 5.1g Carbohydrates: 53.5g

Cinnamon Streusel Raspberry Cake

Total Time Taken: 1 ¼ hours
Yield: 12 Servings
Ingredients:

Cake:
- ¼ cup canola oil
- ½ cup butter, softened
- ½ teaspoon salt
- ¾ cup whole milk
- 1 cup fresh raspberries Cinnamon
- 1 teaspoon vanilla extract
- 2 cups all-purpose flour
- 2 eggs
- 2 teaspoons baking powder

Streusel:
- ¼ cup light brown sugar
- ½ cup all-purpose flour
- ½ cup butter, chilled
- 1 pinch salt
- 1 teaspoon cinnamon powder

Directions:
1. To prepare the cake, sift the flour, baking powder and salt in a container.
2. In a separate container, combine the butter, oil and eggs until creamy. Stir in the milk and vanilla then fold in the flour.
3. Put in the raspberries then spoon the batter in a 8x8-inch cake pan coated with baking paper.
4. Make the cinnamon by mixing all the ingredients in a container until grainy.
5. Spread the streusel over the cake and preheat your oven and bake at 350F for about forty minutes or until fragrant and golden brown.
6. Let the cake cool in the pan and serve, sliced.

Nutritional Content of One Serving:

Calories: 309 Fat: 21.4g Protein: 4.4g Carbohydrates: 25.3g

Citrus Poppy Seed Bundt Cake

Total Time Taken: 1 ¼ hours
Yield: 12 Servings

Ingredients:
- ½ cup butter, softened
- ½ cup canola oil
- ½ teaspoon salt
- 1 cup sour cream
- 1 cup white sugar
- 1 lemon, zested and juiced
- 1 lime, zested and juiced
- 2 cups all-purpose flour
- 2 eggs
- 2 tablespoons poppy seeds
- 2 teaspoons baking powder

Directions:
1. Mix the canola oil, butter and sugar in a container until creamy and pale.
2. Stir in the eggs and mix thoroughly then put in the sour cream.
3. Combine in the lime zest and juice, as well as the lemon zest and juice.
4. Fold in the remaining ingredients then spoon the batter in a greased Bundt cake pan.
5. Pre-heat the oven and bake at 350F for about forty minutes or until it rises significantly and starts to appear golden-brown.
6. Let the cake cool in the pan before you serve.

Nutritional Content of One Serving:

Calories: 350 Fat: 22.4g Protein: 4.1g Carbohydrates: 35.2g

Classic Fruit Cake

Total Time Taken: 2 hours
Yield: 16 Servings
Ingredients:
- ½ cup dates, pitted and chopped
- ½ cup dried apricots, chopped
- ½ cup dried cranberries
- ½ cup dried pineapple, chopped
- ½ cup fresh orange juice
- ½ cup sliced almonds
- ½ teaspoon baking powder
- ½ teaspoon salt
- 1 cup brandy
- 1 cup butter, softened
- 1 cup golden raisins
- 1 cup light brown sugar
- 1 cup sultanas

- 1 teaspoon baking soda
- 2 cups all-purpose flour
- 2 tablespoons orange zest
- 4 eggs

Directions:

1. Mix the dried fruits and brandy in a container. Allow to soak up for minimum an hour.
2. Mix the butter and sugar in a container until creamy and pale.
3. Put in the orange zest and orange juice and mix thoroughly then mix in the eggs, one at a time.
4. Fold in the flour, almonds, baking soda, baking powder and salt.
5. Put in the fruits and stir lightly using a spatula.
6. Spoon the batter in a 9-inch round cake pan coated with baking paper.
7. Pre-heat the oven and bake at 350F for 55-60 minutes. The cake is done when a toothpick inserted in the center comes out clean.
8. Let the cake cool in the pan then serve, sliced.

Nutritional Content of One Serving:

Calories: 290 Fat: 14.4g Protein: 4.4g Carbohydrates: 37.2g

Coconut Carrot Bundt Cake

Total Time Taken: 1 ¼ hours
Yield: 10 Servings

Ingredients:

- ½ cup coconut milk
- ½ cup crushed pineapple
- ½ teaspoon salt
- 1 ¼ cups all-purpose flour
- 1 cup canola oil
- 1 cup coconut flakes
- 1 cup light brown sugar
- 1 cup shredded coconut
- 1 tablespoon orange zest
- 1 teaspoon vanilla extract
- 2 cups grated carrots
- 2 teaspoons baking powder
- 4 eggs

Directions:

1. Mix the eggs and sugar in a container until volume increases to twice what it was.
2. Stir in the oil and vanilla then put in the orange zest, coconut, carrots, pineapple and coconut milk.
3. Fold in the flour, baking powder and salt then pour the batter in a 9-inch round cake pan coated with baking paper.
4. Pre-heat the oven and bake at 350F for about forty minutes or until a toothpick inserted in the center comes out clean.
5. Let the cake cool in the pan and serve, sliced.

Nutritional Content of One Serving:

Calories: 430 Fat: 31.9g Protein: 4.9g Carbohydrates: 33.3g

Coconut Raspberry Cake

Total Time Taken: 1 hour
Yield: 8 Servings
Ingredients:

- ¼ cup coconut milk
- ½ cup butter, softened
- ½ cup coconut oil, melted
- ½ teaspoon salt
- 1 3/4 cups all-purpose flour
- 1 cup fresh raspberries
- 1 cup shredded coconut
- 1 cup white sugar
- 1 teaspoon baking soda
- 4 eggs

Directions:

1. **Mix** the flour, shredded coconut, salt and baking soda in a container.

2. In a separate container, mix the butter, coconut oil and sugar in a container. **Stir thoroughly to mix** until fluffy then put in the eggs, one at a time, and **mix thoroughly** .

3. **Stir in** the coconut oil then fold in the dry ingredients.

4. Spoon the batter in a 9-inch cake pan coated with baking paper.

5. Top with fresh raspberries and preheat your oven and bake at 350F for around forty minutes or **until a golden-brown colour is achieved and it rises significantly.**

6. **The cake tastes best chilled** .

Nutritional Content of One Serving:
Calories: 505 Fat: 32.8g Protein: 6.4g Carbohydrates: 49.8g

Cranberry Upside Down Cake

Total Time Taken: 1 hour
Yield: 10 Servings
Ingredients:

- ¼ teaspoon salt
- ½ cup butter, melted and chilled
- 1 ½ cups all-purpose flour
- ½ cup light brown sugar
- ½ teaspoon baking powder
- 1 cup fresh cranberries
- 1 cup white sugar
- 1 teaspoon vanilla extract
- 6 eggs

Directions:

1. Position the cranberries at the bottom of a round cake pan. Drizzle with brown sugar.

2. Mix the eggs and sugar in a container until fluffy and volume increases to twice what it was.
3. Stir in the butter and stir lightly.
4. Fold in the flour, baking powder and salt.
5. Pour the batter over the cranberries and preheat your oven and bake at 350F for about forty minutes or until it rises significantly and starts to appear golden-brown.
6. When finished, flip the cake upside down on a platter and serve chilled.

Nutritional Content of One Serving:

Calories: 297 Fat: 12.0g Protein: 5.4g Carbohydrates: 42.8g

Cream Bundt Cake

Total Time Taken: 1 hour
Yield: 10 Servings
Ingredients:
- ½ teaspoon salt
- 1 ½ cups heavy cream
- 1 cup white sugar
- 1 teaspoon vanilla extract
- 2 cups all-purpose flour
- 2 teaspoons baking powder
- 3 eggs

Directions:
1. Sift the flour, baking powder and salt.
2. Whip the heavy cream on moderate speed until soft peaks form. Carry on whipping until firm.
3. Stir in the eggs, one at a time, then put in the sugar and mix thoroughly.
4. Fold in the flour then spoon the batter in a Bundt cake pan lined using butter.
5. Pre-heat the oven and bake at 350F for around forty minutes or until a toothpick inserted in the center comes out clean.
6. Let the cake cool in the pan for about ten minutes then move to a platter.

Nutritional Content of One Serving:

Calories: 249 Fat: 8.2g Protein: 4.6g Carbohydrates: 40.2g

Cream Cheese Apple Cake

Total Time Taken: 1 ¼ hours

Yield: 10 Servings

Ingredients:
- ½ cup canola oil
- ½ teaspoon salt
- 1 ½ cups white sugar
- 1 cup cream cheese
- 1 teaspoon vanilla extract
- 2 cups all-purpose flour
- 2 red apples, peeled, cored and diced
- 2 teaspoons baking powder

- 3 eggs

Directions:
1. Mix the cream cheese, canola oil and sugar in a container until pale and creamy.
2. Put in the eggs and mix thoroughly then mix in the vanilla, followed by the rest of the dry ingredients.
3. Combine in the apples then spoon the batter in a 9-inch round cake pan coated with baking paper.
4. Pre-heat the oven and bake at 350F for about fifty minutes or until it rises significantly and starts to appear golden-brown.
5. Let the cake cool in the pan before you serve.

Nutritional Content of One Serving:
Calories: 421 Fat: 20.6g Protein: 6.1g Carbohydrates: 55.4g

Cream Cheese Pumpkin Cake

Total Time Taken: 1 ¼ hours
Yield: 14 Servings
Ingredients:

Cake:
- ½ teaspoon ground cloves
- ½ teaspoon ground ginger
- ½ teaspoon salt
- 1 ½ cups pumpkin puree
- 1 cup canola oil
- 1 teaspoon cinnamon powder
- 1 teaspoon ground ginger
- 2 cups all-purpose flour
- 2 cups white sugar
- 2 teaspoons baking soda
- 4 eggs

Cream cheese frosting:
- ½ cup butter, softened
- 1 cup cream cheese
- 1 cup powdered sugar

Directions:
1. For the cake, combine the pumpkin puree, sugar, eggs and canola oil in a container.
2. Stir in the remaining ingredients and stir until incorporated, don't over mix it!
3. Pour the batter in a 10-inch round cake pan coated with baking paper.
4. Pre-heat the oven and bake at 350F for about forty-five minutes or until it rises significantly and starts to appear golden-brown.
5. Let the cake cool in the pan then move to a platter.
6. For the frosting, combine all the ingredients in a container. Spread the frosting over the cake and serve fresh or place in your refrigerator.

Nutritional Content of One Serving:
Calories: 487 Fat: 29.5g Protein: 5.0g Carbohydrates: 53.6g

Cream Cheese Pumpkin Cake

Total Time Taken: 1 ¼ hours
Yield: 14 Servings
Ingredients:

Cake:
- ½ teaspoon ground cloves
- ½ teaspoon ground ginger
- ½ teaspoon salt
- 1 ½ cups pumpkin puree
- 1 cup canola oil
- 1 teaspoon cinnamon powder
- 1 teaspoon ground ginger
- 2 cups all-purpose flour
- 2 cups white sugar
- 2 teaspoons baking soda
- 4 eggs

Cream cheese frosting:
- ½ cup butter, softened
- 1 cup cream cheese
- 1 cup powdered sugar

Directions:

1. For the cake, combine the pumpkin puree, sugar, eggs and canola oil in a container.
2. Stir in the remaining ingredients and stir until incorporated, don't over mix it!
3. Pour the batter in a 10-inch round cake pan coated with baking paper.
4. Pre-heat the oven and bake at 350F for about forty-five minutes or until it rises significantly and starts to appear golden-brown.
5. Let the cake cool in the pan then move to a platter.
6. For the frosting, combine all the ingredients in a container. Spread the frosting over the cake and serve fresh or place in your refrigerator.

Nutritional Content of One Serving:

Calories: 487 Fat: 29.5g Protein: 5.0g Carbohydrates: 53.6g

Dark Chocolate Coffee Cake

Total Time Taken: 1 ¼ hours
Yield: 8 Servings

Ingredients:
- ¼ cup cocoa powder
- ¼ cup sour cream
- ½ cup light brown sugar
- ½ teaspoon salt
- 1 ½ cups all-purpose flour
- 1 teaspoon baking powder
- 1 teaspoon vanilla extract

- 3 oz. dark chocolate, melted
- 4 eggs
- 4 tablespoons butter, softened

Directions:
1. Mix the butter and chocolate, then mix in the eggs, sugar, vanilla and sour cream.
2. Fold in the flour, cocoa powder, baking powder and salt and stir lightly using a spatula.
3. Spoon the batter in a 9-inch round cake pan and preheat your oven and bake at 350F for around forty minutes or until it passes the toothpicks test.
4. Let the cake cool in the pan before you serve.

Nutritional Content of One Serving:
Calories: 282 Fat: 13.2g Protein: 6.8g Carbohydrates: 35.4g

Dark Rum Pecan Cake

Total Time Taken: 1 ¼ hours
Yield: 10 Servings
Ingredients:

Cake:
- ¼ cup sour cream
- ½ cup light brown sugar
- ½ cup white sugar
- ½ teaspoon baking powder
- ½ teaspoon salt
- ¾ cup butter, softened
- 1 ½ cups all-purpose flour
- 1 cup ground pecans
- 1 teaspoon baking soda
- 3 eggs

Glaze:
- 1 cup powdered sugar
- 2 tablespoons dark rum

Directions:
1. To prepare the cake, combine the flour, pecans, baking soda, baking powder and salt in a container.
2. In a separate container, combine the butter and sugars until creamy. Put in the eggs, one after another, then mix in the sour cream and mix thoroughly.
3. Fold in the flour mixture then spoon the batter in a 9-inch round cake pan covered with parchment paper.
4. Pre-heat the oven and bake at 350F for around forty minutes until a golden-brown colour is achieved and well risen then transfer the cake on a platter and allow to cool.
5. For the glaze, combine the sugar with dark rum. Sprinkle the glaze over the chilled cake and serve immediately.

Nutritional Content of One Serving:
Calories: 350 Fat: 17.5g Protein: 4.1g Carbohydrates: 44.0g

Decadent Chocolate Cake

Total Time Taken: 1 hour
Yield: 10 Servings
Ingredients:
- ¼ cup all-purpose flour
- ½ cup cocoa powder
- ½ teaspoon salt
- 1 cup butter, softened
- 2/3 cup white sugar
- 3 cups dark chocolate chips
- 6 eggs, separated

Directions:
1. Melt the butter and chocolate chips in a heatproof container over a hot water bath.
2. Mix the egg yolks and sugar in a container until fluffy and pale.
3. Stir in the melted chocolate, then put in the cocoa powder, flour and salt.
4. Whip the egg whites until fluffy and firm. Fold the meringue into the batter then pour the batter in a 9-inch round cake pan.
5. Pre-heat the oven and bake at 350F for around forty minutes or until well risen.
6. *The cake tastes best chilled.*

Nutritional Content of One Serving:
Calories: 439 Fat: 31.2g Protein: 7.0g Carbohydrates: 42.3g

Devils Bundt Cake

Total Time Taken: 1 ¼ hours
Yield: 14 Servings
Ingredients:
Cake:
- ¼ teaspoon baking soda
- ½ teaspoon salt
- 1 ½ cups white sugar
- 1 cup butter, softened
- 1 cup cocoa powder
- 1 cup hot water
- 1 cup sour cream
- 1 cup white chocolate chips
- 2 ½ cups all-purpose flour
- 2 teaspoons baking powder
- 4 eggs

Glaze:
- ½ cup heavy cream
- ¾ cup dark chocolate chips

Directions:
1. For the cake, combine the cocoa powder, water and sour cream in a container.

89

2. In a separate container, sift the flour, baking powder, baking soda and salt.
3. Mix the butter and sugar in a container until fluffy. Put in the eggs, one at a time and mix thoroughly.
4. Stir in the cocoa powder mixture then fold in the flour.
5. Put in the chocolate chips then spoon the batter in a Bundt cake lined using butter.
6. Preheat your oven and bake the cake for about forty minutes or until a toothpick inserted in the center comes out clean.
7. Let the cake cool in the pan then move to a platter.
8. For the glaze, combine the two ingredients in a heatproof container and place over low heat. Melt them together then sprinkle the glaze over the cake.
9. Serve immediately or place in your refrigerator.

Nutritional Content of One Serving:

Calories: 456 Fat: 26.1g Protein: 6.9g Carbohydrates: 54.6g

Duo Bundt Cake

Total Time Taken: 1 ¼ hours
Yield: 14 Servings

Ingredients:
- ¼ cup cocoa powder
- ¼ cup hot water
- ½ cup butter, softened
- ½ cup cream cheese
- ½ teaspoon baking soda
- ½ teaspoon salt
- 1 cup buttermilk
- 2 cups white sugar
- 2 teaspoons baking powder
- 3 cups all-purpose flour
- 3 eggs
- 4 oz. dark chocolate, melted

Directions:
1. Mix the butter and sugar in a container until creamy and fluffy.
2. Stir in the chocolate and eggs and mix thoroughly, then put in the cream cheese.
3. Sift the flour, baking powder, baking soda and salt then fold it in the batter.
4. Divide the batter in half. Combine one half with the cocoa powder and hot water.
5. Spoon the white batter in a greased Bundt cake pan.
6. Top with the cocoa batter and preheat your oven and bake at 350F for about fifty minutes or until well risen and it passes the toothpick test.
7. Let the cake cool in the pan then move to a platter.

Nutritional Content of One Serving:

Calories: 360 Fat: 13.4g Protein: 6.1g Carbohydrates: 56.1g

Fluffy Pear Bundt Cake

Total Time Taken: 1 ¼ hours
Yield: 14 Servings

Ingredients:

- ½ cup whole milk
- ½ teaspoon salt
- 1 ½ cups white sugar
- 1 cup canola oil
- 1 teaspoon vanilla extract
- 2 teaspoons baking powder
- 2 teaspoons pumpkin pie spice
- 3 cups all-purpose flour
- 3 eggs
- 3 pears, peeled, cored and diced

Directions:

1. Mix the flour, baking powder, salt and pumpkin pie spice in a container.
2. In a separate container, combine the canola oil with sugar and eggs until volume increases to twice what it was.
3. Put in the vanilla extract and milk then fold in the flour, followed by the pears.
4. Spoon the batter in a greased Bundt cake pan and preheat your oven and bake at 350F for about fifty minutes or until a toothpick comes out clean after being inserted into the center of the cake.
5. Let the cake cool in the pan then serve, sliced.

Nutritional Content of One Serving:

Calories: 363 Fat: 17.1g Protein: 4.4g Carbohydrates: 49.7g

French Apple Cake

Total Time Taken: 1 ¼ hours
Yield: 8 Servings

Ingredients:

- ¼ cup brandy
- ¼ teaspoon salt
- ½ cup butter, softened
- ½ teaspoon cinnamon powder
- 1 ½ cups all-purpose flour
- 1 cup light brown sugar
- 1 teaspoon baking powder
- 2 eggs
- 3 red apples, peeled, cored and sliced

Directions:

1. Sift the flour, baking powder and salt in a container.
2. Mix the eggs, sugar, brandy and butter in a container until fluffy and pale.
3. Fold in the flour then spoon the batter in a 8-inch round cake pan.

4. Top with apple slices and preheat your oven and bake at 350F for around forty minutes or until a golden-brown colour is achieved and it rises significantly.
5. *The cake tastes best chilled.*

Nutritional Content of One Serving:

Calories: 315 Fat: 12.9g Protein: 4.1g Carbohydrates: 45.5g

Fruit and Brandy Cake

Total Time Taken: 1 ½ hours
Yield: 16 Servings

Ingredients:
- ¼ cup black treacle
- ¼ cup candied ginger, chopped
- ¼ cup honey
- ½ cup dried apricots, chopped
- ½ cup dried pineapple, chopped
- ½ cup golden syrup
- 1 cup brandy
- 1 cup butter, softened
- 1 cup dark brown sugar
- 1 cup golden raisins
- 1 cup heavy cream
- 1 teaspoon baking soda
- 1 teaspoon lemon zest
- 1 teaspoon orange zest
- 11 cup dried black currants
- 3 cups all-purpose flour
- 6 eggs

Directions:
1. Mix the dried fruits with brandy in a container and allow to soak up for a few hours, preferably overnight.
2. Mix the golden syrup, treacle, honey, brown sugar, cream, butter, lemon zest and orange zest in a container until creamy.
3. Stir in the eggs, one at a time, then put in the flour. and baking soda.
4. Fold in the dried fruits and stir lightly using a spatula.
5. Spoon the batter in a 10-inch round cake pan , preheat your oven and bake at 330F for an hour or until a toothpick comes out clean after being inserted into the center of the cake. If the toothpick is not clean, continue baking for 10 additional minutes and check again.
6. Let the cake cool in the pan then move to a platter and slice.

Nutritional Content of One Serving:

Calories: 450 Fat: 16.3g Protein: 5.2g Carbohydrates: 73.3g

Fruity Bundt Cake

Total Time Taken: 1 ¼ hours
Yield: 12 Servings
Ingredients:

- ¼ cup dried apricots, chopped
- ¼ cup golden raisins
- ½ cup candied cherries, chopped
- ½ cup chopped almonds
- ½ cup chopped pecans
- 1 ½ cups white sugar
- 1 ½ teaspoons baking powder
- 1 cup butter, softened
- 1 cup cream cheese, room temperature
- 1 teaspoon vanilla extract
- 2 cups all-purpose flour
- 4 eggs

Directions:

1. Mix the cream cheese, butter and sugar in a container until fluffy and creamy.
2. Stir in the eggs, one at a time, then put in the eggs and vanilla.
3. Stir thoroughly to mix then fold in the rest of the ingredients.
4. Spoon the batter in a greased Bundt cake pan and preheat your oven and bake at 350F for about forty minutes or until it rises significantly and starts to appear golden-brown.
5. Let the cake cool in the pan before you serve.

Nutritional Content of One Serving:

Calories: 447 Fat: 26.6g Protein: 6.8g Carbohydrates: 48.0g

Fudgy Chocolate Cake

Total Time Taken: 1 hour
Yield: 10 Servings
Ingredients:

- ½ cup butter, melted
- ½ cup cocoa powder
- ½ cup sour cream
- ½ teaspoon baking soda
- ½ teaspoon salt
- 1 3/4 cups all-purpose flour
- 1 cup hot coffee
- 1 cup white sugar
- 1 teaspoon baking powder
- 2 eggs
- 4 oz. dark chocolate, melted

Directions:

1. Mix the butter and chocolate in a container. Stir in the coffee, eggs and sour cream, as well as sugar.

2. Stir thoroughly to mix then fold in the remaining ingredients.
3. Spoon the batter in a 9-inch round cake pan , preheat your oven and bake at 330F for about fifty minutes.
4. Let the cake cool in the pan before you serve.

Nutritional Content of One Serving:

Calories: 344 Fat: 16.6g Protein: 5.5g Carbohydrates: 46.6g

Fudgy Chocolate Cake

Total Time Taken: 1 hour
Yield: 10 Servings
Ingredients:

- ¼ teaspoon salt
- ½ cup cocoa powder
- ¾ cup all-purpose flour
- 1 cup butter
- 1 cup ground walnuts
- 1 cup white sugar
- 2 cups dark chocolate chips
- 3 eggs

Directions:

1. Mix the chocolate chips and butter in a container and place over a hot water bath. Melt it over heat until the desired smoothness is achieved.
2. Put in the sugar and mix thoroughly then mix in the eggs.
3. Fold in the flour, cocoa powder, salt and walnuts then spoon the batter in a 8- inch round cake pan coated with baking paper.
4. Pre-heat the oven and bake at 350F for a little more than half an hour.
5. Let the cake cool in the pan before you serve.

Nutritional Content of One Serving:

Calories: 490 Fat: 34.1g Protein: 8.2g Carbohydrates: 46.9g

Funfetti Cake

Total Time Taken: 1 hour
Yield: 8 Servings
Ingredients:

- ¼ cup butter, melted
- ½ cup canola oil
- ½ cup funfetti sprinkles
- ½ cup whole milk
- ½ teaspoon salt
- 1 ½ cups all-purpose flour
- 1 ½ teaspoons baking powder
- 1 cup white sugar
- 1 teaspoon vanilla extract

- 3 eggs

Directions:
1. Mix the flour, baking powder, salt and sprinkles in a container.
2. In a separate container, mix the canola oil, butter and sugar and mix thoroughly. Put in the eggs and stir thoroughly for five minutes.
3. Stir in the vanilla and milk and mix thoroughly then pour this mixture over the dry ingredients and stir lightly.
4. Spoon the batter in a 9-inch cake pan coated with baking paper and preheat your oven and bake at 350F for around forty minutes.
5. Let the cake cool in the pan and serve, sliced.

Nutritional Content of One Serving:
Calories: 392 Fat: 21.8g Protein: 5.1g Carbohydrates: 46.0g

Ganache Chocolate Cake

Total Time Taken: 1 ¼ hours
Yield: 8 Servings
Ingredients:

Cake:
- ¼ cup butter, melted and cooled **Ganache:**
- ¼ cup cocoa powder
- ¼ teaspoon salt
- ¾ cup all-purpose flour
- 1 cup dark chocolate, chopped
- 1 teaspoon baking powder
- 1 teaspoon vanilla extract
- 2/3 cup heavy cream
- 6 eggs, room temperature
- 2/3 cup white sugar

Directions:
1. To prepare the cake, combine the eggs, sugar and vanilla in the container of your stand mixer for about five to seven minutes until its volume increases to almost three times it was.
2. Fold in the flour, cocoa powder, salt and baking powder with the help of a wooden spoon or spatula, being cautious not to deflate the eggs.
3. Progressively fold in the melted butter.
4. Pour the batter in a 10-inch cake pan coated with baking paper and preheat your oven and bake at 350F for around forty minutes.
5. Let cool in the pan then move to a platter.
6. For the ganache, bring the cream to the boiling point then turn off heat and mix in the chocolate. Stir until melted and smooth then let cool to room temperature.
7. Spoon the ganache over the cake and serve immediately.

Nutritional Content of One Serving:
Calories: 358 Fat: 19.4g Protein: 7.7g Carbohydrates: 40.5g

German Fruit Bundt Cake

Total Time Taken: 1 ¼ hours
Yield: 10 Servings

Ingredients:

- ¼ cup dark brown sugar
- ¼ cup dried cranberries
- ¼ cup golden raisins
- ½ teaspoon salt
- 1 cup butter, softened
- 1 cup white sugar
- 1 teaspoon cinnamon powder
- 2 cups all-purpose flour
- 2 eggs
- 2 pears, peeled, cored and diced
- 2 teaspoons baking powder

Directions:

1. Mix the flour, baking powder, salt and cinnamon in a container.
2. In a separate container, mix the butter with the sugars and mix thoroughly. Stir in the eggs, one at a time and mix thoroughly.
3. Fold in the flour mixture then put in the pears, raisins and cranberries.
4. Spoon the batter in a Bundt cake pan lined using butter and preheat your oven and bake the cake at 350F for around forty minutes or until a golden-brown colour is achieved and it passes the toothpick test.
5. Let the cake cool down and serve, sliced.

Nutritional Content of One Serving:

Calories: 393 Fat: 19.6g Protein: 4.1g Carbohydrates: 52.7g

Matcha Chocolate Cake

Total Time Taken: 1 ¼ hours
Yield: 8 Servings
Ingredients:

Cake:

- ¼ cup butter, melted
- ½ teaspoon salt
- 1 ¼ cups all-purpose flour
- 1 ½ teaspoons matcha powder
- 1 cup white sugar
- 1 teaspoon baking powder Chocolate
- 4 eggs
- 4 tablespoons hot water

Glaze:

- ¼ cup butter
- 1 cup dark chocolate chips

Directions:

1. For the cake, sift the flour with salt, matcha powder and baking powder.
2. Mix the eggs and white sugar until volume increases to twice what it was.
3. Stir in the melted butter and hot water then fold in the flour mixture.
4. Spoon the batter in a 9-inch round cake pan coated with baking paper.
5. Preheat your oven and bake the cake for around forty minutes or until a toothpick inserted in the center comes out clean.
6. For the glaze, mix the chocolate chips and butter in a heatproof container and place over a hot water bath. Melt them together until the desired smoothness is achieved.
7. Sprinkle the glaze over the cake and serve immediately or place in your refrigerator.

Nutritional Content of One Serving:

Calories: 371 Fat: 17.9g Protein: 5.9g Carbohydrates: 51.0g

Matcha Pound Cake

Total Time Taken: 1 hour
Yield: 10 Servings
Ingredients:

- ¼ teaspoon salt
- ½ cup butter, softened
- ½ cup light brown sugar
- 1 cup all-purpose flour
- 1 tablespoon lemon juice
- 1 teaspoon baking powder
- 1 teaspoon lemon zest
- 2 teaspoons matcha powder
- 4 eggs, separated

Directions:

1. Sift the flour, salt, baking powder and matcha powder in a container.
2. Mix the butter with sugar until creamy and pale. Stir in the egg yolks and mix thoroughly. Put in the lemon zest and lemon juice and give it a good mix.
3. Fold in the flour.
4. Whip the egg whites until fluffy and firm. Fold the meringue into the cake batter.
5. Pour the batter in a loaf cake pan coated with baking paper.
6. Pre-heat the oven and bake at 350F for about forty minutes or until a toothpick inserted into the center of the cake comes out clean.
7. *The cake tastes best chilled.*

Nutritional Content of One Serving:

Calories: 185 Fat: 11.1g Protein: 3.6g Carbohydrates: 18.1g

Meringue Black Forest Cake

Total Time Taken: 2 ½ hours
Yield: 8 Servings

Ingredients:

- ¼ teaspoon salt
- ½ teaspoon cream of tartar
- 1 ½ cups dark chocolate chips
- 1 cup heavy cream
- 1 cup sour cherries, pitted
- 1 cup white sugar
- 1 teaspoon vanilla extract
- 2 tablespoons cocoa powder
- 4 egg whites

Directions:

1. Mix the egg whites, cream of tartar and salt in a container for minimum five minutes or until firm and fluffy.
2. Put in the sugar, progressively, whipping until shiny and firm.
3. Fold in the cocoa powder then spoon the meringue on a large baking sheet coated with baking paper, shaping it into two 8-inch rounds.
4. Pre-heat the oven and bake at 250F for about two hours.
5. Bring the cream to the boiling point in a saucepan. Put in the chocolate and stir until it melts completely. Allow this cream to cool down then put in the vanilla.
6. Layer the baked meringue with chocolate cream and sour cherries.
7. *Serve the cake fresh.*

Nutritional Content of One Serving:

Calories: 275 Fat: 11.8g Protein: 3.9g Carbohydrates: 44.1g

Milk Chocolate Chunk Cake

Total Time Taken: 1 1/5 hours
Yield: 12 Servings

Ingredients:

- ½ cup chocolate syrup
- ½ cup cocoa powder
- ½ teaspoon baking soda
- ½ teaspoon salt
- 1 cup butter, softened
- 1 cup buttermilk
- 1 cup white sugar
- 1 teaspoon baking powder
- 1 teaspoon vanilla extract
- 2 cups all-purpose flour
- 4 eggs
- 8 oz. milk chocolate, chopped

Directions:
1. Sift the flour, cocoa powder, baking powder, baking soda and salt.
2. Mix the butter with sugar until creamy and fluffy. Put in the chocolate syrup then mix in the eggs and vanilla.
3. Fold in the flour, alternating it with buttermilk. Begin and finish with flour.
4. Put in the chocolate chunks then spoon the batter in a round cake pan coated with baking paper.
5. Pre-heat the oven and bake at 350F for about forty minutes or until a toothpick comes out clean after being inserted into the center of the cake.

Nutritional Content of One Serving:

Calories: 449 Fat: 23.4g Protein: 7.2g Carbohydrates: 55.2g

Mississippi Mud Cake

Total Time Taken: 1 ¼ hours
Yield: 12 Servings

Ingredients:
- ½ cup cocoa powder
- ½ teaspoon salt
- 1 cup buttermilk
- 1 cup canola oil
- 1 cup hot coffee
- 1 teaspoon baking powder
- 1 teaspoon baking soda
- 2 ½ cups all-purpose flour
- 2 cups white sugar
- 2 eggs
- 2 teaspoons vanilla extract

Directions:
1. Mix the sugar, eggs, coffee, oil, vanilla and buttermilk in a container.
2. In a separate container, mix the cocoa powder, salt, flour, baking soda and baking powder then mix in the coffee mixture.
3. Pour the batter in a 10-inch round cake pan covered with parchment paper.
4. Pre-heat the oven and bake at 330F for about fifty minutes.
5. Let the cake cool in the pan and serve, sliced.

Nutritional Content of One Serving:

Calories: 410 Fat: 19.8g Protein: 5.0g Carbohydrates: 56.5g

Moist Apple Cake

Total Time Taken: 1 ½ hours
Yield: 14 Servings

Ingredients:
- ¼ cup maple syrup
- ½ teaspoon salt
- 1 ½ cups light brown sugar

- 1 cup butter, softened
- 1 teaspoon cinnamon powder
- 1 teaspoon ground cardamom
- 1 teaspoon ground ginger
- 2 cups applesauce
- 2 eggs
- 2 green apples, peeled, cored and diced
- 2 teaspoons baking soda
- 3 cups all-purpose flour

Directions:

1. Mix the flour, baking soda, salt and spices in a container.
2. In a separate container, mix the butter, sugar and maple syrup and stir thoroughly for a few minutes.
3. Stir in the eggs and applesauce then fold in the flour mixture.
4. Put in the apples then spoon the batter in a 10-inch round cake pan coated with baking paper.
5. Pre-heat the oven and bake at 350F for about fifty minutes or until a toothpick inserted into the center of the cake comes out clean.
6. Let the cake cool in the pan and serve, sliced.

Nutritional Content of One Serving:

Calories: 326 Fat: 14.1g Protein: 3.9g Carbohydrates: 47.2g

Moist Chocolate Cake

Total Time Taken: 1 ¼ hours
Yield: 12 Servings

Ingredients:

- ½ cup canola oil
- ½ cup cocoa powder
- ½ teaspoon salt
- 1 ½ teaspoon baking powder
- 1 cup buttermilk
- 1 cup hot coffee
- 1 teaspoon vanilla extract
- 2 cups all-purpose flour
- 2 cups white sugar
- 2 eggs

Directions:

1. Mix the sugar, eggs and canola oil in a container until creamy.
2. Stir in the vanilla, coffee and buttermilk then put in the remaining ingredients.
3. Pour the batter in a 9-inch round cake pan coated with baking paper.
4. Pre-heat the oven and bake at 350F for about forty-five minutes or until a toothpick comes out clean after being inserted into the center of the cake.
5. Let the cake cool in the pan before you serve.

Nutritional Content of One Serving:

Calories: 310 Fat: 10.7g Protein: 4.4g Carbohydrates: 52.6g

Moist Pumpkin Cake

Total Time Taken: 1 ¼ hours
Yield: 12 Servings

Ingredients:

- ¼ teaspoon ground nutmeg
- ½ teaspoon ground ginger
- ½ teaspoon salt
- 1 ½ cups pumpkin puree
- 1 cup canola oil
- 1 teaspoon cinnamon powder
- 2 cups white sugar
- 2 teaspoons baking powder
- 3 cups all-purpose flour
- 4 eggs

Directions:

1. Mix the sugar, canola oil and eggs in a container until creamy and volume increases to twice what it was.
2. Stir in the pumpkin puree, then fold in the remaining ingredients.
3. Pour the batter in a 9-inch round cake pan coated with baking paper.
4. Pre-heat the oven and bake at 350F for around forty minutes or until well risen and fragrant.
5. Let the cake cool in the pan and serve, sliced.

Nutritional Content of One Serving:

Calories: 432 Fat: 20.1g Protein: 5.4g Carbohydrates: 60.2g

Molasses Pear Bundt Cake

Total Time Taken: 1 ¼ hours
Yield: 10 Servings

Ingredients:

- ½ cup light brown sugar
- ½ cup molasses
- ½ cup sour cream
- ½ cup whole milk
- ½ teaspoon ground ginger
- ½ teaspoon salt
- 1 cup butter, softened
- 1 teaspoon all-spice
- 1 teaspoon baking powder
- 1 teaspoon baking soda
- 1 teaspoon cinnamon powder
- 2 cups all-purpose flour
- 2 pears, peeled, cored and diced
- 3 eggs

Directions:
1. Mix the butter, molasses and sugar in a container until creamy and pale.
2. Stir in the eggs, one at a time, stirring thoroughly after each addition.
3. Mix the flour with baking powder, baking soda, salt and spices.
4. Mix the milk with cream.
5. Fold the flour into the butter mixture, alternating it with the milk and sour cream mix.
6. Put in the pears then spoon the batter in a greased Bundt cake pan.
7. Pre-heat the oven and bake at 350F for about forty minutes or until a toothpick inserted in the center comes out clean.
8. Let the cake cool in the pan for about ten minutes then flip over on a platter.
9. Serve chilled.

Nutritional Content of One Serving:
Calories: 405 Fat: 22.9g Protein: 5.3g Carbohydrates: 46.3g

Morello Cherry Cake

Total Time Taken: 1 ¼ hours
Yield: 12 Servings

Ingredients:
- ¼ cup brandy
- ½ cup cocoa powder
- ½ cup cocoa powder
- ½ cup coconut oil, melted
- ½ cup white sugar
- ½ teaspoon salt
- ¾ cup all-purpose flour
- 1 cup almond flour
- 1 cup maple syrup
- 1 cup Morello cherries
- 3 eggs

Directions:
1. Mix the maple syrup, coconut oil, brandy and eggs in a container.
2. Stir in the sugar and mix thoroughly.
3. Fold in the cocoa powder, almond flour, all-purpose flour, salt and cocoa powder.
4. Spoon the batter in a 9-inch round cake pan and top with cherries.
5. Pre-heat the oven and bake at 350F for forty minutes.
6. *The cake tastes best chilled.*

Nutritional Content of One Serving:
Calories: 270 Fat: 12.4g Protein: 4.2g Carbohydrates: 40.9g

Natural Red Velvet Cake

Total Time Taken: 1 ¼ hours
Yield: 10 Servings
Ingredients:

Cake:
- ¼ cup white sugar
- ½ cup canola oil
- ½ cup light brown sugar
- ½ teaspoon cinnamon powder
- ½ teaspoon salt
- 1 ¼ cups all-purpose flour
- 1 teaspoon baking powder
- 2 beetroots, peeled and pureed
- 2 eggs
- 2 tablespoons cornstarch

Frosting:
- ¼ cup butter, softened
- 1 cup cream cheese
- 1 cup powdered sugar

Directions:

1. For the cake, combine the beetroot puree, canola oil, eggs and sugar in a container.
2. Stir in the remaining ingredients and mix thoroughly.
3. Pour the batter in a 8-inch round cake pan coated with baking paper.
4. Pre-heat the oven and bake at 350F for forty minutes.
5. When finished, allow the cake to cool in the pan then transfer the cake on a platter.
6. For the frosting, combine all the ingredients in a container until fluffy.
7. Cover the cake with the frosting and serve it fresh.

Nutritional Content of One Serving:

Calories: 395 Fat: 24.7g Protein: 4.8g Carbohydrates: 40.1g

Olive Oil Pistachio Cake

Total Time Taken: 1 hour
Yield: 10 Servings
Ingredients:
- ½ cup corn meal
- ½ cup extra virgin olive oil
- ½ cup ground pistachios
- ½ cup white sugar
- 3 eggs
- ½ cup whole milk
- ½ teaspoon salt
- 1 cup all-purpose flour
- 1 teaspoon baking powder

- 1 teaspoon baking soda
- 2 tablespoons orange zest

Directions:
1. Mix the dry ingredients in a container.
2. In a separate container, mix the oil, sugar, eggs and orange zest and stir thoroughly for a few minutes until volume increases to twice what it was.
3. Stir in the milk, followed by the dry ingredients.
4. Pour the batter in 10-inch round cake pan coated with baking paper.
5. Preheat your oven and bake the cake for around forty minutes.
6. The cake tastes best chilled.

Nutritional Content of One Serving:

Calories: 221 Fat: 12.1g Protein: 4.0g Carbohydrates: 26.1g

Orange Chocolate Cake

Total Time Taken: 1 ¼ hours
Yield: 12 Servings

Ingredients:
- ½ cup candied orange peel, chopped
- ½ teaspoon salt
- 1 cup white sugar
- 1 teaspoon baking soda
- 2 cups ground almonds
- 4 eggs
- 8 oz. dark chocolate, melted

Directions:
1. Mix the eggs with sugar until fluffy and pale.
2. Stir in the melted chocolate then put in the almonds, baking soda and salt.
3. Fold in the candied orange peel then pour the batter in 1 8-inch round cake pan coated with baking paper.
4. Pre-heat the oven and bake at 350F for about half an hour.
5. Let the cake cool in the pan before you serve.

Nutritional Content of One Serving:

Calories: 280 Fat: 15.0g Protein: 6.7g Carbohydrates: 32.4g

Orange Chocolate Mud Cake

Total Time Taken: 1 ¼ hours
Yield: 10 Servings

Ingredients:
- ½ cup brewed coffee
- ½ cup candied orange peel, chopped
- ½ teaspoon salt
- ¾ cup cocoa powder

- 1 ½ cups all-purpose flour
- 1 cup butter, softened
- 1 tablespoon orange zest
- 1 teaspoon baking soda
- 1 teaspoon vanilla extract
- 2 cups white sugar
- 2 tablespoons cornstarch
- 4 eggs

Directions:

1. Mix the sugar and butter in a container until fluffy and pale.
2. Put in the coffee, eggs, vanilla and orange zest.
3. Stir in the remaining ingredients and mix thoroughly.
4. Pour the batter in a 9-inch round cake pan coated with baking paper.
5. Preheat your oven and bake the cake for about fifty minutes or until the cake looks set.
6. *The cake tastes best chilled.*

Nutritional Content of One Serving:

Calories: 433 Fat: 21.2g Protein: 5.6g Carbohydrates: 60.9g

Orange Pound Cake

Total Time Taken: 1 ¼ hours
Yield: 16 Servings

Ingredients:

- ½ teaspoon salt
- 1 ½ cups butter, softened
- 1 cup sour cream
- 1 orange, zested and juiced
- 1 teaspoon vanilla extract
- 2 cups white sugar
- 2 teaspoons baking powder
- 3 cups all-purpose flour
- 6 eggs

Directions:

1. Sift the flour with salt and baking powder.
2. Mix the butter with sugar for five minutes until creamy and fluffy.
3. Put in the vanilla, orange zest and orange juice and mix thoroughly.
4. Stir in the sour cream then fold in the flour mixture.
5. Pour the batter in a large loaf cake pan coated with baking paper.
6. Pre-heat the oven and bake at 330F for forty minutes then turn the heat on 350F for another ten minutes.
7. Let the cake cool in the pan and serve, sliced.

Nutritional Content of One Serving:

Calories: 393 Fat: 22.2g Protein: 5.2g Carbohydrates: 45.3g

Orange Pumpkin Bundt Cake

Total Time Taken: 1 ¼ hours
Yield: 12 Servings

Ingredients:

- ½ teaspoon cinnamon powder
- ½ teaspoon ground cardamom
- ½ teaspoon ground ginger
- ½ teaspoon salt
- ¾ cup butter, softened
- 1 ¼ cups white sugar
- 1 ½ teaspoons baking soda
- 1 cup pumpkin puree
- 1 orange, zested and juiced
- 1 teaspoon vanilla extract
- 2 ½ cups all-purpose flour
- 4 eggs

Directions:

1. Mix the butter with sugar in a container until creamy and fluffy.
2. Stir in the eggs and vanilla and mix thoroughly then put in the orange zest and juice, as well as pumpkin puree.
3. Fold in the rest of the ingredients then spoon the batter in a loaf cake pan coated with baking paper.
4. Preheat your oven and bake the cake for about forty minutes.
5. Let the cake cool in the pan before you serve.

Nutritional Content of One Serving:

Calories: 311 Fat: 13.3g Protein: 5.0g Carbohydrates: 44.4g

Orange Ricotta Cake

Total Time Taken: 1 ¼ hours
Yield: 10 Servings

Ingredients:

- ½ cup all-purpose flour
- ½ cup white chocolate, chopped
- ¾ cup white sugar
- 1 cup fresh raspberries
- 1 teaspoon baking powder
- 1 teaspoon orange zest
- 1 teaspoon vanilla extract
- 3 cups ricotta cheese
- 3 eggs

Directions:

1. Mix the ricotta cheese, vanilla, orange zest, sugar and eggs in a container.
2. Stir in rest of the ingredients then spoon the batter in a 9-inch round cake pan coated with baking paper.

3. Pre-heat the oven and bake at 350F for around forty minutes or until a golden-brown colour is achieved.
4. The cake tastes best chilled.

Nutritional Content of One Serving:

Calories: 255 Fat: 10.1g Protein: 11.4g Carbohydrates: 30.5g

Parsnip Carrot Cake

Total Time Taken: 1 ½ hours
  Yield: 12 Servings

Ingredients:
- ¼ cup white sugar
- ½ cup walnuts, chopped
- ½ teaspoon salt
- 1 cup canola oil
- 1 cup crushed pineapple
- 1 cup grated carrots
- 1 cup grated parsnips
- 1 cup light brown sugar
- 1 teaspoon baking powder
- 1 teaspoon baking soda
- 1 teaspoon cinnamon powder
- 1 teaspoon ground ginger
- 2 cups all-purpose flour
- 4 eggs

Directions:
1. Mix the flour, salt, baking soda, baking powder and spices in a container.
2. In a separate container, combine the eggs with the sugars until fluffy and pale.
3. Put in the oil then mix in the carrots, parsnips, pineapple and walnuts.
4. Fold in the dry ingredients you readied a while back.
5. Pour the batter in a 9-inch round cake pan coated with baking paper.
6. Pre-heat the oven and bake at 350F for about forty minutes or until a toothpick inserted in the center comes out clean.
7. Sprinkle with powdered sugar and serve chilled.

Nutritional Content of One Serving:

Calories: 371 Fat: 23.0g Protein: 5.5g Carbohydrates: 37.6g

Peach Brandy Cake

Total Time Taken: 1 ½ hours
  Yield: 10 Servings
  Ingredients:

Cake:
- ½ cup butter, melted
- ½ teaspoon salt

- 1 cup sweet red win
- 1 cup white sugar
- 1 teaspoon baking powder
- 1 teaspoon ground cardamom
- 2 cups almond flour
- 4 peaches, pitted and sliced Brandy
- 5 eggs

Glaze:
- 1 cup powdered sugar
- 1 tablespoon brandy

Directions:
1. To prepare the cake, combine the almond flour, baking powder, salt and cinnamon.
2. In a separate container, combine the sugar and eggs until fluffy and pale. Put in the butter and mix thoroughly, then mix in the red wine.
3. Fold in the almond flour then pour the batter in a 9-inch round cake pan coated with baking paper.
4. Top with sliced peaches and preheat your oven and bake at 350F for 45 minutes or until a toothpick comes out clean after being inserted into the center of the cake.
5. Let the cake cool in the pan then move it to a platter.
6. For the glaze, combine the sugar with brandy. Sprinkle the glaze over the cake and serve it fresh.

Nutritional Content of One Serving:

Calories: 317 Fat: 15.8g Protein: 8.3g Carbohydrates: 37.4g

Peach Meringue Cake

Total Time Taken: 1 ½ hours
Yield: 10 Servings
Ingredients:

Cake:
- ½ cup butter, softened
- ½ cup canola oil
- ½ cup plain yogurt
- ½ teaspoon salt
- ¾ cup white sugar
- 1 teaspoon baking soda
- 1 teaspoon vanilla extract
- 2 cups all-purpose flour
- 3 eggs
- 3 peaches, pitted and sliced

Meringue:
- ½ cup white sugar
- 1 teaspoon vanilla extract
- 3 egg whites

Directions:
1. For the cake, combine the butter, oil and sugar in a container until fluffy and creamy.

2. Stir in the egg, vanilla and yogurt and mix thoroughly.
3. Fold in the flour, baking soda and salt then spoon the batter in a round cake pan coated with baking paper.
4. Top with peach slices and preheat your oven and bake at 350F for about forty minutes or until it rises significantly and starts to appear golden-brown.
5. While the cake bakes, combine the egg whites and sugar in a heatproof container.
6. Place over a hot water bath and mix with a whisk until the mixture is hot.
7. Turn off the heat and continue mixing until firm and shiny. Put in the vanilla and mix thoroughly.
8. Spoon the meringue over the hot cake and allow to cool.
9. *Serve immediately.*

Nutritional Content of One Serving:

Calories: 411 Fat: 21.9g Protein: 6.4g Carbohydrates: 48.5g

Peach Upside Down Cake

Total Time Taken: 1 hour
Yield: 8 Servings
Ingredients:
- ¼ cup butter, melted
- ¼ cup whole milk
- ¼ teaspoon salt
- 1 egg
- ½ cup light brown sugar
- ½ cup sour cream
- 1 cup all-purpose flour
- 1 teaspoon baking powder
- 2 tablespoons butter
- 4 peaches, sliced

Directions:
1. Position the peaches at the bottom of a 9-inch round cake pan coated with baking paper.
2. Drizzle with brown sugar and top with a few pieces of butter.
3. For the batter, combine the flour, baking powder and salt in a container. Put in the rest of the ingredients and stir for a few seconds to mix.
4. Spoon the batter over the peaches and preheat your oven and bake at 350F for about half an hour.
5. When finished, flip the cake upside down on a platter.
6. Serve chilled.

Nutritional Content of One Serving:

Calories: 231 Fat: 12.7g Protein: 3.6g Carbohydrates: 26.8g

Peanut Butter Chocolate Bundt Cake

Total Time Taken: 1 ¼ hours
Yield: 10 Servings
Ingredients:
- ¼ cup butter, softened

- ½ cup cocoa powder
- ½ cup dark chocolate chips
- ½ teaspoon baking soda
- ½ teaspoon salt
- 1 cup buttermilk
- 1 cup light brown sugar
- 1 cup smooth peanut butter
- 1 teaspoon vanilla extract
- 2 cups all-purpose flour
- 2 teaspoons baking powder
- 3 eggs

Directions:
1. Sift the flour, baking powder, baking soda, salt and cocoa powder.
2. Mix the peanut butter, butter and sugar in a container until creamy and light.
3. Put in the eggs and mix thoroughly then mix in the vanilla.
4. Fold in the flour, alternating it with buttermilk. Begin and finish with flour.
5. Put in the chocolate chips then spoon the batter in a Bundt cake pan lined using butter.
6. Preheat your oven and bake the cake for about forty minutes or until it rises significantly and starts to appear golden-brown.
7. When finished, flip the cake upside down on a platter and serve chilled.

Nutritional Content of One Serving:
Calories: 407 Fat: 21.6g Protein: 12.8g Carbohydrates: 46.5g

Peanut Butter Jelly Cake

Total Time Taken: 1 ½ hours
Yield: 12 Servings

Ingredients:
- ½ cup butter, softened
- ½ cup cranberry jelly
- ½ cup light brown sugar
- ½ cup peanut butter
- ½ cup whole milk
- ½ teaspoon salt
- 1 cup white sugar
- 1 teaspoon vanilla extract
- 2 cups all-purpose flour
- 2 eggs
- 2 tablespoons canola oil
- 2 teaspoons baking powder

Directions:
1. Sift the flour, baking powder and salt.
2. Mix the peanut butter, butter, canola oil and sugars in a container until creamy and fluffy.
3. Stir in the eggs and vanilla and mix thoroughly.
4. Fold in the flour mixture, alternating it with the milk. Begin and finish with flour.

5. Spoon the batter in a round cake pan coated with baking paper.
6. Pre-heat the oven and bake at 350F for about forty minutes or until a toothpick inserted into the center of the cake comes out clean.
7. When finished, brush the cake with cranberry jelly and serve it fresh.

Nutritional Content of One Serving:

Calories: 334 Fat: 16.7g Protein: 6.2g Carbohydrates: 42.0g

Pear Brownie Cake

Total Time Taken: 1 ¼ hours
Yield: 10 Servings

Ingredients:
- ¼ cup cocoa powder
- ¼ teaspoon salt
- ½ cup all-purpose flour
- ½ cup butter, softened
- ½ cup white sugar
- 1 cup dark chocolate chips
- 2 pears, peeled, cored and diced
- 4 eggs

Directions:
1. Mix the butter and chocolate in a heatproof container over a hot water bath. Melt them together until the desired smoothness is achieved.
2. Put in the eggs, one at a time, then mix in the sugar.
3. Fold in the flour, cocoa powder and salt then spoon the batter in a 8-inch round cake pan coated with baking paper.
4. Top with pear dices and preheat your oven and bake at 350F for 25 minutes.
5. Let the cake cool in the pan before you serve.

Nutritional Content of One Serving:

Calories: 252 Fat: 14.6g Protein: 4.3g Carbohydrates: 30.5g

Pear Cinnamon Bundt Cake

Total Time Taken: 1 ¼ hours
Yield: 10 Servings

Ingredients:
- ½ cup buttermilk
- ½ teaspoon ground ginger
- ½ teaspoon salt
- 1 ½ cups light brown sugar
- 1 cup butter, melted
- 1 teaspoon cinnamon powder
- 2 cups all-purpose flour
- 2 pears, peeled, cored and diced
- 2 teaspoons baking powder

- 4 eggs

Directions:
1. Mix the flour, cinnamon, ginger, baking powder and salt in a container.
2. In a separate container, mix the butter, sugar, eggs and buttermilk and mix thoroughly. Pour this mixture over the dry ingredients then fold in the pears.
3. Spoon the batter in a Bundt cake pan lined using butter.
4. Pre-heat the oven and bake at 350F for around forty minutes or until golden and it rises significantly.
5. Let the cake cool in the pan before you serve.

Nutritional Content of One Serving:

Calories: 392 Fat: 20.6g Protein: 5.6g Carbohydrates: 48.0g

Pecan Butter Cake

Total Time Taken: 1 ¼ hours
Yield: 12 Servings

Ingredients:
- ½ cup butter, softened
- ½ teaspoon salt
- 1 ½ cups pecans, chopped
- 1 ½ teaspoons baking powder
- 1 cup pecan butter
- 1 cup white sugar
- 1 teaspoon lemon zest
- 1 teaspoon vanilla extract
- 2 cups all-purpose flour
- 4 eggs

Directions:
1. Mix the two types of butter with sugar until creamy and light.
2. Stir in the eggs, one at a time, then put in the vanilla and lemon zest then fold in the dry ingredients.
3. Spoon the batter in a 9-inch round cake pan coated with baking paper.
4. Pre-heat the oven and bake at 350F for about forty minutes or until it rises significantly and starts to appear golden-brown.
5. Let the cake cool in the pan then sprinkle it with powdered sugar and serve.

Nutritional Content of One Serving:

Calories: 377 Fat: 24.2g Protein: 6.2g Carbohydrates: 37.9g

Pecan Carrot Bundt Cake

Total Time Taken: 1 ½ hours
Yield: 14 Servings

Ingredients:
- ¼ cup orange juice
- ½ cup dark brown sugar

- ½ teaspoon baking powder
- ½ teaspoon cardamom powder
- ½ teaspoon salt
- 1 cup butter, softened
- 1 cup crushed pineapple
- 1 cup white sugar
- 1 tablespoon lemon zest
- 1 tablespoon orange zest
- 1 teaspoon baking soda
- 1 teaspoon cinnamon powder
- 2 ½ cups all-purpose flour
- 2 cups grated carrots
- 4 eggs

Directions:

1. Sift the flour, baking soda, baking powder, salt and spices in a container.
2. In a separate container, combine the butter and sugars until creamy and fluffy.
3. Stir in the eggs, one at a time, then put in the citrus zest, carrots, orange juice and pineapple.
4. Fold in the flour and stir lightly using a spatula.
5. Pour the batter in a greased Bundt cake pan.
6. Pre-heat the oven and bake at 350F for about fifty minutes or until a toothpick inserted into the center of the cake comes out clean.
7. Let the cake cool in the pan before you serve.

Nutritional Content of One Serving:

Calories: 304 Fat: 14.6g Protein: 4.3g Carbohydrates: 40.4g

Pecan Rum Cake

Total Time Taken: 1 ¼ hours
Yield: 12 Servings
Ingredients:

Cake:
- ¼ cup dark rum
- ½ cup whole milk
- ½ teaspoon salt
- 1 ¼ cups all-purpose flour
- 1 cup butter, softened
- 1 cup ground pecans
- 1 cup white sugar
- 1 teaspoon baking soda
- 1 teaspoon vanilla extract
- 3 eggs

Glaze:
- 1 cup powdered sugar
- 1 tablespoon dark rum

Directions:

1. For the cake, combine the flour with baking soda, salt and pecans.
2. In a separate container, combine the butter and sugar until fluffy and creamy.
3. Stir in the eggs, one after another, then put in the vanilla, rum and milk and mix thoroughly.
4. Fold in the pecan and flour mixture then spoon the batter in a 8-inch round cake pan coated with baking paper.
5. Pre-heat the oven and bake at 350F for around forty minutes or until well risen and fragrant.
6. Let the cake cool in the pan then move to a platter.
7. For the glaze, combine the ingredients in a container. Sprinkle the glaze over the cake and serve fresh.

Nutritional Content of One Serving:

Calories: 329 Fat: 17.8g Protein: 3.3g Carbohydrates: 37.3g

Peppermint Chocolate Cake

Total Time Taken: 1 ¼ hours
Yield: 10 Servings
Ingredients:

Cake:
- ½ cup canola oil
- 1 cup buttermilk
- ½ cup cocoa powder
- ½ cup hot coffee
- ½ teaspoon baking soda
- ½ teaspoon salt
- 1 ½ cups all-purpose flour
- 1 teaspoon baking powder
- 1 teaspoon vanilla extract

Frosting:
- ½ cup butter, softened
- 1 ½ cups powdered sugar
- 1 teaspoon peppermint extract
- 3 oz. dark chocolate, melted and cooled

Directions:
1. To prepare the cake, combine the dry ingredients in a container and the wet ingredients in a separate container.
2. Combine the flour mixture with the wet ingredients and stir for a few seconds to mix.
3. Pour the batter in a 9-inch cake pan coated with baking paper.
4. Pre-heat the oven and bake at 350F for about 35 minutes.
5. Let the cake cool in the pan then move to a platter.
6. For the frosting, combine the butter with the sugar until creamy and fluffy.
7. Put in the peppermint extract and the melted chocolate and mix thoroughly.
8. Frost the top of the cake with this chocolate buttercream and serve immediately or place in your refrigerator.

Nutritional Content of One Serving:

Calories: 384 Fat: 23.6g Protein: 4.3g Carbohydrates: 41.2g

Pistachio Bundt Cake

Total Time Taken: 1 hour
 Yield: 10 Servings
Ingredients:

- ½ teaspoon salt
- ¾ cup butter, softened
- 1 ½ cups all-purpose flour
- 1 ½ teaspoons baking powder
- 1 cup ground pistachio
- 1 cup white sugar
- 1 teaspoon vanilla extract
- 4 eggs

Directions:

1. Mix the butter and sugar until pale and light. Stir in the eggs and vanilla and mix thoroughly.
2. Fold in the flour, pistachio, baking powder and salt then spoon the batter in a greased Bundt cake pan.
3. Pre-heat the oven and bake at 350F for about forty minutes or until it rises significantly and starts to appear golden- brown.
4. Let the cake cool in the pan before you serve.

Nutritional Content of One Serving:

Calories: 292 Fat: 15.7g Protein: 4.3g Carbohydrates: 34.9g

Pistachio Cake

Total Time Taken: 1 hour
 Yield: 8 Servings
Ingredients:

- ¼ cup whole milk
- ¼ teaspoon cinnamon powder
- ¼ teaspoon salt
- ½ cup all-purpose flour
- ½ cup butter, softened
- ½ cup white sugar
- ½ teaspoon ground cardamom
- 1 cup ground pistachio
- 1 teaspoon baking powder
- 1 teaspoon lemon zest
- 2 eggs

Directions:

1. Mix the pistachio, flour, salt, baking powder, cardamom and cinnamon in a container.
2. Mix the butter and sugar in a container until fluffy and light. Stir in the eggs and milk, as well as lemon zest.
3. Fold in the flour and pistachio mixture then spoon the batter in a 8-inch round cake pan coated with baking paper.

4. Pre-heat the oven and bake at 350F for around forty minutes.
5. The cake tastes best chilled, dusted with powdered sugar.

Nutritional Content of One Serving:

Calories: 214 Fat: 14.1g Protein: 3.2g Carbohydrates: 20.1g

Plum Polenta Cake

Total Time Taken: 1 hour
Yield: 8 Servings
Ingredients:

- ½ cup butter, softened
- ½ cup honey
- ½ pound plums, pitted and sliced
- ½ teaspoon salt
- ½ teaspoon salt
- 1 cup instant polenta flour
- 1 tablespoon lemon zest
- 1 teaspoon baking soda
- 2 cups whole milk
- 4 eggs

Directions:

1. Mix the butter with honey until creamy and firm. Stir in the eggs, one at a time, then put in the milk and lemon zest.
2. Fold in the polenta flour, baking soda and salt then pour the batter in a 9-inch round cake pan coated with baking paper.
3. Top with plum slices and preheat your oven and bake at 350F for around forty minutes or until a golden-brown colour is achieved and it rises significantly.
4. Let the cake cool in the pan then serve, sliced.

Nutritional Content of One Serving:

Calories: 298 Fat: 15.7g Protein: 7.1g Carbohydrates: 33.7g

Pomegranate Cake

Total Time Taken: 1 ½ hours
Yield: 10 Servings
Ingredients:

White cake:

- ½ teaspoon salt
- ¾ cup whole milk
- 1 ¼ cups butter, softened
- 1 ½ cups all-purpose flour
- 1 ½ teaspoons baking powder
- 1 cup white sugar
- 1 teaspoon lemon zest
- 1 teaspoon vanilla extract

- 4 eggs whites

Pomegranate frosting:
- ¼ cup pomegranate juice
- 1 cup white sugar 1 pinch salt
- 4 egg whites

Directions:
1. Mix the flour with sugar, baking powder, salt and butter in a container until grainy.
2. Combine the egg whites with milk, vanilla and lemon zest in a container then pour this mixture over the flour mixture.
3. Stir slowly until mixed then spoon the batter into two 7-inch circular cake pans coated with baking paper.
4. Pre-heat the oven and bake at 350F for about half an hour.
5. Let the cakes cool in the pan then level them and cut each cake in half along the length.
6. For the frosting, combine all the ingredients in a heatproof container and place over a hot water bath. Keep over heat, stirring constantly, until the mixture is hot.
7. Turn off the heat and whip using an electric mixer for minimum seven minutes until firm and shiny.
8. Use half of the frosting to fill the cake and the rest of the frosting to frost the cake.
9. Serve immediately or place in your refrigerator.

Nutritional Content of One Serving:
Calories: 449 Fat: 23.8g Protein: 5.7g Carbohydrates: 55.8g

Poppy Seed Lemon Bundt Cake

Total Time Taken: 1 ¼ hours
Yield: 12 Servings

Ingredients:
- ½ cup cornstarch
- ½ cup sour cream
- ½ teaspoon salt
- 1 cup butter, softened
- 1 cup white sugar
- 1 tablespoon lemon zest
- 1 teaspoon baking powder
- 1 teaspoon baking soda
- 1 teaspoon vanilla extract
- 2 cups all-purpose flour
- 2 tablespoons lemon juice
- 2 tablespoons poppy seeds
- 4 eggs

Directions:
1. Sift the flour, cornstarch, baking powder, baking soda and salt then mix it with the poppy seeds.
2. Mix the butter and sugar in a container until creamy and fluffy.
3. Stir in the eggs, lemon zest and lemon juice and mix thoroughly.
4. Fold in the flour mixture then put in the sour cream and mix thoroughly.

5. Spoon the batter in a greased Bundt cake pan and preheat your oven and bake at 350F for about forty minutes or until a toothpick comes out clean after being inserted into the center of the cake.
6. Let the cake cool in the pan before you serve.

Nutritional Content of One Serving:

Calories: 346 Fat: 19.7g Protein: 4.8g Carbohydrates: 38.7g

Rainbow Cake

Total Time Taken: 1 hour
Yield: 10 Servings
Ingredients:

- ½ cup sour cream
- ½ teaspoon baking soda
- ½ teaspoon salt
- 1 ½ cups white sugar
- 1 cup butter, softened
- 1 teaspoon baking powder
- 1 teaspoon vanilla extract
- 2 ½ cups all-purpose flour
- 2 whole eggs
- 3 egg whites
- Red, green, blue and yellow food coloring

Directions:

1. Mix the butter and sugar in a container until fluffy and creamy.
2. Stir in the eggs, egg whites, vanilla and sour cream and stir thoroughly for a few minutes.
3. Mix the flour with baking powder, baking soda and salt then fold it in the batter.
4. Divide the batter into 4 smaller containers then add a drop of food colouring into each container and stir gently using a spoon in each batch of batter.
5. Spoon the colourful batter into a 9-inch cake pan coated with baking paper.
6. Use a toothpick to swirl the batter around until colours are blended.
7. Pre-heat the oven and bake at 350F for around forty minutes.
8. Let the cake cool in the pan then serve, sliced.

Nutritional Content of One Serving:

Calories: 433 Fat: 22.0g Protein: 6.0g Carbohydrates: 54.8g

Raspberry Chocolate Cake

Total Time Taken: 1 ¼ hours
Yield: 10 Servings

Ingredients:

- ½ cup butter, melted
- ½ teaspoon baking powder
- ½ teaspoon salt
- 1 ¼ cups all-purpose flour
- 1 cup white sugar

- 1 teaspoon vanilla extract
- 2 cups fresh raspberries
- 3 oz. dark chocolate, melted
- 6 eggs

Directions:
1. Mix the eggs and sugar in a container until its volume increases to almost three times it was.
2. Stir in the melted butter and chocolate, as well as vanilla.
3. Fold in the baking powder and salt then put in the raspberries and stir lightly.
4. Pour the batter in a 9-inch round cake pan and preheat your oven and bake at 350F for around forty minutes or until a toothpick inserted into the center of the cake comes out clean.
5. Let cool in the pan then serve, sliced.

Nutritional Content of One Serving:
Calories: 311 Fat: 14.7g Protein: 6.0g Carbohydrates: 40.3g

Raspberry Chocolate Mud Cake

Total Time Taken: 1 ½ hours
Yield: 12 Servings

Ingredients:
- ½ cup buttermilk
- ½ cup cocoa powder
- ½ cup heavy cream
- ½ teaspoon salt
- 1 ½ cups fresh raspberries
- 1 ½ cups white sugar
- 1 cup butter, softened
- 1 cup dark chocolate chips
- 1 cup hot water
- 2 cups all-purpose flour
- 2 tablespoons brandy
- 2 teaspoons baking powder
- 3 eggs

Directions:
1. Mix the butter and chocolate chips in a heatproof container and place over a hot water bath. Melt them together until the desired smoothness is achieved.
2. Stir in the sugar and hot water and mix thoroughly.
3. Put in the buttermilk, cream, eggs and brandy.
4. Fold in the dry ingredients and mix thoroughly.
5. Put in the raspberries and pour the batter in a 9-inch round cake pan coated with baking paper.
6. Pre-heat the oven and bake at 350F for 50 minutes.
7. Let the cake cool in the pan and serve, sliced.

Nutritional Content of One Serving:
Calories: 415 Fat: 21.8g Protein: 5.6g Carbohydrates: 52.5g

Raspberry Ganache Cake

Total Time Taken: 1 ¼ hours
Yield: 8 Servings
Ingredients:

Cake:
- ¼ teaspoon salt
- ½ cup butter, softened
- ½ cup white sugar
- 1 cup all-purpose flour
- 1 cup fresh raspberries
- 1 teaspoon baking powder
- 4 eggs

Ganache:
- ½ cup heavy cream
- 1 cup dark chocolate chips

Directions:
1. For the cake, combine the butter and sugar in a container until fluffy. Put in the eggs, one at a time, then mix in the flour, salt and baking powder.
2. Spoon the batter in a 8-inch round cake pan coated with baking paper.
3. Top with raspberries and preheat your oven and bake at 350F for around forty minutes or until it rises significantly and starts to appear golden-brown.
4. Let the cake cool in the pan then move to a platter.
5. For the ganache, bring the cream to the boiling point in a saucepan. Turn off the heat and mix in the chocolate. Combine until melted.
6. Sprinkle the ganache over the cake and serve the cake chilled.

Nutritional Content of One Serving:

Calories: 341 Fat: 20.7g Protein: 5.8g Carbohydrates: 37.0g

Raspberry Lemon Olive Oil Cake

Total Time Taken: 1 hour
Yield: 10 Servings
Ingredients:
- ¼ cup butter, softened
- ¼ cup whole milk
- ¼ teaspoon baking soda
- ½ teaspoon salt
- ¾ cup extra virgin olive oil
- 1 ¾ cups all-purpose flour
- 1 cup fresh raspberries
- 1 cup white sugar
- 1 teaspoon baking powder
- 2 tablespoons lemon zest
- 4 eggs

Directions:

1. Mix the flour, baking powder, baking soda and salt in a container or platter.
2. In a separate container, mix the oil, butter and sugar and mix thoroughly. Stir in the eggs, one at a time, then put in the milk and lemon zest.
3. Fold in the dry ingredients then put in the raspberries.
4. Spoon the batter in a round cake pan coated with baking paper and preheat your oven and bake at 350F for around forty minutes or until a toothpick inserted into the center of the cake comes out clean.

The cake tastes best chilled.

Nutritional Content of One Serving:

Calories: 361 Fat: 22.0g Protein: 4.9g Carbohydrates: 39.1g

Raspberry Matcha Cake

Total Time Taken: 1 ¼ hours
Yield: 10 Servings

Ingredients:

- ½ teaspoon salt
- 1 ½ cups all-purpose flour
- 1 cup fresh raspberries
- 1 tablespoons matcha powder
- 1 teaspoon vanilla extract
- 2 teaspoons baking powder
- 2/3 cup butter, softened
- 2/3 cup white sugar
- 4 eggs

Directions:

1. Sift the flour, matcha powder, baking powder and salt in a container.
2. Mix the butter and sugar until fluffy and creamy.
3. Put in the eggs, one at a time, and mix thoroughly after each addition. Stir in the vanilla then fold in the flour.
4. Put in the raspberries then spoon the batter in a loaf cake pan coated with baking paper.
5. Pre-heat the oven and bake at 350F for around forty minutes or until a toothpick inserted into the center of the cake comes out clean.
6. *The cake tastes best chilled.*

Nutritional Content of One Serving:

Calories: 262 Fat: 14.3g Protein: 4.4g Carbohydrates: 30.3g

Raspberry Ricotta Cake

Total Time Taken: 1 hour
Yield: 10 Servings
Ingredients:

- ¼ cup cocoa powder

- ¼ teaspoon salt
- ½ cup butter, softened
- ¾ cup white sugar
- 1 cup hot water
- 1 cup raspberries
- 1 cup ricotta cheese
- 2 cups all-purpose flour
- 2 teaspoons baking powder

Directions:
1. Mix the ricotta cheese, butter and sugar in a container until creamy.
2. Put in the water and mix thoroughly.
3. Fold in the flour, cocoa powder, baking powder and salt.
4. Put in the raspberries then spoon the batter in a 9-inch round cake pan coated with baking paper.
5. Pre-heat the oven and bake at 350F for forty minutes or until a toothpick inserted into the center of the cake comes out clean.
6. The cake tastes best chilled.

Nutritional Content of One Serving:
Calories: 275 Fat: 11.8g Protein: 6.0g Carbohydrates: 38.5g

Rhubarb Upside Down Cake

Total Time Taken: 1 ¼ hours
Yield: 10 Servings

Ingredients:
- ½ cup sour cream
- ½ cup white sugar
- ½ teaspoon salt
- ¾ cup butter, softened
- ¾ cup white sugar
- 1 ½ teaspoons baking powder
- 1 teaspoon vanilla extract
- 2 cups all-purpose flour
- 3 eggs
- 4 rhubarb stalks, peeled and sliced

Directions:
1. Position the stalks of rhubarb in a 9-inch round cake pan coated with baking paper.
2. Top with ½ cup white sugar.
3. Mix the butter with
4. 1 cup sugar until fluffy and pale.
5. Put in the eggs and sour cream and mix thoroughly.
6. Stir in the vanilla then fold in the flour, baking powder and salt.
7. Pour the batter in the pan and preheat your oven and bake at 350F for about forty minutes.
8. When finished, flip the cake upside down on a platter.

Nutritional Content of One Serving:
Calories: 357 Fat: 17.8g Protein: 4.9g Carbohydrates: 46.0g

Rich Vanilla Cake

Total Time Taken: 1 hour
Yield: 10 Servings
Ingredients:

- ½ teaspoon salt
- 1 cup butter, softened
- 1 cup white sugar
- 1 tablespoon vanilla extract
- 2 cups all-purpose flour
- 2 egg whites
- 2 teaspoons baking powder
- 6 egg yolks

Directions:

1. Mix the butter, sugar and vanilla in a container until fluffy and creamy.
2. Put in the egg yolks and whole eggs, one at a time, stirring thoroughly after each addition.
3. Fold in the flour, baking powder and salt then spoon the batter in a 9-inch round cake pan coated with baking paper.
4. Pre-heat the oven and bake at 350F for around forty minutes or until a toothpick inserted into the center of the cake comes out clean.
5. Let the cake cool in the pan before you serve.

Nutritional Content of One Serving:

Calories: 369 Fat: 21.4g Protein: 5.1g Carbohydrates: 40.1g

Rum Pineapple Upside Down Cake

Total Time Taken: 1 ¼ hours
Yield: 10 Servings

Ingredients:

- ¼ cup butter, melted
- ¼ cup light rum
- ¼ teaspoon salt
- 1 ½ teaspoons baking powder
- 1 can pineapple rings, drained
- 1 cup white sugar
- 2 cups all-purpose flour
- 4 eggs

Directions:

1. Position the pineapple rings at the bottom of a 9-inch round cake pan coated with baking paper.
2. Mix the eggs and sugar in a container until volume increases to twice what it was.
3. Stir in the rum and melted butter then fold in the flour, baking powder and salt.
4. Pour the batter over the pineapple and preheat your oven and bake at 350F for around forty minutes.
5. When finished, flip it over on a platter and let cool before you serve.

Nutritional Content of One Serving:

Calories: 254 Fat: 6.6g Protein: 4.9g Carbohydrates: 41.7g

Snickerdoodle Bundt Cake

Total Time Taken: 1 ½ hours
Yield: 12 Servings
Ingredients:

Filling:
- 1 cup white sugar
- 1 tablespoon cinnamon powder

Cake:
- ½ teaspoon baking soda
- ½ teaspoon salt
- 1 cup butter, softened
- 1 cup sour cream
- 1 cup white sugar
- 1 teaspoon baking powder
- 1 teaspoon ground ginger
- 2 ½ cups all-purpose flour
- 2 tablespoons dark brown sugar
- 3 eggs

Directions:
1. For the filling, combine the sugar with cinnamon in a container.
2. For the cake, sift the flour, ginger, baking powder, baking soda and salt.
3. Mix the butter and sugars in a container until fluffy and light.
4. Put in the eggs, one at a time, then mix in the sour cream.
5. Fold in the flour then spoon half of the batter in a greased Bundt cake pan. Drizzle with the cinnamon sugar mixture then top with the rest of the batter.
6. Pre-heat the oven and bake at 350F for about forty-five minutes or until a golden-brown colour is achieved and a toothpick inserted into the center of the cake comes out clean.
7. *The cake tastes best chilled.*

Nutritional Content of One Serving:

Calories: 419 Fat: 20.7g Protein: 4.9g Carbohydrates: 55.9g

Sour Cherry Chocolate Cake

Total Time Taken: 1 ¼ hours
Yield: 10 Servings

Ingredients:
- ¼ cup whole milk
- ½ cup cocoa powder
- ½ teaspoon salt
- 1 cup all-purpose flour
- 1 cup butter, softened
- 1 cup heavy cream, whipped

- 1 cup sour cherries, pitted
- 1 cup white sugar
- 1 teaspoon baking powder
- 1 teaspoon vanilla extract
- 4 eggs

Directions:

1. Sift the flour with cocoa, salt and baking powder.
2. Mix the butter with sugar and vanilla until creamy. Put in the eggs, one at a time, then fold in the flour mixture.
3. Put in the cherries then spoon the batter in a 9-inch round cake pan coated with baking paper.
4. Pre-heat the oven and bake at 350F for around forty minutes or until a toothpick comes out clean after being inserted into the center of the cake.
5. Let the cake cool then move to a platter and cover it in whipped cream.
6. Serve fresh or place in your refrigerator.

Nutritional Content of One Serving:

Calories: 373 Fat: 25.5g Protein: 5.0g Carbohydrates: 35.0g

Spiced Pumpkin Sheet Cake

Total Time Taken: 1 ¼ hours
Yield: 16 Servings

Ingredients:

- ¼ teaspoon baking soda
- ½ cup walnuts, chopped
- ½ teaspoon ground cloves
- ½ teaspoon ground star anise
- ½ teaspoon salt
- 1 ½ cups pumpkin puree
- 1 ½ cups white sugar
- 1 cup canola oil
- 1 teaspoon cinnamon powder
- 1 teaspoon ground ginger
- 2 cups all-purpose flour
- 2 teaspoons baking powder
- 4 eggs

Directions:

1. Sift the flour, baking powder, baking soda, salt and spices in a container.
2. Mix the sugar, canola oil and eggs in a container until pale and fluffy.
3. Stir in the pumpkin puree then incorporate the flour, ½ cup at a time, mixing gently using a spatula.
4. Fold in the walnuts then spoon the batter in a 10x10 inch rectangle pan coated with baking paper.
5. Pre-heat the oven and bake at 350F for around forty minutes or until a toothpick inserted into the center of the cake comes out clean.
6. The cake tastes best chilled, cut into small squares.

Nutritional Content of One Serving:

Calories: 297 Fat: 17.3g Protein: 4.2g Carbohydrates: 33.5g

Spiced Walnut Cake

Total Time Taken: 1 hour
Yield: 8 Servings
Ingredients:

3 eggs

- ¼ cup canola oil
- ½ teaspoon ground cardamom
- ½ teaspoon ground ginger
- ½ teaspoon salt
- ¾ cup all-purpose flour
- 1 cup ground walnuts
- 1 cup white sugar
- 1 teaspoon baking soda
- 1 teaspoon cinnamon powder

Directions:

1. Mix the eggs and sugar in a container until fluffy and volume increases to twice what it was.
2. Stir in the canola oil then fold in the walnuts, cinnamon, ginger, cardamom, flour, salt and baking soda.
3. Pour the batter in a 8-inch round cake pan coated with baking paper.
4. Pre-heat the oven and bake at 350F for around forty minutes or until it rises completely and is aromatic.
5. Let the cake cool in the pan and serve, sliced.

Nutritional Content of One Serving:

Calories: 318 Fat: 17.8g Protein: 7.1g Carbohydrates: 35.8g

Spicy Chocolate Cake

Total Time Taken: 1 hour
Yield: Servings 6
Ingredients:

- ¼ cup canola oil
- ¼ teaspoon cinnamon powder
- ½ cup cocoa powder
- ½ teaspoon salt
- 1 ½ cups all-purpose flour
- 1 cup hot coffee
- 1 teaspoon baking soda
- 1 teaspoon vanilla extract
- 1/2 teaspoon chili powder
- 2 oz. dark chocolate, chopped

Directions:

1. Sift the flour with cocoa powder, chili, cinnamon, baking soda and salt.
2. Mix the canola oil with coffee and chocolate and stir until it melts completely.
3. Put in the vanilla, then fold in the flour mixture.

4. Pour the batter in a 9-inch round cake pan covered with parchment paper and preheat your oven and bake at 350F for around forty minutes or until a toothpick comes out clean after being inserted into the center of the cake.
5. The cake tastes best chilled.

Nutritional Content of One Serving:

Calories: 264 Fat: 13.2g Protein: 5.3g Carbohydrates: 33.6g

Strawberry Cake

Total Time Taken: 1 ½ hours
Yield: 12 Servings
Ingredients:

Cake:
- ½ cup canola oil
- ½ cup coconut milk
- ½ teaspoon salt
- 1 cup white sugar
- 1 teaspoon vanilla extract
- 2 cups all-purpose flour
- 2 teaspoons baking powder
- 4 eggs

Strawberry buttercream:
- ¼ cup strawberry puree
- 1 cup butter
- 3 cups powdered sugar

Directions:
1. For the cake, combine the flour, baking powder and salt in a container.
2. In a separate container, combine the sugar, canola oil and eggs in a container until volume increases to twice what it was.
3. Stir in the milk and vanilla then fold in the dry ingredients.
4. Spoon the batter in two 9-inch circular cake pans and preheat your oven and bake at 350F for half an hour.
5. Let the cakes cool in the pan then level them up.
6. For the buttercream, combine the butter and sugar in a container until firm and fluffy.
7. Stir in the strawberry puree and mix thoroughly.
8. Fill the cake with half of the buttercream then use the rest of the buttercream to cover the cake.
9. Serve immediately or place in your refrigerator.

Nutritional Content of One Serving:

Calories: 522 Fat: 28.6g Protein: 4.4g Carbohydrates: 64.6g

Strawberry Crumble Cake

Total Time Taken: 1 ¼ hours
Yield: 12 Servings
Ingredients:

Cake:
- ¼ cup canola oil
- ¼ teaspoon salt
- ½ teaspoon baking powder
- 1 ½ cups all-purpose flour
- 1 cup plain yogurt
- 1 cup white sugar
- 1 teaspoon vanilla extract
- 2 cups fresh strawberries, sliced
- 6 eggs

Crumble:
- ¼ cup chilled butter
- ½ cup all-purpose flour
- 2 tablespoons white sugar

Directions:
1. For the cake, combine the eggs, sugar and vanilla in a container until fluffy and twofold in volume at least.
2. Stir in the yogurt and oil then fold in the flour, baking powder and salt.
3. Pour the batter in a 9-inch round cake pan coated with baking paper.
4. Top with strawberries.
5. For the streusel, combine all the ingredients in a container until grainy.
6. Top the cake with streusel and preheat your oven and bake at 350F for 45 minutes or until a toothpick comes out clean after being inserted into the center of the cake.
7. *The cake tastes best chilled.*

Nutritional Content of One Serving:

Calories: 275 Fat: 11.1g Protein: 6.3g Carbohydrates: 38.2g

Strawberry Lemon Olive Oil Cake

Total Time Taken: 1 ¼ hours
Yield: 10 Servings

Ingredients:
- ¼ teaspoon salt
- ¾ cup olive oil
- ¾ cup white sugar
- 1 ¼ cups all-purpose flour
- 1 ½ cups strawberries, sliced
- 1 lemon, zested and juiced
- 1 teaspoon baking powder
- 4 eggs

Directions:

1. Mix the eggs, oil and sugar in a container until fluffy and pale.
2. Put in the lemon zest and juice and mix thoroughly.
3. Fold in the flour, baking powder and salt then spoon the batter in a 9-inch round cake pan coated with baking paper.
4. Top with strawberries and preheat your oven and bake at 350F for about forty minutes.
5. Let the cake cool in the pan before you serve.

Nutritional Content of One Serving:

Calories: 277 Fat: 17.1g Protein: 4.0g Carbohydrates: 29.5g

Strawberry Polenta Cake

Total Time Taken: 1 ¼ hours
Yield: 10 Servings

Ingredients:

- ¼ cup butter, melted
- ¼ teaspoon salt
- ½ cup white sugar
- 1 cup polenta flour
- 1 teaspoon baking soda
- 1 teaspoon vanilla extract
- 2 cups strawberries, sliced
- 2 cups water
- 2 cups whole milk
- 2 tablespoons all-purpose flour

Directions:

1. Mix the polenta flour, flour, salt and baking soda in a container.
2. Stir in the milk, water, sugar, vanilla and melted butter.
3. Pour the batter in a 8x8-inch and top with strawberry slices.
4. Pre-heat the oven and bake at 350F for around forty minutes or until a toothpick inserted into the center of the cake comes out clean.
5. When finished, take it out of the oven, let cool down then cut into small squares.
6. *Serve immediately.*

Nutritional Content of One Serving:

Calories: 147 Fat: 6.4g Protein: 2.4g Carbohydrates: 20.7g

Strawberry Yogurt Cake

Total Time Taken: 1 hour
Yield: 8 Servings
Ingredients:

- ½ cup butter, softened
- 1 cup all-purpose flour
  - 1 cup strawberries, sliced
- 1 cup white sugar

- 1 teaspoon baking powder
- 1 teaspoon vanilla extract
- 1/2 cup plain yogurt
- 3 eggs

Directions:
1. Mix the butter and sugar until softened and creamy.
2. Put in the eggs, one at a time, then mix in the yogurt and vanilla.
3. Fold in the flour and baking powder using a spatula then put in the strawberries.
4. Pour the batter in a round cake pan coated with baking paper.
5. Pre-heat the oven and bake at 350F for about forty minutes or until a toothpick inserted into the center of the cake comes out clean.
6. Let the cake cool in the pan before you serve.

Nutritional Content of One Serving:
Calories: 295 Fat: 13.5g Protein: 4.8g Carbohydrates: 39.9g

Sultana Cake

Total Time Taken: 1 ½ hours
Yield: 10 Servings

Ingredients:
- ¼ cup orange marmalade
- ¼ teaspoon salt
- ½ cup brandy
- ½ cup butter, softened
- 1 ½ cups sultanas
- 1 cup all-purpose flour
- 1 cup white sugar
- 1 teaspoon baking soda
- 2 eggs
- 2 tablespoons dark brown sugar

Directions:
1. Mix the sultanas with the brandy and allow to soak up for about half an hour.
2. Mix the butter, sugars and marmalade in a container until creamy.
3. Put in the eggs and mix thoroughly.
4. Fold in the flour, salt and baking soda then put in the sultanas.
5. Spoon the batter in a 8-inch round cake pan coated with baking paper.
6. Pre-heat the oven and bake at 350F for about fifty minutes or until a toothpick inserted into the center of the cake comes out clean.
7. Let the cake cool down before you serve.

Nutritional Content of One Serving:
Calories: 262 Fat: 10.2g Protein: 2.7g Carbohydrates: 40.7g

Summer Fruit Cake

Total Time Taken: 1 ¼ hours
Yield: 12 Servings

Ingredients:

- ½ cup butter, softened
- ½ cup canola oil
- 1 cup all-purpose flour
- 1 cup cherries, pitted
- 1 cup ground almonds
- 1 cup mixed berries
- 1 cup white sugar
- 1 teaspoon baking powder
- 1 teaspoon vanilla extract
- 6 eggs

Directions:

1. Mix the butter, oil and sugar in a container until creamy and fluffy. Put in the vanilla and eggs, one at a time, and mix thoroughly.
2. Stir in the almonds, flour and baking powder then pour the batter in a 9-inch round cake pan coated with baking paper.
3. Top with berries and cherries and preheat your oven and bake at 350F for 40- 45 minutes or until it rises significantly and starts to appear golden-brown.
4. Let the cake cool in the pan and serve, sliced.

Nutritional Content of One Serving:

Calories: 341 Fat: 23.0g Protein: 5.7g Carbohydrates: 29.9g

Sweet Potato Bundt Cake

Total Time Taken: 1 hour
Yield: 10 Servings
Ingredients:

- 1 cup sweet potato puree
- 2 eggs
- ½ cup sour cream
- ¼ cup canola oil
- 1 teaspoon vanilla extract
- 2 cups all-purpose flour
- 2 teaspoons baking powder
- ½ teaspoon salt
- ½ cup dark chocolate chips
- 3/4 cup maple syrup

Directions:

1. Mix the potato puree, maple syrup, eggs, sour cream, canola oil and vanilla in a container.
2. Stir in the remaining ingredients then spoon the batter in a greased Bundt cake pan.

3. Pre-heat the oven and bake at 350F for about forty minutes or until a toothpick comes out clean after being inserted into the center of the cake.
4. Let the cake cool in the pan then serve, sliced.

Nutritional Content of One Serving:

Calories: 294 Fat: 10.7g Protein: 5.0g Carbohydrates: 45.9g

Tahini Cake

Total Time Taken: 1 ¼ hours
Yield: 10 Servings

Ingredients:
- ½ cup butter, softened
- ½ cup tahini paste
- ½ teaspoon baking soda
- ½ teaspoon salt
- 1 cup buttermilk
- 1 cup white sugar
- 1 teaspoon baking powder
- 1 teaspoon vanilla extract
- 2 cups all-purpose flour
- 2 eggs

Directions:

1. **Mix** the tahini paste, butter and sugar in a container and give it a good mix.

2. **Stir in** the eggs, one at a time, then put in the vanilla and buttermilk.

3. Fold in the flour, baking powder, baking soda and salt then spoon the batter in a round cake pan coated with baking paper.

4. Pre-heat the oven and bake at 350F **for about forty minutes** or until the cake is well risen and seems golden brown.

5. Let the cake cool in the pan and serve, sliced.

Nutritional Content of One Serving:

Calories: 343 Fat: 17.0g Protein: 6.6g Carbohydrates: 43.1g

The Ultimate Chocolate Cake

Total Time Taken: 1 ¼ hours
Yield: 14 Servings
Ingredients:

Cake:
- ¼ cup canola oil
- ½ cup cocoa powder
- ½ teaspoon salt
- 1 ½ cups white sugar
- 1 cup butter, softened

- 1 cup buttermilk
- 2 ½ cups all-purpose flour
- 2 egg yolks
- 2 teaspoons baking powder
- 4 eggs

Frosting:
- 1 ½ cups dark chocolate chips
- 1 cup heavy cream

Directions:
1. Mix the butter and sugar in a container until creamy and fluffy.
2. Stir in the eggs and egg yolks and mix thoroughly.
3. Put in the buttermilk and oil and mix thoroughly then fold in the dry ingredients.
4. Pour the batter in a 10-inch round cake pan and preheat your oven and bake at 350F for 45 minutes or until the toothpick inserted in the center of the cake comes out clean.
5. Let the cake cool in the pan then move to a platter.
6. For the frosting, bring the cream to the boiling point then turn off the heat and put in the chocolate. let the frosting cool in your refrigerator for a few hours then whip it using an electric mixer until fluffy.
7. Sprinkle the chocolate frosting over the cake and serve it fresh.

Nutritional Content of One Serving:

Calories: 442 Fat: 26.3g Protein: 6.6g Carbohydrates: 50.3g

Tiramisu Cake

Total Time Taken: 2 hours
Yield: 12 Servings
Ingredients:
- ¼ cup Grand Marnier
- 1 cup powdered sugar
- 1 tablespoon vanilla extract
- 10 oz. ladyfingers
- 2 cups brewed coffee
- 2 cups heavy cream, whipped
- 2 cups mascarpone cheese

Directions:
1. Coat a 9-inch round cake pan using plastic wrap.
2. Mix the mascarpone cheese with sugar then fold in the whipped cream.
3. Mix the coffee and Grand Marnier in a container.
4. Immerse the ladyfingers in the coffee mixture and layer them at the bottom of the pan.
5. Top with 1/3 of the cream, followed by an additional layer of ladyfingers.
6. Carry on until you run out of ingredients and place in your fridge at least an hour.
7. *The cake tastes best chilled.*

Nutritional Content of One Serving:

Calories: 285 Fat: 14.9g Protein: 7.6g Carbohydrates: 26.0g

Tropical Carrot Cake

Total Time Taken: 1 ½ hours
Yield: 16 Servings
Ingredients:

Cake:

- ¼ cup dark brown sugar
- 1 cup vegetable oil
- ½ cup chopped walnuts
- 1 cup shredded coconut

Frosting:

- ½ teaspoon ground cloves
- 1 cup white sugar
- ½ teaspoon ground ginger
- ½ teaspoon salt
- 1 cup butter, softened
- 1 cup cream cheese, softened
- 2 ½ cups powdered sugar
- 1 cup crushed pineapple (with juice)
- 1 teaspoon baking powder
- 1 teaspoon cinnamon powder
- 1 teaspoon vanilla extract
- 1 teaspoon vanilla extract
- 4 carrots, grated
- 2 cups all-purpose flour
- 1 teaspoon baking soda
- 4 eggs

Directions:

1. For the cake, combine the flour, baking soda, baking powder, spices and salt in a container.
2. Combine the sugars, oil, eggs and vanilla in a container and stir thoroughly until volume increases to twice what it was.
3. Stir in the carrots, pineapple, walnuts and coconut then put in the dry ingredients.
4. Pour the batter in two 9-inch cake pans and preheat your oven and bake at 350F for around forty minutes or until it rises and looks golden brown.
5. Let the cakes cool in the pans then level them and set aside for later.
6. For the frosting, combine the cream cheese, butter, sugar and vanilla in a container for minimum five minutes until firm and fluffy.
7. Use half of the frosting to fill the cakes and the second half to garnish them.

Nutritional Content of One Serving:

Calories: 529 Fat: 35.5g Protein: 5.5g Carbohydrates: 50.1g

Vanilla Cardamom Cake

Total Time Taken: 1 ¼ hours
 Yield: 12 Servings
 Ingredients:

Cake:

- ¼ teaspoon salt
- ½ cup canola oil
- 1 ½ cups all-purpose flour
- 1 cup white sugar
- 1 teaspoon baking powder
- 1 teaspoon cardamom powder
- 6 eggs

Frosting:

- ½ cup butter, softened
- 1 ½ cups powdered sugar
- 1 cup cream cheese
- 1 teaspoon vanilla extract

Directions:

1. For the cake, sift the flour with baking powder, salt and cardamom.
2. Mix the eggs with sugar until fluffy and pale.
3. Put in the oil and mix thoroughly then fold in the flour.
4. Pour the batter in a 9-inch round cake pan coated with baking paper.
5. Pre-heat the oven and bake at 350F for about forty minutes.
6. When finished, allow the cake to cool in the pan then cut it in half along the length.
7. For the frosting, combine the butter and cream cheese in a container until fluffy. Put in the vanilla and sugar and continue mixing for minimum five minutes until pale.
8. Use half of the frosting as filling and the second half to cover the cake.
9. *Serve the cake fresh.*

Nutritional Content of One Serving:

Calories: 427 Fat: 25.9g Protein: 5.9g Carbohydrates: 44.6g

Vanilla Funfetti Cake

Total Time Taken: 1 ½ hours
 Yield: 12 Servings
 Ingredients:

Cake:

- ½ cup sprinkles
- ½ teaspoon salt
- 1 ½ teaspoons baking powder
- 1 cup butter, softened
- 1 cup sour cream
- 1 cup white sugar
- 1 teaspoon vanilla extract

- 2 cups all-purpose flour
- 3 eggs

Frosting:
- ½ cup butter, softened
- 1 ½ cups powdered sugar
- 1 teaspoon vanilla extract

Directions:
1. For the cake, combine the butter and sugar in a container until fluffy and creamy.
2. Put in the eggs and vanilla and stir thoroughly for a few minutes.
3. Stir in the sour cream then fold in the flour, baking powder and salt, as well as sprinkles.
4. Spoon the batter in a 9-inch round cake pan coated with baking paper.
5. Pre-heat the oven and bake at 350F for about forty minutes or until it rises significantly and starts to appear golden-brown.
6. For the frosting, combine the butter, sugar and vanilla and stir thoroughly until fluffy and
7. pale.
8. Top the cake with frosting and serve it fresh.

Nutritional Content of One Serving:

Calories: 464 Fat: 28.3g Protein: 4.4g Carbohydrates: 50.0g

Vanilla Genoise Cake

Total Time Taken: 1 hour
Yield: 8 Servings
Ingredients:

- 6 eggs
- ¼ teaspoon baking powder
- ¼ teaspoon salt
- ¾ cup white sugar
- 1 cup all-purpose flour
- 1 teaspoon vanilla extract

Directions:
1. Mix the eggs, sugar and vanilla in a container until fluffy and light.
2. Fold in the flour, salt and baking powder then spoon the batter in a 8-inch round cake pan coated with baking paper.
3. Pre-heat the oven and bake at 350F for about half an hour or until it rises significantly and starts to appear golden-brown.
4. Let the cake cool down before you serve.

Nutritional Content of One Serving:

Calories: 176 Fat: 3.4g Protein: 5.8g Carbohydrates: 31.1g

Vanilla Strawberry Cake

Total Time Taken: 1 ½ hours
Yield: 10 Servings
Ingredients:

Cake:
- ¼ cup sour cream
- ½ cup butter, softened
- ½ cup whole milk
- ½ teaspoon baking soda
- ½ teaspoon salt
- 1 ½ cups all-purpose flour
- 1 cup white sugar
- 1 teaspoon baking powder
- 1 teaspoon vanilla extract
- 4 egg whites

Filling:
- ½ cup butter, softened
- 1 cup fresh strawberries, sliced
- 2 cups powdered sugar
- 2 teaspoons vanilla extract

Directions:
1. For the cake, sift the flour with baking powder, baking soda and salt in a container.
2. Put in the sugar and butter and stir until grainy.
3. Combine the egg whites, milk and sour cream, as well as vanilla in a container. Pour this mixture over the dry ingredients and stir only until blended.
4. Spoon the batter in two 8-inch circular cake pans coated with baking paper.
5. For the filling, combine the butter with sugar for five minutes until fluffy and creamy. Put in the vanilla and mix thoroughly.
6. Fill the cake with the buttercream and strawberry slices.
7. Serve it fresh.

Nutritional Content of One Serving:

Calories: 435 Fat: 20.3g Protein: 4.2g Carbohydrates: 60.6g

Vanilla White Chocolate Chip Cake

Total Time Taken: 1 ¼ hours
Yield: 12 Servings

Ingredients:
- ½ teaspoon salt
- 1 ½ teaspoons baking powder
- 1 cup butter, softened
- 1 cup white chocolate chips
- 1 cup white sugar
- 1 cup whole milk

- 1 tablespoon vanilla extract
- 2 cups all-purpose flour
- 4 eggs

Directions:
1. Mix the butter and sugar in a container until fluffy and pale.
2. Stir in the eggs, one at a time, then put in the vanilla and milk.
3. Stir in the flour, baking powder and salt then fold in the chocolate chips.
4. Spoon the batter in a 9-inch round cake pan coated with baking paper.
5. Pre-heat the oven and bake at 350F for about forty minutes.
6. Let the cake cool in the pan and serve, sliced.

Nutritional Content of One Serving:

Calories: 387 Fat: 22.2g Protein: 5.6g Carbohydrates: 42.4g

Victoria Sponge Cake With Strawberries

Total Time Taken: 1 ¼ hours
Yield: 8 Servings

Ingredients:
- ¼ teaspoon salt
- 1 ¼ cups all-purpose flour
- 1 cup butter, softened
- 1 cup fresh strawberries, sliced
- 1 cup heavy cream, whipped
- 1 cup white sugar
- 1 teaspoon baking powder
- 4 eggs

Directions:
1. Mix the butter and sugar in a container until light and creamy.
2. Stir in the eggs, one at a time, then fold in the flour, salt and baking powder.
3. Spoon the batter in a 9-inch round cake pan covered with parchment paper and preheat your oven and bake at 350F for about half an hour or until it rises significantly and starts to appear golden-brown.
4. Let the cake cool down then take it out of the pan and cut it in half along the length.
5. Fill the cake with whipped cream and strawberries and garnish it with a dust of powdered sugar.

Nutritional Content of One Serving:

Calories: 458 Fat: 31.0g Protein: 5.5g Carbohydrates: 42.2g

Walnut Banana Cake

Total Time Taken: 1 ¼ hours
Yield: 10 Servings

Ingredients:
- ¼ cup whole milk
- ½ teaspoon salt

- 1 cup butter, softened
- 1 cup ground walnuts
- 1 cup light brown sugar
- 1 teaspoon cinnamon powder
- 2 cups all-purpose flour
- 2 teaspoons baking soda
- 3 ripe bananas, mashed
- 4 eggs

Directions:
1. Mix the flour, walnuts, baking soda, salt and cinnamon in a container.
2. In a separate container, combine the butter and sugar until creamy, then put in the eggs, one at a time.
3. Put in the milk and bananas then fold in the flour mixture.
4. Spoon the batter into a 10-inch round cake pan coated with baking paper.
5. Pre-heat the oven and bake at 350F or until a toothpick inserted into the center of the cake comes out clean.
6. Let the cake cool completely and serve, sliced.

Nutritional Content of One Serving:
Calories: 446 Fat: 28.1g Protein: 8.6g Carbohydrates: 43.1g

Walnut Carrot Cake

Total Time Taken: 1 ½ hours
Yield: 16 Servings
Ingredients:

Cake:
- ½ cup ground walnuts
- ½ teaspoon salt
- 1 cup canola oil
- 1 cup chopped walnuts
- 1 cup crushed pineapple
- 1 cup white sugar
- 1 teaspoon all-spice powder
- 1 teaspoon baking powder
- 1 teaspoon baking soda
- 1 teaspoon cinnamon powder
- 2 cups all-purpose flour
- 2 cups grated carrots
- 3 eggs

Frosting:
- ¼ cup butter
- 1 cup cream cheese, softened
- 3 cups powdered sugar

Directions:

1. To prepare the cake, combine the dry ingredients in a container and the wet ingredients in another container.
2. Pour the wet ingredients over the dry ones and mix using a spatula.
3. Pour the batter in 9-inch round cake pan coated with baking paper.
4. Preheat your oven and bake the cake at 350F for about forty minutes or until they pass the toothpick test.
5. Let the cakes cool completely.
6. For the frosting, combine the cream cheese and butter in a container until creamy.
7. Put in the sugar, progressively, stirring thoroughly after each addition.
8. Whip the frosting thoroughly until fluffy.
9. Fill the cake with 1/3 of the frosting and cover it with the rest of the cream cheese frosting.
10. Serve the cake fresh or place in your refrigerator.

Nutritional Content of One Serving:

Calories: 483 Fat: 29.5g Protein: 6.8g Carbohydrates: 51.3g

Walnut Coffee Cake

Total Time Taken: 2 hours
Yield: 16 Servings
Ingredients:

Walnut cake:
- ¼ cup whole milk
- ½ teaspoon salt
- 1 cup butter, softened
- 1 cup ground walnuts
- 1 cup white sugar
- 1 teaspoon vanilla extract
- 2 cups all-purpose flour
- 2 teaspoons baking powder
- 4 eggs

Coffee buttercream:
- 1 cup butter, softened
- 1 teaspoon vanilla extract
- 2 ½ cups powdered sugar
- 2 teaspoons instant coffee

Directions:
1. For the cake, combine the flour, baking powder, walnuts and salt in a container.
2. In a separate container, combine the butter and sugar until creamy. Stir in the eggs, one at a time, then put in the milk and vanilla.
3. Fold in the flour and stir lightly using a spatula.
4. Pour the batter in a round cake pan coated with baking paper and preheat your oven and bake at 350F for around forty minutes.
5. Let the cake cool in the pan then move to a platter.
6. For the buttercream, combine the butter until creamy and light. Put in the sugar, progressively and stir thoroughly for a few minutes until firm.

7. Mix the vanilla with the coffee then add it into the buttercream. Stir thoroughly to mix.
8. Cover the cake with the buttercream and serve it fresh.

Nutritional Content of One Serving:

Calories: 449 Fat: 29.0g Protein: 5.2g Carbohydrates: 44.5g

Walnut Honey Pound Cake

Total Time Taken: 1 ¼ hours
Yield: 12 Servings

Ingredients:
- ½ cup butter, softened
- ½ teaspoon salt
- 1 ½ cups walnuts, chopped
- 1 cup honey
- 1 cup whole milk
- 1 teaspoon vanilla extract
- 2 cups all-purpose flour
- 2 eggs
- 2 teaspoons baking powder

Directions:
1. Sift the flour, baking powder and salt in a container.
2. In a separate container, combine the butter and honey until fluffy. Stir in the eggs and vanilla and mix thoroughly.
3. Put in the flour mixture, alternating it with the milk.
4. Fold in the walnuts then spoon the batter in a 9-inch round cake pan coated with baking paper.
5. Pre-heat the oven and bake at 350F for about forty minutes or until it rises significantly and starts to appear golden-brown.
6. Let the cake cool in the pan and serve, sliced.

Nutritional Content of One Serving:

Calories: 351 Fat: 18.5g Protein: 7.6g Carbohydrates: 42.1g

White Chocolate Blackberry Cake

Total Time Taken: 2 hours
Yield: 10 Servings
Ingredients:

Sponge cake:
- ¼ teaspoon salt
- ½ cup white sugar
- ½ teaspoon baking powder
- 1 cup all-purpose flour
- 5 eggs

Filling:
- 1 ½ cups heavy cream

- 2 ½ cups white chocolate chips
- 2 cups fresh blackberries

Directions:

1. For the sponge cake, whip the eggs, sugar and salt in a container until volume increases to twice what it was.
2. Fold in the flour and baking powder then spoon the batter in a 8-inch round cake pan coated with baking paper.
3. Pre-heat the oven and bake at 350F for around forty minutes then allow the cake to cool in the pan.
4. Slice the cake in half along the length.
5. For the filling, bring the cream to the boiling point in a saucepan. Turn off the heat and put in the chocolate. Stir until melted then let cool in your refrigerator.
6. Whip the white chocolate cream for at least two minutes until fluffy.
7. Fill the cake with half of the cream and half of the blackberries. Cover the cake with the rest of the cream and garnish with blackberries.
8. The cake tastes best chilled.

Nutritional Content of One Serving:

Calories: 418 Fat: 22.8g Protein: 7.3g Carbohydrates: 48.3g

Whole Pear Sponge Cake

Total Time Taken: 2 hours
Yield: 14 Servings
Ingredients:

- ¼ cup canola oil
- ¼ cup honey
- ¼ teaspoon salt
- ½ cup butter, softened
- ½ cup cocoa powder
- ½ cup sour cream
- 1 ½ cups all-purpose flour
- 1 cinnamon stick
- 1 teaspoon baking soda
- 2 cups white wine
- 2 eggs
- 2 star anise
- 4 pears

Directions:

1. Peel the pears and place them in a saucepan. Put in the star anise, cinnamon, honey and wine and cook over low heat for about half an hour. Let cool and then position the pears in a 9-inch round cake pan coated with baking paper.
2. Mix the butter, canola oil and eggs in a container until creamy.
3. Put in the sour cream and mix thoroughly then fold in the flour, cocoa powder, baking soda and salt.
4. Spoon the batter over the pears.
5. Preheat your oven and bake the cake for 45 minutes or until a toothpick inserted into the center of the cake comes out clean.

6. Let the cake cool before you serve.

Nutritional Content of One Serving:

Calories: 257 Fat: 13.5g Protein: 3.4g Carbohydrates: 27.6g

Yeasted Plum Cake

Total Time Taken: 2 hours

Yield: 16 Servings

Ingredients:

- ¼ cup butter, melted
- ½ cup light brown sugar
- ½ cup warm milk
- ½ teaspoon salt
- 1 ¼ teaspoons instant yeast
- 1 cup warm water
- 1 pound plums, pitted and sliced
- 1 tablespoon lemon zest
- 1 teaspoon vanilla extract
- 2 eggs
- 3 cups all-purpose flour

Directions:

1. Mix the flour, salt and yeast in a container.
2. Put in the water, milk, butter, eggs, vanilla and lemon zest and knead the dough minimum ten minutes until it looks and feels elastic.
3. Allow the dough to rest for an hour then roll it into a rectangle and move it to a sheet cake pan coated with baking paper.
4. Top with plums and drizzle with brown sugar.
5. Pre-heat the oven and bake at 350F for about forty minutes or until it rises significantly and starts to appear golden-brown.
6. Let the cake cool in the pan before you serve.

Nutritional Content of One Serving:

Calories: 150 Fat: 3.9g Protein: 3.7g Carbohydrates: 25.1g

Yogurt Bundt Cake

Total Time Taken: 1 ¼ hours

Yield: 12 Servings

Ingredients:

- ½ teaspoon salt
- 1 ½ cups plain yogurt
- 1 ½ cups white sugar
- 1 cup butter, softened
- 1 teaspoon baking powder
- 1 teaspoon baking soda
- 2 tablespoons lemon juice

- 2 tablespoons lemon zest
- 3 cups all-purpose flour
- 6 eggs, separated

Directions:
1. Mix the egg yolks with sugar until pale and fluffy. Stir in the butter and mix thoroughly.
2. Put in the lemon zest and juice then mix in the yogurt.
3. Fold in the flour, baking powder, baking soda and salt.
4. Spoon the batter in a greased Bundt cake pan and preheat your oven and bake at 350F for about forty minutes or until a toothpick inserted into the center of the cake comes out clean.
5. Let the cake cool in the pan before transferring on a platter.

Nutritional Content of One Serving:

Calories: 398 Fat: 18.2g Protein: 7.9g Carbohydrates: 51.7g

Yogurt Strawberry Cake

Total Time Taken: 1 hour
Yield: 8 Servings
Ingredients:
- ½ cup cornstarch
- ½ teaspoon salt
- ¾ cup canola oil
- ¾ cup white sugar
- 1 ½ cups all-purpose flour
- 1 cup plain yogurt
- 1 cup strawberries, sliced
- 1 teaspoon baking powder
- 1 teaspoon vanilla extract
- 2 eggs

Directions:
1. Mix the canola oil, sugar, eggs and vanilla in a container until fluffy.
2. Stir in the yogurt and mix thoroughly then fold in the flour, cornstarch, baking powder and salt then pour the batter in a 9-inch round cake pan covered with parchment paper.
3. Top the cake with fresh strawberries and preheat your oven and bake at 350F for about forty minutes or until a toothpick inserted in the center comes out cleans.
4. Let the cake cool in the pan before you serve.

Nutritional Content of One Serving:

Calories: 412 Fat: 22.2g Protein: 5.7g Carbohydrates: 47.9g

Almond Poppy Seed Muffins

Total Time Taken: 1 hour
Yield: 12 Servings
Ingredients:
- ¼ teaspoon salt
- ½ cup butter, melted

- ½ cup sour cream
- ½ cup white sugar
- 1 ½ cups almond flour
- 1 pinch salt
- 1 teaspoon baking powder
- 1 teaspoon lemon zest
- 1 teaspoon vanilla extract
- 2 eggs
- 2 tablespoons poppy seeds

Directions:
1. Mix the almond flour, baking powder, salt and poppy seeds in a container.
2. In another container, combine the sugar, butter, eggs, sour cream, lemon zest and salt. Pour this mixture over the dry ingredients and mix thoroughly.
3. Spoon the batter in a muffin tin covered with muffin papers.
4. Pre-heat the oven and bake at 350F for about twenty minutes or until a golden-brown colour is achieved and it rises significantly.
5. Let the muffins cool in the pan before you serve.

Nutritional Content of One Serving:

Calories: 159 Fat: 12.8g Protein: 2.3g Carbohydrates: 10.2g

Almond Rose Cupcakes

Total Time Taken: 1 ½ hours
Yield: 12 Servings
Ingredients:

Cupcakes:
- ¼ cup all-purpose flour
- ¼ teaspoon salt
- ½ cup butter, softened
- ½ cup white sugar
- 1 /2 teaspoon almond extract
- 1 ¼ cups almond flour
- 1 ½ teaspoons baking powder
- 1 teaspoon rose water
- 2 eggs

Frosting:
- 1 cup butter, softened
- 1 teaspoon rose water Rose petals to garnish
- 2 cups powdered sugar

Directions:
1. To make the cupcakes, combine the butter and sugar in a container until creamy and fluffy. Put in the rose water and almond extract, as well as the eggs and mix thoroughly.
2. Fold in the flours, salt and baking powder and mix using a spatula.
3. Spoon the batter in a muffin tin covered with muffin papers and preheat your oven and bake at 350F for about twenty minutes or until it rises significantly and starts to appear golden-brown.

4. Let cool in the pan.
5. To make the frosting, combine the butter and sugar in a container until creamy and fluffy and
6. pale.
7. Put in the rose water and mix thoroughly.
8. Pipe the frosting on top of each cupcake and garnish with rose petals.

Nutritional Content of One Serving:

Calories: 350 Fat: 25.3g Protein: 2.1g Carbohydrates: 31.3g

Banana Mascarpone Cupcakes

Total Time Taken: 1 ½ hours
Yield: 12 Servings
Ingredients:

Cupcakes:

- ¼ cup canola oil
- ½ cup oat flour
- ½ teaspoon salt
- 1 ½ cups all-purpose flour
- 1 cup buttermilk
- 1 teaspoon vanilla extract
- 2 bananas, mashed
- 2 eggs
- 2 teaspoons baking powder

Frosting:

- 1 ½ cups mascarpone cheese
- 1 cup powdered sugar
- 1 teaspoon vanilla extract

Directions:

1. To make the cupcakes, combine the bananas, eggs, vanilla, oil and buttermilk in a container.
2. Put in the remaining ingredients and mix thoroughly.
3. Spoon the batter in a muffin tin covered with muffin papers.
4. Pre-heat the oven and bake at 350F for about twenty minutes or until a golden-brown colour is achieved and it rises significantly.
5. Let them cool in the pan.
6. To make the frosting, combine the mascarpone cheese and sugar in a container until pale and fluffy.
7. Put in the vanilla and mix thoroughly.
8. Apply the frosting on top of the cupcakes and serve them fresh.

Nutritional Content of One Serving:

Calories: 244 Fat: 9.9g Protein: 7.4g Carbohydrates: 31.5g

Banana Olive Oil Muffins

Total Time Taken: 1 hour
Yield: 12 Servings
Ingredients:

- ¼ cup extra virgin olive oil
- ½ cup buttermilk
- ½ cup light brown sugar
- ½ teaspoon salt
- 1 ½ cups all-purpose flour
- 1 ½ teaspoons baking powder
- 1 tablespoon lemon juice
- 1 teaspoon lemon zest
- 2 bananas, mashed
- 2 eggs

Directions:

1. Mix the eggs and sugar in a container until creamy. Put in the olive oil and lemon zest and mix thoroughly. Stir in the lemon juice and bananas, as well as the buttermilk.
2. Fold in the flour, salt and baking powder then spoon the batter in a muffin tin covered with muffin papers.
3. Pre-heat the oven and bake at 350F for about twenty minutes or until it rises significantly and seems golden.

These muffins taste best chilled.

Nutritional Content of One Serving:

Calories: 149 Fat: 5.2g Protein: 3.1g Carbohydrates: 23.3g

Banana Peanut Butter Cups Muffins

Total Time Taken: 1 hour
Yield: 12 Servings
Ingredients:

- ½ cup light brown sugar
- ½ peanut butter cups, chopped
- ½ teaspoon salt
- 1 ½ cups all-purpose flour
- 1 cup buttermilk
- 1 teaspoon baking soda
- 1 teaspoon vanilla extract
- 2 bananas, mashed
- 2 eggs

Directions:

1. Mix the bananas, eggs, buttermilk and vanilla in a container.
2. Put in the sugar, flour, salt and baking soda and mix using a spatula.
3. Fold in the peanut butter cups then spoon the batter in a muffin tin covered with muffin papers.

4. Preheat your oven and bake the muffins at 350F for about twenty minutes or until a golden-brown colour is achieved and it rises significantly.

These muffins taste best chilled.

Nutritional Content of One Serving:

Calories: 180 Fat: 6.5g Protein: 6.1g Carbohydrates: 25.5g

Banana Peanut Butter Muffins

Total Time Taken: 1 hour
Yield: 12 Servings
Ingredients:
- ¼ cup canola oil
- ¼ cup smooth peanut butter
- ½ cup buttermilk
- ½ cup light brown sugar
- ½ teaspoon salt
- 1 ½ cups all-purpose flour
- 1 teaspoon baking soda
- 1 teaspoon vanilla extract
- 2 eggs
- 2 ripe bananas, mashed

Directions:
1. Mix the peanut butter, bananas, oil, eggs and buttermilk in a container.
2. Put in the vanilla and mix thoroughly then fold in the remaining ingredients.
3. Spoon the batter in 12 muffin cups covered with muffin papers.
4. Preheat your oven and bake the muffins at 350F for about twenty minutes or until it rises significantly and becomes aromatic.

These muffins taste best chilled.

Nutritional Content of One Serving:

Calories: 185 Fat: 8.3g Protein: 4.4g Carbohydrates: 24.0g

Banana Pear Muffins

Total Time Taken: 1 hour
Yield: 12 Servings
Ingredients:
- ¼ cup buttermilk
- ¼ cup canola oil
- ¼ teaspoon salt
- ½ cup white sugar
- ½ cup whole wheat flour
- ½ teaspoon ground ginger
- 1 cup all-purpose flour
- 1 egg

- 1 teaspoon baking soda
- 1 teaspoon cinnamon powder
- 2 bananas, mashed
- 2 pears, cored and diced

Directions:
1. Mix the bananas, egg, oil, buttermilk and sugar in a container.
2. Put in the flours, salt, spices and baking soda and stir for a few seconds to mix just until incorporated.
3. Fold in the pears then spoon the batter in a muffin tin covered with muffin papers.
4. Pre-heat the oven and bake at 350F for about twenty minutes or until a golden-brown colour is achieved and fragrant.

These muffins taste best chilled.

Nutritional Content of One Serving:
Calories: 173 Fat: 5.2g Protein: 2.6g Carbohydrates: 30.4g

Banana Yogurt Muffins

Total Time Taken: 1 hour
Yield: 12 Servings
Ingredients:
- ½ cup canola oil
- ½ cup light brown sugar
- ½ teaspoon baking soda
- ½ teaspoon salt
- 1 bananas, mashed
- 1 cup plain yogurt
- 1 egg
- 1 teaspoon baking powder
- 2 cups all-purpose flour

Directions:
1. Mix the bananas, yogurt, egg, sugar and oil in a container until creamy.
2. Put in the remaining ingredients and stir for a few seconds to mix.
3. Spoon the batter in a muffin tin covered with muffin papers.
4. Preheat your oven and bake the muffins at 350F for about twenty minutes or until a golden-brown colour is achieved and it rises significantly.

These muffins taste best chilled.

Nutritional Content of One Serving:
Calories: 208 Fat: 9.9g Protein: 3.9g Carbohydrates: 25.7g

Basic Chocolate Muffins

Total Time Taken: 1 hour
Yield: 12 Servings
Ingredients:

- 2 tablespoons cocoa powder
- 2 eggs
- 2 cups all-purpose flour
- 1 teaspoon vanilla extract
- 1 ½ teaspoons baking powder
- ¾ cup light brown sugar
- ½ cup milk
- ½ cup canola oil
- ¼ teaspoon salt

Directions:

1. Mix the flour, cocoa powder, salt and baking powder.
2. Mix the sugar and oil in a container for a couple of minutes. Put in the eggs, vanilla and milk and mix thoroughly.
3. Fold in the flour then spoon the batter in a muffin tin covered with muffin papers of your desire.
4. Pre-heat the oven and bake at 350F for about twenty minutes or until a toothpick inserted into them comes out dry.

These muffins taste best chilled.

Nutritional Content of One Serving:

Calories: 210 Fat: 10.3g Protein: 3.6g Carbohydrates: 26.2g

Basic Muffins

Total Time Taken: 1 hour
Yield: 12 Servings
Ingredients:

- ¼ teaspoon salt
- ½ cup canola oil
- ½ teaspoon baking powder
- ½ teaspoon baking soda
- ¾ cup white sugar
- 1 cup whole milk
- 1 egg
- 1 teaspoon vanilla extract
- 2 ¼ cups all-purpose flour

Directions:

1. Mix the flour, sugar, salt, baking powder and baking soda in a container.
2. Stir in the egg, oil, milk and vanilla and stir for a few seconds to mix.
3. Spoon the batter in a muffin tin covered with muffin papers and preheat your oven and bake at 350F for about twenty minutes or until it rises significantly and seems golden.

These muffins taste best chilled.

Nutritional Content of One Serving:

Calories: 231 Fat: 10.3g Protein: 3.5g Carbohydrates: 31.5g

Beetroot Raspberry Muffins

Total Time Taken: 1 ½ hours
Yield: 12 Servings

Ingredients:

- ½ cup buttermilk
- ½ cup canola oil
- ½ cup white sugar
- ½ teaspoon salt
- 1 ½ teaspoons baking powder
- 1 cup beetroot puree
- 1 cup fresh raspberries
- 1 egg
- 1 teaspoon vanilla extract
- 2 cups all-purpose flour

Directions:

1. Mix the beetroot puree, egg, buttermilk and oil in a container.
2. Put in the sugar and vanilla and mix thoroughly then fold in the flour, salt and baking powder.
3. Fold in the raspberries then spoon the batter in a muffin tin coated with baking muffin papers.
4. Pre-heat the oven and bake at 350F for about twenty minutes or until it rises significantly and starts to appear golden-brown.

These muffins taste best chilled.

Nutritional Content of One Serving:

Calories: 206 Fat: 9.8g Protein: 3.2g Carbohydrates: 26.8g

Black Bottom Muffins

Total Time Taken: 1 hour
Yield: 12 Servings
Ingredients:

- ¼ cup white sugar
- ½ cup butter, melted
- ½ cup light brown sugar
- ½ teaspoon salt
- 1 ½ cups almond flour
- 1 cup cream cheese
- 1 egg
- 1 teaspoon baking powder
- 1/3 cup all-purpose flour
- 2 eggs

Directions:

1. Mix the cream cheese,
2. 1 egg and ¼ cup sugar in a container.
3. Spoon the mixture into 12 muffin cups covered with muffin papers.
   4. **Combine**
5. 2 eggs with butter and sugar until pale.
6. Put in the flour, almond flour, baking powder and salt.
7. Spoon the batter over the cream cheese mixture.
8. Preheat your oven and bake the muffins at 350F for about twenty minutes or until well risen.

These muffins taste best chilled.

Nutritional Content of One Serving:

Calories: 223 Fat: 17.3g Protein: 4.0g Carbohydrates: 14.3g

Black Forest Cupcakes

Total Time Taken: 1 ½ hours
Yield: 12 Servings
Ingredients:

Cupcakes:

- ¼ cup cocoa powder
- ½ cup canola oil
- ½ teaspoon salt
- 1 ¼ cups all-purpose flour
- 1 cup brewed coffee
- 1 egg
- 1 teaspoon baking soda
- 1 teaspoon vanilla extract

Frosting:

- 1 cup sour cherries, pitted
- 2 cups heavy cream, whipped

Directions:

1. To make the cupcakes, combine the coffee, oil, egg and vanilla in a container.
2. Stir in the flour, cocoa powder, salt and baking soda and stir for a few seconds to mix.
3. Pour the batter in a muffin tin covered with muffin papers.
4. Pre-heat the oven and bake at 350F for about twenty minutes or until it rises significantly and becomes aromatic.
5. Let the muffins cool to room temperature.
6. Spread the whipped cream on top of each muffin and decorate with sour cherries.

Nutritional Content of One Serving:

Calories: 264 Fat: 17.2g Protein: 2.7g Carbohydrates: 25.4g

Black Forest Muffins

Total Time Taken: 1 hour
Yield: 12 Servings
Ingredients:

- ¼ cup canola oil
- ¼ cup cocoa powder
- ¼ teaspoon salt
- ½ cup brewed coffee
- ½ teaspoon baking soda
- 1 ½ cups all-purpose flour
- 1 cup buttermilk
- 1 cup cherries, pitted
- 1 teaspoon baking powder
- 1 teaspoon vanilla extract
- 2 eggs

Directions:

1. Mix the eggs, buttermilk, coffee, oil and vanilla and mix thoroughly.
2. Fold in the flour, cocoa powder, baking soda, baking powder and salt then put in the cherries and mix them in gently.
3. Spoon the batter in a muffin tin coated with baking muffin papers and preheat your oven and bake at 350F for about twenty minutes or until well risen.

These muffins taste best chilled.

Nutritional Content of One Serving:

Calories: 128 Fat: 5.8g Protein: 3.6g Carbohydrates: 15.9g

Black Magic Cupcakes

Total Time Taken: 1 ½ hours
Yield: 14 Servings
Ingredients:

Cupcakes:

- ¼ cup butter, softened
- ¼ teaspoon salt
- ½ cup buttermilk
- ½ cup canola oil
- ¾ cup cocoa powder
- 1 ½ cups all-purpose flour
- 1 ½ teaspoons baking powder
- 1 cup white sugar
- 1 teaspoon instant coffee
- 1 teaspoon vanilla extract
- 2 eggs

Frosting:

- ¼ cup cocoa powder
- 1 cup butter, softened
- 1 teaspoon instant coffee
- 2 cups powdered sugar
- 2 tablespoons milk

Directions:

1. To make the cupcakes, combine the butter, oil and sugar in a container until creamy and pale.
2. Put in the eggs and mix thoroughly. Stir in the vanilla and buttermilk then put in the remaining ingredients and mix using a spatula.
3. Spoon the batter in a muffin tin covered with muffin papers.
4. Preheat your oven and bake the muffins at 350F for about twenty minutes or until a toothpick inserted into them comes out dry.
5. Let cool in the pan.
6. To make the frosting, combine the butter in a container until creamy and pale.
7. Put in the sugar, progressively, then whip until fluffy.
8. Stir in the coffee, cocoa powder and milk and mix for a few additional minutes.
9. Spoon the frosting in a pastry bag and top each cupcake with it.

The cupcakes taste best chilled.

Nutritional Content of One Serving:

Calories: 412 Fat: 25.9g Protein: 3.8g Carbohydrates: 45.8g

Black Sesame Cupcakes With Cream Cheese Frosting

Total Time Taken: 1 ½ hours
Yield: 14 Servings
Ingredients:

Cupcakes:

- ¼ cup black sesame powder
- ½ teaspoon salt
- ¾ cup milk
- 1 ½ cups all-purpose flour
- 1 cup white sugar
- 1 teaspoon baking powder
- 1 teaspoon vanilla extract
- 2 eggs
- 2/3 cup butter, softened

Frosting:

- 1 cup cream cheese
- 2/3 cup butter, softened
- 3 cups powdered sugar

Directions:

1. To make the cupcakes, combine the butter and sugar in a container until fluffy and airy. Put in the eggs, one at a time, then mix in the milk and vanilla.
2. Fold in the dry ingredients and mix using a spatula.
3. Spoon the batter into 12 muffin cups covered with muffin papers.
4. Preheat your oven and bake the cupcakes at 350F for about twenty minutes or until the cupcakes pass the toothpick test.
5. Let cool in the pan.
6. To make the frosting, combine the butter and cream cheese in a container until creamy.
7. Put in the sugar and continue stirring thoroughly until fluffy and pale.
8. Spoon the frosting in a pastry bag and top each cupcake with it.

Nutritional Content of One Serving:

Calories: 445 Fat: 25.0g Protein: 4.0g Carbohydrates: 53.3g

Blackberry Bran Muffins

Total Time Taken: 1 hour
Yield: 12 Servings
Ingredients:
- ¼ cup honey
- ¼ cup light brown sugar
- ¼ cup rice bran oil
- ½ cup wheat bran
- ½ teaspoon salt
- ¾ cup milk
- 1 cup all-purpose flour
- 1 cup fresh blackberries
- 1 teaspoon baking soda
- 2 eggs

Directions:
1. Mix the flour, wheat bran, baking soda and salt in a container.
2. Stir in the eggs, milk, honey, sugar and oil and stir for a few seconds to mix.
3. Fold in the blackberries then spoon the batter in a muffin tin covered with muffin papers.
4. Pre-heat the oven and bake at 350F for about twenty minutes or until it rises significantly and seems golden.

These muffins taste best chilled.

Nutritional Content of One Serving:

Calories: 140 Fat: 5.8g Protein: 3.1g Carbohydrates: 20.2g

Blackberry Muffins

Total Time Taken: 1 hour
Yield: 10 Servings
Ingredients:
- ½ cup rolled oats
- ½ teaspoon salt

- 1 ½ cups all-purpose flour
- 1 cup buttermilk
- 1 cup fresh blackberries
- 1 teaspoon baking soda
- 1 teaspoon vanilla extract
- 2 eggs
- 2/3 cup white sugar

Directions:
1. Mix the flour, oats, baking soda, salt and sugar in a container.
2. Put in the eggs, buttermilk and vanilla and stir swiftly to combine.
3. Fold in the blackberries then scoop the batter in a muffin tin covered with muffin papers.
4. Preheat your oven and bake the muffins at 350F for about twenty minutes or until it rises significantly and seems golden.

These muffins taste best chilled.

Nutritional Content of One Serving:
Calories: 164 Fat: 1.6g Protein: 4.6g Carbohydrates: 33.1g

Blackberry Oat Bran Muffins

Total Time Taken: 1 hour
Yield: 12 Servings
Ingredients:
- 2 eggs
- 1 teaspoon vanilla extract
- 1 cup buttermilk
- 1 cup blackberries
- 1 ½ teaspoons baking powder
- 1 ½ cups all-purpose flour
- ½ teaspoon cinnamon powder
- ½ cup white sugar
- ½ cup oat bran
- ½ cup butter, melted
- ¼ teaspoon salt

Directions:
1. Mix the flour, oat bran, baking powder, salt and cinnamon in a container.
2. In a separate container, mix the butter, sugar, eggs, buttermilk and vanilla. Pour this mixture over the dry ingredients and give them a quick whisk.
3. Fold in the blackberries then spoon the batter in a muffin tin lined using muffin papers of your choice.
4. Pre-heat the oven and bake at 350F for about twenty minutes or until it rises significantly and seems golden.

These muffins taste best chilled.

Nutritional Content of One Serving:
Calories: 188 Fat: 9.0g Protein: 3.9g Carbohydrates: 24.5g

Blackberry White Chocolate Muffins

Total Time Taken: 1 hour
Yield: 12 Servings
Ingredients:
- 2 teaspoons baking powder
- 2 eggs
- 2 cups all-purpose flour
- 1 teaspoon vanilla extract
- 1 cup milk
- 1 cup blueberries
- ½ teaspoon salt
- ½ cup white sugar
- ½ cup white chocolate chips
- ½ cup canola oil
- ¼ cup shredded coconut

Directions:
1. Mix the flour, baking powder, salt, sugar, coconut and chocolate chips in a container.
2. Stir in the milk, eggs, canola oil and vanilla and mix using a spatula.
3. Fold in the blueberries then spoon the batter in a muffin tin coated with baking muffin papers.
4. Preheat your oven and bake the muffins at 350F for about twenty minutes or until it rises significantly and starts to appear golden-brown.

These muffins taste best chilled.

Nutritional Content of One Serving:

Calories: 261 Fat: 13.3g Protein: 4.3g Carbohydrates: 31.9g

Blueberry Banana Muffins

Total Time Taken: 1 hour
Yield: 12 Servings
Ingredients:
- ½ cup canola oil
- ½ teaspoon cinnamon powder
- ½ teaspoon salt
- 1 cup all-purpose flour
- 1 cup fresh blueberries
- 1 cup plain yogurt
- 1 cup wheat flour
- 2 bananas, mashed
- 2 eggs
- 2 teaspoons baking powder

Directions:
1. Mix the flours, cinnamon, salt and baking powder in a container.
2. Put in the remaining ingredients and stir for a few seconds to mix.

3. Fold in the blueberries then spoon the batter in a muffin tin lined.
4. Pre-heat the oven and bake at 350F for about twenty minutes or until it rises significantly and starts to appear golden-brown.

These muffins taste best chilled.

Nutritional Content of One Serving:

Calories: 206 Fat: 10.4g Protein: 4.5g Carbohydrates: 24.0g

Blueberry Cheese Muffins

Total Time Taken: 1 hour
Yield: 12 Servings
Ingredients:

- ¼ cup white rice flour
- ¼ teaspoon salt
- ½ cup coconut flour
- ½ cup cream cheese
- ½ cup sorghum flour
- ½ cup tapioca flour
- ¾ cup butter, melted
- 1 ½ teaspoons baking powder
- 1 cup fresh blueberries
- 1 cup milk
- 1 cup white sugar
- 2 eggs

Directions:

1. Mix the butter, sugar and eggs in a container until creamy.
2. Put in the milk and mix thoroughly then mix in the flours, salt and baking powder.
3. Put in the blueberries then spoon the batter in a muffin tin coated with baking muffin papers.
4. Top each muffin with a dollop of cream cheese and preheat your oven and bake at 350F for about twenty minutes or until a golden-brown colour is achieved and it rises significantly.
5. Let the muffins cool to room temperature before you serve.

Nutritional Content of One Serving:

Calories: 314 Fat: 17.1g Protein: 4.3g Carbohydrates: 38.6g

Blueberry Frosted Cupcakes

Total Time Taken: 1 ½ hours
Yield: 12 Servings
Ingredients:

Cupcakes:

- ½ cup butter, softened
- 2 tablespoons dark brown sugar
- 3 eggs
- 1 teaspoon vanilla extract

- 1 ¾ cups all-purpose flour
- 1 teaspoon baking powder
- ½ teaspoon salt
- 1 cup buttermilk
- 1 cup fresh blueberries
- 2/3 cup white sugar

Frosting:
- ¼ cup blueberry puree
- 1 cup butter, softened
- 2 ½ cups powdered sugar

Directions:
1. To make the cupcakes, combine the butter and sugars in a container until fluffy and pale.
2. Put in the eggs and vanilla and mix thoroughly then fold in the flour, baking powder and salt.
3. Stir in the buttermilk then fold in the blueberries.
4. Spoon the batter in 12 muffin cups covered with muffin papers.
5. Preheat your oven and bake the cupcakes at 350F for about twenty minutes or until it rises significantly and starts to appear golden-brown.
6. Let the cupcakes cool down in the pan.
7. To make the frosting, combine the butter and sugar in a container until fluffy and pale, at least five minutes.
8. Put in the blueberry puree and mix thoroughly.
9. Spoon the frosting into a pastry bag and top the cupcakes with it.

Nutritional Content of One Serving:
Calories: 463 Fat: 24.5g Protein: 4.3g Carbohydrates: 58.8g

Blueberry Lemon Cupcakes

Total Time Taken: 1 ½ hours
Yield: 12 Servings
Ingredients:

Cupcakes:
- ½ cup butter, softened
- ½ teaspoon salt
- 1 ½ teaspoons baking powder
- 1 ¾ cups all-purpose flour
- 1 cup fresh blueberries
- 1 cup white sugar
- 1 tablespoon lemon zest
- 1 teaspoon vanilla extract
- 2 tablespoons lemon juice
- 3 eggs

Frosting:
- ½ cup butter
- 1 cup white sugar
- 3 lemons, zested and juiced

- 4 egg yolks

Directions:

1. To make the cupcakes, combine the butter and sugar in a container until fluffy and creamy.
2. Put in the eggs and mix thoroughly then mix in the lemon zest, lemon juice and vanilla.
3. Fold in the flour, salt, baking powder and blueberries.
4. Spoon the batter in a muffin tin covered with muffin papers.
5. Pre-heat the oven and bake at 350F for about twenty minutes or until a toothpick inserted into them comes out dry.
6. Let them cool in the pan.
7. To make the frosting, combine all the ingredients in a heatproof container and place over a hot water bath.
8. Cook the mixture for about twenty minutes, stirring all the time with a whisk until it thickens and it looks smooth and shiny.
9. Let cool and then top each cupcake with the lemon cream.

Nutritional Content of One Serving:

Calories: 374 Fat: 18.2g Protein: 4.6g Carbohydrates: 51.1g

Blueberry Oatmeal Muffins

Total Time Taken: 1 hour
Yield: 12 Servings
Ingredients:

- ¼ teaspoon salt
- ½ cup canola oil
- ½ teaspoon baking soda
- ¾ cup light brown sugar
- 1 cup all-purpose flour
- 1 cup buttermilk
- 1 cup fresh blueberries
- 1 cup oat flour
- 1 teaspoon baking powder
- 2 eggs

Directions:

1. Mix the flours, baking powder, baking soda, salt and sugar in a container.
2. Put in the eggs, buttermilk and canola oil and mix thoroughly.
3. Fold in the blueberries then spoon the batter in a muffin tin covered with muffin papers of your desire.
4. Pre-heat the oven and bake at 350F for about twenty minutes or until it rises significantly and starts to appear golden-brown.
5. Let cool in the pan before you serve.

Nutritional Content of One Serving:

Calories: 209 Fat: 10.6g Protein: 3.8g Carbohydrates: 25.1g

Blueberry Poppy Seed Muffins

Total Time Taken: 1 hour

Yield: 12 Servings

Ingredients:

- ½ cup canola oil
- ½ cup white sugar
- ½ teaspoon salt
- 1 1/2 cups all-purpose flour 2 teaspoons baking powder
- 1 cup fresh blueberries
- 1 cup plain yogurt
- 1 tablespoon lemon juice
- 1 tablespoon lemon zest
- 2 eggs
- 2 tablespoons poppy seeds

Directions:

1. Mix the eggs, yogurt, lemon zest, lemon juice and oil in a container.
2. Put in the sugar and mix thoroughly then fold in the remaining ingredients.
3. Spoon the batter in a muffin tin covered with muffin papers and preheat your oven and bake at 350F for about twenty minutes or until a toothpick inserted into them comes out dry.
4. *Best served chilled.*

Nutritional Content of One Serving:

Calories: 210 Fat: 10.9g Protein: 4.1g Carbohydrates: 24.4g

Blueberry White Chocolate Muffins

Total Time Taken: 1 hour

Yield: 12 Servings

Ingredients:

- ¼ cup canola oil
- ½ cup shredded coconut
- ½ cup white chocolate chips
- ½ teaspoon salt
- 1 1/2 cups all-purpose flour
- 1 cup milk
- 1 teaspoon vanilla extract
- 2 eggs
- 2 teaspoons baking powder

Directions:

1. Mix the flour, baking powder, salt, coconut and chocolate chips in a container.
2. Put in the remaining ingredients and mix thoroughly.
3. Spoon the batter in a muffin tin lined with special muffin papers.
4. Preheat your oven and bake the muffins at 350F for about twenty minutes or until a golden-brown colour is achieved and it rises significantly.

These muffins taste best chilled.

Nutritional Content of One Serving:

Calories: 169 Fat: 9.2g Protein: 3.7g Carbohydrates: 18.1g

Bourbon Glazed Pumpkin Muffins

Total Time Taken: 1 hour

Yield: 12 Servings

Ingredients:

Muffins:

- ¼ cup coconut oil
- ½ cup buttermilk
- ½ cup white sugar
- ½ teaspoon ground ginger
- ½ teaspoon salt
- 1 ½ cups whole wheat flour
- 1 cup pumpkin puree
- 1 egg
- 1 teaspoon cinnamon powder
- 2 teaspoons baking powder

Glaze:

- 1 ½ cups powdered sugar
- 2 tablespoons bourbon

Directions:

1. For the muffins, combine the dry ingredients in a container.
2. Put in the wet ingredients and stir for a few seconds to mix.
3. Spoon the batter in a muffin tin covered with muffin papers.
4. Pre-heat the oven and bake at 350F for about twenty minutes.
5. When finished, let cool in the pan.
6. For the glaze, combine the ingredients in a container.
7. Sprinkle the glaze over each muffin and serve the muffins chilled.

Nutritional Content of One Serving:

Calories: 208 Fat: 5.2g Protein: 2.6g Carbohydrates: 37.8g

Bran Flax Blueberry Muffins

Total Time Taken: 1 hour

Yield: 12 Servings

Ingredients:

- 2 teaspoons baking powder
- 2 eggs
- 1 teaspoon vanilla extract
- 1 red apple, peeled and grated
- 1 cup milk
- 1 cup grated carrots
- 1 cup blueberries

- 1 ½ cups all-purpose flour
- ½ teaspoon salt
- ½ cup raisins
- ½ cup oat bran
- ½ cup ground flax seeds
- ½ cup canola oil

Directions:
1. Mix the flour, flax seeds, oat bran, baking powder and salt in a container.
2. Put in the milk, eggs, canola oil and vanilla and stir for a few seconds to mix.
3. Fold in the carrots, apple, raisins and blueberries then spoon the batter in a muffin tin covered with muffin papers.
4. Preheat your oven and bake the muffins at 350F for about twenty minutes or until a toothpick inserted into the center of a muffin comes out clean.

These muffins taste best chilled.

Nutritional Content of One Serving:
Calories: 227 Fat: 12.1g Protein: 4.9g Carbohydrates: 25.9g

Breakfast Muffins

Total Time Taken: 1 hour
Yield: 16 Servings
Ingredients:
- 2 teaspoons baking powder
- 2 eggs
- 1 cup rolled oats
- 1 cup milk
- 1 cup grated carrots
- 1 cup golden raisins
- 1 banana, mashed
- 1 ½ cups all-purpose flour
- ½ teaspoon salt
- ½ teaspoon ground nutmeg
- ½ teaspoon ground ginger
- ½ teaspoon cinnamon powder
- ½ cup shredded coconut
- ½ cup olive oil

Directions:
1. Mix the oats, flour, baking powder, salt and spices in a container. Stir in the raisins and coconut.
2. Put in the olive oil, eggs, milk, carrots and banana and mix using a spatula.
3. Spoon the batter in a muffin tin lined using muffin papers of your choice.
4. Pre-heat the oven and bake at 350F for about twenty minutes or until well risen and a toothpick inserted into the center of a muffin comes out clean.

These muffins taste best chilled.

Nutritional Content of One Serving:

Calories: 178 Fat: 8.5g Protein: 3.6g Carbohydrates: 23.5g

Brooklyn Blackout Cupcakes

Total Time Taken: 1 ½ hours

Yield: 12 Servings

Ingredients:

Cupcakes:

- ¼ teaspoon salt
- ½ cup butter, softened
- ½ cup buttermilk
- ½ cup cocoa powder
- ½ teaspoon baking soda
- 1 cup all-purpose flour
- 1 cup white sugar
- 1 teaspoon baking powder
- 1 teaspoon vanilla extract
- 2 eggs
- 2 teaspoons instant coffee

Frosting:

- ¼ cup white sugar
- 1 cup milk
- 1 pinch salt
- 1 teaspoon instant coffee
- 2 tablespoons butter
- 2 tablespoons cocoa powder
- 2 tablespoons cornstarch

Directions:

1. To make the cupcakes, combine the butter and sugar in a container until creamy.
2. Put in the eggs, one at a time, and mix thoroughly then mix in the coffee powder, buttermilk and vanilla.
3. Put in the flour, cocoa powder, baking soda, baking powder and salt and mix using a spatula or whisk.
4. Pour the batter in a muffin tin covered with muffin papers and preheat your oven and bake at 350F for about twenty minutes or until a toothpick inserted into them comes out dry.
5. Let cool down in the pan.
6. To make the frosting, bring the milk to the boiling point in a saucepan.
7. In a container, mix the remaining ingredients.
8. Pour in the milk and mix thoroughly then return on low heat and cook until it becomes thick.
9. Let the frosting cool down then spoon it over each cupcake.

The cupcakes taste best chilled.

Nutritional Content of One Serving:

Calories: 242 Fat: 11.5g Protein: 3.9g Carbohydrates: 34.2g

Brown Butter Banana Cupcakes

Total Time Taken: 1 ½ hours
Yield: Servings 20
Ingredients:

Cupcakes:
- ¼ cup coconut oil, melted
- ¼ teaspoon salt
- ½ cup brown butter
- ½ cup buttermilk
- ½ teaspoon baking soda
- ¾ cup light brown sugar
- ¾ cup whole wheat flour
- 1 cup all-purpose flour
- 1 teaspoon baking powder
- 2 bananas, mashed
- 2 eggs

Frosting:
- ½ teaspoon cinnamon powder
- 1 cup butter, softened
- 2 cups powdered sugar

Directions:

1. To make the cupcakes, combine the flours, salt, baking soda and baking powder in a container.
2. In a separate container, combine the butter, coconut oil and sugar in a container until fluffy and creamy.
3. Put in the eggs and mix thoroughly then mix in the buttermilk and bananas.
4. Fold in the flour then spoon the batter in a muffin tin covered with muffin papers.
5. Pre-heat the oven and bake at 350F for about twenty minutes or until it is aromatic and appears golden.
6. Let cool in the pan.
7. To make the frosting, combine all the ingredients in a container for about five to seven minutes until pale and fluffy.
8. Top each cupcake with the butter frosting.

Best served chilled.

Nutritional Content of One Serving:

Calories: 331 Fat: 18.5g Protein: 5.3g Carbohydrates: 37.0g

Brown Butter Banana Muffins

Total Time Taken: 1 hour
Yield: 12 Servings
Ingredients:
- ¼ teaspoon salt
- ½ cup butter

- ½ teaspoon baking powder
- ½ teaspoon baking soda
- ¾ cup light brown sugar
- 1 cup all-purpose flour
- 1 cup ground walnuts
- 1/2 cup milk
- 2 eggs
- 4 bananas, mashed

Directions:
1. Put the butter in a saucepan and place over medium flame. Cook the butter until it starts to turn golden brown, slightly caramelized.
2. Mix the butter, sugar, milk and eggs in a container.
3. Stir in the walnuts, flour, baking soda, salt and baking powder.
4. Spoon the batter in a muffin tin lined with special muffin papers and preheat your oven and bake at 350F for about twenty minutes or until it rises significantly and starts to appear golden-brown.

These muffins taste best chilled.

Nutritional Content of One Serving:

Calories: 255 Fat: 15.0g Protein: 5.4g Carbohydrates: 27.5g

Brown Butter Chocolate Chip Muffins

Total Time Taken: 1 ¼ hours
 Yield: 14 Servings

Ingredients:
- ¼ teaspoon salt
- ½ cup brown butter
- ½ cup dark chocolate chips
- ¾ cup milk
- ¾ cup white sugar
- 1 ½ cups all-purpose flour
- 1 ½ teaspoons baking powder
- 2 eggs

Directions:
1. Mix the brown butter and sugar in a container until creamy. Put in the eggs and milk and mix thoroughly then mix in the flour, baking powder and salt.
2. Spoon the batter in a muffin tin covered with muffin papers.
3. Top with chocolate chips and preheat your oven and bake at 350F for about twenty minutes or until it rises significantly and starts to appear golden-brown.
4. When finished, let cool in the pan before you serve.

Nutritional Content of One Serving:

Calories: 267 Fat: 10.6g Protein: 7.4g Carbohydrates: 36.4g

Brown Butter Streusel Pumpkin Muffins

Total Time Taken: 1 hour
Yield: 12 Servings
Ingredients:

Muffins:
- ¼ cup canola oil
- ½ cup buttermilk
- ½ cup light brown sugar
- ½ teaspoon baking powder
- ½ teaspoon baking soda
- 1 ½ cups all-purpose flour
- 1 cup pumpkin puree
- 1 pinch salt
- 1 teaspoon pumpkin pie spices
- 1 teaspoon vanilla extract
- 2 eggs

Streusel:
- ¼ cup brown sugar
- ½ cup all-purpose flour
- 1 pinch salt
- 2 tablespoons light brown sugar
- 2 tablespoons pumpkin seeds

Directions:
1. For the muffins, combine the wet ingredients in a container.
2. Put in the dry ingredients and stir for a few seconds to mix.
3. Spoon the batter in a muffin tin covered with muffin papers.
4. For the streusel, combine all the ingredients in a container and stir until grainy.
5. Spread the streusel over the muffins and preheat your oven and bake at 350F for about twenty minutes or until they're fragrant and it rises significantly.
6. Let cool in the pan before you serve.

Nutritional Content of One Serving:

Calories: 187 Fat: 6.3g Protein: 4.0g Carbohydrates: 29.0g

Brown Sugar Bourbon Cupcakes

Total Time Taken: 1 hour
Yield: 12 Servings
Ingredients:

Cupcakes:
- ¼ teaspoon salt
- ½ cup butter, softened
- ½ cup heavy cream
- 1 ½ teaspoons baking powder
- 1 ¾ cups all-purpose flour

- 1 cup light brown sugar
- 1 teaspoon vanilla extract
- 2 tablespoons bourbon
- 3 eggs

Frosting:
- ½ cup dark brown sugar
- 1 cup butter, softened
- 1 cup powdered sugar

Directions:
1. To make the cupcakes, combine the sugar and butter in a container until creamy.
2. Put in the cream, vanilla and bourbon and mix thoroughly.
3. Stir in the eggs and stir thoroughly until blended.
4. Fold in the flour, salt and baking powder then spoon the batter in a muffin tin covered with muffin papers.
5. Pre-heat the oven and bake at 350F for about twenty minutes or until a toothpick inserted into them comes out dry.
6. Let cool in the pan.
7. To make the frosting, combine all the ingredients in a container for about five to seven minutes or until fluffy and pale.
8. Top the cupcakes with the frosting and serve them fresh.

Nutritional Content of One Serving:
Calories: 418 Fat: 26.2g Protein: 3.6g Carbohydrates: 42.2g

Butternut Almond Muffins

Total Time Taken: 1 hour
Yield: 12 Servings
Ingredients:
- ¼ cup canola oil
- ¼ cup sliced almonds
- ½ cup golden syrup
- ½ teaspoon salt
- 1 ½ teaspoons baking powder
- 1 cup all-purpose flour
- 1 cup almond flour
- 1 cup butternut squash puree
- 1 teaspoon pumpkin pie spices
- 1 teaspoon vanilla extract
- 2 eggs

Directions:
1. Mix the butternut squash puree, golden syrup, eggs, vanilla and canola oil in a container.
2. Put in the flours, salt, baking powder and spices and stir lightly.
3. Spoon the batter in a muffin tin covered with muffin papers and top with sliced almonds.
4. Pre-heat the oven and bake at 350F for about twenty minutes or until a golden-brown colour is achieved and it rises significantly.

These muffins taste best chilled.

Nutritional Content of One Serving:

Calories: 158 Fat: 7.6g Protein: 3.0g Carbohydrates: 20.9g

Cakey Blueberry Muffins

Total Time Taken: 1 hour
Yield: 12 Servings
Ingredients:

- ¼ cup cornstarch
- ¼ teaspoon salt
- ½ cup canola oil
- ¾ cup white sugar
- 1 ½ cups all-purpose flour
- 1 ½ teaspoons baking powder
- 1 cup blueberries
- 1 teaspoon vanilla extract
- 2 eggs
- 2/3 cup sour cream

Directions:

1. Mix the eggs and sugar in a container until volume increases to twice what it was. Stir in the vanilla and oil and mix thoroughly then put in the sour cream and stir thoroughly until blended.
2. Fold in the flour, cornstarch, salt and baking powder then fold in the blueberries.
3. Spoon the batter in a muffin tin covered with muffin papers.
4. Pre-heat the oven and bake at 350F for about twenty minutes or until a toothpick inserted into them comes out dry.

These muffins taste best chilled.

Nutritional Content of One Serving:

Calories: 241 Fat: 12.7g Protein: 3.0g Carbohydrates: 29.6g

Caramel Vanilla Cupcakes

Total Time Taken: 1 ½ hours
Yield: 12 Servings
Ingredients:

Cupcakes:

- 2 eggs
- 1/3 cup butter, melted
- 1 teaspoon vanilla extract
- 1 egg
- 1 cup milk
- 1 ¾ cups all-purpose flour
- 1 ½ teaspoons baking powder
- ¼ teaspoon salt

Frosting:
- 2 cups powdered sugar
- 1 teaspoon vanilla extract
- 1 cup butter, softened
- ½ cup caramel sauce

Directions:
1. To make the cupcakes, combine the flour, salt and baking powder in a container.
2. Combine the eggs, butter, milk, egg and vanilla then pour this mixture over the flour. Give it a quick mix then spoon the batter in a muffin tin covered with muffin papers.
3. Pre-heat the oven and bake at 350F for about twenty minutes or until it rises significantly and starts to appear golden-brown. Let them cool down.
4. To make the frosting, combine the butter in a container until fluffy. Put in the sugar and vanilla and keep mixing for five minutes.
5. Pipe the frosting over the cupcakes and sprinkle them with caramel sauce.

These cupcakes taste best when fresh.

Nutritional Content of One Serving:

Calories: 388 Fat: 22.2g Protein: 4.3g Carbohydrates: 44.3g

Caribbean Muffins

Total Time Taken: 1 hour
Yield: 12 Servings
Ingredients:
- ¼ cup wheat bran
- ¼ teaspoon salt
- ½ cup shredded coconut
- 1 ½ cups all-purpose flour
- 1 ½ teaspoons baking powder
- 1 cup buttermilk
- 1 cup crushed pineapple
- 1 egg
- 1 mango, peeled and diced
- 2 tablespoons chia seeds

Directions:
1. Mix the flour, wheat bran, salt, baking powder, chia seeds and coconut in a container.
2. Put in the egg, buttermilk and pineapple and mix thoroughly.
3. Fold in the mango then spoon the batter in a muffin tin covered with muffin papers.
4. Preheat your oven and bake the muffins at 350F for about twenty minutes or until it rises significantly and starts to appear golden-brown.

These muffins taste best chilled.

Nutritional Content of One Serving:

Calories: 130 Fat: 3.5g Protein: 4.3g Carbohydrates: 21.0g

Carrot Cake Pecan Muffins

Total Time Taken: 1 hour
Yield: 12 Servings
Ingredients:
- ¼ teaspoon salt
- ½ cup canola oil
- ½ cup crushed pineapple
- ½ cup light brown sugar
- ½ cup milk
- ½ cup walnuts, chopped
- ½ teaspoon ground ginger
- 1 ½ cups all-purpose flour
- 1 cup grated carrot
- 1 egg
- 1 teaspoon baking soda
- 1 teaspoon cinnamon powder

Directions:
1. Mix the flour, salt, baking soda, cinnamon and ginger.
2. Put in the milk, egg, oil, sugar, carrot, pineapple and walnuts and mix thoroughly.
3. Spoon the batter in a muffin tin covered with muffin papers.
4. Pre-heat the oven and bake at 350F for about twenty minutes or until it rises significantly and becomes aromatic.
5. Serve the muffins chilled or store them in an airtight container for maximum four days.

Nutritional Content of One Serving:

Calories: 210 Fat: 12.9g Protein: 3.8g Carbohydrates: 20.8g

Carrot White Chocolate Muffins

Total Time Taken: 1 hour
Yield: 12 Servings
Ingredients:
- ¼ cup canola oil
- ¼ teaspoon baking soda
- ½ cup plain yogurt
- ½ cup white chocolate chips
- ½ cup white sugar
- ½ cup whole wheat flour
- ½ teaspoon salt
- ½ teaspoon salt
- 1 cup all-purpose flour
- 1 cup crushed pineapple
- 1 cup grated carrots
- 1 egg
- 1 teaspoon baking powder

Directions:
1. Mix the egg and sugar in a container until pale and light.
2. Put in the oil and yogurt and mix thoroughly.
3. Fold in the flours, salt, baking powder, baking soda and salt.
4. Put in the crushed pineapple, carrots and chocolate chips.
5. Spoon the batter in a muffin tin covered with muffin papers and preheat your oven and bake at 350F for about twenty minutes or until a toothpick inserted into the center of a muffin comes out clean.

These muffins taste best chilled.

Nutritional Content of One Serving:
Calories: 190 Fat: 7.5g Protein: 3.2g Carbohydrates: 28.1g

Chai Vanilla Frosted Cupcakes

Total Time Taken: 1 ½ hours
Yield: 12 Servings
Ingredients:

Cupcakes:
- ½ cup butter, softened
- 2 eggs
- 1 teaspoon vanilla extract
- 1 ½ cups all-purpose flour
- 1 teaspoon baking powder
- ½ teaspoon baking soda
- ¼ teaspoon cinnamon powder
- ¼ teaspoon ground ginger
- ¼ teaspoon ground star anise
- ¼ teaspoon ground cardamom
- 2/3 cup white sugar
- 2/3 cup buttermilk

Frosting:
- 1 cup butter, softened
- 1 teaspoon vanilla extract
- 2 cups powdered sugar

Directions:
1. To make the cupcakes, combine the butter and sugar in a container until creamy and firm.
2. Put in the eggs and vanilla, then mix in the buttermilk.
3. Put in the flour, baking powder, baking soda, cinnamon powder, ginger, star anise and cardamom, as well as a pinch of salt.
4. Pour the batter in a muffin tin covered with muffin papers and preheat your oven and bake at 350F for about twenty minutes or until a golden-brown colour is achieved.
5. Let cool down in the pan.
6. To make the frosting, combine the butter in a container until creamy and light.
7. Put in the sugar, ½ cup at a time, and stir thoroughly for at least five minutes.
8. Put in the vanilla and mix thoroughly.

9. Top each cupcake with the frosting and serve fresh.

Nutritional Content of One Serving:

Calories: 399 Fat: 24.0g Protein: 3.2g Carbohydrates: 44.1g

Cherry Coconut Muffins

Total Time Taken: 1 hour
Yield: 12 Servings
Ingredients:
- ¼ cup canola oil
- ½ cup white sugar
- ½ teaspoon salt
- ¾ cup coconut milk
- 1 cup all-purpose flour
- 1 cup cherries, pitted
- 1 cup shredded coconut
- 1 teaspoon baking soda
- 2 eggs

Directions:
1. Mix the eggs and sugar in a container until fluffy and pale. Put in the oil and milk and mix thoroughly.
2. Fold in the coconut, flour, salt, baking soda and cherries.
3. Spoon the batter in a muffin tin covered with muffin papers.
4. Preheat your oven and bake the muffins at 350F for about twenty minutes or until a toothpick inserted into them comes out dry.

These muffins taste best chilled.

Nutritional Content of One Serving:

Calories: 185 Fat: 11.2g Protein: 2.6g Carbohydrates: 19.9g

Cherry Muffins

Total Time Taken: 1 hour
Yield: 10 Servings
Ingredients:
- ¼ teaspoon salt
- ½ cup butter, melted
- ½ cup white sugar
- 1 cup all-purpose flour
- 1 cup cherries, pitted
- 1 teaspoon baking powder
- 1 teaspoon vanilla extract
- 4 eggs

Directions:
1. Mix the eggs, sugar and vanilla in a container until its volume increases to almost three times it was.

2. Stir in the butter and mix thoroughly.
3. Fold in the flour, salt and baking powder.
4. Put in the cherries then spoon the batter in a muffin tin covered with muffin papers.
5. Preheat your oven and bake the muffins at 350F for about twenty minutes or until a golden-brown colour is achieved and it rises significantly.

These muffins taste best chilled.

Nutritional Content of One Serving:
Calories: 200 Fat: 11.1g Protein: 3.6g Carbohydrates: 22.0g

Chocolate Avocado Cupcakes

Total Time Taken: 1 ½ hours
Yield: 12 Servings
Ingredients:

Cupcakes:
- 1 large avocado, mashed
- 1 cup coconut milk
- 1 teaspoon vanilla extract
- 1 egg
- 2 egg whites
- 1 cup whole wheat flour
- 1 cup all-purpose flour
- ¼ teaspoon salt
- 2 teaspoons baking powder
- ½ cup cocoa powder
- 2/3 cup coconut sugar

Frosting:
- ¼ cup cocoa powder
- ½ teaspoon vanilla extract
- 1 large avocado, mashed
- 2 tablespoons coconut oil
- 2 tablespoons coconut sugar

Directions:
1. To make the cupcakes, combine the avocado, coconut sugar, coconut milk, vanilla, egg and egg whites in a container until creamy.
2. Put in the remaining ingredients and stir swiftly to combine.
3. Spoon the batter in a muffin tin covered with muffin papers.
4. Pre-heat the oven and bake at 350F for about twenty minutes or until a toothpick inserted in the muffins comes out clean.
5. Let cool in the pan.
6. To make the frosting, combine all the ingredients in a blender or food processor and pulse until well mixed.
7. Pipe the frosting over each cupcake and serve fresh.

Nutritional Content of One Serving:

Calories: 280 Fat: 14.8g Protein: 5.3g Carbohydrates: 36.0g

Chocolate Candied Orange Muffins

Total Time Taken: 1 hour

Yield: 12 Servings

Ingredients:

- ¼ cup candied orange peel, chopped
- ½ cup canola oil
- ½ cup dark chocolate chips
- ½ cup fresh orange juice
- ½ cup plain yogurt
- ½ cup white sugar
- ½ teaspoon salt
- 1 ½ cups all-purpose flour
- 1 ½ teaspoons baking powder
- 1 teaspoon orange zest
- 2 eggs

Directions:

1. Mix the sugar, orange juice, eggs, oil, yogurt and orange zest in a container.
2. Stir in the flour, salt, baking powder, chocolate chips and orange peel and mix using a spatula.
3. Pour the batter in a muffin tin covered with muffin papers and preheat your oven and bake at 350F for about twenty minutes or until a toothpick inserted into them comes out dry.

These muffins taste best chilled.

Nutritional Content of One Serving:

Calories: 217

Fat:11.4g Protein: 3.5g Carbohydrates: 26.3g

Chocolate Chip Cinnamon Muffins

Total Time Taken: 1 hour

Yield: 12 Servings

Ingredients:

- ¼ cup milk
- ½ cup butter, melted
- ½ cup dark chocolate chips
- ½ cup white sugar
- ½ teaspoon salt
- 1 cup all-purpose flour
- 1 teaspoon baking powder
- 1 teaspoon cinnamon powder
- 1 teaspoon orange zest
- 1 teaspoon vanilla extract
- 2 tablespoons dark brown sugar

- 4 eggs

Directions:
1. Mix the eggs and sugars in a container until fluffy and pale.
2. Put in the vanilla, orange zest and melted butter.
3. Fold in the flour, cinnamon, salt and baking powder then put in the milk and chocolate chips.
4. Spoon the batter in a muffin tin covered with muffin papers.
5. Pre-heat the oven and bake at 350F for about twenty minutes or until a golden-brown colour is achieved and it rises significantly.

These muffins taste best chilled.

Nutritional Content of One Serving:
Calories: 191 Fat: 10.7g Protein: 3.5g Carbohydrates: 21.7g

Chocolate Chip Muffins

Total Time Taken: 1 hour
Yield: 12 Servings
Ingredients:
- ½ cup canola oil
- ½ cup chocolate chips
- ½ cup white sugar
- ½ teaspoon salt
- 1 ½ teaspoons baking powder
- 1 cup all-purpose flour
- 1 cup whole wheat flour
- 1 egg
- 1 teaspoon vanilla extract
- 2/3 cup milk

Directions:
1. Mix the flours, baking powder and salt in a container.
2. Put in the sugar, egg, milk, oil and vanilla and mix using a spatula.
3. Fold in the chocolate chips then spoon the batter in a muffin tin covered with muffin papers.
4. Preheat your oven and bake the muffins at 350F for about twenty minutes or until a golden-brown colour is achieved and it rises significantly.

These muffins taste best chilled.

Nutritional Content of One Serving:
Calories: 238 Fat: 12.0g Protein: 3.6g Carbohydrates: 29.4g

Chocolate Chunk Cupcakes

Total Time Taken: 1 ½ hours
Yield: 12 Servings
Ingredients:
Cupcakes:
- ½ cup butter, melted

- ½ cup sour cream
- ½ cup white sugar
- ½ teaspoon salt
- 2 cups all-purpose flour
- 2 eggs
- 2 teaspoons baking powder
- 4 oz. dark chocolate, chopped

Frosting:
- 1 ½ cups heavy cream, whipped
- 2 oz. dark chocolate, chopped

Directions:
1. To make the cupcakes, combine the butter, sugar and eggs in a container until pale.
2. Put in the sour cream and mix thoroughly.
3. Fold in the flour, baking powder and salt then fold in the dark chocolate.
4. Spoon the batter in a muffin tin covered with muffin papers.
5. Preheat your oven and bake the cupcakes at 350F for about twenty minutes or until a golden-brown colour is achieved and it rises significantly.
6. Let the cupcakes cool then top each of them with a dollop of whipped cream.
7. Drizzle each cream with chopped chocolate and serve.

Nutritional Content of One Serving:
Calories: 334 Fat: 20.4g Protein: 4.8g Carbohydrates: 33.9g

Chocolate Cupcakes With Peanut Butter Frosting

Total Time Taken: 1 ½ hours
Yield: 16 Servings
Ingredients:

Cupcakes:
- ¼ teaspoon salt
- ½ cup butter, softened
- ½ cup cocoa powder
- ½ cup sour cream
- 1 ½ cups all-purpose flour
- 1 ½ teaspoons baking powder
- 1 cup buttermilk
- 1 cup white sugar
- 1 teaspoon vanilla extract
- 3 eggs

Frosting:
- ½ cup butter, softened
- 1 cup powdered sugar
- 1 cup smooth peanut butter
- 1 teaspoon vanilla extract

- 2 tablespoons heavy cream

Directions:
1. To make the cupcakes, combine the butter and sugar in a container until creamy and pale.
2. Put in the eggs and mix thoroughly then mix in the vanilla, sour cream and buttermilk.
3. Fold in the flour, cocoa powder, salt and baking powder then spoon the batter in a muffin tin covered with muffin papers.
4. Preheat your oven and bake the muffins at 350F for about twenty minutes.
5. Let the cupcakes cool down.
6. To make the frosting, combine the peanut butter, butter and sugar in a container until fluffy and pale.
7. Put in the vanilla and cream and continue whipping for five minutes until fluffy and airy.
8. Garnish the cupcakes with the peanut butter frosting.

These cupcakes taste best when fresh.

Nutritional Content of One Serving:
Calories: 363 Fat: 23.3g Protein: 7.7g Carbohydrates: 35.0g

Chocolate Drizzle Cupcakes

Total Time Taken: 1 ½ hours
Yield: 12 Servings
Ingredients:

Cupcakes:
- ¼ cup brewed coffee
- ¼ cup canola oil
- ¼ cup cocoa powder
- ½ teaspoon salt
- 1 ½ cups all-purpose flour
- 1 ½ teaspoons baking powder
- 1 cup buttermilk
- 1 teaspoon vanilla extract
- 2 eggs

Frosting:
- 1 cup butter, softened
- 1 tablespoon cocoa powder
- 1 tablespoon dark rum
- 2 cups powdered sugar

Directions:
1. To make the cupcakes, combine the flour, salt, baking powder and cocoa powder in a container.
2. Put in the eggs, vanilla, buttermilk, coffee and canola oil and stir for a few seconds to mix.
3. Pour the batter in 12 muffin cups covered with muffin papers and preheat your oven and bake at 350F for about twenty minutes or until a toothpick inserted into them comes out dry.
4. Let cool down.
5. To make the frosting, combine the butter until fluffy. Put in the sugar and mix for about five to seven minutes or until pale and light.

6. Stir in the rum and mix thoroughly.
7. Top each cupcake with the frosting and serve them fresh.

Nutritional Content of One Serving:

Calories: 338 Fat: 21.3g Protein: 3.8g Carbohydrates: 34.5g

Chocolate Graham Cupcakes

Total Time Taken: 1 ½ hours
Yield: 12 Servings
Ingredients:

Cupcakes:
- ¼ cup whole milk
- ½ cup all-purpose flour
- ½ cup crushed graham crackers
- ½ teaspoon salt
- 1 cup butter, softened
- 1 cup light brown sugar
- 1 cup whole wheat flour
- 1 teaspoon baking soda
- 1 teaspoon vanilla extract
- 1/2 teaspoon cinnamon powder
- 4 eggs

Frosting:
- ½ cup crushed graham crackers
- 1 cup heavy cream
- 2 cups dark chocolate chips

Directions:
1. To make the cupcakes, combine the butter and sugar in a container until pale and creamy.
2. Put in the vanilla and eggs, one at a time and mix thoroughly.
3. Fold in the flours, graham crackers, salt, baking soda and cinnamon powder, alternating it with the milk.
4. Spoon the batter in a muffin tin coated with baking muffin papers.
5. Pre-heat the oven and bake at 350F for about twenty minutes or until the cupcakes pass the toothpick test.
6. Let cool in the pan.
7. To make the frosting, bring the cream to a boil in a saucepan. Turn off the heat and put in the chocolate. Stir until melted and smooth then let cool down.
8. Apply the frosting on top of each cupcake and drizzle with crushed graham crackers.

Nutritional Content of One Serving:

Calories: 421 Fat: 26.9g Protein: 5.8g Carbohydrates: 43.2g

Chocolate Malt Cupcakes

Total Time Taken: 1 hour
Yield: Servings 18
Ingredients:

Cupcakes:

- ¼ cup canola oil
- ½ teaspoon baking soda
- ½ teaspoon salt
- ¾ cups cocoa powder
- 1 cup malted milk powder
- 1 cup milk
- 1 cup sour cream
- 1 teaspoon baking powder
- 1 teaspoon vanilla extract
- 2 ¼ cups all-purpose flour
- 4 eggs

Frosting:

- ½ cup malted milk powder
- 1 ½ cups butter, softened
- 1 teaspoon vanilla extract
- 2 cups powdered sugar

Directions:

1. To make the cupcakes, combine the milk, milk powder, eggs, sour cream, vanilla and oil in a container.
2. Put in the flour, cocoa powder, salt, baking soda and baking powder and mix using a spatula.
3. Spoon the batter in a muffin tin covered with muffin papers.
4. Pre-heat the oven and bake at 350F for about twenty minutes or until a toothpick inserted into them comes out dry.
5. Let cool down before you serve.
6. To make the frosting, combine the butter in a container until airy.
7. Put in the milk powder and mix 2 minutes on high speed, then mix in the sugar and vanilla and continue mixing for five minutes on high speed.
8. Pipe the frosting on top of the cupcakes and serve them fresh.

Nutritional Content of One Serving:

Calories: 389 Fat: 23.6g Protein: 5.8g Carbohydrates: 41.3g

Chocolate Peanut Butter Cupcakes

Total Time Taken: 1 ½ hours
Yield: 12 Servings
Ingredients:

Cupcakes:

- ¼ cup smooth peanut butter
- ¼ teaspoon salt

- ½ cup butter, softened
- ½ cup sour cream
- 1 cup all-purpose flour
- 1 cup almond flour
- 1 teaspoon baking powder
- 1 teaspoon vanilla extract
- 2 eggs

Frosting:
- 1 cup heavy cream
- 1 teaspoon vanilla extract
- 2 cups dark chocolate chips

Directions:
1. To make the cupcakes, combine the butter and peanut butter in a container until creamy.
2. Put in the eggs and sour cream and mix thoroughly. Stir in the vanilla too.
3. Put in the flours, salt and baking powder and mix them using a spatula.
4. Spoon the batter in 12 muffin cups covered with muffin papers.
5. Preheat your oven and bake the cupcakes at 350F for about twenty minutes or until it rises significantly and seems golden.
6. Let them cool in the pan.
7. To make the frosting, bring the cream to a boil in a saucepan.
8. Turn off the heat and put in the chocolate chips. Stir until melted and smooth then allow to cool.
9. Spoon the frosting on top of each cupcake.

Nutritional Content of One Serving:
Calories: 312 Fat: 23.4g Protein: 5.8g Carbohydrates: 23.9g

Chocolate Pear Muffins

Total Time Taken: 1 hour
Yield: 12 Servings
Ingredients:
- ½ cup buttermilk
- ½ cup light brown sugar
- ½ cup milk
- ½ teaspoon salt
- 1 1/3 cups all-purpose flour
- 1 teaspoon baking powder
- 1/3 cup cocoa powder
- 2 eggs
- 2 pears, peeled and diced

Directions:
1. Mix the eggs, milk, sugar and buttermilk in a container.
2. Stir in the dry ingredients and stir for a few seconds to mix.
3. Fold in the pears then spoon the batter in a muffin tin covered with muffin papers.
4. Preheat your oven and bake the muffins at 350F for about twenty minutes or until well risen.

These muffins taste best chilled.

Nutritional Content of One Serving:
Calories: 119 Fat: 1.5g Protein: 3.6g Carbohydrates: 24.4g

Chocolate Pretzel Muffins

Total Time Taken: 1 ½ hours
Yield: 12 Servings
Ingredients:

Cupcakes:
- ¼ cup canola oil
- ¼ cup cocoa powder
- ¼ teaspoon salt
- ½ cup brewed coffee
- 1 ¼ cups all-purpose flour
- 1 ½ teaspoons baking powder
- 1 cup buttermilk
- 1 teaspoon vanilla extract
- 2 eggs

Frosting:
- ½ cup dark chocolate chips, melted and chilled
- 1 cup butter, softened
- 1 cup pretzels2 cups powdered sugar
- , crushed

Directions:
1. To make the cupcakes, combine the flour, cocoa powder, salt and baking powder in a container.
2. Put in the remaining ingredients and stir for a few seconds to mix.
3. Pour the batter in a muffin tin covered with muffin papers.
4. Pre-heat the oven and bake at 350F for about twenty minutes or until a toothpick inserted into the center of a muffin comes out clean.
5. Let cool down.
6. To make the frosting, combine the butter and sugar in a container until fluffy and pale.
7. Stir in the chocolate and mix thoroughly.
8. Top each cupcake with the frosting and drizzle with pretzels.

These cupcakes taste best when fresh.

Nutritional Content of One Serving:

Calories: 368 Fat: 22.6g Protein: 4.3g Carbohydrates: 39.5g

Chocolate Raspberry Crumble Muffins

Total Time Taken: 1 ¼ hours
Yield: 12 Servings
Ingredients:

Muffins:
- ¼ cup cocoa powder

- ½ cup butter, melted
- ½ cup milk
- ½ cup white sugar
- ½ teaspoon salt
- 1 ½ cups all-purpose flour
- 1 cup fresh raspberries
- 1 teaspoon vanilla extract
- 2 teaspoons baking powder
- 3 eggs

Crumble Topping:
- ¼ cup butter, chilled
- ¼ teaspoon salt
- ½ cup all-purpose flour

Directions:
1. For the muffins, combine the eggs, sugar and vanilla in a container until creamy.
2. Stir in the milk and butter and mix thoroughly.
3. Fold in the flour, cocoa powder, salt and baking powder then spoon the batter in a muffin pan coated with muffin papers.
4. For the topping, combine the ingredients in a container until grainy.
5. Top the muffins with the crumble topping and preheat your oven and bake at 350F for about twenty minutes or until well risen.

These muffins taste best chilled.

Nutritional Content of One Serving:
Calories: 241 Fat: 13.3g Protein: 4.4g Carbohydrates: 27.5g

Chocolate Raspberry Cupcakes

Total Time Taken: 1 ½ hours
Yield: 12 Servings
Ingredients:

Cupcakes:
- 2 eggs
- 1 teaspoon vanilla extract
- ¼ cup milk
- 1 ½ cups all-purpose flour
- ½ teaspoon salt
- 1 ½ teaspoons baking powder
- ¼ cup cocoa powder
- 2/3 cup butter, softened
- 2/3 cup white sugar

Frosting:
- ½ cup dark chocolate chips, melted and chilled
- 1 cup butter, softened
- 1 cup cream cheese

- 2 cups powdered sugar

Directions:
1. To make the cupcakes, combine the butter and sugar in a container until fluffy and airy.
2. Put in the eggs and vanilla and mix thoroughly. Stir in the milk.
3. Fold in the flour, salt, baking powder and cocoa and mix using a spatula.
4. Spoon the batter in a muffin tin covered with muffin papers and preheat your oven and bake at 350F for about twenty minutes or until well risen.
5. Let them cool in the pan.
6. For frosting, combine the cream cheese and butter in a container until pale.
7. Put in the sugar, progressively, and mix for five minutes on high speed.
8. Stir in the melted chocolate then spoon a dollop of frosting over each cupcake and serve fresh.

Nutritional Content of One Serving:
Calories: 512 Fat: 34.9g Protein: 5.1g Carbohydrates: 48.5g

Chocolate Spice Cupcakes

Total Time Taken: 1 ½ hours
Yield: 12 Servings
Ingredients:

Cupcakes:
- ¼ cup cocoa powder
- ½ cup white sugar
- ½ teaspoon cinnamon powder
- ½ teaspoon ground ginger
- ½ teaspoon ground star anise
- ½ teaspoon salt
- ¾ cup milk
- 1 ¼ cups all-purpose flour
- 1 ½ teaspoons baking powder
- 1 teaspoon vanilla extract
- 1/2 cup butter, softened
- 2 eggs

Frosting:
- ½ cup heavy cream
- 1 cup dark chocolate chips

Directions:
1. To make the cupcakes, combine the butter, sugar and vanilla in a container until fluffy and pale.
2. Put in the eggs and mix thoroughly then mix in the milk.
3. Fold in the flour, cocoa powder, salt, baking powder, cinnamon, ginger and star anise.
4. Spoon the batter in a muffin tin covered with muffin papers.
5. Preheat your oven and bake the cupcakes at 350F for about twenty minutes or until it rises completely and is aromatic.
6. Let the cupcakes cool down.
7. To make the frosting, bring the cream to a boil in a saucepan. Turn off the heat and mix in the chocolate chips. Stir until melted then spoon the frosting over each cupcake.

8. Serve immediately or store them in an airtight container.

Nutritional Content of One Serving:

Calories: 235 Fat: 13.6g Protein: 4.0g Carbohydrates: 27.4g

Chocolate Tahini Muffins

Total Time Taken: 1 hour

Yield: 12 Servings

Ingredients:

- ¼ cup cocoa powder
- ¼ cup light brown sugar
- ¼ cup maple syrup
- ¼ cup milk
- ¼ cup tahini paste
- ¼ teaspoon salt
- 1 ½ cups all-purpose flour
- 1 teaspoon baking powder
- 1 teaspoon vanilla extract
- 4 eggs

Directions:

1. Mix the eggs, tahini paste, maple syrup, sugar, vanilla and milk in a container.
2. Put in the flour, cocoa powder, salt and baking powder and stir for a few seconds to mix.
3. Spoon the batter in a muffin tin coated with baking muffin papers.
4. Pre-heat the oven and bake at 350F for about twenty minutes or until a toothpick inserted in the center of the muffins comes out clean.
5. Allow the muffins to cool to room temperature in the pan.

Nutritional Content of One Serving:

Calories: 144 Fat: 4.6g Protein: 4.8g Carbohydrates: 21.9g

Chunky Banana Muffins

Total Time Taken: 1 hour

Yield: 12 Servings

Ingredients:

- ¼ cup butter, melted
- ¼ teaspoon salt
- ½ cup cocoa powder
- ½ cup light brown sugar
- 1 ½ cups all-purpose flour
- 1 cup buttermilk
- 1 teaspoon vanilla extract
- 2 bananas, sliced
- 2 eggs
- 2 tablespoons molasses
- 2 teaspoons baking powder

185

Directions:
1. Mix the eggs and sugar in a container until pale and light. Put in the molasses and vanilla and mix thoroughly.
2. Stir in the butter and buttermilk then put in the flour, cocoa powder, salt and baking powder.
3. Fold in the banana slices and spoon the batter in a muffin tin lined using muffin papers of your choice.
4. Pre-heat the oven and bake at 350F for about twenty minutes. When finished, allow them to cool in the pan before you serve.

Nutritional Content of One Serving:
Calories: 169 Fat: 5.4g Protein: 4.1g Carbohydrates: 28.3g

Cinnamon Apple Cupcakes

Total Time Taken: 1 ½ hours
Yield: 12 Servings
Ingredients:

Cupcakes:
- ¼ cup milk
- ½ cup butter, softened
- ½ cup light brown sugar
- ½ teaspoon salt
- 1 ½ cups all-purpose flour
- 1 teaspoon baking powder
- 1 teaspoon grated ginger
- 1 teaspoon vanilla extract
- 2 red apples, cored and diced
- 3 eggs

Frosting:
- 1 cup butter, softened
- 1 teaspoon cinnamon powder
- 1 teaspoon vanilla extract
- 2 cups powdered sugar

Directions:
1. To make the cupcakes, combine the butter and sugar in a container until fluffy and creamy.
2. Put in the eggs, one at a time, and mix thoroughly then mix in the vanilla and ginger.
3. Fold in the flour, salt and baking powder, alternating it with milk. Fold in the apples.
4. Spoon the batter in a muffin tin covered with muffin papers.
5. Preheat your oven and bake the cupcakes at 350F for about twenty minutes. Let the cupcakes cool in the pan.
6. To make the frosting, combine the butter in a container until fluffy. Put in the sugar and mix thoroughly then mix in the cinnamon and vanilla. Whip on high speed for five minutes.
7. Top each cupcake with the frosting and serve them fresh.

Nutritional Content of One Serving:
Calories: 398 Fat: 24.4g Protein: 3.5g Carbohydrates: 42.7g

Cinnamon Autumn Muffins

Total Time Taken: 1 hour
Yield: 12 Servings
Ingredients:

- ½ cup butter, melted
- ½ cup butternut squash cubes
- ½ cup milk
- ½ teaspoon salt
- 1 apple, cored and diced
- 1 pear, cored and diced
- 1 teaspoon cinnamon powder
- 1 teaspoon vanilla extract
- 2 cups all-purpose flour
- 2 eggs
- 2 teaspoons baking powder
- 2/3 cup light brown sugar

Directions:

1. Mix the flour, salt, baking powder, cinnamon and sugar in a container.
2. Put in the butter, eggs, milk and vanilla and mix thoroughly.
3. Fold in the apple, pear and butternut squash cubes.
4. Spoon the batter in a muffin tin coated with baking muffin papers.
5. Pre-heat the oven and bake at 350F for about twenty minutes or until it rises significantly and seems golden.

These muffins taste best chilled.

Nutritional Content of One Serving:

Calories: 208 Fat: 8.9g Protein: 3.6g Carbohydrates: 29.1g

Cinnamon Blueberry Muffins

Total Time Taken: 1 hour
Yield: 12 Servings
Ingredients:

- ½ cup butter, melted
- ½ cup light brown sugar
- ½ cup milk
- ½ teaspoon cinnamon powder
- ½ teaspoon salt
- 1 cup blueberries
- 1 teaspoon baking soda
- 2 cups all-purpose flour
- 2 eggs

Directions:

1. Mix the flour, sugar, salt, baking soda and cinnamon in a container.

2. Put in the milk, eggs and melted butter and fold in the blueberries then spoon the batter in a muffin tin covered with muffin papers.
3. Preheat your oven and bake the muffins at 350F for about twenty minutes or until it rises significantly and starts to appear golden-brown.

These muffins taste best chilled.

Nutritional Content of One Serving:

Calories: 189 Fat: 8.8g Protein: 3.6g Carbohydrates: 24.1g

Cinnamon Plum Muffins

Total Time Taken: 1 hour
Yield: 12 Servings
Ingredients:
- ¼ cup canola oil
- ½ cup ground walnuts
- ½ cup light brown sugar
- ½ teaspoon ground ginger
- 1 ½ cups all-purpose flour
- 1 cup buttermilk
- 1 egg
- 1 teaspoon baking soda
- 1 teaspoon cinnamon powder
- 1 teaspoon vanilla extract
- 6 plums, pitted and diced

Directions:
1. Mix the flour, sugar, baking soda, cinnamon, ginger and walnuts in a container.
2. Put in the remaining ingredients and mix thoroughly. Put in the plums as well.
3. Spoon the batter in a muffin tin lined using muffin papers of your choice.
4. Pre-heat the oven and bake at 350F for about twenty minutes or until it rises significantly and starts to appear golden-brown.

These muffins taste best chilled.

Nutritional Content of One Serving:

Calories: 177 Fat: 8.4g Protein: 4.2g Carbohydrates: 22.0g

Citrus Coconut Muffins

Total Time Taken: 1 hour
Yield: 12 Servings
Ingredients:
- ¼ cup milk
- ½ cup butter, melted
- ½ cup white sugar
- ½ teaspoon salt
- 1 cup coconut flakes

- 1 teaspoon lemon zest
- 1 teaspoon lime zest
- 1 teaspoon orange zest
- 2 cups all-purpose flour
- 2 eggs
- 2 teaspoons baking powder

Directions:
1. Mix the eggs and sugar in a container until pale and light. Put in the melted butter and citrus zest and mix thoroughly.
2. Fold in the dry ingredients, as well as the coconut flakes then spoon the batter in 12 muffin cups covered with muffin papers.
3. Preheat your oven and bake the muffins at 350F for about twenty minutes or until a golden-brown colour is achieved and it rises significantly.
4. Let cool in the pan before you serve.

Nutritional Content of One Serving:
Calories: 213 Fat: 10.9g Protein: 3.5g Carbohydrates: 26.1g

Citrus Iced Coconut Cupcakes

Total Time Taken: 1 ¼ hours
Yield: 12 Servings
Ingredients:

Cupcakes:
- ¼ teaspoon salt
- ½ cup coconut butter
- ½ cup coconut flakes
- ½ cup coconut milk
- ½ cup white sugar
- 1 ½ cups all-purpose flour
- 1 ½ teaspoons baking powder
- 2 eggs

Icing:
- 1 ½ cups powdered sugar
- 1 tablespoon lime juice
- 1 teaspoon lemon zest
- 1 teaspoon lime zest

Directions:
1. To make the cupcakes, combine the coconut butter and sugar until creamy.
2. Put in the eggs, one at a time, then mix in the coconut milk.
3. Fold in the flour, coconut flakes, salt and baking powder then spoon the batter in a muffin tin covered with muffin papers.
4. Preheat your oven and bake the muffins at 350F for about twenty minutes or until a golden-brown colour is achieved and it rises significantly. Let them cool in the pan.
5. For the icing, combine all the ingredients in a container.
6. Sprinkle the icing over each cupcake and serve them fresh.

Nutritional Content of One Serving:

Calories: 212 Fat: 6.2g Protein: 3.1g Carbohydrates: 37.7g

Coconut Caramel Cupcakes

Total Time Taken: 1 ½ hours

Yield: 14 Servings

Ingredients:

Cupcakes:

- ½ cup butter, softened
- ½ cup coconut cream
- ½ cup coconut milk
- ½ teaspoon salt
- 1 ½ cups all-purpose flour
- 1 cup white sugar
- 1 teaspoon vanilla extract
- 2 teaspoons baking powder
- 2/3 cup shredded coconut
- 3 eggs

Frosting:

- ½ cup caramel sauce
- 1 cup butter, softened
- 1 cup coconut flakes
- 1 teaspoon vanilla extract
- 2 cups powdered sugar

Directions:

1. To make the cupcakes, combine the butter and sugar in a container until fluffy and pale.
2. Put in the eggs and mix thoroughly then mix in the coconut cream, milk and vanilla.
3. Fold in the flour, coconut, salt and baking powder.
4. Spoon the batter in a muffin tin covered with muffin papers and preheat your oven and bake at 350F for about twenty minutes or until a golden-brown colour is achieved and it rises significantly.
5. Let the cupcakes cool down.
6. To make the frosting, combine the butter and sugar in a container for about five to seven minutes or until fluffy and pale.
7. Put in the vanilla and mix thoroughly. Top each cupcake with the frosting then garnish with coconut flakes.
8. Just before you serve, sprinkle the cupcakes with caramel sauce.

Nutritional Content of One Serving:

Calories: 462 Fat: 28.1g Protein: 3.7g Carbohydrates: 52.2g

Coconut Cupcakes

Total Time Taken: 1 ½ hours
Yield: 12 Servings
Ingredients:

Cupcakes:
- ½ cup butter, softened
- ½ cup shredded coconut
- ½ teaspoon salt
- ¾ cup coconut milk
- ¾ cup white sugar
- 1 ½ teaspoons baking powder
- 1 ¾ cup all-purpose flour
- 1 teaspoon vanilla extract
- 3 eggs

Frosting:
- ½ cup butter, softened
- ½ cup cream cheese, softened
- 1 teaspoon vanilla extract
- 2 cups powdered sugar

Directions:
1. To make the cupcakes, combine the butter, sugar and vanilla in a container until fluffy and pale.
2. Put in the eggs, one at a time, then fold in the flour, baking powder, salt and coconut, alternating it with milk. Begin with flour and finish with flour.
3. Spoon the batter in 12 muffin cups covered with muffin papers.
4. Pre-heat the oven and bake at 350F for about twenty minutes or until it rises significantly and starts to appear golden-brown.
5. Let the cupcakes cool in the pan.
6. To make the frosting, combine the butter, cream cheese and sugar in a container for five minutes or until fluffy and pale.
7. Stir in the vanilla and mix thoroughly then spoon the frosting in a pastry bag and top the cupcakes with it.

Nutritional Content of One Serving:

Calories: 425 Fat: 24.7g Protein: 4.6g Carbohydrates: 48.4g

Coconut Flakes Cupcakes

Total Time Taken: 1 ½ hours
Yield: 12 Servings
Ingredients:

Cupcakes:
- ¼ teaspoon salt
- ½ cup butter, softened
- ½ cup white sugar

- 1 cup all-purpose flour
- 1 cup shredded coconut
- 1 teaspoon baking powder
- 1 teaspoon coconut extract
- 3 eggs

Frosting:
- 1 cup butter, softened
- 1 cup coconut flakes
- 2 cups powdered sugar

Directions:
1. To make the cupcakes, combine the butter and sugar in a container until pale and light.
2. Put in the coconut extract and eggs and mix thoroughly.
3. Fold in the flour, salt, baking powder and shredded coconut.
4. Spoon the batter in a muffin tin covered with muffin papers.
5. Preheat your oven and bake the cupcakes at 350F for about twenty minutes or until it rises significantly and seems golden. Let the cupcakes cool down.
6. To make the frosting, combine the butter until pale. Put in the sugar and stir thoroughly for five minutes.
7. Spoon the frosting in a pastry bag and top each cupcake with it.
8. Garnish the frosted cupcakes with coconut flakes.

These cupcakes taste best when fresh.

Nutritional Content of One Serving:
Calories: 415 Fat: 28.7g Protein: 3.2g Carbohydrates: 38.6g

Coconut Lemon Chia Seed Muffins

Total Time Taken: 1 hour
Yield: 10 Servings
Ingredients:
- ¼ cup coconut oil, melted
- ¼ teaspoon salt
- ½ cup honey
- ½ cup milk
- 1 ½ cups almond flour
- 1 teaspoon baking powder
- 1 teaspoon lemon juice
- 1 teaspoon lemon zest
- 1 teaspoon vanilla extract
- 2 tablespoons chia seeds
- 4 eggs

Directions:
1. Mix the chia seeds, almond flour, salt and baking powder in a container.
2. Put in the remaining ingredients and stir for a few seconds to mix.
3. Pour the batter in a muffin tin covered with muffin papers.

4. Pre-heat the oven and bake at 350F for about twenty minutes or until it rises significantly and seems golden.
5. Let the muffins cool in the pan before you serve.

Nutritional Content of One Serving:

Calories: 187 Fat: 11.5g Protein: 4.8g Carbohydrates: 18.0g

Coconut Mango Muffins

Total Time Taken: 1 hour
Yield: 12 Servings
Ingredients:
- ½ cup canola oil
- ½ cup coconut milk
- ½ cup white sugar
- ½ teaspoon salt
- 1 ½ teaspoons baking powder
- 1 cup all-purpose flour
- 1 cup shredded coconut
- 1 mango, peeled and diced
- 1 teaspoon vanilla extract
- 2 eggs

Directions:
1. Mix the oil, eggs, sugar, vanilla and coconut milk in a container.
2. Put in the coconut, flour, salt and baking powder then fold in the mango.
3. Spoon the batter in a muffin tin covered with muffin papers or greased and preheat your oven and bake at 350F for about twenty minutes or until it rises significantly and starts to appear golden-brown.

These muffins taste best chilled.

Nutritional Content of One Serving:

Calories: 220 Fat: 14.6g Protein: 2.5g Carbohydrates: 21.2g

Coconut Muffins

Total Time Taken: 1 hour
Yield: 12 Servings
Ingredients:
- ½ cup canola oil
- ½ cup light brown sugar
- ½ cup quinoa flour
- ½ cup raspberry jam
- ½ cup shredded coconut
- ½ teaspoon salt
- 1 ½ cups all-purpose flour
- 1 egg

- 1 teaspoon baking soda
- 1 teaspoon vanilla extract
- 2/3 cup milk

Directions:
1. Mix the flours, baking soda, salt, coconut and sugar.
2. Stir in the egg, milk, oil and vanilla and stir for a few seconds to mix using a spatula.
3. Spoon the batter in a muffin tin covered with muffin papers.
4. Drop a dollop of raspberry jam on top of each muffin and preheat your oven and bake at 350F for about twenty minutes or until it rises significantly and starts to appear golden-brown.

These muffins taste best chilled.

Nutritional Content of One Serving:
Calories: 237 Fat: 11.5g Protein: 4.4g Carbohydrates: 28.9g

Cranberry Eggnog Muffins

Total Time Taken: 1 hour
Yield: 12 Servings
Ingredients:
- ¼ teaspoon salt
- ½ cup butter, softened
- ½ cup eggnog
- ¾ cup light brown sugar
- 1 cup dried cranberries
- 1 cup eggnog
- 1 teaspoon vanilla extract
- 2 cups all-purpose flour
- 2 eggs
- 2 teaspoons baking powder

Directions:
1. Mix the cranberries and eggnog in a container and set aside for later to soak up.
2. Mix the butter, sugar, eggnog, eggs and vanilla in a container until creamy.
3. Fold in the flour and mix thoroughly then put in the cranberries.
4. Spoon the batter in a muffin tin covered with muffin papers.
5. Pre-heat the oven and bake at 350F for about twenty minutes or until it rises significantly and starts to appear golden-brown.

These muffins taste best chilled.

Nutritional Content of One Serving:
Calories: 238 Fat: 11.0g Protein: 4.4g Carbohydrates: 30.4g

Decadent Brownie Muffins

Total Time Taken: 1 hour
Yield: 12 Servings
Ingredients:

- ¼ teaspoon salt
- ½ teaspoon baking soda
- ¾ cup butter
- 1 ½ cups dark chocolate chips
- 1 cup all-purpose flour
- 1 cup light brown sugar
- 1 teaspoon vanilla extract
- 4 eggs

Directions:

1. Melt the butter and chocolate in a heatproof container over a hot water bath. Let cool down slightly.
2. Mix the eggs and sugar in a container until fluffy and pale. Put in the vanilla then mix in the chocolate mixture.
3. Fold in the flour, baking soda and salt then spoon the batter in a muffin tin covered with muffin papers.
4. Pre-heat the oven and bake at 350F for about fifteen minutes or until set.
5. *Let cool in the pan then serve.*

Nutritional Content of One Serving:

Calories: 278 Fat: 17.1g Protein: 4.1g Carbohydrates: 30.0g

Deep Chocolate Pumpkin Muffins

Total Time Taken: 1 hour
Yield: 12 Servings
Ingredients:

- ¼ cup cocoa powder
- ¼ teaspoon cinnamon powder
- ½ cup buttermilk
- ½ cup canola oil
- ½ cup dark chocolate chips
- ½ teaspoon baking powder
- 1 ½ cups all-purpose flour
- 1 cup pumpkin puree
- 1 pinch nutmeg
- 1 teaspoon baking soda
- 1 teaspoon vanilla extract
- 2/3 cup light brown sugar
- 3 eggs

Directions:

1. Mix the eggs and sugar in a container until fluffy and pale.
2. Put in the canola oil and vanilla, as well as buttermilk and pumpkin puree.

195

3. Fold in the dry ingredients then put in the chocolate chips.
4. Spoon the batter in a muffin tin covered with muffin papers.
5. Preheat your oven and bake the muffins at 350F for about twenty minutes or until a toothpick inserted into them comes out dry.
6. Let cool in the pan before you serve.

Nutritional Content of One Serving:

Calories: 223 Fat: 12.0g Protein: 4.2g Carbohydrates: 26.5g

Double Berry Cupcakes

Total Time Taken: 1 ½ hours

Yield: 12 Servings

Ingredients:

Cupcakes:
- ½ cup almond flour
- ½ cup butter, softened
- ½ cup white sugar
- ½ teaspoon salt
- 1 ¼ cups all-purpose flour
- 1 ½ teaspoons baking powder
- 1 cup fresh strawberries, sliced
- 1 teaspoon vanilla extract
- 2 eggs
- 2/3 cup buttermilk

Frosting:
- 1 cup fresh raspberries
- 2 cups heavy cream

Directions:
1. To make the cupcakes, combine the butter and sugar in a container until creamy and pale. Put in the eggs and vanilla and mix thoroughly.
2. Stir in the buttermilk then fold in the flours, salt and baking powder.
3. Put in the strawberries and stir lightly.
4. Spoon the batter in a muffin tin coated with baking muffin papers and preheat your oven and bake at 350F for about twenty minutes or until a golden-brown colour is achieved and it rises significantly.
5. Let them cool in the pan.
6. Apply whipped cream on top of each cupcake and garnish with raspberries.

Nutritional Content of One Serving:

Calories: 249 Fat: 16.7g Protein: 3.7g Carbohydrates: 22.3g

Double Chocolate Cupcakes

Total Time Taken: 1 ½ hours
Yield: 12 Servings
Ingredients:

Cupcakes:
- ½ cup canola oil
- ½ cup cocoa powder
- ½ teaspoon salt
- ¾ cup white sugar
- 1 ½ cups all-purpose flour
- 1 cup brewed coffee
- 1 teaspoon baking soda
- 1 teaspoon lemon juice
- 1 teaspoon vanilla extract
- 2 eggs

Frosting:
- 1 cup heavy cream
- 1 teaspoon vanilla extract
- 2 cups dark chocolate chips

Directions:
1. To make the cupcakes, combine all the ingredients in a container and stir for a few seconds to mix.
2. Pour the batter into 12 muffin cups covered with muffin papers.
3. Preheat your oven and bake the cupcakes at 350F for about twenty minutes or until well risen and set.
4. Let cool in the pan.
5. To make the frosting, bring the cream to a boil in a saucepan.
6. Put in the chocolate chips and stir thoroughly until melted. Stir in the vanilla and mix thoroughly.
7. Let the frosting cool down.

Apply the frosting on top of each cupcake.

Nutritional Content of One Serving:

Calories: 333 Fat: 19.5g Protein: 4.7g Carbohydrates: 40.1g

Double Chocolate Muffins

Total Time Taken: 1 hour
Yield: 12 Servings
Ingredients:
- ½ cup canola oil
- ½ cup cocoa powder
- ½ cup dark chocolate chips
- ½ cup whole milk
- ½ teaspoon salt
- 1 ½ cups all-purpose flour

- 1 teaspoon baking powder
- 1 teaspoon vanilla extract
- 2 eggs

Directions:
1. Mix the flour, cocoa powder, salt and baking powder in a container.
2. Put in the remaining ingredients and stir for a few seconds to mix with a whisk.
3. Spoon the batter into 12 muffin cups covered with muffin papers and preheat your oven and bake at 350F for about twenty minutes.

These muffins taste best chilled.

Nutritional Content of One Serving:
Calories: 186 Fat: 12.1g Protein: 3.8g Carbohydrates: 18.0g

Double Chocolate Nutella Muffins

Total Time Taken: 1 hour
Yield: 12 Servings
Ingredients:
- ¼ cup cocoa powder
- ¼ cup white sugar
- ¼ teaspoon salt
- ½ cup canola oil
- ½ cup chopped hazelnuts
- ½ cup dark chocolate chips
- ½ cup milk
- ½ cup Nutella
- ½ teaspoon baking soda
- 1 teaspoon baking powder
- 1 teaspoon vanilla extract
- 2 cups all-purpose flour
- 3 eggs

Directions:
1. Mix the Nutella, eggs, vanilla, oil and milk in a container.
2. Put in the flour, cocoa powder, sugar, salt, baking powder and baking soda and stir for a few seconds to mix.
3. Fold in the chocolate chips then spoon the batter in a muffin tin lined using muffin papers of your choice.
4. Top with chopped hazelnuts and preheat your oven and bake at 350F for about twenty minutes or until a toothpick inserted into them comes out dry.
5. Let cool in the pan before you serve or storing away.

Nutritional Content of One Serving:
Calories: 258 Fat: 15.0g Protein: 5.1g Carbohydrates: 27.5g

Duo Chocolate Chip Muffins

Total Time Taken: 1 hour
Yield: 12 Servings
Ingredients:
- ½ cup canola oil
- ½ cup dark chocolate chips
- ½ cup white chocolate chips
- ½ teaspoon salt
- 1 ½ teaspoons baking powder
- 1 cup milk
- 1 cup white sugar
- 2 cups all-purpose flour
- 2 eggs

Directions:
1. Mix the oil and sugar in a container. Put in the eggs and mix thoroughly then mix in the milk.
2. Fold in the flour, salt and baking powder then put in the chocolate chips.
3. Spoon the batter in a muffin tin covered with muffin papers and preheat your oven and bake at 350F for about twenty minutes or until a golden-brown colour is achieved.

These muffins taste best chilled.

Nutritional Content of One Serving:
Calories: 301 Fat: 14.0g Protein: 4.5g Carbohydrates: 41.4g

Eggless Pumpkin Muffins

Total Time Taken: 1 hour
Yield: 12 Servings
Ingredients:
- ¼ teaspoon salt
- ½ cup coconut oil, melted
- ½ cup maple syrup
- 1 cup pumpkin puree
- 1 teaspoon lemon juice
- 1 teaspoon pumpkin pie spices
- 1 teaspoon vanilla extract
- 2 cups all-purpose flour
- 2 teaspoons baking powder
- 3/4 cup almond milk

Directions:
1. Mix the wet ingredients in a container.
2. Put in the remaining ingredients and stir for a few seconds to mix.
3. Spoon the batter in a muffin tin covered with muffin papers and preheat your oven and bake at 350F for about twenty minutes or until a toothpick inserted into them comes out dry.

These muffins taste best chilled.

Espresso Sour Cream Cupcakes

Total Time Taken: 1 ½ hours
Yield: 12 Servings
Ingredients:

Cupcakes:
- 1 teaspoon vanilla extract
- 2 eggs
- ½ cup sour cream
- ¼ cup brewed espresso
- 1 ½ cups all-purpose flour
- ½ teaspoon salt
- 1 ½ teaspoons baking powder
- ¼ cup cornstarch
- 2/3 cup butter, softened
- 2/3 cup white sugar

Frosting:
- 1 cup butter, softened
- 1 teaspoon vanilla extract
- 2 cups powdered sugar
- 2 teaspoons instant coffee

Directions:
1. To make the cupcakes, combine the butter and sugar in a container until pale and creamy.
2. Put in the vanilla and eggs and mix thoroughly. Stir in the espresso and sour cream.
3. Put in the remaining ingredients and mix using a spatula.
4. Spoon the batter in a muffin tin covered with muffin papers.
5. Pre-heat the oven and bake at 350F for about twenty minutes or until it rises significantly and starts to appear golden-brown.
6. Let the cupcakes cool in the pan.
7. To make the frosting, combine the butter and sugar in a container for minimum five minutes or until pale and creamy.
8. Put in the coffee and vanilla and mix thoroughly.
9. Spoon the frosting in a pastry bag and top the cupcakes with it.

These are best enjoyed fresh.

Nutritional Content of One Serving:
Calories: 447 Fat: 28.5g Protein: 3.1g Carbohydrates: 46.4g

Extra Chocolate Muffins

Total Time Taken: 1 hour
Yield: 12 Servings
Ingredients:
- ¼ cup cocoa powder
- ½ cup dark chocolate chips
- ½ cup light brown sugar
- ½ cup white chocolate chips
- ½ teaspoon baking powder
- ½ teaspoon baking soda
- ½ teaspoon salt
- 1 ¾ cups all-purpose flour
- 1 cup milk
- 1/3 cup canola oil
- 2 eggs

Directions:
1. Mix the dry ingredients in a container then put in the wet ingredients.
2. Fold in the chocolate chips then spoon the batter in a muffin cups covered with muffin papers.
3. Preheat your oven and bake the muffins at 350F for about twenty minutes or until well risen.

These muffins taste best chilled.

Nutritional Content of One Serving:
Calories: 229 Fat: 11.2g Protein: 4.5g Carbohydrates: 29.5g

Fig Walnut Muffins

Total Time Taken: 1 hour
Yield: 12 Servings
Ingredients:
- ¼ teaspoon baking soda
- ¼ teaspoon salt
- ½ cup shredded coconut
- ½ cup white sugar
- 1 ½ cups whole wheat flour
- 1 cup coconut milk
- 1 cup ground walnuts
- 1 egg
- 1 pinch cinnamon powder
- 1 teaspoon baking powder
- 1 teaspoon vanilla extract
- 1/3 cup olive oil
- 6 fresh figs, quartered

Directions:

1. Mix the flour, baking powder, baking soda, salt, cinnamon, sugar, coconut and walnuts in a container.
2. Put in the remaining ingredients and mix thoroughly.
3. Pour the batter in a muffin tin covered with muffin papers and top with figs.
4. Pre-heat the oven and bake at 350F for about twenty minutes or until a toothpick inserted into them comes out dry.
5. Let the muffins cool in the pan before you serve.

Nutritional Content of One Serving:

Calories: 289 Fat: 18.2g Protein: 5.5g Carbohydrates: 29.3g

Flaxseed Pumpkin Muffins

Total Time Taken: 1 hour
Yield: 12 Servings
Ingredients:

- ¼ cup canola oil
- ¼ cup ground flaxseeds
- ¼ teaspoon baking soda
- ¼ teaspoon salt
- ½ cup buttermilk
- 1 ¼ cups all-purpose flour
- 1 cup pumpkin puree
- 1 egg
- 1 teaspoon baking powder
- 1 teaspoon pumpkin pie spices
- 1 teaspoon vanilla extract

Directions:
1. Mix the flour, flaxseeds, spices, baking powder, baking soda and salt in a container.
2. Put in the remaining ingredients and mix thoroughly.
3. Spoon the batter in a muffin tin lined with special muffin papers.
4. Preheat your oven and bake the muffins at 350F for about twenty minutes or until a toothpick inserted into them comes out dry.
5. Let cool in the pan before you serve.

Nutritional Content of One Serving:

Calories: 118 Fat: 5.9g Protein: 2.8g Carbohydrates: 13.1g

Fragrant Date Banana Muffins

Total Time Taken: 1 ¼ hours
Yield: 12 Servings

Ingredients:

- ¼ teaspoon salt
- ½ cup butter, melted
- ½ cup light brown sugar
- 1 ½ cups all-purpose flour

- 1 cup dates, pitted and chopped
- 2 eggs
- 2 teaspoons baking powder
- 4 bananas, mashed

Directions:
1. Mix the butter, eggs, bananas and sugar in a container.
2. Put in the flour, baking powder and salt and stir swiftly to combine.
3. Fold in the dates then spoon the batter in a muffin tin covered with muffin papers.
4. Pre-heat the oven and bake at 350F for about twenty minutes or until it rises significantly and starts to appear golden-brown.
5. *Let cool down before you serve.*

Nutritional Content of One Serving:
Calories: 236 Fat: 8.7g Protein: 3.4g Carbohydrates: 38.4g

Fresh Ginger Muffins

Total Time Taken: 1 hour
Yield: 12 Servings
Ingredients:
- ½ cup butter, softened
- ½ cup light brown sugar
- ½ teaspoon salt
- 1 ½ teaspoons grated ginger
- 1 cup buttermilk
- 1 teaspoon vanilla extract
- 2 cups all-purpose flour
- 2 eggs
- 2 teaspoons baking powder

Directions:
1. Mix the butter, eggs, buttermilk, ginger and vanilla in a container.
2. Stir in the sugar and mix thoroughly.
3. Fold in the flour, salt and baking powder then spoon the batter in a muffin tin covered with muffin papers.
4. Pre-heat the oven and bake at 350F for about twenty minutes or until it rises significantly and starts to appear golden-brown.

These muffins taste best chilled.

Nutritional Content of One Serving:
Calories: 188 Fat: 8.8g Protein: 3.9g Carbohydrates: 23.5g

Fudgy Chocolate Date Muffins

Total Time Taken: 1 hour
Yield: 12 Servings
Ingredients:
- ¼ cup cornstarch
- ¼ cup milk
- ½ cup cocoa powder
- ½ cup fresh orange juice
- ½ teaspoon salt
- 1 cup all-purpose flour
- 1 cup dates, pitted
- 1 teaspoon baking soda
- 1 teaspoon orange zest
- 1 teaspoon vanilla extract
- 2 eggs

Directions:
1. Mix the dates, orange juice, orange zest, eggs and vanilla in a blender and pulse until the desired smoothness is achieved. Put in the milk and mix thoroughly.
2. Fold in the remaining ingredients and mix thoroughly.
3. Pour the batter in a muffin tin covered with muffin papers.
4. Preheat your oven and bake the muffins at 350F for about twenty minutes or until a toothpick inserted into the center of a muffin comes out clean.

These muffins taste best chilled.

Nutritional Content of One Serving:

Calories: 117 Fat: 1.5g Protein: 3.3g Carbohydrates: 24.9g

Fudgy Chocolate Muffins

Total Time Taken: 1 hour
Yield: 12 Servings
Ingredients:
- ½ cup canola oil
- ½ teaspoon salt
- 1 ¾ cups all-purpose flour
- 1 cup dark chocolate chips
- 1 cup milk
- 1 egg
- 1 teaspoon vanilla extract
- 2 tablespoons cocoa powder
- 2 teaspoons baking powder
- 3 oz. dark chocolate

Directions:

1. Mix the dark chocolate and canola oil in a heatproof container and place over a hot water bath. Melt them together until smooth then turn off heat and put in the egg, milk, sugar and vanilla.
2. Fold in the flour, cocoa powder, baking powder and salt then put in the chocolate chips.
3. Spoon the batter in a muffin tin covered with muffin papers.
4. Preheat your oven and bake the muffins at 350F for about twenty minutes or until well risen and a toothpick inserted into the center of a muffin comes out clean.

These muffins taste best chilled.

Nutritional Content of One Serving:

Calories: 250 Fat: 14.9g Protein: 4.4g Carbohydrates: 26.7g

Funfetti Banana Muffins

Total Time Taken: 1 hour
Yield: 12 Servings
Ingredients:
- ¼ cup colourful sprinkles
- ¼ teaspoon salt
- ½ cup almond flour
- ½ cup canola oil
- ½ cup milk
- ½ cup white sugar
- 1 ½ cups all-purpose flour
- 1 teaspoon baking powder
- 1 teaspoon vanilla extract
- 2 eggs

Directions:
1. Mix the eggs and sugar in a container until fluffy and pale.
2. Put in the oil, vanilla and milk and mix thoroughly.
3. Fold in the flours, salt and baking powder then put in the sprinkles.
4. Spoon the batter in a muffin tin covered with muffin papers and preheat your oven and bake at 350F for about twenty minutes or until a golden-brown colour is achieved and it rises significantly.
5. *Let cool down before you serve.*

Nutritional Content of One Serving:

Calories: 204 Fat: 11.2g Protein: 3.3g Carbohydrates: 23.3g

Funfetti Cream Cheese Cupcakes

Total Time Taken: 1 ½ hours
Yield: 12 Servings
Ingredients:

Cupcakes:
- ½ cup colourful sprinkles
- ½ cup butter, softened
- ½ cup milk

- ½ cup sour cream
- ½ teaspoon baking soda
- ½ teaspoon salt
- 1 ¾ cups all-purpose flour
- 1 teaspoon baking powder
- 1 teaspoon vanilla extract
- 2 eggs
- 2/3 cup white sugar

Frosting:
- ½ cup butter, softened
- 1 cup cream cheese
- 2 cups powdered sugar
- Sprinkles to garnish

Directions:
1. To make the cupcakes, combine the butter and sugar in a container until creamy and pale.
2. Put in the eggs and mix thoroughly then mix in the sour cream, milk and vanilla.
3. Fold in the sprinkles then spoon the batter in a muffin tin coated with baking muffin papers.
4. Pre-heat the oven and bake at 350F for about twenty minutes or until it rises significantly and starts to appear golden-brown.
5. Let the cupcakes cool down.
6. To make the frosting, combine the cream cheese and butter in a container until pale.
7. Put in the sugar and mix thoroughly for about five to seven minutes or until fluffy and light.
8. Garnish the cupcakes with cream cheese frosting.
9. *Top with colourful sprinkles.*

Nutritional Content of One Serving:

Calories: 438 Fat: 25.7g Protein: 5.2g Carbohydrates: 48.6g

German Chocolate Cupcakes

Total Time Taken: 1 ½ hours
Yield: Servings 18
Ingredients:

Cupcakes:
- 1 cup butter, softened
- ¼ cup light brown sugar
- 2 eggs
- 1 teaspoon vanilla extract
- 1 cup buttermilk
- ½ cup sour cream
- 1 cup cocoa powder
- ¼ teaspoon salt
- 1 ½ teaspoons baking powder
- ½ teaspoon baking soda
- 2/3 cup white sugar
- 1 3/4 cups all-purpose flour

Frosting:
- ½ cup pecans, chopped
- 1 cup butter, softened
- 1 cup evaporated milk
- 1 cup light brown sugar
- 1 cup sliced almonds
- 2 cups shredded coconut

Directions:
1. To make the cupcakes, combine the butter, sugars and vanilla in a container until fluffy and pale.
2. Put in the eggs, one at a time, and mix thoroughly then mix in the buttermilk and sour cream.
3. Fold in the flour, cocoa powder, salt, baking powder and baking soda.
4. Spoon the batter in a muffin tin covered with muffin papers.
5. Pre-heat the oven and bake at 350F for about twenty minutes.
6. To make the frosting, combine the butter, sugar and evaporated milk in a container until creamy and fluffy.
7. Put in the coconut, almonds and pecans and mix thoroughly.
8. Top each cupcake with the frosting and serve them fresh.

Nutritional Content of One Serving:
Calories: 415 Fat: 30.4g Protein: 6.1g Carbohydrates: 34.4g

Ginger Pineapple Muffins

Total Time Taken: 1 hour
Yield: 12 Servings
Ingredients:
- ½ cup canola oil
- ½ cup milk
- ½ cup shredded coconut
- ½ teaspoon cinnamon powder
- ½ teaspoon salt
- ¾ cup light brown sugar
- 1 ½ cups all-purpose flour
- 1 ½ teaspoons baking powder
- 1 cup crushed pineapple
- 1 egg
- 1 teaspoon ground ginger

Directions:
1. Mix the oil and sugar until creamy. Put in the egg and mix thoroughly then mix in the milk and mix very well.
2. Fold in the flour, coconut, salt, baking powder, ginger and cinnamon and mix thoroughly.
3. Fold in the pineapple then spoon the batter in a muffin tin covered with muffin papers.
4. Pre-heat the oven and bake at 350F for about twenty minutes or until it rises significantly and starts to appear golden-brown.

These muffins taste best chilled.

Calories: 202 Fat: 10.9g Protein: 2.6g Carbohydrates: 24.1g

Gingerbread Muffins

Total Time Taken: 1 hour
Yield: 12 Servings
Ingredients:

- ½ cup raisins
- ½ cup wheat bran
- ½ cup white sugar
- ½ teaspoon ground ginger
- ½ teaspoon ground star anise
- ½ teaspoon salt
- 1 ½ cups all-purpose flour
- 1 cup buttermilk
- 1 egg
- 1 teaspoon cinnamon powder
- 1 teaspoon vanilla extract
- 2 tablespoons dark molasses

Directions:

1. Mix the dry ingredients in a container.
2. Put in the wet ingredients and stir for a few seconds to mix.
3. Spoon the batter in a muffin tin covered with muffin papers.
4. Preheat your oven and bake the muffins at 350F for about twenty minutes or until it is aromatic and appears golden.
5. *Best served chilled.*

Nutritional Content of One Serving:

Calories: 137 Fat: 0.8g Protein: 3.4g Carbohydrates: 30.3g

Gluten Free Chocolate Cupcakes With Pumpkin Frosting

Total Time Taken: 1 ½ hours
Yield: 12 Servings
Ingredients:

Cupcakes:

- ¼ cup coconut oil, melted
- ¼ teaspoon salt
- ½ cup buckwheat flour
- ½ cup cocoa powder
- ½ cup coconut flour
- ½ cup maple syrup
- 1 cup shredded coconut

- 1 cup sparkling water
- 1 teaspoon baking soda
- 1 teaspoon vanilla extract

Frosting:
- ¼ teaspoon cinnamon powder
- ¼ teaspoon ground ginger
- ½ cup pumpkin puree
- ½ cup walnuts
- 1 cup dates, pitted
- 2 tablespoons coconut oil
- 2 tablespoons maple syrup

Directions:
1. To make the cupcakes, combine the flours, shredded coconut, cocoa powder, baking soda and salt in a container.
2. In a separate container, mix the maple syrup, sparkling water, coconut oil and vanilla and mix thoroughly. Put in the dry ingredients and stir for a few seconds to mix.
3. Pour the batter in a muffin tin covered with muffin papers and preheat your oven and bake at 350F for about twenty minutes or until a toothpick inserted into them comes out dry.
4. Let the cupcakes cool down.
5. To make the frosting, place the dates and the rest of the ingredients in a food processor or blender and pulse until well mixed.
6. Top each cupcake with the frosting and serve fresh.

Nutritional Content of One Serving:
Calories: 249 Fat: 13.5g Protein: 3.9g Carbohydrates: 32.8g

Gluten Free Chocolate Muffins

Total Time Taken: 1 hour
Yield: 10 Servings
Ingredients:
- ¼ cup cocoa powder
- ½ cup canola oil
- ½ cup dark chocolate chips
- ½ cup shredded coconut
- ½ cup tapioca flour
- ½ cup white rice flour
- ½ cup white sugar
- ½ teaspoon salt
- 1 teaspoon baking powder
- 1 teaspoon vanilla extract
- 3 eggs

Directions:
1. Mix the eggs, sugar and vanilla in a container until fluffy and pale.
2. Put in the oil then mix in the remaining ingredients.

3. Spoon the batter in a muffin tin covered with muffin papers and preheat your oven and bake at 350F for about twenty minutes or until it rises significantly and becomes aromatic.

These muffins taste best chilled.

Nutritional Content of One Serving:

Calories: 251 Fat: 15.4g Protein: 2.9g Carbohydrates: 28.7g

Gluten Free Maple Muffins

Total Time Taken: 1 hour
Yield: 12 Servings
Ingredients:
- ¼ cup tapioca flour
- ¼ teaspoon salt
- ½ cup butter, melted
- ½ cup coconut flour
- ½ cup maple syrup
- ½ cup sorghum flour
- ¾ cup milk
- 1 ½ teaspoons baking powder
- 1 teaspoon vanilla extract
- 2 eggs
- 2 tablespoons dark brown sugar

Directions:
1. Mix the eggs, butter, maple syrup, sugar and vanilla in a container until creamy.
2. Put in the remaining ingredients and mix thoroughly.
3. Pour the batter in a muffin tin covered with muffin papers.
4. Pre-heat the oven and bake at 350F for about twenty minutes or until a toothpick inserted into the center of a muffin comes out clean.
5. Let the muffins cool to room temperature before you serve.

Nutritional Content of One Serving:

Calories: 203 Fat: 9.7g Protein: 3.1g Carbohydrates: 27.3g

Grain Free Apple Cinnamon

Total Time Taken: 1 ¼ hours
Yield: 12 Servings

Ingredients:
- ¼ cup coconut oil, melted
- ¼ cup honey
- ¼ teaspoon salt
- ½ cup coconut milk
- ½ cup tapioca flour
- ½ teaspoon baking powder
- ½ teaspoon baking soda

- 1 ½ cups almond flour
- 1 teaspoon cinnamon powder
- 1 teaspoon lemon juice
- 1 teaspoon vanilla extract
- 2 red apples, cored and diced
- 3 eggs

Directions:

1. Mix the flours, cinnamon, baking soda, baking powder and salt in a container.
2. Put in the eggs and the remaining ingredients and mix thoroughly.
3. Spoon the batter in a muffin tin coated with baking muffin papers then preheat your oven and bake at 350F for about twenty minutes or until a golden-brown colour is achieved and it rises significantly.

These muffins taste best chilled.

Nutritional Content of One Serving:

Calories: 163 Fat: 9.8g Protein: 2.5g Carbohydrates: 18.5g

Grapefruit Cream Cheese Cupcakes

Total Time Taken: 1 ½ hours
Yield: 12 Servings
Ingredients:

Cupcakes:
- ½ cup butter, softened
- ½ teaspoon salt
- ¾ cup buttermilk
- ¾ cup white sugar
- 1 ½ teaspoons baking powder
- 1 ¾ cups all-purpose flour
- 1 teaspoon grapefruit zest
- 2 eggs

Frosting:
- ½ cup butter
- 1 cup cream cheese
- 1 tablespoon grapefruit zest
- 2 cups powder sugar

Directions:

1. To make the cupcakes, combine the butter and sugar in a container until fluffy and creamy.
2. Put in the zest and eggs and mix thoroughly.
3. Stir in the flour, salt and baking powder then put in the milk and mix thoroughly.
4. Spoon the batter in a muffin tin covered with muffin papers and preheat your oven and bake at 350F for about twenty minutes.
5. Let the cupcakes cool in the pan.
6. To make the frosting, combine the cream cheese and butter in a container until fluffy.
7. Put in the eggs and stir thoroughly for 4-5 minutes then mix in the zest.

8. Garnish each cupcake with frosting and serve them fresh.

Nutritional Content of One Serving:

Calories: 412 Fat: 23.1g Protein: 4.9g Carbohydrates: 48.1g

Harvest Muffins

Total Time Taken: 1 hour
Yield: 12 Servings
Ingredients:

- 2 eggs
- 2 cups all-purpose flour
- 1 teaspoon baking powder
- 1 pear, cored and diced
- 1 cup milk
- 1 apple, cored and diced
- ½ teaspoon ground ginger
- ½ teaspoon cinnamon powder
- ½ teaspoon baking soda
- ½ cup light brown sugar
- ½ cup dried cranberries
- ½ cup butter, melted
- ¼ teaspoon salt

Directions:

1. Mix the flour, baking powder, baking soda, salt, cinnamon, ginger and sugar in a container.
2. Put in the eggs, milk and butter and stir for a few seconds to mix.
3. Fold in the apple, pear and cranberries then spoon the batter in a muffin pan coated with muffin papers.
4. Pre-heat the oven and bake at 350F for about twenty minutes or until it rises significantly and becomes aromatic.
5. Let the muffins cool to room temperature before you serve.

Nutritional Content of One Serving:

Calories: 205 Fat: 9.1g Protein: 3.9g Carbohydrates: 27.4g

Hazelnut Fig Muffins

Total Time Taken: 1 hour
Yield: 12 Servings
Ingredients:

- ¼ cup canola oil
- ½ cup all-purpose flour
- ½ cup light brown sugar
- ½ teaspoon salt
- 1 cup ground hazelnuts
- 1 teaspoon baking powder
- 12 fresh figs

- 4 eggs

Directions:

1. Mix the hazelnuts, flour, salt and baking powder in a container.
2. Mix the eggs and sugar in a container until pale and light. Put in the oil and mix thoroughly.
3. Fold in the flour and hazelnut mixture then pour the batter in a muffin tin covered with muffin papers.
4. Top each muffin with a fig and preheat your oven and bake at 350F for about twenty minutes or until it rises significantly and seems golden.

These muffins taste best chilled.

Nutritional Content of One Serving:

Calories: 190 Fat: 10.0g Protein: 4.0g Carbohydrates: 23.4g

Healthy Chocolate Muffins

Total Time Taken: 1 hour
Yield: 12 Servings
Ingredients:

- ¼ teaspoon salt
- ½ cup cocoa powder
- ½ cup low fat milk
- ½ cup maple syrup
- 1 ½ cups whole wheat flour
- 1 ½ teaspoons baking powder
- 1 cup plain yogurt
- 1 egg
- 1 teaspoon vanilla extract

Directions:

1. Mix the flour, baking powder, salt and cocoa powder in a container.
2. Put in the remaining ingredients and stir for a few seconds to mix.
3. Spoon the batter in a muffin tin covered with muffin papers and preheat your oven and bake at 350F for about twenty minutes or until a toothpick inserted into them comes out dry.
4. Let cool in the pan before you serve.

Nutritional Content of One Serving:

Calories: 125 Fat: 1.4g Protein: 4.2g Carbohydrates: 25.0g

Honey Cardamom Cupcakes

Total Time Taken: 1 ½ hours
Yield: 12 Servings
Ingredients:

Cupcakes:

- ½ cup butter, softened
- ½ cup honey
- ½ teaspoon salt

- 1 ½ cups all-purpose flour
- 1 ½ teaspoons baking powder
- 1 teaspoon ground cardamom
- 1 teaspoon vanilla extract
- 1/3 cup milk
- 2 eggs
- 2 tablespoons dark brown sugar

Frosting:
- ¼ cup honey
- 1 cup butter, softened
- 1 teaspoon vanilla extract
- 2 cups powdered sugar

Directions:
1. To make the cupcakes, combine the butter, honey and sugar in a container until fluffy and pale. Put in the vanilla and eggs and mix thoroughly.
2. Fold in the flour, salt, baking powder and cardamom, alternating them with milk.
3. Spoon the batter in a muffin tin covered with muffin papers.
4. Pre-heat the oven and bake at 350F for about twenty minutes or until a golden-brown colour is achieved.
5. Let them cool in the pan.
6. To make the frosting, combine the butter and sugar in a container for about five to seven minutes until fluffy and pale. Stir in the vanilla and mix thoroughly.
7. Spoon the frosting into a pastry and top each cupcake with it.
8. Sprinkle the frosted cupcakes with honey.

Nutritional Content of One Serving:

Calories: 425 Fat: 24.1g Protein: 3.1g Carbohydrates: 51.7g

Honey Lemon Muffins

Total Time Taken: 1 hour
Yield: 12 Servings
Ingredients:
- ¼ cup canola oil
- ¼ cup honey
- ¼ teaspoon salt
- ½ cup milk
- ½ cup white chocolate chips
- 1 ½ cups all-purpose flour
- 1 ½ teaspoons baking powder
- 1 tablespoon lemon zest
- 2 eggs
- 2 tablespoons lemon juice

Directions:
1. Mix the flour, salt and baking powder in a container.
2. Put in the remaining ingredients and mix thoroughly.

3. Spoon the batter in a muffin tin coated with baking muffin papers and preheat your oven and bake at 350F for about twenty minutes or until it rises significantly and starts to appear golden-brown.
4. *Let cool down before you serve.*

Nutritional Content of One Serving:

Calories: 174 Fat: 7.9g Protein: 3.3g Carbohydrates: 23.0g

Honey Nutmeg Peach Muffins

Total Time Taken: 1 hour
Yield: 12 Servings
Ingredients:
- ¼ cup honey
- ¼ teaspoon salt
- ½ cup buttermilk
- ½ cup ground walnuts
- ½ cup white sugar
- ½ teaspoon ground nutmeg
- 1 ½ cups all-purpose flour
- 1 banana, mashed
- 1 teaspoon baking soda
- 2 eggs
- 2 peaches, pitted and diced

Directions:
1. Mix the dry ingredients in a container.
2. Stir in the eggs, honey, banana and buttermilk and stir for a few seconds to mix.
3. Fold in the peaches and spoon the batter in a muffin tin covered with muffin papers.
4. Pre-heat the oven and bake at 350F for about twenty minutes or until it rises significantly and starts to appear golden-brown.
5. Let the muffins cool in the pan before you serve.

Nutritional Content of One Serving:

Calories: 172 Fat: 4.1g Protein: 4.4g Carbohydrates: 31.0g

Honey Pear Muffins

Total Time Taken: 1 hour
Yield: 12 Servings
Ingredients:
- ¼ cup butter, melted
- ¼ teaspoon ground nutmeg
- ½ cup buttermilk
- ½ cup light brown sugar
- ½ teaspoon cinnamon powder
- ½ teaspoon salt
- 1 ½ cups all-purpose flour
- 1 ½ teaspoons baking powder

- 1 teaspoon vanilla extract
- 2 eggs
- 2 pears, cored and diced

Directions:
1. Mix the dry ingredients in a container and the wet ingredients in a separate container.
2. Combine the two mixtures together and mix quickly with a whisk or spatula.
3. Fold in the pears then spoon the batter in a muffin tin covered with muffin papers.
4. Preheat your oven and bake the muffins at 350F for about twenty minutes or until a golden-brown colour is achieved and it rises significantly.

These muffins taste best chilled.

Nutritional Content of One Serving:
Calories: 150 Fat: 4.9g Protein: 3.0g Carbohydrates: 24.1g

Honey Pumpkin Muffins

Total Time Taken: 1 hour
Yield: 12 Servings
Ingredients:
- 2 teaspoons baking powder
- 2 tablespoons pumpkin seeds
- 2 eggs
- 1 teaspoon vanilla extract
- 1 cup pumpkin puree
- 1 cup oat flour
- 1 cup all-purpose flour
- ½ cup honey
- ¼ teaspoon salt

Directions:
1. Mix the honey, pumpkin puree, vanilla and eggs in a container.
2. Put in the remaining ingredients then pour the batter in a muffin tin covered with muffin papers of your desire.
3. Pre-heat the oven and bake at 350F for about twenty minutes or until it rises significantly and starts to appear golden-brown.

These muffins taste best chilled.

Nutritional Content of One Serving:
Calories: 138 Fat: 2.1g Protein: 3.6g Carbohydrates: 27.2g

Honey Spiced Muffins

Total Time Taken: 1 hour
Yield: 12 Servings
Ingredients:
- ½ cup butter, melted
- ½ cup honey

- ½ teaspoon cinnamon powder
- ½ teaspoon ground cardamom
- ½ teaspoon ground ginger
- ½ teaspoon ground star anise
- ½ teaspoon salt
- 1 cup all-purpose flour
- 1 cup ground almonds
- 1 teaspoon baking soda
- 1 teaspoon vanilla extract
- 2 eggs
- 2 tablespoons dark brown sugar

Directions:
1. Mix the butter, eggs, honey and sugar in a container.
2. Stir in the remaining ingredients and mix using a spatula just until incorporated.
3. Pour the batter in a muffin tin covered with muffin papers.
4. Pre-heat the oven and bake at 350F for about twenty minutes or until it rises completely and is aromatic.

These muffins taste best chilled.

Nutritional Content of One Serving:
Calories: 213 Fat: 12.5g Protein: 3.9g Carbohydrates: 23.1g

Hummingbird Muffins

Total Time Taken: 1 ½ hours
Yield: 12 Servings

Ingredients:
- ¼ teaspoon cinnamon powder
- ½ cup canola oil
- ½ cup crushed pineapple
- ½ cup grated carrots
- ½ cup shredded coconut
- ½ cup walnuts, chopped
- ½ cup white sugar
- ½ teaspoon salt
- 1 ½ cups all-purpose flour
- 1 ½ teaspoons baking powder
- 1 teaspoon orange zest
- 1 teaspoon vanilla extract
- 2 bananas, mashed
- 2 eggs

Directions:
1. Mix the eggs and sugar in a container until fluffy and pale.
2. Put in the bananas and oil, as well as vanilla and mix thoroughly.

3. Fold in the flour, salt, baking powder and cinnamon then put in the coconut, walnuts, pineapple, carrots and orange zest.
4. Pour the batter in a muffin tin covered with muffin papers.
5. Preheat your oven and bake the muffins at 350F for about twenty minutes or until a golden-brown colour is achieved and it rises significantly.

These muffins taste best chilled.

Nutritional Content of One Serving:

Calories: 247 Fat: 14.2g Protein: 4.2g Carbohydrates: 27.6g

Intense Chocolate Cupcakes

Total Time Taken: 1 ½ hours
Yield: 12 Servings
Ingredients:

Cupcakes:
- ¼ cup canola oil
- ¼ cup cocoa powder
- ½ cup buttermilk
- ½ teaspoon baking powder
- ½ teaspoon salt
- 1 ½ cups all-purpose flour
- 1 cup brewed coffee
- 1 egg
- 1 teaspoon baking soda
- 1 teaspoon vanilla extract
- 3 oz. dark chocolate

Frosting:
- 1 cup butter, softened
- 2 cups powdered sugar
- 2 tablespoons cocoa powder
- 2 tablespoons heavy cream

Directions:
1. To make the cupcakes, combine the wet ingredients in a container. Put in the dry ingredients and stir swiftly to combine.
2. Pour the cupcakes in 12 muffin cups covered with muffin papers.
3. Preheat your oven and bake the cupcakes at 350F for about twenty minutes.
4. To make the frosting, combine the butter and sugar in a container until fluffy and pale.
5. Put in the remaining ingredients and mix thoroughly.
6. Spoon the frosting in a pastry bag and top each cupcake with it.

Nutritional Content of One Serving:

Calories: 374 Fat: 23.9g Protein: 3.7g Carbohydrates: 38.3g

Lemon Blueberry Muffins

Total Time Taken: 1 hour
Yield: 12 Servings
Ingredients:

- ½ cup white sugar
- ½ teaspoon salt
- 1 cup buttermilk
- 1 cup fresh blueberries
- 1 tablespoon lemon zest
- 1 teaspoon vanilla extract
- 2 cups all-purpose flour
- 2 eggs
- 2 tablespoons chia seeds
- 2 teaspoons baking powder

Directions:

1. Mix the flour, baking powder, salt, chia seeds and sugar in a container.
2. Put in the remaining ingredients and mix using a spatula.
3. Spoon the batter into 12 muffin cups covered with muffin papers.
4. Preheat your oven and bake the muffins at 350F for about twenty minutes or until it rises significantly and starts to appear golden-brown.

These muffins taste best chilled.

Nutritional Content of One Serving:

Calories: 146 Fat: 1.9g Protein: 4.4g Carbohydrates: 27.7g

Lemon Chia Seed Muffins

Total Time Taken: 1 hour
Yield: 12 Servings
Ingredients:

- ¼ teaspoon salt
- ½ cup coconut oil, melted
- ½ teaspoon baking soda
- 1 ½ teaspoons baking powder
- 1 cup plain yogurt
- 1 cup white sugar
- 1 teaspoon vanilla extract
- 2 cups all-purpose flour
- 2 eggs
- 2 tablespoons chia seeds

Directions:

1. Mix the chia seeds, flour, baking powder, baking soda and salt in a container.
2. Put in the yogurt, coconut oil, vanilla, sugar and eggs and stir for a few seconds to mix.
3. Spoon the batter in a muffin tin covered with muffin papers.

4. Pre-heat the oven and bake at 350F for about twenty minutes or until a toothpick inserted into them comes out dry.

These muffins taste best chilled.

Nutritional Content of One Serving:

Calories: 269 Fat: 11.9g Protein: 5.3g Carbohydrates: 36.2g

Lemon Curd Cupcakes

Total Time Taken: 1 ½ hours
Yield: 12 Servings

Ingredients:
- ½ cup almond flour
- ½ teaspoon salt
- ¾ cup butter, softened
- ¾ cup white sugar
- 1 ½ cups all-purpose flour
- 1 cup lemon curd
- 1 tablespoon lemon zest
- 1 teaspoon vanilla extract
- 2 tablespoons lemon juice
- 2 teaspoons baking powder
- 3 eggs

Directions:
1. Mix the butter and sugar in a container until pale and fluffy.
2. Put in the eggs, one at a time, and mix thoroughly then mix in the lemon zest and juice, as well as vanilla.
3. Fold in the flours, salt and baking powder then spoon the batter in 12 muffin cups covered with muffin papers.
4. Preheat your oven and bake the cupcakes at 350F for about twenty minutes or until it rises significantly and starts to appear golden-brown.
5. When finished, let cool and top each cupcake with a dollop of lemon curd.

Nutritional Content of One Serving:

Calories: 311 Fat: 21.4g Protein: 4.7g Carbohydrates: 30.7g

Lemon Fig Muffins

Total Time Taken: 1 hour
Yield: 12 Servings
Ingredients:
- ½ cup buttermilk
- ½ cup white sugar
- ½ teaspoon salt
- 1 cup all-purpose flour
- 1 cup ground almonds

- 1 lemon, zested and juiced
- 1 teaspoon baking soda
- 1/3 cup butter, melted
- 3 eggs
- 4 fresh figs, chopped

Directions:

1. Mix the butter, sugar, eggs, buttermilk, lemon zest and lemon juice in a container until creamy.
2. Put in the flour, salt and baking soda and mix using a spatula.
3. Fold in the figs then spoon the batter in a muffin tin covered with muffin papers.
4. Pre-heat the oven and bake at 350F for about twenty minutes or until a toothpick inserted into them comes out dry.
5. *Best served chilled.*

Nutritional Content of One Serving:

Calories: 197 Fat: 10.4g Protein: 4.8g Carbohydrates: 23.0g

Lemon Glazed Apple Cider Muffins

Total Time Taken: 1 hour
Yield: 12 Servings
Ingredients:

- ¼ teaspoon salt
- ½ cup apple cider
- ½ cup coconut oil
- ½ cup light brown sugar
- ½ teaspoon baking soda
- ½ teaspoon cinnamon powder
- 1 cup powdered sugar
- 1 tablespoon lemon juice
- 1 teaspoon baking powder
- 1 teaspoon vanilla extract
- 2 cups all-purpose flour
- 2 eggs
- 2 red apples, cored and diced

Directions:

1. Mix the coconut oil and sugar in a container for a couple of minutes. Put in the eggs and vanilla and mix thoroughly.
2. Stir in the apple cider then fold in the flour, baking powder, baking soda, salt and cinnamon and mix using a spatula.
3. Fold in the apples then spoon the batter in a muffin tin covered with muffin papers.
4. Pre-heat the oven and bake at 350F for about twenty minutes or until set and golden brown.
5. For the glaze, combine the lemon juice and sugar in a container.
6. Sprinkle the mixture over the muffins and serve chilled.

Nutritional Content of One Serving:

Calories: 249 Fat: 10.1g Protein: 3.2g Carbohydrates: 37.5g

Lemon Poppy Seed Muffins

Total Time Taken: 1 hour
Yield: 12 Servings
Ingredients:

- ½ cup canola oil
- ½ cup milk
- ½ cup white sugar
- ½ teaspoon salt
- 1 ½ teaspoons baking powder
- 1 ¾ cups all-purpose flour
- 1 tablespoon lemon zest
- 2 eggs
- 2 tablespoons lemon juice
- 2 tablespoons poppy seeds

Directions:

1. Mix the flour, salt, baking powder and poppy seeds in a container.
2. In a separate container, combine the eggs and sugar until fluffy and pale. Put in the oil and milk and mix thoroughly then mix in the lemon zest and juice.
3. Fold in the flour mixture then spoon the batter in 12 muffin cups covered with muffin papers.
4. Preheat your oven and bake the muffins at 350F for about twenty minutes or until a golden-brown colour is achieved and it rises significantly.

These muffins taste best chilled.

Nutritional Content of One Serving:

Calories: 203 Fat: 10.9g Protein: 3.4g Carbohydrates: 23.6g

Lemon Ricotta Muffins

Total Time Taken: 1 hour
Yield: 12 Servings
Ingredients:

- ¼ cup milk
- ½ cup butter, melted
- ½ cup ricotta cheese
- ½ teaspoon salt
- 1 ½ teaspoons baking powder
- 1 cup all-purpose flour
- 1 cup almond flour
- 1 tablespoon lemon zest
- 1 teaspoon vanilla extract
- 2 eggs

Directions:

1. Mix the butter, vanilla, eggs, ricotta, milk and lemon zest in a container.
2. Put in the flours, salt and baking powder and mix using a spatula.

3. Spoon the batter in 12 muffin cups coated with baking muffin papers of your desire.
4. Pre-heat the oven and bake at 350F for about twenty minutes or until it rises significantly and starts to appear golden-brown.

These muffins taste best chilled.

Nutritional Content of One Serving:
Calories: 148 Fat: 10.6g Protein: 3.9g Carbohydrates: 9.7g

Loaded Muffins

Total Time Taken: 1 ¼ hours
Yield: 10 Servings

Ingredients:
- ¼ cup canola oil
- ¼ cup cocoa powder
- ¼ cup dried apricots, chopped
- ¼ cup dried cranberries
- ½ cup milk
- ½ teaspoon salt
- 1 ½ cups all-purpose flour
- 1 ½ teaspoons baking powder
- 2 eggs
- 2 tablespoons candied orange peel, chopped

Directions:
1. Mix the dry ingredients in a container.
2. Put in the remaining ingredients and stir for a few seconds to mix.
3. Spoon the batter in a muffin tin covered with muffin papers.
4. Preheat your oven and bake the muffins at 350F for about twenty minutes or until a golden-brown colour is achieved and it rises significantly.

These muffins taste best chilled.

Nutritional Content of One Serving:
Calories: 145 Fat: 7.1g Protein: 3.9g Carbohydrates: 17.5g

Mango Buttermilk Muffins

Total Time Taken: 1 hour
Yield: 12 Servings
Ingredients:
- ¼ cup canola oil
- ¼ teaspoon salt
- ½ cup white sugar
- 1 ½ cups buttermilk
- 1 mango, peeled and diced
- 1 teaspoon baking soda
- 1 teaspoon vanilla extract

- 2 cups all-purpose flour
- 2 eggs

Directions:
1. Mix the flour, sugar, salt and baking soda in a container.
2. Put in the eggs, buttermilk, oil and vanilla and stir for a few seconds to mix.
3. Fold in the mango then spoon the batter in a muffin tin covered with muffin papers.
4. Preheat your oven and bake the muffins at 350F for about twenty minutes or until it rises significantly and starts to appear golden-brown.

These muffins taste best chilled.

Nutritional Content of One Serving:

Calories: 171 Fat: 5.7g Protein: 4.1g Carbohydrates: 25.8g

Maple Spice Muffins

Total Time Taken: 1 hour
Yield: 12 Servings
Ingredients:
- ¼ teaspoon salt
- ½ cup canola oil
- ½ cup dark chocolate chips
- ½ cup milk
- ½ cup walnuts, chopped
- ½ teaspoon all-spice powder
- ½ teaspoon cinnamon powder
- ½ teaspoon ground ginger
- ¾ cup maple syrup
- 1 egg
- 1 teaspoon vanilla extract
- 2 ¼ cups all-purpose flour
- 2 teaspoons baking powder

Directions:
1. Mix the flour, salt, baking powder and spices in a container.
2. Put in the remaining ingredients and stir thoroughly until blended.
3. Fold in the walnuts and chocolate chips then spoon the batter in a muffin tin covered with muffin papers.
4. Pre-heat the oven and bake at 350F for about twenty minutes or until a toothpick inserted into them comes out dry.

These muffins taste best chilled.

Nutritional Content of One Serving:

Calories: 285 Fat: 14.3g Protein: 4.8g Carbohydrates: 36.0g

Maple Syrup Pecan Cupcakes

Total Time Taken: 1 ½ hours
Yield: 12 Servings
Ingredients:

Cupcakes:
- ¼ cup butter, softened
- ¼ cup heavy cream
- ¼ cup maple syrup
- ½ cup white sugar
- ½ teaspoon salt
- 1 cup all-purpose flour
- 1 cup dates, pitted and chopped
- 1 cup ground pecans
- 1 teaspoon baking powder
- 1 teaspoon vanilla extract
- 2 eggs

Frosting:
- ¼ cup maple syrup
- 1 cup butter, softened

Directions:

1. For the syrup, combine the butter, cream, sugar and maple syrup in a container until pale and creamy.
2. Put in the eggs and vanilla and mix thoroughly.
3. Fold in the pecans, flour, salt and baking powder then put in the dates.
4. Spoon the batter in a muffin tin covered with muffin papers.
5. Pre-heat the oven and bake at 350F for about twenty minutes or until a golden-brown colour is achieved and it rises significantly.
6. Let them cool in the pan.
7. To make the frosting, combine the butter and cream in a container.
8. Sprinkle the frosting over each cupcake and serve fresh.

Nutritional Content of One Serving:

Calories: 343 Fat: 21.9g Protein: 2.7g Carbohydrates: 36.8g

Matcha Strawberry Cupcakes

Total Time Taken: 1 ½ hours
Yield: 14 Servings
Ingredients:

Cupcakes:
- ¼ cup cornstarch
- ½ cup butter, softened
- ½ teaspoon salt
- 1 ½ cups all-purpose flour
- 1 cup white sugar

- 1 tablespoon matcha
- 1 teaspoon baking powder
- 1 teaspoon vanilla extract
- 2/3 cup whole milk
- 3 eggs

Frosting:
- 1 cup butter, softened
- 1 cup fresh strawberries, sliced
- 2 cups powdered sugar

Directions:
1. To make the cupcakes, combine the butter and sugar in a container until fluffy and pale.
2. Put in the eggs and vanilla and mix thoroughly.
3. Fold in the dry ingredients, alternating them with milk.
4. Spoon the batter in a muffin tin covered with muffin papers.
5. Preheat your oven and bake the cupcakes at 350F for about twenty minutes or until well risen.
6. Let the cupcakes cool down.
7. To make the frosting, combine the butter and sugar in a container until airy and fluffy.
8. Spoon the frosting into a pastry bag and top the cupcakes with it. Top each cupcake with a strawberry and serve fresh.

Nutritional Content of One Serving:
Calories: 377 Fat: 21.2g Protein: 3.2g Carbohydrates: 45.3g

Mexican Chocolate Muffins

Total Time Taken: 1 hour
Yield: 12 Servings
Ingredients:
- ¼ cup cocoa powder
- ¼ cup milk
- ¼ teaspoon baking soda
- ¼ teaspoon salt
- ½ cup butter, melted
- ½ teaspoon chili powder
- ¾ cup white sugar
- 1 ½ cups all-purpose flour
- 1 cup dark chocolate chips
- 1 egg
- 1 teaspoon baking powder
- 3 bananas, mashed

Directions:
1. Mix the flour, cocoa powder, sugar, salt, baking powder, baking soda and chili powder.
2. Put in the bananas, egg, butter and milk and stir for a few seconds to mix.
3. Fold in the chocolate chips then spoon the batter in a muffin tin covered with muffin papers.
4. Preheat your oven and bake the muffins at 350F for about twenty minutes or until it rises significantly and becomes aromatic.

These muffins taste best chilled.

Nutritional Content of One Serving:
Calories: 257 Fat: 11.3g Protein: 3.6g Carbohydrates: 39.4g

Milk Chocolate Cupcakes

Total Time Taken: 1 ½ hours
Yield: 12 Servings
Ingredients:

Cupcakes:
- ½ cup butter, softened
- ½ teaspoon salt
- ¾ cup white sugar
- 1 cup milk
- 1 teaspoon vanilla extract
- 2 cups all-purpose flour
- 2 eggs
- 2 teaspoons baking powder

Frosting:
- ½ cup milk chocolate chips, melted and chilled
- 1 cup butter, softened
- 2 cups powdered sugar

Directions:
1. To make the cupcakes, combine the butter and sugar until fluffy and pale.
2. Put in the eggs, one at a time, then mix in the vanilla and milk.
3. Put in the flour, baking powder and salt and mix using a spatula.
4. Spoon the batter into 12 muffin cups covered with muffin papers.
5. Preheat your oven and bake the cupcakes at 350F for about twenty minutes or until a golden-brown colour is achieved and it rises significantly.
6. Let cool down.
7. To make the frosting, combine the butter in a container until fluffy and pale.
8. Put in the sugar and stir thoroughly for five minutes.
9. Stir in the chocolate and mix thoroughly.
   10. Spoon the frosting in a pastry bag and top each cupcake with it.

These cupcakes taste best when fresh.

Nutritional Content of One Serving:
Calories: 438 Fat: 25.0g Protein: 4.0g Carbohydrates: 51.3g

Milky Banana Muffins

Total Time Taken: 1 hour
Yield: 12 Servings
Ingredients:
- ¼ cup canola oil

- ½ cup heavy cream
- ½ teaspoon salt
- 1 ½ cups all-purpose flour
- 1 teaspoon baking soda
- 1 teaspoon vanilla extract
- 2 bananas, mashed
- 2 eggs

Directions:

1. Mix the bananas, eggs, cream, oil and vanilla in a container.
2. Put in the flour, salt and baking soda then spoon the batter in a muffin tin covered with muffin papers.
3. Preheat your oven and bake the muffins at 350F for about twenty minutes or until it rises significantly and becomes aromatic.

These muffins taste best chilled.

Nutritional Content of One Serving:

Calories: 143 Fat: 7.3g Protein: 2.8g Carbohydrates: 16.7g

Millet Flour Plum Muffins

Total Time Taken: 1 hour
Yield: 12 Servings
Ingredients:
- ¼ cup coconut oil, melted
- ¼ teaspoon salt
- ½ cup light brown sugar
- 1 cup almond milk
- 1 cup millet flour
- 1 cup whole wheat flour
- 1 teaspoon baking soda
- 2 eggs
- 6 plums, pitted and sliced

Directions:

1. Mix the flours, salt, sugar and baking soda in a container.
2. Put in the remaining ingredients and mix thoroughly.
3. Fold in the plums then spoon the batter in a muffin tin lined with special muffin papers.
4. Preheat your oven and bake the muffins at 350F for about twenty minutes or until a golden-brown colour is achieved and it rises significantly.
5. *Let cool down before you serve.*

Nutritional Content of One Serving:

Calories: 210 Fat: 10.7g Protein: 4.0g Carbohydrates: 26.2g

Minty Chocolate Cupcakes

Total Time Taken: 1 ½ hours
Yield: 12 Servings
Ingredients:

Cupcakes:
- ¼ cup canola oil
- ½ cup cocoa powder
- ½ teaspoon baking powder
- ½ teaspoon salt
- 1 ½ cups all-purpose flour
- 1 cup buttermilk
- 1 cup white sugar
- 1 teaspoon baking soda
- 1 teaspoon vanilla extract
- 2 eggs

Frosting:
- 1 ½ cups dark chocolate chips
- 1 teaspoon peppermint extract
- 2 tablespoons butter
- 2/3 cup heavy cream

Directions:
1. To make the cupcakes, combine the flour, cocoa powder, sugar, baking soda, baking powder and salt in a container.
2. Put in the buttermilk, eggs, canola oil and vanilla and stir swiftly to combine.
3. Spoon the batter in a muffin cup covered with muffin papers.
4. Preheat your oven and bake the cupcakes at 350F for about twenty minutes or until well risen.
5. Let cool in the pan.
6. To make the frosting, bring the cream to the boiling in a saucepan. Turn off the heat and mix in the chocolate chips. Stir until melted and smooth then put in the peppermint extract and butter and mix thoroughly.
7. Let the frosting cool then put the frosting on top of each cupcake.

Best served chilled.

Nutritional Content of One Serving:
Calories: 298 Fat: 14.5g Protein: 5.0g Carbohydrates: 42.0g

Mixed Berry Buttermilk Muffins

Total Time Taken: 1 hour
Yield: 12 Servings
Ingredients:
- ¼ cup olive oil
- ½ cup white sugar

- ½ teaspoon baking soda
- ½ teaspoon salt
- 1 ¼ cups buttermilk
- 1 cup mixed berries
- 1 egg
- 1 teaspoon baking powder
- 1 teaspoon vanilla extract
- 2 cups all-purpose flour

Directions:

1. Mix the flour, salt, baking powder and baking soda in a container.
2. Put in the egg, olive oil, buttermilk and vanilla and mix thoroughly then mix in the sugar.
3. Fold in the berries then spoon the batter in a muffin tin lined using muffin papers of your choice.
4. Preheat your oven and bake the muffins at 350F for about twenty minutes or until a toothpick inserted into them comes out dry.

These muffins taste best chilled.

Nutritional Content of One Serving:

Calories: 167 Fat: 5.0g Protein: 3.5g Carbohydrates: 27.1g

Mocha Chocolate Chip Banana Muffins

Total Time Taken: 1 hour

Yield: 12 Servings

Ingredients:

- ¼ teaspoon salt
- ½ cup dark chocolate chips
- ½ cup light brown sugar
- ½ cup milk
- ½ teaspoon baking soda
- 1 ½ cups all-purpose flour
- 1 teaspoon baking powder
- 1 teaspoon vanilla extract
- 2 bananas, mashed
- 2 eggs
- 2 teaspoons instant coffee

Directions:

1. Mix the bananas, eggs, instant coffee, vanilla, milk and sugar in a container.
2. Stir in the remaining ingredients and mix thoroughly.
3. Fold in the chocolate chips then spoon the batter in 12 muffin cups covered with muffin papers.
4. Pre-heat the oven and bake at 350F for about twenty minutes or until a golden-brown colour is achieved and it rises significantly.

These muffins taste best chilled.

Nutritional Content of One Serving:

Calories: 138 Fat: 2.5g Protein: 3.4g Carbohydrates: 26.5g

Mocha Cupcakes

Total Time Taken: 1 ½ hours
Yield: 14 Servings
Ingredients:

Cupcakes:

- ½ cup canola oil
- ½ cup espresso
- ½ cup sour cream
- ½ teaspoon salt
- 1 cup light brown sugar
- 1 teaspoon vanilla extract
- 2 cups all-purpose flour
- 2 eggs
- 2 teaspoons baking powder

Frosting:

- ½ cup butter, softened
- ½ cup dark chocolate chips, melted
- 1 cup cream cheese
- 1 teaspoon instant coffee
- 2 cups powdered sugar

Directions:

1. To make the cupcakes, combine the oil and sugar in a container for a couple of minutes then put in the eggs and mix thoroughly.
2. Stir in the vanilla, sour cream and espresso then put in the flour, baking powder and salt.
3. Pour the batter in a muffin tin covered with muffin papers.
4. Preheat your oven and bake the cupcakes at 350F for about twenty minutes.
5. Let cool in the pan.
6. To make the frosting, combine the cream cheese and butter in a container until pale. Put in the sugar and continue whipping until fluffy.
7. Stir in the coffee and melted chocolate.
8. Spoon the frosting in a pastry bag and top the cupcakes with it.

These cupcakes taste best when fresh.

Nutritional Content of One Serving:

Calories: 404 Fat: 23.8g Protein: 4.5g Carbohydrates: 44.9g

Mocha Madness Cupcakes

Total Time Taken: 1 ½ hours
Yield: 12 Servings
Ingredients:

Cupcakes:

- ¼ teaspoon salt
- ½ cup canola oil

- ½ cup cocoa powder
- ½ cup water
- 1 ½ cups all-purpose flour
- 1 cup white sugar
- 1 teaspoon apple cider vinegar
- 1 teaspoon baking soda
- 1 teaspoon instant coffee
- 2 eggs
- 2 teaspoon vanilla extract

Frosting:
- ½ cup white sugar 1 pinch salt
- 1 cup butter, softened
- 1 cup dark chocolate chips, melted and cooled
- 1 teaspoon instant coffee
- 2 egg whites

Directions:
1. To make the cupcakes, combine the eggs and sugar in a container until fluffy and pale.
2. Put in the vanilla, vinegar, water, coffee and oil and mix thoroughly.
3. Stir in the dry ingredients then pour the batter in a muffin tin covered with muffin papers.
4. Preheat your oven and bake the cupcakes at 350F for about twenty minutes or until a toothpick inserted into them comes out dry.
5. Let cool in the pan.
6. To make the frosting, combine the egg whites, sugar and salt in a container and place over a hot water bath. Keep on heat until the sugar has melted then remove and start whipping until firm and shiny and chilled.
7. Put in the butter, all at once, and mix a few minutes until it comes together into a silky cream.
8. Stir in the chocolate and coffee and mix thoroughly.
9. Pipe the frosting over each cupcake and serve them fresh.

Nutritional Content of One Serving:
Calories: 437 Fat: 28.5g Protein: 4.6g Carbohydrates: 45.8g

Moist Banana Muffins

Total Time Taken: 1 hour
Yield: 12 Servings
Ingredients:
- 3 bananas, mashed
- 2 eggs
- 2 cups all-purpose flour
- 1 teaspoon vanilla extract
- 1 teaspoon baking soda
- 1 teaspoon baking powder
- 1 cup white sugar
- ½ cup dark chocolate chips
- ½ cup canola oil

Directions:
1. Mix the flour, baking soda, baking powder and sugar in a container.
2. Put in the remaining ingredients and stir for a few seconds to mix.
3. Fold in the chocolate chips then spoon the batter in a muffin tin covered with muffin papers.
4. Pre-heat the oven and bake at 350F for about twenty minutes or until it rises significantly and becomes aromatic.
5. Serve the muffins chilled or store them in an airtight container.

Nutritional Content of One Serving:
Calories: 280 Fat: 11.4g Protein: 3.7g Carbohydrates: 42.9g

Moist Banana Muffins

Total Time Taken: 1 hour
Yield: 12 Servings
Ingredients:
- 3 bananas, mashed
- 1 teaspoon vanilla extract
- 2 eggs
- ½ cup sour cream
- ½ cup coconut oil, melted
- 2 cups all-purpose flour
- ¼ teaspoon salt
- 2 teaspoons baking powder
- 2/3 cup white sugar

Directions:
1. Mix the bananas, sugar, vanilla, eggs, sour cream and coconut oil in a container.
2. Put in the flour, salt and baking powder and stir swiftly to combine.
3. Spoon the batter in a muffin tin covered with muffin papers.
4. Pre-heat the oven and bake at 350F for about twenty minutes or until a toothpick inserted into the center of a muffin comes out clean.

These muffins taste best chilled.

Nutritional Content of One Serving:
Calories: 255 Fat: 12.1g Protein: 3.7g Carbohydrates: 34.6g

Moist Chocolate Coffee Cupcakes

Total Time Taken: 1 ½ hours
Yield: 12 Servings
Ingredients:

Cupcakes:
- ¼ cup canola oil
- ½ cup buttermilk
- ½ cup cocoa powder
- ½ teaspoon salt

- 1 ½ cups all-purpose flour
- 1 cup brewed coffee
- 1 egg
- 1 teaspoon baking soda
- 1 teaspoon instant coffee
- 1 teaspoon vanilla extract

Frosting:
- 1 cup heavy cream
- 1 teaspoon vanilla extract
- 2 cups dark chocolate chips

Directions:
1. To make the cupcakes, combine the cocoa powder, flour, salt and baking soda in a container.
2. Stir in the egg, coffee, instant coffee, buttermilk, oil and vanilla and mix thoroughly.
3. Pour the batter in a muffin tin covered with muffin papers.
4. Preheat your oven and bake the cupcakes at 350F for about twenty minutes or until well risen. Let them cool in the pan.
5. To make the frosting, bring the cream to a boil. Turn off the heat and
6. put in the chocolate. Stir until melted and smooth then let cool to room temperature.
7. Stir in the vanilla then whip the cream using an electric mixer just until pale and firm.
8. Garnish each cupcake with whipped frosting and serve them fresh.

Nutritional Content of One Serving:
Calories: 244 Fat: 14.6g Protein: 4.6g Carbohydrates: 28.1g

Morning Glory Muffins

Total Time Taken: 1 hour
Yield: 12 Servings
Ingredients:
- 3 eggs
- 2 tablespoons chia seeds
- 1 teaspoon baking soda
- 1 cup grated carrots
- 1 ¾ cups all-purpose flour
- ½ teaspoon salt
- ½ teaspoon baking powder
- ½ cup walnuts, chopped
- ½ cup shredded coconut
- ½ cup raisins
- ½ cup canola oil
- ½ cup applesauce

Directions:
1. Mix the flour, baking soda, baking powder and salt in a container.
2. Put in the eggs, canola oil and applesauce and stir for a few seconds to mix.
3. Fold in the carrots, raisins, walnuts, coconut and chia seeds then spoon the batter in a muffin tin covered with muffin papers.

4. Pre-heat the oven and bake at 350F for about twenty minutes or until it rises significantly and starts to appear golden-brown.

These muffins taste best chilled.

Nutritional Content of One Serving:

Calories: 259 Fat: 16.2g Protein: 6.0g Carbohydrates: 23.7g

Morning Muffins

Total Time Taken: 1 ¼ hours
 Yield: 12 Servings

Ingredients:
- ¼ teaspoon salt
- ½ cup dried cranberries
- ½ cup light brown sugar
- ½ cup oat flour
- 1 ½ cups all-purpose flour
- 1 apple, cored and diced
- 1 cup buttermilk
- 1 cup grated carrots
- 1 teaspoon baking soda
- 1 teaspoon vanilla extract
- 2 eggs

Directions:
1. Mix the eggs and sugar in a container until pale and airy.
2. Put in the vanilla and buttermilk and mix thoroughly.
3. Fold in the flours, salt and baking soda then put in the carrots, cranberries and apple.
4. Spoon the batter in a muffin tin lined using muffin papers of your choice.
5. Pre-heat the oven and bake at 350F for about twenty minutes or until a toothpick inserted into them comes out dry.

These muffins taste best chilled.

Nutritional Content of One Serving:

Calories: 129 Fat: 1.3g Protein: 3.8g Carbohydrates: 25.0g

Muesli Apple Muffins

Total Time Taken: 1 hour
Yield: 16 Servings
Ingredients:
- ½ cup canola oil
- ½ teaspoon cinnamon powder
- ½ teaspoon salt
- 1 ½ cups milk
- 1 cup muesli
- 2 ½ cups all-purpose flour

- 2 eggs
- 2 red apples, cored and diced
- 2 teaspoons baking powder

Directions:

1. Mix the flour, salt, baking powder, cinnamon and muesli in a container.
2. Put in the eggs, canola oil and milk and mix thoroughly using a spatula.
3. Fold in the apples then spoon the batter in a muffin tin lined using muffin papers of your choice.
4. Pre-heat the oven and bake at 350F for about twenty minutes or until it rises significantly and starts to appear golden-brown.
5. Serve the muffins chilled or store them in an airtight container.

Nutritional Content of One Serving:

Calories: 182 Fat: 8.4g Protein: 4.0g Carbohydrates: 23.5g

Multigrain Muffins

Total Time Taken: 1 hour
Yield: 12 Servings
Ingredients:

- ¼ cup canola oil
- ¼ teaspoon salt
- ½ cup all-purpose flour
- ½ cup light brown sugar
- ½ cup walnuts
- ½ cup wheat bran
- 1 ½ cups buttermilk
- 1 cup whole wheat flour
- 2 eggs
- 2 tablespoons pumpkin seeds
- 2 tablespoons sunflower seeds
- 2 teaspoons baking powder

Directions:

1. Mix the flours, bran, baking powder and salt in a container.
2. Put in the eggs, buttermilk, oil, sugar, walnuts and seeds and mix using a spatula.
3. Spoon the batter in a muffin tin covered with muffin papers and preheat your oven and bake at 350F for about twenty minutes or until it rises significantly and starts to appear golden-brown.

These muffins taste best chilled.

Nutritional Content of One Serving:

Calories: 192 Fat: 9.8g Protein: 5.6g Carbohydrates: 22.2g

Nutella Peanut Butter Cupcakes

Total Time Taken: 1 ½ hours
Yield: 12 Servings
Ingredients:

Cupcakes:

- ¼ cup butter, softened
- ¼ teaspoon salt
- ½ cup buttermilk
- ½ cup smooth peanut butter
- ¾ cup light brown sugar
- 1 ½ cups all-purpose flour
- 1 ½ teaspoons baking powder
- 1 teaspoon vanilla extract
- 2 eggs

Frosting:

- 1 cup Nutella

Directions:

1. To make the cupcakes, combine the peanut butter, butter, sugar and vanilla in a container until creamy.
2. Put in the eggs and buttermilk and mix thoroughly.
3. Fold in the remaining ingredients then spoon the batter in a muffin tin covered with muffin papers.
4. Pre-heat the oven and bake at 350F for about twenty minutes or until it rises significantly and starts to appear golden-brown.
5. When chilled, top with Nutella and serve fresh.

Nutritional Content of One Serving:

Calories: 221 Fat: 11.2g Protein: 5.8g Carbohydrates: 25.7g

Nutella Stuffed Strawberry Muffins

Total Time Taken: 1 hour
Yield: 12 Servings
Ingredients:

- ¼ teaspoon salt
- ½ cup canola oil
- ½ cup Nutella
- ¾ cup milk
- 1 cup strawberries, sliced
- 1 cup white sugar
- 1 teaspoon vanilla extract
- 2 cups all-purpose flour
- 2 eggs
- 2 teaspoons baking powder

Directions:

1. Mix the eggs and sugar in a container until fluffy and pale.

2. Put in the vanilla and oil and mix thoroughly.
3. Stir in the milk then put in the flour, salt and baking powder and mix using a spatula.
4. Spoon half of the batter evenly in a muffin tin covered with muffin papers.
5. Top with a dollop of Nutella then spoon the rest of the batter over the Nutella.
6. Pre-heat the oven and bake at 350F for about twenty minutes or until fluffy and golden brown.
7. Let cool in the pan before you serve.

Nutritional Content of One Serving:

Calories: 259 Fat: 11.4g Protein: 3.8g Carbohydrates: 36.5g

Nutty Chocolate Chip Muffins

Total Time Taken: 1 hour
Yield: 12 Servings
Ingredients:
- 2 eggs
- 1 teaspoon vanilla extract
- 1 teaspoon baking powder
- 1 cup white sugar
- 1 cup walnuts, chopped
- 1 cup buttermilk
- 1 ½ cups all-purpose flour
- ½ teaspoon baking soda
- ½ cup dark chocolate chips
- ½ cup cocoa powder
- ¼ teaspoon salt
- ¼ cup canola oil

Directions:
1. Mix the flour, cocoa powder, sugar, baking soda, baking powder and salt in a container.
2. Put in the eggs, oil, vanilla and buttermilk and stir for a few seconds to mix.
3. Fold in the walnuts and chocolate chips then pour the batter in a muffin tin lined using muffin papers of your choice.
4. Pre-heat the oven and bake at 350F for about twenty minutes or until a toothpick inserted into them comes out dry.

These muffins taste best chilled.

Nutritional Content of One Serving:

Calories: 275 Fat: 13.6g Protein: 6.7g Carbohydrates: 36.2g

Nutty Double Chocolate Muffins

Total Time Taken: 1 hour
Yield: 12 Servings
Ingredients:
- ¼ cup canola oil
- ¼ cup cocoa powder
- ½ cup ground hazelnuts

- ½ teaspoon salt
- 1 1/2 cup all-purpose flour
- 1 cup dark chocolate chips
- 1 cup milk
- 1 cup white sugar
- 1 egg
- 1 teaspoon baking powder
- 1 teaspoon vanilla extract

Directions:
1. Mix the flour, cocoa powder, ground hazelnuts, salt, baking powder and sugar in a container.
2. Put in the egg, canola oil, milk and vanilla and stir for a few seconds to mix.
3. Fold in the chocolate chips then spoon the batter in a muffin tin covered with muffin papers.
4. Preheat your oven and bake the muffins at 350F for about twenty minutes or until a toothpick inserted into them comes out dry.

These muffins taste best chilled.

Nutritional Content of One Serving:
Calories: 247 Fat: 10.3g Protein: 4.2g Carbohydrates: 38.0g

Oatmeal Carrot Muffins

Total Time Taken: 1 hour
Yield: 12 Servings
Ingredients:
- 2 eggs
- 2 cups grated carrots
- 1 teaspoon baking powder
- 1 cup rolled oats
- 1 cup buttermilk
- 1 cup all-purpose flour
- ½ teaspoon ground ginger
- ½ teaspoon cinnamon powder
- ½ teaspoon baking soda
- ½ cup light brown sugar
- ½ cup crushed pineapple
- ½ cup canola oil
- ¼ teaspoon salt

Directions:
1. Mix the oats, flour, baking soda, baking powder, salt, cinnamon, ginger and sugar in a container.
2. Stir in the eggs, oil and buttermilk and stir for a few seconds to mix.
3. Fold in the carrots and pineapple then spoon the batter in a muffin tin covered with muffin papers.
4. Preheat your oven and bake the muffins at 350F for about twenty minutes or until it rises significantly and starts to appear golden-brown.

These muffins taste best chilled.

Nutritional Content of One Serving:

Calories: 197 Fat: 10.5g Protein: 3.8g Carbohydrates: 22.5g

Oatmeal Cranberry Muffins

Total Time Taken: 1 hour

Yield: 12 Servings

Ingredients:

- ¼ cup candied orange peel, diced
- ¼ cup light brown sugar
- ¼ cup milk
- ¼ cup olive oil
- ¼ teaspoon salt
- 1 cup all-purpose flour
- 1 cup fresh cranberries
- 1 cup rolled oats
- 1 teaspoon vanilla extract
- 2 bananas, mashed
- 2 eggs
- 2 tablespoons ground flaxseeds
- 2 teaspoons baking powder

Directions:

1. Mix the bananas, eggs, milk, olive oil, sugar and vanilla in a container.
2. Fold in the flour, flaxseeds, oats, baking powder and salt then put in the cranberries and orange peel.
3. Spoon the batter in a muffin tin covered with muffin papers.
4. Pre-heat the oven and bake at 350F for about twenty minutes or until it rises completely and is aromatic.
5. Let cool in the pan before you serve.

Nutritional Content of One Serving:

Calories: 157 Fat: 6.0g Protein: 3.5g Carbohydrates: 22.4g

Orange Almond Muffins

Total Time Taken: 1 ½ hours

Yield: 12 Servings

Ingredients:

- ½ teaspoon salt
- 1 cup white sugar
- 1 teaspoon baking powder
- 1 teaspoon vanilla extract
- 2 cups almond flour
- 2 small oranges
- 6 eggs

Directions:

1. Put the oranges in a saucepan and cover them with water. Boil the oranges for about half an hour until softened. Drain the oranges well and place them in a blender. Pulse until the desired smoothness is achieved.
2. Mix the eggs and sugar in a container until fluffy and pale.
3. Stir in the oranges then fold in the almond flour, baking powder and salt.
4. Spoon the batter in a muffin tin covered with muffin papers.
5. Preheat your oven and bake the muffins at 350F for about twenty minutes or until it rises significantly and starts to appear golden-brown.
6. Let the muffins cool to room temperature before you serve.

Nutritional Content of One Serving:

Calories: 130 Fat: 4.5g Protein: 3.9g Carbohydrates: 20.0g

Orange Glazed Cupcakes

Total Time Taken: 1 ½ hours
Yield: 12 Servings
Ingredients:

Cupcakes:
- ¼ cup candied ginger, chopped
- ¼ cup molasses
- ¼ teaspoon salt
- ½ cup butter, softened
- ½ teaspoon baking powder
- ½ teaspoon ground cloves
- ½ teaspoon ground ginger
- 1 cup light brown sugar
- 1 cup sour cream
- 1 tablespoon orange zest
- 1 teaspoon baking soda
- 1 teaspoon cinnamon powder
- 1 teaspoon grated ginger
- 2 cups all-purpose flour
- 2 eggs

Glaze:
- 1 cup powdered sugar
- 1 tablespoon orange juice
- 1 teaspoon vanilla extract

Directions:
1. To make the cupcakes, combine the butter, molasses and sugar in a container until creamy and pale.
2. Put in the sour cream, orange zest, ginger and eggs and mix thoroughly.
3. Fold in the flour, salt, baking soda, baking powder, cinnamon, ginger and cloves.
4. Fold in the ginger and mix using a spatula.
5. Spoon the batter in a muffin tin coated with baking muffin papers.
6. Pre-heat the oven and bake at 350F for about twenty minutes or until it rises significantly and becomes aromatic.

7. Let them cool down in the pan.
8. For the glaze, combine all the ingredients in a container.
9. Sprinkle the glaze over the cupcakes and serve them fresh.

Nutritional Content of One Serving:

Calories: 304 Fat: 12.7g Protein: 3.8g Carbohydrates: 44.6g

Orange Iced Cupcakes

Total Time Taken: 1 ¼ hours
Yield: 12 Servings

Ingredients:
- ¼ cup candied orange peel, diced
- ½ cup butter, softened
- ½ cup buttermilk
- ½ teaspoon salt
- ¾ cup white sugar
- 1 ½ teaspoons baking powder
- 1 ¾ cups all-purpose flour
- 1 teaspoon vanilla extract
- 3 eggs

Frosting:
- 1 ½ cups powdered sugar
- 1 tablespoon butter, melted
- 1 tablespoon orange juice
- 1 teaspoon orange zest

Directions:
1. To make the cupcakes, combine the butter and sugar in a container until fluffy and pale.
2. Put in the eggs and mix thoroughly then mix in the vanilla and buttermilk.
3. Fold in the flour, baking powder, salt and orange peel then spoon the batter in a muffin tin covered with muffin papers.
4. Pre-heat the oven and bake at 350F for about twenty minutes or until a toothpick inserted into them comes out dry. Let them cool in the pan.
5. For the glaze, combine all the ingredients in a container and mix thoroughly.
6. Sprinkle each cupcake with frosting.

Nutritional Content of One Serving:

Calories: 272 Fat: 10.0g Protein: 3.7g Carbohydrates: 42.9g

Orange Olive Oil Muffins

Total Time Taken: 1 hour
Yield: 12 Servings
Ingredients:
- ¼ cup olive oil
- ¼ teaspoon salt
- ½ cup fresh orange juice

242

- ½ cup sliced almonds
- 1 cup all-purpose flour
- 1 cup almond flour
- 1 cup white sugar
- 1 tablespoon orange zest
- 1 teaspoon baking powder
- 1 teaspoon vanilla extract
- 4 eggs

Directions:

1. Mix the eggs and sugar in a container until fluffy and pale.
2. Put in the orange juice, oil, vanilla and orange zest and mix thoroughly.
3. Fold in the flours, salt and baking powder then spoon the batter in a muffin tin coated with baking muffin papers.
4. Top each muffin with sliced almonds and preheat your oven and bake at 350F for about twenty minutes or until it rises significantly and starts to appear golden-brown.

These muffins taste best chilled.

Nutritional Content of One Serving:

Calories: 200 Fat: 8.9g Protein: 4.4g Carbohydrates: 27.5g

Orange Pecan Muffins

Total Time Taken: 1 ¼ hours
Yield: 12 Servings

Ingredients:

- ¼ cup fresh orange juice
- ¼ teaspoon cinnamon
- ¼ teaspoon salt
- ½ cup dried cranberries
- ½ cup milk
- ½ cup white sugar
- 1 ½ teaspoons baking powder
- 1 ¾ cups all-purpose flour
- 1 cup pecans, chopped
- 1 tablespoon orange zest
- 2 eggs
- 6 tablespoons butter, melted

Directions:

1. Mix the flour, salt, baking powder, sugar and cinnamon in a container.
2. Put in the eggs, butter, milk, orange juice and orange zest and stir for a few seconds to mix.
3. Fold in the pecans and cranberries then spoon the batter in a muffin tin coated with baking muffin papers.
4. Preheat your oven and bake the muffins at 350F for about twenty minutes or until it rises significantly and seems golden.
5. *Let cool down before you serve.*

Orange Poppy Seed Muffins

Total Time Taken: 1 ½ hours
Yield: 12 Servings

Ingredients:
- ½ cup coconut oil
- ½ cup whole wheat flour
- ½ teaspoon salt
- 1 ½ teaspoon baking powder
- 1 cup all-purpose flour
- 1 orange, washed
- 1 teaspoon vanilla extract
- 2 tablespoons poppy seed
- 3 eggs

Directions:
1. Put the orange in a saucepan and cover it with water. Cook until softened then drain and place the orange in a blender.
2. Put in the coconut oil, eggs and vanilla and blend until the desired smoothness is achieved.
3. Stir in the flours, salt, baking powder and poppy seed and mix using a spatula.
4. Spoon the batter in a muffin tin covered with muffin papers and preheat your oven and bake at 350F for about twenty minutes or until it rises significantly and seems golden.

These muffins taste best chilled.

Nutritional Content of One Serving:
Calories: 168 Fat: 11.0g Protein: 3.4g Carbohydrates: 14.5g

Orange Soda Cupcakes

Total Time Taken: 1 ½ cups
Yield: 12 Servings
Ingredients:

Cupcakes:
- ¼ cup vegetable oil
- ¼ teaspoon salt
- ½ cup butter, softened
- ½ cup white sugar 3 egg whites
- 1 ¼ cups orange soda
- 1 ½ cups all-purpose flour
- 1 ½ teaspoons baking powder
- 1 cup cream cheese
- 1 teaspoon orange zest **Frosting:**
- 1 teaspoon vanilla extract

- 2 cups powdered sugar
- 2 tablespoons heavy cream

Directions:

1. To make the cupcakes, combine the egg whites, oil, orange soda and orange zest in a container.
2. Put in the remaining ingredients then spoon the batter in a muffin tin covered with muffin papers.
3. Pre-heat the oven and bake at 350F for about twenty minutes or until a toothpick inserted into them comes out dry.
4. Let cool in the pan.
5. To make the frosting, combine the butter and cream cheese in a container until fluffy.
6. Put in the sugar and mix for five minutes on high speed.
7. Stir in the cream and vanilla and mix for 1 additional minute.
8. Pipe the frosting over each cupcake and serve them fresh.

Nutritional Content of One Serving:

Calories: 368 Fat: 20.1g Protein: 4.1g Carbohydrates: 44.4g

Orange Yogurt Muffins

Total Time Taken: 1 hour
Yield: 12 Servings
Ingredients:

- ¼ cup candied orange peel, chopped
- ½ cup canola oil
- ½ teaspoon salt
- 1 cup plain yogurt
- 1 egg
- 1 orange, zested and juice
- 2 cups all-purpose flour
- 2 teaspoons baking powder

Directions:

1. Mix the flour, baking powder and salt in a container.
2. Put in the yogurt, orange zest, orange juice, oil and egg and mix thoroughly.
3. Fold in the orange peel then spoon the batter in a muffin tin lined using muffin papers of your choice.
4. Pre-heat the oven and bake at 350F for about twenty minutes or until it rises significantly and starts to appear golden-brown.

These muffins taste best chilled.

Nutritional Content of One Serving:

Calories: 186 Fat: 9.9g Protein: 3.9g Carbohydrates: 20.1g

Oreo Cream Cupcakes

Total Time Taken: 1 ½ hours
Yield: 12 Servings
Ingredients:

Cupcakes:
- ¼ teaspoon salt
- 1 cup butter, softened
- 1 cup buttermilk
- 1 cup white sugar
- 1 tablespoon vanilla extract
- 2 cups all-purpose flour
- 2 eggs
- 2 teaspoons baking powder
- 6 Oreo cookies, crushed

Topping:
- 2 cups heavy cream, whipped
- 6 Oreo cookies, chopped

Directions:
1. To make the cupcakes, combine the flour, salt, baking powder and sugar in a container.
2. Put in the butter and stir until grainy.
3. In a small container, mix the eggs, buttermilk and vanilla. Pour this mixture progressively over the flour and mix for a minute on high speed.
4. Spoon the batter in a muffin tin covered with muffin papers.
5. Pre-heat the oven and bake at 350F for about twenty minutes or until it rises significantly and starts to appear golden-brown.
6. Let cool down before you serve.

Nutritional Content of One Serving:

Calories: 412 Fat: 25.8g Protein: 4.9g Carbohydrates: 41.9g

Passionfruit Cupcakes

Total Time Taken: 1 ½ hours
Yield: 12 Servings
Ingredients:

Cupcakes:
- ¼ cup passionfruit juice
- ½ cup butter, softened
- ½ cup milk
- ½ cup white sugar
- ½ teaspoon salt
- 1 ½ teaspoons baking powder
- 1 13/4 cups all-purpose flour
- 1 teaspoon vanilla extract
- 2 eggs

Frosting:
- 1 cup butter, softened
- 2 cups powdered sugar
- 2 tablespoons passionfruit juice

Directions:
1. To make the cupcakes, combine the butter and sugar in a container until pale and light.
2. Put in the eggs and mix thoroughly then mix in the vanilla, passionfruit juice and milk.
3. Fold in the flour, salt and baking powder then spoon the batter in a muffin tin covered with muffin papers.
4. Pre-heat the oven and bake at 350F for about twenty minutes or until a golden-brown colour is achieved.
5. Let the cupcakes cool down.
6. To make the frosting, combine the butter and sugar in a container for five minutes until pale.
7. Stir in the passionfruit juice and mix thoroughly.
8. Top each cupcake with the frosting and serve fresh.

Nutritional Content of One Serving:

Calories: 494 Fat: 24.4g Protein: 6.1g Carbohydrates: 63.8g

Peach and Cream Muffins

Total Time Taken: 1 hour
Yield: 12 Servings
Ingredients:
- ¼ teaspoon salt
- ½ cup white sugar
- 1 cup butter, melted
- 1 cup sour cream
- 1 teaspoon vanilla extract
- 2 cups all-purpose flour
- 2 peaches, pitted and diced
- 2 teaspoons baking powder

Directions:
1. Mix the butter, sour cream, sugar and vanilla in a container until creamy.
2. Put in the flour, baking powder and salt then fold in the peaches.
3. Spoon the batter in a muffin tin covered with muffin papers and preheat your oven and bake at 350F for about twenty minutes or until a golden-brown colour is achieved and it rises significantly.

These muffins taste best chilled.

Nutritional Content of One Serving:

Calories: 292 Fat: 19.6g Protein: 3.1g Carbohydrates: 27.1g

Peachy Muffins

Total Time Taken: 1 hour
Yield: 12 Servings
Ingredients:

- ½ cup canola oil
- ½ cup plain yogurt
- ½ cup whole wheat flour
- ½ teaspoon salt
- ¾ cup white sugar
- 1 cup all-purpose flour
- 1 teaspoon baking soda
- 2 eggs
- 2 peaches, pitted and diced
- 2 tablespoons chia seeds

Directions:

1. Mix the flours, salt, chia seeds and baking soda in a container.
2. Mix the oil, sugar and eggs in another container and whip until volume increases to twice what it was.
3. Put in the yogurt then mix in the flour. Fold in the peaches.
4. Spoon the batter in a muffin tin covered with muffin papers.
5. Preheat your oven and bake the muffins at 350F for about twenty minutes or until it rises significantly and starts to appear golden-brown.

These muffins taste best chilled.

Nutritional Content of One Serving:

Calories: 219 Fat: 10.9g Protein: 3.8g Carbohydrates: 26.9g

Peanut Butter Banana Cupcakes

Total Time Taken: 1 ½ hours
Yield: 12 Servings
Ingredients:

Cupcakes:
- ¼ teaspoon salt
- ½ cup canola oil
- ½ cup milk
- 1 ¾ cups all-purpose flour
- 1 egg
- 1 teaspoon baking soda
- 1 teaspoon vanilla extract
- 2 bananas, mashed

Frosting:
- ½ cup smooth peanut butter
- 1 cup cream cheese

- 1 cup powdered sugar

Directions:
1. To make the cupcakes, combine the bananas, canola oil, milk, egg and vanilla.
2. Stir in the flour, salt and baking soda then spoon the batter in a muffin tin covered with muffin papers.
3. Pre-heat the oven and bake at 350F for about twenty minutes or until it rises significantly and starts to appear golden-brown.
4. To make the frosting, combine all the ingredients in a container until creamy and fluffy.
5. Apply the frosting on top of each cupcake and serve them fresh.

Nutritional Content of One Serving:
Calories: 345 Fat: 22.1g Protein: 7.0g Carbohydrates: 31.5g

Pear and Ginger Muffins

Total Time Taken: 1 hour
Yield: 12 Servings
Ingredients:
- ¼ teaspoon salt
- ½ cup buttermilk
- ½ cup canola oil
- ½ cup dark chocolate chips
- ½ cup light brown sugar
- 1 ½ cups all-purpose flour
- 1 teaspoon baking soda
- 1 teaspoon grated ginger
- 1 teaspoon vanilla extract
- 2 eggs
- 2 pears, cored and diced

Directions:
1. Mix the eggs and sugar in a container until fluffy and pale. Stir in the oil and mix thoroughly then put in the buttermilk and mix thoroughly.
2. Stir in the vanilla and ginger then fold in the flour, salt and baking powder.
3. Put in the pears and dark chocolate and stir lightly using a spatula.
4. Spoon the batter in a muffin tin covered with muffin papers and preheat your oven and bake at 350F for about twenty minutes or until it rises significantly and starts to appear golden-brown.

These muffins taste best chilled.

Nutritional Content of One Serving:
Calories: 220 Fat: 11.4g Protein: 3.4g Carbohydrates: 27.2g

Pecan Pie Muffins

Total Time Taken: 1 hour

Yield: 10 Servings

Ingredients:

- 2 eggs
- 1 teaspoon vanilla extract
- 1 cup light brown sugar
- 1 cup butter, melted
- 1 ½ cups pecans, chopped
- ½ cup all-purpose flour
- ¼ teaspoon salt

Directions:

1. Mix the eggs and sugar in a container until fluffy and volume increases to twice what it was.
2. Put in the vanilla and melted butter and mix thoroughly.
3. Fold in the flour, pecans and salt then spoon the batter in a muffin tin covered with muffin papers.
4. Pre-heat the oven and bake at 350F for about twenty minutes or until a golden-brown colour is achieved.

These muffins taste best chilled.

Nutritional Content of One Serving:

Calories: 264 Fat: 20.3g Protein: 2.1g Carbohydrates: 19.3g

Persimmon Muffins

Total Time Taken: 1 hour

Yield: 12 Servings

Ingredients:

- ½ cup butter, melted
- ½ cup whole wheat flour
- ½ teaspoon cinnamon powder
- ½ teaspoon ground ginger
- ½ teaspoon salt
- ¾ cup buttermilk
- 1 ½ cups all-purpose flour
- 1 teaspoon vanilla extract
- 2 eggs
- 2 persimmon fruits, diced
- 2 teaspoons baking powder

Directions:

1. Mix the flours, salt, baking powder, ginger and cinnamon in a container.
2. Stir in the eggs, butter, buttermilk and vanilla and stir for a few seconds to mix.
3. Fold in the persimmon then spoon the batter in a muffin tin covered with muffin papers.
4. Pre-heat the oven and bake at 350F for about twenty minutes or until it rises significantly and starts to appear golden-brown.

5. Serve the muffins chilled or store them in an airtight container for maximum four days.

Nutritional Content of One Serving:

Calories: 182 Fat: 8.7g Protein: 3.8g Carbohydrates: 22.4g

Pink Coconut Cupcakes

Total Time Taken: 1 ½ hours
Yield: 12 Servings
Ingredients:

Cupcakes:
- ½ cup butter, softened
- ½ cup shredded coconut
- ½ cup white sugar
- ½ teaspoon salt
- 1 ½ cups all-purpose flour
- 1 teaspoon baking powder
- 1 teaspoon vanilla extract
- 2 eggs
- 2/3 cup whole milk

Frosting:
- ½ teaspoon pink food coloring
- 1 cup butter, softened
- 2 cups powdered sugar
- 2 tablespoons heavy cream

Directions:
1. To make the cupcakes, combine the butter, sugar and vanilla in a container until fluffy and pale.
2. Put in the eggs and mix thoroughly then fold in the flour, salt, baking powder and coconut, alternating it with milk.
3. Spoon the batter in a muffin tin covered with muffin papers and preheat your oven and bake at 350F for about twenty minutes or until a golden-brown colour is achieved and it rises significantly.
4. Let the cupcakes cool down.
5. To make the frosting, combine the butter and sugar in a container until fluffy and pale.
6. Put in the cream and food colouring and continue mixing a few additional minutes until airy.
7. Spoon the frosting on top of each cupcake before you serve.

Nutritional Content of One Serving:

Calories: 410 Fat:26.4g Protein: 3.4g Carbohydrates: 41.7g

Pink Lemonade Cupcakes

Total Time Taken: 1 ½ hours
Yield: 12 Servings
Ingredients:

Cupcakes:
- ¼ teaspoon salt

- ½ cup milk
- ¾ cup butter, softened
- 1 cup white sugar
- 1 drop red food coloring
- 1 egg white
- 1 tablespoon lemon zest
- 1 teaspoon vanilla extract
- 2 ½ cups all-purpose flour
- 2 eggs
- 2 tablespoons lemon juice
- 2 teaspoons baking powder

Frosting:
- 1 cup butter
- 1 drop red food coloring
- 2 cups powdered sugar

Directions:
1. To make the cupcakes, combine the butter and sugar in a container until fluffy and pale.
2. Put in the eggs and egg white and mix thoroughly.
3. Stir in the vanilla, lemon juice, lemon zest, milk and food colouring and mix thoroughly.
4. Put in the dry ingredients and fold them in using a spatula.
5. Spoon the batter in a muffin tin covered with muffin papers.
6. Pre-heat the oven and bake at 350F for about twenty minutes or until a golden-brown colour is achieved and it rises significantly.
7. Let cool in the pan.
8. To make the frosting, combine the butter in a container until fluffy. Put in the sugar and continue mixing for a few minutes on high speed.
9. Put in the food colouring then pipe the frosting over each cupcake.

The cupcakes taste best chilled.

Nutritional Content of One Serving:
Calories: 442 Fat: 24.1g Protein: 3.9g Carbohydrates: 54.6g

Pink Velvet Cupcakes

Total Time Taken: 1 ½ hours
Yield: 12 Servings
Ingredients:

Cupcakes:
- ¼ teaspoon red food coloring
- ½ cup sour cream
- ½ cup white sugar
- ½ teaspoon salt
- 1 ½ teaspoon baking powder
- 1 2/3 cups all-purpose flour
- 1 egg

- 1 teaspoon vanilla extract

Frosting:
- 1 cup butter, softened
- 1 teaspoon vanilla extract
- 2 cups powdered sugar

Directions:
1. To make the cupcakes, combine the egg and sugar until pale. Put in the vanilla and mix thoroughly then mix in the sour cream and food coloring.
2. Stir in the remaining ingredients and stir for a few seconds to mix.
3. Spoon the batter in 12 muffin cups covered with muffin papers.
4. Preheat your oven and bake the cupcakes at 350F for about twenty minutes or until the cupcake pass the toothpick test.
5. Let the cupcakes cool down.
6. To make the frosting, combine the butter until pale. Put in the sugar and stir thoroughly until blended.
7. Stir in the vanilla and mix thoroughly then spoon the buttercream in a pastry bag and pipe on each cupcake.

Nutritional Content of One Serving:
Calories: 336 Fat: 17.9g Protein: 2.7g Carbohydrates: 42.3g

Plum Whole Wheat Muffins

Total Time Taken: 1 hour
Yield: 12 Servings
Ingredients:
- ¼ cup all-purpose flour
- ¼ cup canola oil
- ½ cup buttermilk
- ½ teaspoon salt
- 1 ½ cups whole wheat flour
- 1 tablespoon chia seeds
- 1 teaspoon vanilla extract
- 2 eggs
- 2 teaspoons baking powder
- 4 plums, pitted and diced

Directions:
1. Mix the flours, baking powder, salt and chia seeds in a container.
2. Put in the remaining ingredients and stir for a few seconds to mix using a spatula.
3. Spoon the batter in a muffin tin covered with muffin papers.
4. Preheat your oven and bake the muffins at 350F for about twenty minutes or until it rises significantly and seems golden.

These muffins taste best chilled.

Nutritional Content of One Serving:
Calories: 142 Fat: 6.4g Protein: 3.8g Carbohydrates: 17.4g

Pumpkin Apple Muffins

Total Time Taken: 1 ¼ hours
Yield: 12 Servings

Ingredients:

- 2 red apples, cored and diced
- 2 eggs
- 1 teaspoon pumpkin pie spices
- 1 teaspoon baking soda
- 1 cup pumpkin puree
- 1 ½ cups whole wheat flour
- ½ teaspoon salt
- ½ teaspoon baking powder
- ½ cup light brown sugar
- ½ cup canola oil
- ½ cup all-purpose flour
- ¼ cup milk

Directions:

1. Mix the flours, baking soda, baking powder, salt and spices in a container.
2. Put in the eggs, pumpkin puree, milk, oil and sugar and stir for a few seconds to mix.
3. Fold in the apples then spoon the batter in a muffin tin covered with muffin papers.
4. Pre-heat the oven and bake at 350F for about twenty minutes or until it rises significantly and starts to appear golden-brown.

These muffins taste best chilled.

Nutritional Content of One Serving:

Calories: 215 Fat: 10.2g Protein: 3.6g Carbohydrates: 28.2g

Pumpkin Apple Streusel Muffins

Total Time Taken: 1 ¼ hours
Yield: 14 Servings
Ingredients:

Muffins:

- ¼ cup canola oil
- ¼ teaspoon salt
- ½ cup oat flour
- 1 ¼ cups pumpkin puree
- 1 cup white sugar
- 1 teaspoon baking powder
- 1 teaspoon baking soda
- 1 teaspoon pumpkin pie spices
- 2 apples, peeled and diced
- 2 cups all-purpose flour
- 2 eggs

Streusel:
- ¼ cup butter
- ¼ cup rolled oats
- ½ cup all-purpose flour
- 1 pinch salt
- 2 tablespoons dark brown sugar

Directions:
1. For the muffins, combine the flours, sugar, baking soda, baking powder, salt and spices in a container.
2. Put in the pumpkin puree, eggs, canola oil and apples and stir for a few seconds to mix.
3. Spoon the batter in a muffin tin covered with muffin papers.
4. Pre-heat the oven and bake at 350F for about twenty minutes or until it rises completely and is aromatic.
5. *Let cool down before you serve.*

Nutritional Content of One Serving:

Calories: 252 Fat: 8.5g Protein: 4.1g Carbohydrates: 41.5g

Pumpkin Chocolate Chip Muffins

Total Time Taken: 1 hour
Yield: 12 Servings
Ingredients:
- 2 eggs
- 1 teaspoon vanilla extract
- 1 teaspoon baking soda
- 1 cup pumpkin puree
- 1 ½ cups all-purpose flour
- ½ teaspoon ground star anise
- ½ teaspoon ground ginger
- ½ teaspoon cinnamon powder
- ½ cup oat flour
- ½ cup dark chocolate chips
- ¼ teaspoon salt
- ¼ cup canola oil

Directions:
1. Mix the pumpkin puree, oil, eggs and vanilla in a container and mix thoroughly.
2. Fold in the flours, salt, baking soda and spices.
3. Spoon the batter in a muffin tin covered with muffin papers.
4. Preheat your oven and bake the muffins at 350F for about twenty minutes or until it rises significantly and starts to appear golden-brown.

These muffins taste best chilled.

Nutritional Content of One Serving:

Calories: 155 Fat: 7.1g Protein: 3.6g Carbohydrates: 19.8g

Pumpkin Nutella Muffins

Total Time Taken: 1 hour
Yield: 12 Servings
Ingredients:

- ¼ teaspoon salt
- ½ cup coconut oil, melted
- ½ cup Nutella
- ½ teaspoon ground ginger
- ½ teaspoon ground nutmeg
- 1 ½ cups pumpkin puree
- 1 cup white sugar
- 1 teaspoon baking powder
- 1 teaspoon baking soda
- 1 teaspoon cinnamon powder
- 1 teaspoon vanilla extract
- 2 cups all-purpose flour
- 2 eggs

Directions:

1. Mix the flour, sugar, baking powder, baking soda, salt, cinnamon, nutmeg and ginger.
2. Put in the eggs, vanilla, pumpkin puree and coconut oil and stir for a few seconds to mix.
3. Spoon the batter in a muffin tin covered with muffin papers.
4. Drop a spoonful of Nutella on top of each muffin then swirl it with a toothpick.
5. Pre-heat the oven and bake at 350F for about twenty minutes or until it rises significantly and starts to appear golden-brown.

These muffins taste best chilled.

Nutritional Content of One Serving:

Calories: 256 Fat: 11.1g Protein: 3.6g Carbohydrates: 37.2g

Pumpkin Pecan Crunch Muffins

Total Time Taken: 1 ¼ hours
Yield: 12 Servings
Ingredients:

Muffins:

- ¼ cup butter, chilled
- ¼ teaspoon salt
- ½ cup all-purpose flour
- ½ cup coconut milk Pecan crunch:
- ½ cup coconut oil, melted
- ½ cup ground pecans
- ½ cup light brown sugar
- ½ cup pecans, chopped
- 1 ½ cups all-purpose flour

- 1 cup pumpkin puree
- 1 teaspoon baking soda
- 1 teaspoon pumpkin pie spices
- 2 eggs
- 2 tablespoons light brown sugar

Directions:

1. For the muffins, combine the dry ingredients in a container.
2. Put in the remaining ingredients, all at once, and stir for a few seconds to mix just until incorporated.
3. Spoon the batter in a muffin tin coated with baking muffin papers.
4. For the pecan crunch, combine the ingredients in a container until sandy.
5. Spread the crunch over the muffins and preheat your oven and bake at 350F for about twenty minutes or until the top is crunchy and golden brown.
6. Let cool in the pan before you serve.

Nutritional Content of One Serving:

Calories: 274 Fat: 18.0g Protein: 3.8g Carbohydrates: 26.0g

Pure Vanilla Muffins

Total Time Taken: 1 hour
Yield: 10 Servings
Ingredients:

- ¼ cup sour cream
- ½ cup canola oil
- ½ cup white sugar
- ½ teaspoon salt
- 1 ½ cups all-purpose flour
- 1 teaspoon baking powder
- 1 teaspoon vanilla extract
- 2 eggs

Directions:

1. Mix the eggs and sugar in a container until pale and light.
2. Put in the canola oil, vanilla and sour cream and mix thoroughly.
3. Fold in the flour, salt and baking powder then spoon the batter in a muffin tin covered with muffin papers.
4. Pre-heat the oven and bake at 350F for about twenty minutes or until it rises significantly and seems golden.

These muffins taste best chilled.

Nutritional Content of One Serving:

Calories: 229 Fat: 13.2g Protein: 3.2g Carbohydrates: 24.9g

Quick Coffee Muffins

Total Time Taken: 1 hour
Yield: 12 Servings
Ingredients:

- ¼ cup brewed espresso
- ¼ teaspoon salt
- ½ cup canola oil
- ½ cup hot water
- ½ teaspoon baking soda
- ¾ cup cocoa powder
- 1 ½ cups white sugar
- 1 ¾ cups all-purpose flour
- 1 cup buttermilk
- 1 teaspoon baking powder
- 1 teaspoon vanilla extract
- 2 eggs

Directions:

1. Mix the dry ingredients in a container.
2. Put in the remaining ingredients and stir for a few seconds to mix.
3. Pour the batter in a muffin tin covered with muffin papers and preheat your oven and bake at 350F for about twenty minutes or until a toothpick inserted into them comes out dry.
4. *Let cool down before you serve.*

Nutritional Content of One Serving:

Calories: 277 Fat: 10.9g Protein: 4.6g Carbohydrates: 44.1g

Quinoa Cranberry Muffins

Total Time Taken: 1 hour
Yield: 12 Servings
Ingredients:

- ¼ cup all-purpose flour
- ¼ cup butter, melted
- ¼ cup white sugar
- ¼ teaspoon salt
- ½ cup quinoa flour
- 1 cup cranberries
- 1 cup plain yogurt
- 1 cup whole wheat flour
- 2 eggs
- 2 tablespoons sunflower seeds
- 2 teaspoons baking powder

Directions:

1. Mix the flours, salt, baking powder, sunflower seeds in a container.
2. Put in the yogurt, eggs, sugar and butter and stir for a few seconds to mix.

258

3. Fold in the cranberries then spoon the batter in a muffin tin coated with baking muffin papers.
4. Pre-heat the oven and bake at 350F for about twenty minutes or until it rises significantly and seems golden.
5. *Let cool down before you serve.*

Nutritional Content of One Serving:

Calories: 149 Fat: 5.7g Protein: 5.2g Carbohydrates: 18.1g

Quinoa Peach Muffins

Total Time Taken: 1 hour
Yield: 12 Servings
Ingredients:

- 2 cups all-purpose flour
- 1 teaspoon vanilla extract
- 1 teaspoon baking powder
- 1 egg
- 1 cup cooked quinoa
- 1 cup buttermilk
- ¾ cups light brown sugar
- ½ teaspoon baking soda
- ¼ teaspoon salt
- ¼ cup canola oil

Directions:

1. Mix the quinoa, canola oil, egg, buttermilk and vanilla in a container.
2. Stir in the sugar and mix thoroughly then put in the flour, salt, baking powder and baking soda.
3. Spoon the batter in a muffin tin covered with muffin papers.
4. Pre-heat the oven and bake at 350F for about twenty minutes or until well risen.
5. *Let cool down before you serve.*

Nutritional Content of One Serving:

Calories: 217 Fat: 6.1g Protein: 5.3g Carbohydrates: 35.1g

Almond Blueberry Cookies

Total Time Taken: 1 ¼ hours
Yield: 20 Servings

Ingredients:

- ½ cup butter, softened
- 1 teaspoon lemon zest
- 1 egg
- ¼ cup whole milk
- 1 teaspoon almond extract
- 1 ¼ cups all-purpose flour
- 1 cup ground almonds
- ¼ teaspoon salt
- ½ teaspoon baking soda

- ½ cup dried blueberries
- ¼ cup sliced almonds
- 2/3 cup white sugar

Directions:
1. Mix the butter, sugar and lemon zest in a container until fluffy and pale.
2. Put in the egg and milk and mix thoroughly then fold in the flour, ground almonds, baking soda, salt and blueberries.
3. Drop spoonfuls of batter on a baking tray covered with parchment paper and top each cookie with almond slices.
4. Preheat your oven and bake the cookies at 350F for about fifteen minutes or until a golden-brown colour is achieved and fragrant.
5. Serve Chilled or store them in an airtight container for maximum 1 week.

Nutritional Content of One Serving:
Calories: 136 Fat: 8.0g Protein: 2.5g Carbohydrates: 14.6g

Almond Cookies

Total Time Taken: 1 ¼ hours
Yield: 20 Servings

Ingredients:
- ½ cup butter, softened
- 1 teaspoon almond extract
- 2 egg yolks
- 1 ½ cups all-purpose flour
- ½ cup almond flour
- ¼ teaspoon salt
- 1 teaspoon baking powder
- ½ cup sliced almonds
- 2/3 cup white sugar

Directions:
1. Mix the butter, sugar and almond extract in a container until fluffy and pale.
2. Put in the egg yolks and stir thoroughly until blended.
3. Fold in the flours, salt and baking powder.
4. Drop spoonfuls of batter on a baking sheet coated with baking paper.
5. Top each cookie with sliced almonds and preheat your oven and bake at 350F for about fifteen minutes until a golden-brown colour is achieved on the edges.
6. These cookies taste best chilled.

Nutritional Content of One Serving:
Calories: 124 Fat: 6.7g Protein: 1.9g Carbohydrates: 14.7g

Amaretti Cookies

Total Time Taken: 1 ¼ hours
Yield: 10 Servings

Ingredients:

- ¼ cup all-purpose flour
- ¼ teaspoon salt 2 egg whites
- ½ cup light brown sugar
- ½ teaspoon baking powder
- 1 teaspoon vanilla extract
- 2 cups almond flour

Directions:

1. Whip the egg whites with salt and vanilla in a container until fluffy.
2. Put in the sugar and continue mixing until shiny and firm.
3. Drop spoonfuls of batter on a baking tray coated with baking paper.
4. Pre-heat the oven and bake at 350F for about twenty minutes or until a golden-brown colour is achieved and crisp.
5. *These cookies taste best chilled.*

Nutritional Content of One Serving:

Calories: 76 Fat: 2.8g Protein: 2.2g Carbohydrates: 10.9g

Amaretti Cookies

Total Time Taken: 1 hour
Yield: 10 Servings

Ingredients:

- 2 cups almond flour
- 1 teaspoon vanilla extract
- ½ teaspoon almond extract
- 2 egg whites
- 2/3 cup light brown sugar

Directions:

1. Mix the egg whites until fluffy.
2. Put in the vanilla and sugar and continue whipping until shiny and firm.
3. Fold in the almond flour then drop spoonfuls of batter on a baking tray coated with baking paper.
4. Preheat your oven and bake the cookies at 350F for about fifteen minutes or until a golden-brown colour is achieved on the edges.
5. These cookies taste best chilled.

Nutritional Content of One Serving:

Calories: 74 Fat: 2.8g Protein: 1.9g Carbohydrates: 10.8g

American Chocolate Chunk Cookies

Total Time Taken: 1 ¼ hours
 Yield: 20 Servings

Ingredients:
- ½ cup smooth peanut butter
- ½ cup light brown sugar
- 1 egg
- 1 teaspoon vanilla extract
- 1 cup all-purpose flour
- ¼ teaspoon salt
- ½ teaspoon baking powder
- ½ cup peanuts, chopped
- 3 oz. dark chocolate, chopped
- 1/3 cup butter, softened

Directions:
1. Mix the peanut butter, butter and sugar in a container until fluffy and creamy.
2. Put in the egg and vanilla and mix thoroughly.
3. Fold in the flour, salt, baking powder, peanuts and dark chocolate.
4. Drop spoonfuls of batter on a baking tray coated with baking paper.
5. Preheat your oven and bake the cookies at 350F for about fifteen minutes or until a golden-brown colour is achieved on the edges.
    6. *These cookies taste best chilled.*

Nutritional Content of One Serving:

Calories: 149 Fat: 9.7g Protein: 3.9g Carbohydrates: 12.8g

Anzac Cookies

Total Time Taken: 1 ¼ hours
 Yield: 20 Servings

Ingredients:
- ¼ teaspoon salt
- ½ cup shredded coconut
- ½ teaspoon baking soda
- ¾ cup all-purpose flour
- ¾ cup butter, melted
- 1 cup rolled oats
- 1 teaspoon lemon juice
- 4 tablespoons golden syrup

Directions:
1. Mix the oats, coconut, flour, baking soda and salt in a container.
2. Put in the rest of the ingredients and mix thoroughly.
3. Make small balls of dough and place them in a baking tray coated with baking paper.
4. Flatten the cookies slightly then preheat your oven and bake at 350F for about fifteen minutes or until a golden-brown colour is achieved on the edges.

5. *These cookies taste best chilled.*

Nutritional Content of One Serving:

Calories: 112 Fat: 7.9g Protein: 1.2g Carbohydrates: 9.8g

Apricot Coconut Cookies

Total Time Taken: 1 ½ hours
 Yield: 25 Servings

Ingredients:
- ¼ cup light brown sugar
- ¼ teaspoon salt
- ½ cup butter, softened
- ½ cup dark chocolate chips
- ½ cup dried apricots, chopped
- ½ cup rolled oats
- ½ cup white sugar
- ½ teaspoon baking soda
- 1 cup all-purpose flour
- 1 cup shredded coconut
- 1 teaspoon vanilla extract
- 2 eggs

Directions:
1. Mix the flour, coconut, oats, apricots, salt and baking soda in a container.
2. In a separate container, mix the butter and the sugars and vanilla and mix thoroughly.
3. Fold in the flour mixture and the chocolate chips.
4. Drop spoonful of batter on a baking sheet coated with baking paper.
5. Pre-heat the oven and bake at 350F for about fifteen minutes or until a golden-brown colour is achieved on the edges.
6. Let the cookies cool before you serve.

Nutritional Content of One Serving:

Calories: 107 Fat: 5.9g Protein: 1.5g Carbohydrates: 12.8g

Banana Chocolate Chip Cookies

Total Time Taken: 1 ¼ hours
 Yield: 20 Servings

Ingredients:
- ¼ teaspoon salt
- ½ cup butter, melted
- ½ cup dark chocolate chips
- ½ cup white sugar
- 1 ½ cups all-purpose flour
- 1 egg
- 1 teaspoon baking powder
- 1 teaspoon vanilla extract

- 2 bananas, mashed

Directions:
1. Combine all the dry ingredients in a container.
2. Put in the rest of the ingredients and mix thoroughly using a spatula.
3. Drop spoonfuls of batter on a baking tray covered with parchment paper.
4. Preheat your oven and bake the cookies at 350F for about fifteen minutes or until a golden-brown colour is achieved on the edges.
5. *These cookies taste best chilled.*

Nutritional Content of One Serving:
Calories: 122 Fat: 5.8g Protein: 1.6g Carbohydrates: 17.0g

Banana Chocolate Cookies

Total Time Taken: 1 ¼ hours
Yield: 20 Servings

Ingredients:
- ¼ cup butter, softened
- ¼ cup cocoa powder
- ¼ cup coconut oil, melted
- ¼ teaspoon baking soda
- ¼ teaspoon salt
- ½ cup walnuts, chopped
- ½ teaspoon baking powder
- 1 ¾ cups all-purpose flour
- 2 bananas, mashed
- 2/3 cup white sugar

Directions:
1. **Mix** the butter, oil and sugar in a container until creamy and fluffy.

2. **Stir in** the bananas then fold in the flour, baking soda, baking powder, salt and cocoa powder.

3. Put in the walnuts then drop spoonfuls of batter on a baking sheet **coated with baking paper** .

4. **Preheat your oven and bake the cookies at** 350F for **fifteen minutes** or **until aromatic** .

5. **These cookies taste best chilled** .

Nutritional Content of One Serving:
Calories: 141 Fat: 7.2g Protein: 2.2g Carbohydrates: 18.7g

Banana Oatmeal Cookies

Total Time Taken: 1 hour
Yield: 10 Servings
Ingredients:
- ¼ teaspoon baking soda
- 1 cup rolled oats
- 1 pinch salt

264

- 2 tablespoons maple syrup
- 3 ripe bananas, mashed

Directions:
1. Combine all the ingredients in a container.
2. Drop spoonfuls of batter on a baking sheet coated with baking paper.
3. Preheat your oven and bake the cookies at 350F for about ten minutes or until a golden-brown colour is achieved on the edges.
4. *These cookies taste best chilled.*

Nutritional Content of One Serving:
Calories: 73 Fat: 0.7g Protein: 1.5g Carbohydrates: 16.3g

Brown Butter American Cookies

Total Time Taken: 1 ¼ hours
Yield: 20 Servings

Ingredients:
- ¼ teaspoon salt
- ½ cup pecans, chopped
- ½ teaspoon baking soda
- 1 ½ cups all-purpose flour
- 1 cup butter
- 1 cup light brown sugar
- 1 egg
- 1 teaspoon vanilla extract

Directions:
1. Put the butter in a saucepan and melt it then cook it until golden and caramelized. Let cool and then move to a container.
2. Mix the butter and sugar in a fluffy and pale.
3. Put in the egg and vanilla and mix thoroughly then mix in the flour, baking soda, salt and pecans.
4. Drop spoonfuls of batter on a baking tray coated with baking paper.
5. Pre-heat the oven and bake at 350F for about fifteen minutes or until a golden-brown colour is achieved on the edges.
6. *These cookies taste best chilled.*

Nutritional Content of One Serving:
Calories: 152 Fat: 10.0g Protein: 1.4g Carbohydrates: 14.4g

Brown Butter Chocolate Chip Cookies

Total Time Taken: 2 hours
Yield: 20 Servings
Ingredients:
- ¼ teaspoon salt
- ½ cup butter
- ½ teaspoon baking soda
- 1 ½ cups all-purpose flour

- 1 cup dark chocolate chips
- 1 cup light brown sugar
- 1 egg
- 1 egg yolk
- 1 teaspoon baking powder
- 1 teaspoon vanilla extract

Directions:

1. Mix the flour, baking powder, baking soda and salt in a container.
2. Melt the butter in a saucepan until it starts to appear somewhat golden-brown and caramelized. Let cool and then move to a container.
3. Stir in the sugar, egg, egg yolk, vanilla and flour. Stir slowly until mixed using a spatula.
4. Fold in the chocolate chips then drop spoonfuls of dough on a baking sheet coated with baking paper.
5. Freeze the cookies for about half an hour then preheat your oven and bake at 350F for fifteen minutes until a golden-brown colour is achieved.

Best served chilled.

Nutritional Content of One Serving:

Calories: 137 Fat: 6.8g Protein: 1.8g Carbohydrates: 18.5g

Brown Butter Chocolate Oatmeal Cookies

Total Time Taken: 1 ¼ hours
Yield: 30 Servings

Ingredients:

- ¼ teaspoon salt
- ½ cup dark chocolate chips
- 1 1/2 cups rolled oats
- 1 cup all-purpose flour
- 1 cup butter
- 1 cup light brown sugar
- 1 egg
- 1 teaspoon baking soda
- 1 teaspoon vanilla extract

Directions:

1. Melt the butter in a saucepan until it becomes mildly golden.
2. Put in the sugar and mix thoroughly then mix in the egg and vanilla.
3. Put in the oats, flour, baking soda and salt then fold in the chocolate chips.
4. Drop spoonfuls of batter on a baking tray coated with baking paper.
5. Preheat your oven and bake the cookies at 350F for about fifteen minutes or until a golden-brown colour is achieved on the edges.
6. *These cookies taste best chilled.*

Nutritional Content of One Serving:

Calories: 115 Fat: 7.1g Protein: 1.4g Carbohydrates: 12.0g

Brown Sugar Chocolate Chip Cookies

Total Time Taken: 1 ½ hours
Yield: 40 Servings

Ingredients:
- ½ cup white sugar
- ½ teaspoon salt
- 1 ½ cups butter, softened
- 1 ½ cups dark chocolate chips
- 1 cup dark brown sugar
- 1 cup light brown sugar
- 1 teaspoon baking soda
- 1 teaspoon vanilla extract
- 2 eggs
- 3 cups all-purpose flour

Directions:
1. Mix the butter and sugars in a container until creamy and fluffy.
2. Put in the eggs and vanilla and mix thoroughly then fold in the remaining ingredients.
3. Drop spoonfuls of batter on a baking tray coated with baking paper.
4. Preheat your oven and bake the cookies at 350F for about fifteen minutes or until a golden-brown colour is achieved on the edges and crisp.
5. *These cookies taste best chilled.*

Nutritional Content of One Serving:

Calories: 157 Fat: 8.4g Protein: 1.6g Carbohydrates: 19.8g

Butter Vanilla Cookies

Total Time Taken: 1 hour
Yield: 30 Servings
Ingredients:
- ¼ cup cornstarch
- ¼ teaspoon salt
- ½ cup powdered sugar
- 1 cup butter, softened
- 1 egg
- 1 tablespoon vanilla extract
- 2 cups all-purpose flour

Directions:
1. Mix the butter and sugar in a container until fluffy and creamy.
2. Put in the egg and vanilla and mix thoroughly.
3. Fold in the flour, cornstarch and salt and mix thoroughly.
4. Drop spoonfuls of batter on a baking sheet coated with baking paper.
5. Pre-heat the oven and bake at 350F for about fifteen minutes or until a golden-brown colour is achieved on the edges.
6. *These cookies taste best chilled.*

Calories: 100 Fat: 6.4g Protein: 1.1g Carbohydrates: 9.4g

Cakey Chocolate Chip Cookies

Total Time Taken: 1 hour

Yield: 20 Servings

Ingredients:

- ¼ cup coconut oil, melted
- ¼ cup whole milk
- ¼ teaspoon salt
- ½ cup dark chocolate chips
- ½ cup white sugar
- ½ teaspoon baking powder
- 1 ½ cups all-purpose flour
- 1 egg

Directions:

1. Mix the egg and sugar in a container until volume increases to twice what it was.
2. Put in the coconut oil and milk and mix thoroughly.
3. Stir in the remaining ingredients then drop spoonfuls of batter on a baking tray coated with baking paper.
4. Preheat your oven and bake the cookies at 350F for about ten minutes or until it rises and appears golden.
5. Let cool in the pan before you serve.

Nutritional Content of One Serving:

Calories: 96 Fat: 3.9g Protein: 1.6g Carbohydrates: 14.4g

Candied Ginger Oatmeal Cookies

Total Time Taken: 1 hour

Yield: 30 Servings

Ingredients:

- ¼ cup butter, softened
- ½ cup candied ginger, chopped
- ½ cup canola oil
- ½ teaspoon salt
- 1 cup light brown sugar
- 1 teaspoon baking soda
- 1 teaspoon vanilla extract
- 2 cups all-purpose flour
- 2 cups rolled oats
- 2 eggs

Directions:

1. Mix the butter and sugar in a container until creamy and pale.
2. Put in the eggs and mix thoroughly then mix in the vanilla.

3. Fold in the dry ingredients and ginger then drop spoonfuls of batter on a baking sheet coated with baking paper.
4. Preheat your oven and bake the cookies at 350F for about fifteen minutes or until it is aromatic and appears golden-brown on the edges.
5. *These cookies taste best chilled.*

Nutritional Content of One Serving:

Calories: 121 Fat: 5.9g Protein: 2.0g Carbohydrates: 15.0g

Candy Cane Chocolate Cookies

Total Time Taken: 1 ¼ hours
Yield: 20 Servings

Ingredients:
- ¼ cup cocoa powder
- ¼ cup shredded coconut
- ¼ teaspoon salt
- ½ cup butter, softened
- ½ cup crushed candy cane cookies
- ½ teaspoon baking soda
- 1 cup all-purpose flour
- 1 egg
- 1 teaspoon vanilla extract
- 2 tablespoons canola oil
- 2/3 cup light brown sugar

Directions:
1. Mix the butter, canola oil, sugar and vanilla in a container until fluffy and creamy.
2. Stir in the egg then put in the flour, cocoa powder, coconut, baking soda and salt.
3. Fold in the crushed candy then drop spoonfuls of batter on a baking sheet coated with baking paper.
4. Preheat your oven and bake the cookies at 350F for about fifteen minutes or until aromatic and risen.
5. *These cookies taste best chilled.*

Nutritional Content of One Serving:

Calories: 108 Fat: 7.0g Protein: 1.3g Carbohydrates: 10.8g

Cardamom Chocolate Chip Cookies

Total Time Taken: 1 hour
Yield: 20 Servings
Ingredients:
- ½ cup light brown sugar
- ½ cup white sugar
- ½ teaspoon salt
- 1 cup butter, softened
    - 1 cup dark chocolate chips
- 1 teaspoon baking powder

- 1 teaspoon cardamom powder
- 2 ½ cups all-purpose flour
- 2 eggs

Directions:

1. Mix the butter and sugars in a container until creamy and fluffy.
2. Stir in the eggs, one at a time, then put in the flour, salt, baking powder and cardamom powder.
3. Fold in the chocolate chips then drop spoonfuls of batter on a baking sheet coated with baking paper.
4. Pre-heat the oven and bake at 350F for about fifteen minutes.
5. Let the cookies cool in the pan before you serve.

Nutritional Content of One Serving:

Calories: 206 Fat: 11.4g Protein: 2.7g Carbohydrates: 24.7g

Cashew Cranberry Cookies

Total Time Taken: 1 ¼ house
Yield: 30 Servings

Ingredients:

- ¼ teaspoon salt
- ½ cup all-purpose flour
- ½ cup baking soda
- ½ cup coconut oil, melted
- ½ cup light brown sugar
- 1 ½ cups ground cashew nuts
- 1 cup dried cranberries
- 1 teaspoon vanilla extract
- 2 eggs
- 2 tablespoons golden syrup

Directions:

1. Mix the cashew nuts, flour, salt and baking soda in a container.
2. In a separate container, combine the coconut oil, eggs, vanilla, sugar and syrup until creamy.
3. Put in the flour mixture then fold in the cranberries.
4. Drop spoonfuls of batter on a baking sheet coated with baking paper.
5. Preheat your oven and bake the cookies at 350F for about fifteen minutes or until a golden-brown colour is achieved on the edges.
6. *These cookies taste best chilled.*

Nutritional Content of One Serving:

Calories: 106 Fat: 7.7g Protein: 2.0g Carbohydrates: 7.6g

Chewy Coconut Cookies

Total Time Taken: 1 hour
Yield: 20 Servings
Ingredients:

- ¼ cup coconut oil, melted

- ¼ cup cornstarch
- ¼ teaspoon salt
- ½ teaspoon baking soda
- ½ teaspoon coconut extract
- 1 ¼ cups all-purpose flour
- 1 cup shredded coconut
- 1 cup white sugar
- 1 egg
- 1 teaspoon vanilla extract

Directions:

1. Mix the egg and sugar in a container until volume increases to twice what it was. Stir in the coconut oil then put in the coconut oil, vanilla and coconut extract.
2. Fold in the flour, cornstarch, baking soda, salt and coconut.
3. Drop spoonfuls of batter on a baking sheet pan coated with baking paper.
4. Preheat your oven and bake the cookies at 350F for about fifteen minutes or until a golden-brown colour is achieved on the edges.
5. *These cookies taste best chilled.*

Nutritional Content of One Serving:

Calories: 114 Fat: 4.4g Protein: 1.2g Carbohydrates: 18.1g

Chewy Sugar Cookies

Total Time Taken: 1 ¼ hours
Yield: 40 Servings

Ingredients:

- ½ teaspoon salt
- 1 cup butter, softened
- 1 teaspoon baking soda
- 1 teaspoon vanilla extract
- 2 ½ cups all-purpose flour
- 2 cups white sugar
- 2 eggs

Directions:

1. Mix the butter with sugar until creamy and pale. Put in the eggs, one at a time, then mix in the vanilla.
2. Fold in the flour, baking soda and salt then shape the dough into small balls.
3. Put the balls on a baking tray coated with baking paper and flatten them slightly.
4. Preheat your oven and bake the cookies at 350F for about fifteen minutes or until mildly golden brown.
5. *These cookies taste best chilled.*

Nutritional Content of One Serving:

Calories: 110 Fat: 4.9g Protein: 1.1g Carbohydrates: 16.0g

Chili Chocolate Cookies

Total Time Taken: 1 ¼ hours
Yield: 30 Servings

Ingredients:

- ¼ cup dark brown sugar
- ½ cup cocoa powder
- ½ cup white sugar
- ½ teaspoon salt
- 1 cup butter, softened
- 1 cup dark chocolate chips
- 1 teaspoon baking powder
- 1 teaspoon chili powder
- 1 teaspoon vanilla extract
- 2 cups all-purpose flour
- 2 eggs

Directions:

1. Mix the butter and sugars in a container until creamy and fluffy.
2. Put in the vanilla and eggs and mix thoroughly.
3. Fold in the flour, cocoa powder, salt, chili powder and baking powder then put in the chocolate chips.
4. Drop spoonfuls of batter on a baking sheet coated with baking paper.
5. Preheat your oven and bake the cookies at 350F for about fifteen minutes or until risen and fragrant.
6. *These cookies taste best chilled.*

Nutritional Content of One Serving:

Calories: 129 Fat: 7.8g Protein: 1.8g Carbohydrates: 14.5g

Chocolate Buttercream Cookies

Total Time Taken: 1 ½ hours
Yield: 20 Servings
Ingredients:

Cookies:

- ½ cup butter, softened
- ½ cup cocoa powder
- ½ cup coconut oil
- ½ cup powdered sugar
- ½ teaspoon baking powder
- ½ teaspoon salt
- 1 egg
- 2 cups all-purpose flour
- 2 tablespoons whole milk

Filling:

- ½ cup butter, softened
- 1 cup powdered sugar

Directions:

1. For the cookies, combine the flour, cocoa powder, salt and baking powder in a container.
2. In a separate container, combine the coconut oil, butter and sugar in a container until creamy and fluffy.
3. Put in the egg and mix thoroughly, then mix in the flour and the milk.
4. Cover the dough with plastic wrap and store in the refrigerator for about half an hour.
5. Transfer the dough to a floured working surface and roll into a slim sheet.
6. Cut small round cookies and place them on a baking sheet.
7. Pre-heat the oven and bake at 350F for about fifteen minutes.
8. Let the cookies cool to room temperature.
9. For the filling, combine the butter with sugar until fluffy and creamy.
10. Fill the cookies, two by two with the buttercream.
11. Serve fresh or store in an airtight container.

Nutritional Content of One Serving:

Calories: 218 Fat: 15.4g Protein: 2.1g Carbohydrates: 19.8g

Chocolate Chip Pecan Cookies

Total Time Taken: 1 ¼ hours
Yield: 20 Servings

Ingredients:

- ¼ teaspoon salt
- ½ cup butter, softened
- ½ cup chocolate chips
- ½ cup powdered sugar
- ½ teaspoon baking soda
- 1 cup all-purpose flour
- 1 cup ground pecans
- 1 egg
- 2 tablespoon honey

Directions:

1. Mix the butter, sugar and honey in a container until creamy and pale.
2. Put in the egg and mix thoroughly then put in the flour, pecans, baking soda and salt.
3. Fold in the chocolate chips then drop spoonfuls of batter on a baking sheet coated with baking paper.
4. Pre-heat the oven and bake at 350F for about fifteen minutes or until a golden-brown colour is achieved and fragrant.
5. *These cookies taste best chilled.*

Nutritional Content of One Serving:

Calories: 112 Fat: 6.6g Protein: 1.4g Carbohydrates: 12.1g

Chocolate Chunk Cookies

Total Time Taken: 1 ¼ hours
Yield: 20 Servings

Ingredients:
- ¼ teaspoon salt
- ½ cup butter, softened
- 1 ½ cups all-purpose flour
- 1 egg
- 1 teaspoon baking powder
- 2 tablespoons honey
- 2/3 cup light brown sugar
- 4 oz. dark chocolate, chopped

Directions:
1. Mix the butter, honey and sugar in a container until fluffy and pale.
2. Put in the egg and mix thoroughly then mix in the flour, baking powder and salt.
3. Fold in the chocolate then drop spoonfuls of dough on a baking sheet coated with baking paper.
4. Preheat your oven and bake the cookies at 350F for fifteen minutes or until a golden-brown colour is achieved on the edges.
5. *These cookies taste best chilled.*

Nutritional Content of One Serving:

Calories: 133 Fat: 6.6g Protein: 1.8g Carbohydrates: 17.1g

Chocolate Crinkles

Total Time Taken: 2 hours
Yield: 40 Servings
Ingredients:
- ½ cup cocoa powder
- ½ cup coconut oil, melted
- ½ teaspoon salt
- 1 ½ teaspoons baking powder
- 1 teaspoon vanilla extract
- 2 cups all-purpose flour
- 2 cups powdered sugar
- 2 cups white sugar
- 4 eggs
- 4 oz. dark chocolate, melted

Directions:
1. Mix the coconut oil and melted chocolate in a container.
2. Put in the sugar and eggs and mix thoroughly then mix in the vanilla.
3. Fold in the flour, baking powder, cocoa and salt then cover the dough using plastic wrap.
4. Place in your refrigerator for an hour then form small balls of dough and roll them through powdered sugar.

5. Put the cookies on a baking tray coated with baking paper and preheat your oven and bake at 350F for about ten minutes.
6. *These cookies taste best chilled.*

Nutritional Content of One Serving:

Calories: 131 Fat: 4.2g Protein: 1.6g Carbohydrates: 23.1g

Chocolate Dipped Sugar Cookies

Total Time Taken: 1 ¼ hours
Yield: 30 Servings

Ingredients:
- ¼ teaspoon salt
- 1 cup butter, softened
- 1 cup dark chocolate, melted
- 1 cup powdered sugar
- 1 teaspoon baking powder
- 1 teaspoon vanilla extract
- 2 egg yolks
- 3 cups all-purpose flour

Directions:
1. Mix the butter and sugar in a container until pale and fluffy.
2. Stir in the egg yolks and vanilla and mix thoroughly.
3. Fold in the flour, baking powder and salt then wrap the dough in plastic wrap and store in the refrigerator for about half an hour.
4. Transfer the dough to a floured working surface and roll into a slim sheet.
5. Cut cookies using a cookie cutter of your choices and arrange them on a baking sheet coated with baking paper.
6. Pre-heat the oven and bake at 350F for about thirteen minutes or until mildly golden-brown on the edges.
7. When finished, allow the cookies to cool then immerse them in melted chocolate.
8. *These cookies taste best chilled.*

Nutritional Content of One Serving:

Calories: 149 Fat: 8.2g Protein: 2.0g Carbohydrates: 17.0g

Chocolate Drizzled Lavender Cookies

Total Time Taken: 1 ½ hours
Yield: 20 Servings

Ingredients:
- ¼ cup cornstarch
- ¼ teaspoon baking soda
- ¼ teaspoon salt
- ½ cup butter, softened
- ½ cup powdered sugar
- ½ cup white chocolate chips, melted

- 1 ½ cups all-purpose flour
- 1 egg
- 1 egg yolk
- 1 teaspoon lavender buds
- 2 tablespoons whole milk

Directions:
1. Mix the butter with sugar in a container until fluffy and pale.
2. Stir in the egg and egg yolk and mix thoroughly.
3. Put in the milk and mix then fold in the remaining ingredients. Mix the dough then move it to a floured working surface and roll it into a slim sheet.
4. Cut into small cookies using a cookie cutter of your choices.
5. Position the cookies on a baking sheet coated with baking paper.
6. Pre-heat the oven and bake at 350F for about fifteen minutes or until a golden-brown colour is achieved on the edges.
7. When finished, let cool in the pan then sprinkle the cookies with melted chocolate.
8. **Best served chilled.**

Nutritional Content of One Serving:
Calories: 122 Fat: 6.6g Protein: 1.7g Carbohydrates: 14.2g

Chocolate Hazelnut Cookies

Total Time Taken: 1 ½ hours
Yield: 30 Servings

Ingredients:
- ¼ cup cocoa powder
- ¼ teaspoon salt
- ½ cup cream cheese, softened
- ½ cup ground hazelnuts
- 1 ½ cups all-purpose flour
- 1 cup butter, softened
- 1 egg yolk

Directions:
1. Mix the butter, cream cheese and egg yolk in a container until creamy.
2. Put in the salt, flour, cocoa powder and hazelnuts and mix using a spatula.
3. Wrap the plastic wrap and store in the refrigerator for about half an hour.
4. Transfer the dough to a floured working surface and roll it into a slim sheet.
5. Cut into small cookies with a cookie cutter of your choices.
6. Put the cookies in a baking sheet coated with baking paper and preheat your oven and bake at 350F for about ten minutes or until a golden-brown colour is achieved on the edges.
7. These cookies taste best chilled.

Nutritional Content of One Serving:
Calories: 102 Fat: 8.6g Protein: 1.4g Carbohydrates: 5.5g

Chocolate Nutella Cookies

Total Time Taken: 1 ¼ hours
Yield: 30 Servings

Ingredients:

- ¼ cup cocoa powder
- ¼ cup white sugar
- ½ teaspoon baking soda
- ½ teaspoon salt
- ¾ cup light brown sugar
- 1 cup butter, softened
- 1 cup dark chocolate chips
- 1 cup Nutella
- 1 teaspoon vanilla extract
- 2 cups all-purpose flour
- 2 eggs

Directions:

1. Mix the butter and sugars in a container until creamy and fluffy.
2. Put in the Nutella, vanilla and eggs and mix thoroughly.
3. Fold in the remaining ingredients then drop spoonfuls of batter on a baking tray covered with parchment paper.
4. Preheat your oven and bake the cookies at 350F for about fifteen minutes or until a golden-brown colour is achieved.
5. Serve the cookie chilled.

Nutritional Content of One Serving:

Calories: 136 Fat: 8.0g Protein: 1.8g Carbohydrates: 15.5g

Chocolate Orange Shortbread Cookies

Total Time Taken: 1 hour
Yield: 20 Servings
Ingredients:

- ¼ cup cocoa powder
- ¼ teaspoon salt
- ½ cup almond flour
- ½ cup butter, softened
- ½ cup white sugar
- ½ teaspoon baking soda
- 1 ½ cups all-purpose flour
- 1 egg
- 1 tablespoon orange zest
- 1 teaspoon vanilla extract

Directions:

1. Mix the butter, cocoa powder and sugar in a container until fluffy and pale.
2. Put in the egg, vanilla and orange zest and mix thoroughly.

3. Fold in the flour, almond flour, salt and baking soda then transfer the dough on a floured working surface.
4. Roll the dough into a slim sheet then cut small cookies using a cookie cutter of your choice.
5. Preheat your oven and bake the cookies at 350F for about fifteen minutes or until a golden-brown colour is achieved and fragrant.
6. These cookies taste best chilled.

Nutritional Content of One Serving:

Calories: 104 Fat: 5.4g Protein: 1.6g Carbohydrates: 13.0g

Chocolate Pecan Cookies

Total Time Taken: 1 hour
Yield: 10 Servings
Ingredients:
- ¼ teaspoon salt
- ½ cup dark chocolate chips
- 1 cup ground pecans
- 1 teaspoon vanilla extract
- 2 egg whites
- 2/3 cup white sugar

Directions:
1. Whip the egg whites and salt in a container until fluffy and airy.
2. Put in the sugar, progressively, and stir until shiny.
3. Fold in the pecans and chocolate chips then drop spoonfuls of batter on a baking sheet coated with baking paper.
4. Preheat your oven and bake the cookies at 350F for about fifteen minutes or until a z
5. These cookies taste best chilled.

Nutritional Content of One Serving:

Calories: 92 Fat: 2.6g Protein: 1.3g Carbohydrates: 17.6g

Chocolate Sandwich Cookies With Passionfruit Ganache

Total Time Taken: 2 hours
Yield: 30 Servings
Ingredients:

Cookies:
- ½ cup cocoa powder
- ½ teaspoon salt
- 1 cup white sugar
- 1 egg
- 1 teaspoon baking powder
- 1 teaspoon vanilla extract
- 2 cups all-purpose flour

- 2/3 cup butter, softened

Passionfruit Ganache:
- ¼ cup passionfruit juice
- ½ cup heavy cream
- 1 cup white chocolate chips
- 2 tablespoons butter

Directions:
1. For the cookies, combine the flour, cocoa powder, baking powder and salt in a container.
1. In a separate container, combine the butter and sugar until fluffy and pale.
2. Stir in the egg and vanilla and mix thoroughly then fold in the flour.
3. Transfer the dough to a floured working surface and roll it into a slim sheet.
4. Cut 40 small cookies using a round cookie cutter and arrange them on a baking sheet coated with baking paper.
5. For the ganache, bring the cream to a boil. Stir in the chocolate and stir until it melts completely. Put in the passionfruit juice and butter and mix thoroughly. Let cool in your refrigerator.
6. Fill the cookies with chilled ganache.

Nutritional Content of One Serving:

Calories: 143 Fat: 7.8g Protein: 1.7g Carbohydrates: 17.6g

Chocolate Star Anise Cookies

Total Time Taken: 1 ¼ hours
Yield: 20 Servings

Ingredients:
- ½ cup butter, softened
- ½ cup cocoa powder
- ½ cup pecans, chopped
- ½ teaspoon baking soda
- ½ teaspoon salt
- ¾ cup white sugar
- 1 ½ cups all-purpose flour
- 1 egg
- 1 teaspoon ground star anise
- 2 tablespoons coconut oil

Directions:
1. Mix the butter and coconut oil in a container. Put in the sugar and stir until fluffy.
2. Stir in the egg and stir thoroughly until blended.
3. Fold in the remaining ingredients and mix using a spatula.
4. Drop spoonfuls of batter on baking trays covered with parchment paper.
5. Pre-heat the oven and bake at 350F for about fifteen minutes or until risen and fragrant.
6. These cookies taste best chilled.

Nutritional Content of One Serving:

Calories: 129 Fat: 7.1g Protein: 1.8g Carbohydrates: 16.1g

Chunky Peanut Butter Cookies

Total Time Taken: 1 ¼ hours
Yield: 30 Servings

Ingredients:

- ¼ teaspoon salt
- ½ cup butter, softened
- 1 cup light brown sugar
- 1 cup peanut butter, softened
- 1 cup peanuts, chopped
- 1 egg
- 1 teaspoon baking powder
- 2 cups all-purpose flour

Directions:

1. Mix the butter and peanut butter in a container until creamy. Put in the sugar and mix for five minutes until fluffy.
2. Put in the egg and mix thoroughly then fold in the remaining ingredients.
3. Drop spoonfuls of batter on a baking tray coated with baking paper.
4. Preheat your oven and bake the cookies at 350F for about fifteen minutes or until a golden-brown colour is achieved on the edges.
5. Allow the cookies cool down before you serve.

Nutritional Content of One Serving:

Calories: 156 Fat: 10.0g Protein: 4.5g Carbohydrates: 13.7g

Raisin Bran Muffins

Total Time Taken: 1 hour
Yield: 10 Servings

Ingredients:

- ¼ teaspoon ground ginger
- ½ cup canola oil
- ½ cup golden raisins
- ½ cup white sugar
- ½ cup whole milk
- ½ teaspoon cinnamon powder
- ½ teaspoon salt
- 1 cup all-purpose flour
- 1 cup wheat bran
- 2 eggs
- 2 teaspoons baking powder

Directions:

1. Mix the flour, wheat bran, baking powder, salt, cinnamon, ginger and raisins in a container.
2. Put in the sugar, canola oil and eggs, as well as milk and mix using a spatula.
3. Spoon the batter in a muffin tin covered with muffin papers.

4. Preheat your oven and bake the muffins at 350F for about twenty minutes or until it rises significantly and starts to appear golden-brown.
5. *These muffins taste best cold.*

Nutritional Content of One Serving:

Calories: 235 Fat: 12.6g Protein: 3.9g Carbohydrates: 30.1g

Raspberry Jam Muffins

Total Time Taken: 1 hour
Yield: 12 Servings
Ingredients:

- 2 eggs
- 1 teaspoon vanilla extract
- ½ cup canola oil
- ¾ cup sour cream
- 1 ¾ cups all-purpose flour
- ½ teaspoon salt
- 1 ½ teaspoons baking powder
- 1 cup raspberry jam
- 2/3 cup white sugar

Directions:

1. Mix the eggs and sugar in a container until fluffy and pale, minimum volume increases to twice what it was.
2. Stir in the vanilla, sour cream and oil and mix thoroughly.
3. Fold in the flour, salt and baking powder then spoon the batter in a muffin tin coated with baking muffin papers.
4. Spoon the jam over each muffin and preheat your oven and bake at 350F for about twenty minutes or until a golden-brown colour is achieved and it rises significantly.
5. *Let cool down before you serve.*

Nutritional Content of One Serving:

Calories: 298 Fat: 13.0g Protein: 3.4g Carbohydrates: 43.4g

Raspberry Muffins

Total Time Taken: 1 hour
Yield: 10 Servings
Ingredients:

- ½ cup milk
- ½ cup white sugar
- ½ teaspoon salt
- 1 ½ teaspoons baking powder
- 1 cup fresh raspberries
- 1 teaspoon vanilla extract
- 2 cups all-purpose flour
- 3 eggs

Directions:
1. Mix the flour, sugar, salt and baking powder in a container.
2. Put in the remaining ingredients and mix using a spatula.
3. Spoon the batter in a muffin tin covered with muffin papers.
4. Preheat your oven and bake the muffins at 350F for about twenty minutes or until a toothpick inserted into the center of a muffin comes out clean.

These muffins taste best chilled.

Nutritional Content of One Serving:
Calories: 162 Fat: 1.9g Protein: 4.8g Carbohydrates: 31.7g

Raspberry Ricotta Muffins

Total Time Taken: 1 hour
Yield: 12 Servings
Ingredients:
- 2 eggs
- 1/3 cup white sugar
- 1/3 cup butter, softened
- 1 teaspoon vanilla extract
- 1 cup raspberries
- 1 ¾ cups all-purpose flour
- 1 ½ teaspoons baking powder
- ¾ cup ricotta cheese
- ½ cup milk
- ¼ teaspoon salt

Directions:
1. Mix the butter, cheese, sugar, eggs, milk and vanilla in a container.
2. Put in the flour, salt and baking powder then spoon the batter in a muffin tin covered with muffin papers.
3. Top each muffin with fresh raspberries and preheat your oven and bake at 350F for about twenty minutes or until it rises significantly and starts to appear golden-brown.

These muffins taste best chilled.

Nutritional Content of One Serving:
Calories: 176 Fat: 7.5g Protein: 5.1g Carbohydrates: 22.4g

Raspberry Vanilla Cupcakes

Total Time Taken: 1 ½ hours
Yield: 12 Servings
Ingredients:
Cupcakes:
- ½ cup butter, softened
- 2 eggs
- 1 tablespoon vanilla extract

- 1 ½ cups all-purpose flour
- ¼ teaspoon salt
- 1 ½ teaspoons baking powder
- 2/3 cup white sugar
- 2/3 cup buttermilk

Frosting:
- 1 cup fresh raspberries
- 1 teaspoon vanilla extract
- 2 cups heavy cream
- 2 tablespoons powdered sugar

Directions:
1. To make the cupcakes, combine the butter and sugar until pale and light.
2. Put in the eggs, one at a time, then mix in the vanilla and buttermilk.
3. Fold in the flour, salt and baking powder then spoon the batter in a muffin tin covered with muffin papers.
4. Preheat your oven and bake the cupcakes at 350F for about twenty minutes until a toothpick inserted into them comes out dry then allow them to cool down.
5. To make the frosting, whip the cream in a container until airy and puffed up. Put in the sugar and vanilla and mix thoroughly.
6. Drop a dollop of cream over each cupcake and garnish with a few raspberries.

Nutritional Content of One Serving:
Calories: 267 Fat: 16.1g Protein: 3.6g Carbohydrates: 27.3g

Raspberry White Chocolate Muffins

Total Time Taken: 1 hour
Yield: 12 Servings
Ingredients:
- ½ cup sour cream
- ½ cup white chocolate chips
- ½ cup white sugar
- ½ teaspoon salt
- 1 ½ cups all-purpose flour
- 1 cup fresh raspberries
- 1 teaspoon baking powder
- 1 teaspoon vanilla extract
- 2 eggs

Directions:
1. Mix the eggs, sugar and vanilla in a container until fluffy and creamy.
2. Put in the sour cream and mix thoroughly then fold in the dry ingredients.
3. Stir in using a spatula the raspberries and white chocolate.
4. Spoon the batter in a muffin tin covered with muffin papers and preheat your oven and bake at 350F for about twenty minutes or until a golden-brown colour is achieved and it rises significantly.
5. Let the muffins cool to room temperature before you serve.

Nutritional Content of One Serving:

Calories: 164 Fat: 5.2g Protein: 3.4g Carbohydrates: 26.4g

Red Berries Cream Cheese Muffins

Total Time Taken: 1 hour

 Yield: 12 Servings

Ingredients:

- ¼ teaspoon salt
- ½ cup butter, softened
- ½ cup heavy cream
- ½ cup sliced almonds
- ¾ cup white sugar
- 1 ½ cups all-purpose flour
- 1 cup cream cheese
- 1 cup mixed berries
- 1 teaspoon vanilla extract
- 2 eggs
- 2 teaspoons baking powder

Directions:

1. Mix the cream cheese and butter in a container.
2. Put in the sugar and eggs and mix thoroughly. Stir in the cream and vanilla and stir thoroughly until blended.
3. Fold in the flour, salt and baking powder then put in the berries.
4. Spoon the batter in a muffin tin covered with muffin papers.
5. Top the muffins with sliced almonds and preheat your oven and bake at 350F for about twenty minutes or until it rises significantly and starts to appear golden-brown.
6. *Let cool down before you serve.*

Nutritional Content of One Serving:

Calories: 298 Fat: 19.2g Protein: 5.1g Carbohydrates: 27.9g

Red Velvet Cupcakes

Total Time Taken: 1 ½ hours

 Yield: 12 Servings

 Ingredients:

Cupcakes:

- ½ cup buttermilk
- ½ teaspoon baking soda
- ½ teaspoon salt
- ½ teaspoon white wine vinegar
- ¾ cup canola oil
- ¾ cup white sugar
- 1 ½ cups all-purpose flour
- 1 egg
- 1 tablespoon cocoa powder

- 1 teaspoon baking powder
- 1 teaspoon red food coloring
- 1 teaspoon vanilla extract

Frosting:
- ½ cup butter, softened
- 1 cup cream cheese, softened
- 1 teaspoon vanilla extract
- 3 cups powdered sugar

Directions:
1. To make the cupcakes, sift the flour, baking soda, baking powder and cocoa powder in a container.
2. In a separate container, combine the oil, egg and sugar until creamy and pale.
3. Stir in the buttermilk, red food coloring, vinegar and vanilla extract.
4. Spoon the batter in a muffin tin covered with muffin papers.
5. Preheat your oven and bake the cupcakes at 350F for about twenty minutes or until well risen.
6. Let the cupcakes cool in the pan.
7. To make the frosting, combine the cream cheese and butter in a container. Put in the vanilla and mix thoroughly then mix in the sugar and continue mixing for five minutes until fluffy and airy.
8. Spoon the frosting in a pastry bag and top the cupcakes with it.

These cupcakes taste best when fresh.

Nutritional Content of One Serving:
Calories: 489 Fat: 28.7g Protein: 4.0g Carbohydrates: 55.9g

Red Wine Fig Cupcakes

Total Time Taken: 1 ½ hours
Yield: 16 Servings
Ingredients:

Cupcakes:
- ½ cup red wine
- 1 teaspoon vanilla extract
- 2 eggs
- 1 ½ cups all-purpose flour
- ¼ cup cocoa powder
- ¼ teaspoon salt
- 1 ½ teaspoons baking powder
- 2/3 cup butter, softened
- 2/3 cup white sugar

Frosting:
- ½ cup butter, softened
- 1 cup cream cheese
- 2 cups powdered sugar

Fig compote:
- ¼ cup light brown sugar
- ½ cup red wine

- 1 cinnamon stick
- 6 figs, halved

Directions:
1. To make the cupcakes, combine the butter and sugar in a container until creamy. Put in the wine, vanilla and eggs and mix thoroughly.
2. Fold in the flour, cocoa powder, salt and baking powder and mix using a spatula.
3. Spoon the batter in a muffin tin covered with muffin papers.
4. Pre-heat the oven and bake at 350F for about twenty minutes or until it rises significantly and seems golden.
5. Let the muffins cool to room temperature in the pan.
6. To make the frosting, combine the butter and cream cheese in a container until fluffy and pale.
7. Put in the sugar, ½ cup at a time and stir thoroughly for 4-5 minutes until airy.
8. Pipe the frosting over each cupcake.
9. For the compote, mix the ingredients in a saucepan and cook for about five minutes just until softened.
    10. Top rach cupcake with the compote and serve fresh.

Nutritional Content of One Serving:
Calories: 353 Fat: 19.4g Protein: 3.6g Carbohydrates: 40.9g

Rhubarb Strawberry Muffins

Total Time Taken: 1 hour
Yield: 12 Servings
Ingredients:
- ½ cup light brown sugar
- ½ cup milk
- ½ cup whole wheat flour
- ½ teaspoon salt
- 1 cup all-purpose flour
- 1 cup strawberries, sliced
- 1 rhubarb stalk, sliced
- 1 teaspoon baking soda
- 1 teaspoon vanilla extract
- 3 eggs

Directions:
1. Mix the flours, salt and baking soda in a container.
2. Whip the eggs and sugar in a container until pale and light.
3. Put in the milk and vanilla and mix thoroughly.
4. Fold in the flour mixture then put in the rhubarb and strawberries.
5. Spoon the batter in a muffin tin covered with muffin papers.
6. Preheat your oven and bake the muffins at 350F for about twenty minutes or until a golden-brown colour is achieved and fluffy.

These muffins taste best chilled.

Nutritional Content of One Serving:

Calories: 106 Fat: 1.5g Protein: 3.5g Carbohydrates: 19.6g

Rhubarb Streusel Muffins

Total Time Taken: 1 ¼ hours
Yield: 12 Servings
Ingredients: **Muffins:**

- 2 rhubarb stalks, sliced
- 2 eggs
- 2 cups all-purpose flour
- 1 teaspoon baking powder
- 1 cup buttermilk
- ½ teaspoon baking soda
- ½ cup light brown sugar
- ¼ teaspoon salt
- ¼ cup white sugar
- ¼ cup canola oil

Streusel:

- 2 tablespoons white sugar
- 1 pinch salt
- 1 cup all-purpose flour
- ½ cup butter, melted

Directions:

1. For the muffins, combine the flour, baking soda, baking powder, salt and sugars in a container.
2. Put in the eggs, buttermilk and oil and mix using a spatula.
3. Fold in the rhubarb then spoon the batter in a muffin tin coated with baking muffin papers.
4. For the streusel, combine the ingredients in a container until grainy. Spread the
5. streusel over each muffin.
6. Pre-heat the oven and bake at 350F for about twenty minutes or until a golden-brown colour is achieved and it rises significantly.

These muffins taste best chilled.

Nutritional Content of One Serving:

Calories: 289 Fat: 13.4g Protein: 5.0g Carbohydrates: 37.6g

Rich Chocolate Muffins

Total Time Taken: 1 hour
Yield: 12 Servings
Ingredients:

- ¼ teaspoon baking soda
- ½ cup canola oil
- ½ cup cocoa powder
- ½ teaspoon salt
- ¾ cup milk
- 1 ¾ cups all-purpose flour

- 1 cup white sugar
- 1 teaspoon baking powder
- 1 teaspoon vanilla extract
- 2 eggs

Directions:
1. Mix the flour, cocoa powder, salt, baking powder, baking soda and salt in a container.
2. Put in the remaining ingredients and mix thoroughly.
3. Pour the batter in a muffin tin covered with muffin papers.
4. Preheat your oven and bake the muffins at 350F for about twenty minutes.
5. Let them cool in the pan before you serve or storing.

Nutritional Content of One Serving:
Calories: 237 Fat: 10.8g Protein: 3.9g Carbohydrates: 33.6g

Ricotta Lemon Muffins

Total Time Taken: 1 hour
Yield: 12 Servings
Ingredients:
- ¼ cup butter, melted
- ½ cup white sugar
- ½ teaspoon salt
- 1 ½ cups all-purpose flour
- 1 cup ricotta cheese
- 1 tablespoon lemon zest
- 1 teaspoon baking powder
- 1 teaspoon vanilla extract
- 2 eggs

Directions:
1. Mix the cheese, butter, eggs, vanilla and sugar in a container.
2. Put in the flour, salt and baking powder and mix using a spatula.
3. Spoon the batter in a muffin tin covered with muffin papers.
4. Preheat your oven and bake the muffins at 350F for about twenty minutes or until a golden-brown colour is achieved and it rises significantly.

These muffins taste best chilled.

Nutritional Content of One Serving:
Calories: 163 Fat: 6.3g Protein: 4.9g Carbohydrates: 21.7g

S'mores Chocolate Cupcakes

Total Time Taken: 1 ½ hours
Yield: 12 Servings
Ingredients:
Cupcakes:
- ¼ cup cocoa powder

- ¼ teaspoon salt
- ½ cup butter, softened
- ½ cup buttermilk
- ½ cup white sugar
- ½ teaspoon baking soda
- 1 ½ cups all-purpose flour
- 1 teaspoon baking powder
- 1 teaspoon vanilla extract
- 2 eggs
- 2 tablespoons dark brown sugar

Frosting:
- ½ cup crushed graham crackers
- ½ cup dark chocolate chips
- ½ cup white sugar
- 1 teaspoon vanilla extract
- 2 egg whites

Directions:
1. To make the cupcakes, combine the flour, cocoa powder, baking soda, baking powder and salt in a container.
2. Mix the butter and sugars in a separate container until creamy and pale.
3. Put in the eggs, buttermilk and vanilla and mix thoroughly.
4. Fold in the flour mixture then spoon the batter in a muffin tin coated with baking muffin papers.
5. Pre-heat the oven and bake at 350F for about twenty minutes or until it is aromatic and appears golden brown.
6. Let cool in the pan.
7. To make the frosting, combine the egg whites, sugar and vanilla in a container and place over a hot water bath. Keep on heat until the sugar is melted.
8. Turn off the heat and whip using an electric mixer until fluffy, stiff and shiny.
9. Apply the frosting on top of each cupcake and drizzle with chocolate chips and graham crackers.

These cupcakes taste best when fresh.

Nutritional Content of One Serving:
Calories: 255 Fat: 10.6g Protein: 4.4g Carbohydrates: 37.9g

Simple Lavender Cupcakes

Total Time Taken: 1 ½ hours
Yield: 12 Servings
Ingredients:

Cupcakes:
- ½ cup butter, softened
- 2 eggs
- 1 teaspoon vanilla extract
- 1 teaspoon lavender buds
- ½ cup heavy cream

- 1 ½ cups all-purpose flour
- ½ teaspoon salt
- 1 teaspoon baking powder
- 2/3 cup white sugar

Frosting:
- ¾ cup butter, softened
- 1 cup cream cheese
- 2 ½ cups powdered sugar

Directions:
1. To make the cupcakes, combine the butter and sugar in a container until creamy and pale.
2. Put in the eggs and vanilla and mix thoroughly. Stir in the lavender buds and cream and mix thoroughly.
3. Fold in the flour, salt and baking powder then spoon the batter in a muffin tin coated with baking muffin papers.
4. Pre-heat the oven and bake at 350F for about twenty minutes or until it rises significantly and starts to appear golden-brown.
5. Let them cool in the pan.
6. To make the frosting, combine the cream cheese and butter in a container until fluffy.
7. Put in the sugar and stir thoroughly for five minutes on high speed.
8. Top each cupcake with the frosting and serve them fresh.

Nutritional Content of One Serving:
Calories: 466 Fat: 28.8g Protein: 4.4g Carbohydrates: 49.8g

Snickerdoodle Muffins

Total Time Taken: 1 hour
Yield: 12 Servings
Ingredients:

Muffins:
- ½ cup butter, softened
- ½ cup light brown sugar
- ½ teaspoon ground ginger
- ½ teaspoon salt
- 1 teaspoon vanilla extract
- 2 ¼ cups all-purpose flour
- 2 eggs
- 2 teaspoons baking powder
- 2/3 cup buttermilk

Topping:
- 1 teaspoon cinnamon powder
- 2/3 cup white sugar

Directions:
1. For the muffins, combine the butter and sugar in a container.
2. Put in the vanilla and eggs and mix thoroughly then mix in the buttermilk.

3. Fold in the flour, salt, baking powder and ginger then spoon the batter in a muffin tin covered with muffin papers.
4. Pre-heat the oven and bake at 350F for about twenty minutes or until a golden-brown colour is achieved and it rises significantly.
5. For the topping, combine the ingredients in a container.
6. While the muffins are still hot, immerse them in cinnamon sugar.

These muffins taste best chilled.

Nutritional Content of One Serving:
Calories: 236 Fat: 8.8g Protein: 3.9g Carbohydrates: 36.1g

Snickers Cupcakes

Total Time Taken: 1 ½ hours
Yield: 16 Servings
Ingredients:

Cupcakes:
- ¼ teaspoon salt
- ½ cup canola oil
- ½ cup cocoa powder
- 1 ½ cups all-purpose flour
- 1 ½ teaspoons baking powder
- 1 cup buttermilk
- 1 cup light brown sugar
- 1 teaspoon lemon juice
- 1 teaspoon vanilla extract
- 4 eggs

Frosting:
- ½ cup butter, softened
- ½ cup cocoa powder
- ½ cup smooth peanut butter
- 1 teaspoon vanilla extract
- 2 cups powdered sugar

Topping:
- 6 snickers, chopped

Directions:
1. To make the cupcakes, combine the eggs and sugar in a container until fluffy and pale. Put in the oil and mix thoroughly then mix in the buttermilk, lemon juice and vanilla.
2. Fold in the flour, cocoa powder, salt and baking powder then spoon the batter in a muffin tin covered with muffin papers.
3. Preheat your oven and bake the cupcakes at 350F for about twenty minutes or until a toothpick inserted into them comes out dry.
4. Let cool down in the pan.
5. To make the frosting, combine the butter and peanut butter in a container until fluffy.

6. Stir in the sugar, cocoa powder and vanilla and stir thoroughly for a few additional minutes until fluffy and well mixed.
7. Pipe the frosting over each cupcake and serve them fresh.

Nutritional Content of One Serving:

Calories: 399 Fat: 22.4g Protein: 7.4g Carbohydrates: 45.8g

Sour Cream Muffins

Total Time Taken: 1 hour
Yield: 12 Servings
Ingredients:
- ¼ teaspoon salt
- 1 ½ cups sour cream
- 1 cup butter, softened
- 1 teaspoon vanilla extract
- 2 cups all-purpose flour
- 2 teaspoons baking powder

Directions:
1. Mix the butter, vanilla and sour cream in a container until creamy.
2. Put in the flour, salt and baking powder then spoon the batter in a muffin tin coated with baking muffin papers.
3. Pre-heat the oven and bake at 350F for about twenty minutes or until it rises significantly and starts to appear golden-brown.

These muffins taste best chilled.

Nutritional Content of One Serving:

Calories: 275 Fat: 21.6g Protein: 3.2g Carbohydrates: 17.6g

Spelt Zucchini Muffins

Total Time Taken: 1 ¼ hours
Yield: 12 Servings

Ingredients:
- ¼ cup coconut oil, melted
- ¼ cup maple syrup
- ¼ teaspoon salt
- ½ cup plain yogurt
- 1 cup grated zucchinis
- 1 cup spelt flour
- 1 cup whole wheat flour
- 1 egg
- 1 teaspoon baking soda
- 1 teaspoon vanilla extract
- 2 tablespoons chia seeds

Directions:

1. Mix the spelt flour, wheat flour, salt and baking soda in a container.
2. Put in the remaining ingredients and stir for a few seconds to mix.
3. Spoon the batter in a muffin tin covered with muffin papers and preheat your oven and bake at 350F for about twenty minutes or until a toothpick inserted in the center comes out clean.
4. *Let cool down before you serve.*

Nutritional Content of One Serving:

Calories: 169 Fat: 6.9g Protein: 4.7g Carbohydrates: 22.5g

Spiced Cupcakes With Cream Cheese Cupcakes

Total Time Taken: 1 ½ hours
Yield: 16 Servings
Ingredients:

Cupcakes:
- ¼ teaspoon salt
- ½ cup butter, softened
- ½ teaspoon grated ginger
- ½ teaspoon ground cardamom
- ¾ cup plain yogurt
- 1 ½ teaspoons baking powder
- 1 cup white sugar
- 1 teaspoon cinnamon powder
- 1 teaspoon vanilla extract
- 2 cups all-purpose flour
- 2 eggs

Frosting:
- ½ cup butter, softened
- 1 cup cream cheese
- 3 cups powdered sugar

Directions:
1. To make the cupcakes, combine the butter and sugar in a container until fluffy and pale.
2. Put in the eggs and mix thoroughly then mix in the yogurt and vanilla.
3. Fold in the flour, spices, salt and baking powder then spoon the batter in a muffin tin covered with muffin papers.
4. Preheat your oven and bake the cupcakes at 350F for about twenty minutes.
5. To make the frosting, combine the cream cheese and butter in a container until creamy.
6. Put in the sugar, progressively, and stir thoroughly for a few minutes until fluffy.
7. Pipe the frosting over each cupcake and serve the cupcakes fresh.

Nutritional Content of One Serving:

Calories: 361 Fat: 17.4g Protein: 4.2g Carbohydrates: 48.4g

Spiced Strawberry Cupcakes

Total Time Taken: 1 ½ hours
Yield: 12 Servings Ingredients

Cupcakes:
- ¼ teaspoon ground nutmeg
- ½ cup canola oil
- ½ teaspoon baking powder
- ½ teaspoon cinnamon powder
- ½ teaspoon ground ginger
- ½ teaspoon salt
- 1 cup all-purpose flour
- 1 cup milk
- 1 cup white sugar
- 1 egg
- 1 teaspoon apple cider vinegar
- 1 teaspoon baking soda

Frosting:
- ½ cup strawberry puree
- 1 cup butter, softened
- 2 ½ cups powdered sugar

Directions:
1. To make the cupcakes, combine all the ingredients in a container and stir for a few seconds to mix.
2. Pour the batter in a muffin tin coated with baking muffin papers.
3. Pre-heat the oven and bake at 350F for about twenty minutes or until it rises significantly and becomes aromatic.
4. Let cool in the pan.
5. To make the frosting, combine the butter in a container until fluffy. Put in the sugar and mix thoroughly then mix in the strawberry puree.
6. Top each cupcake with the frosting and serve them fresh.

Nutritional Content of One Serving:

Calories: 435 Fat: 25.4g Protein: 2.4g Carbohydrates: 51.8g

Spiced Zucchini Muffins

Total Time Taken: 1 ¼ hours
Yield: 12 Servings

Ingredients:
- ¼ cup honey
- ¼ teaspoon salt
- ½ cup almond butter, softened
- ½ teaspoon cinnamon
- ½ teaspoon ground cardamom
- ½ teaspoon ground ginger
- 1 ½ cups all-purpose flour

- 1 ½ teaspoons baking powder
- 1 apple, cored and grated
- 1 cup grated zucchinis
- 1 teaspoon vanilla extract
- 2 eggs

Directions:

1. Mix the zucchinis, apples, almond butter, honey, eggs and vanilla in a container.
2. Stir in the flour, cinnamon, ginger, cardamom, salt and baking powder.
3. Spoon the batter in a muffin tin covered with muffin papers and preheat your oven and bake at 350F for about twenty minutes or until a toothpick inserted into them comes out dry.
4. *Let cool down before you serve.*

Nutritional Content of One Serving:

Calories: 167 Fat: 6.8g Protein: 4.9g Carbohydrates: 22.6g

Spicy Pineapple Muffins

Total Time Taken: 1 hour

Yield: 12 Servings

Ingredients:

- ¼ teaspoon cayenne pepper
- ½ cup light brown sugar
- ½ cup sultanas
- ½ teaspoon ground ginger
- ½ teaspoon salt
- 1 ½ cups all-purpose flour
- 1 teaspoon baking soda
- 1/3 cup canola oil
- 2 cups crushed pineapple
- 2 eggs

Directions:

1. Mix the flour, salt, baking soda and sultanas in a container.
2. Put in the cayenne pepper and ginger then mix in the remaining ingredients and stir for a few seconds to mix.
3. Spoon the batter in a muffin tin covered with muffin papers.
4. Pre-heat the oven and bake at 350F for about twenty minutes or until it rises significantly and starts to appear golden-brown.
5. Serve the muffins chilled or store them in an airtight container.

Nutritional Content of One Serving:

Calories: 162 Fat: 7.0g Protein: 2.7g Carbohydrates: 22.7g

Sprinkles Chocolate Cupcakes

Total Time Taken: 1 ½ hours
Yield: 12 Servings
Ingredients:

Cupcakes:

- ¼ cup cocoa powder
- ½ cup butter, softened
- ½ teaspoon salt
- 1 ½ cups all-purpose flour
- 1 ½ teaspoons baking powder
- 1 cup white sugar
- 1 cup whole milk
- 1 teaspoon vanilla extract
- 2 eggs

Frosting:

- ½ cup dark chocolate chips, melted
- 1 cup butter, softened
- 2 cups powdered sugar

Directions:

1. To make the cupcakes, combine the butter and sugar in a container until creamy and pale.
2. Put in the eggs and vanilla and mix thoroughly then mix in the flour, cocoa powder, salt and baking powder, alternating them with milk.
3. Spoon the batter in a muffin tin coated with baking muffin papers.
4. Preheat your oven and bake the cupcakes at 350F for about twenty minutes or until a toothpick inserted into them comes out dry.
5. To make the frosting, combine the butter and sugar in a container until fluffy and pale. Put in the melted and cooled chocolate.
6. Garnish the cupcakes with frosting and serve them fresh.

Nutritional Content of One Serving:

Calories: 452 Fat: 26.1g Protein: 4.1g Carbohydrates: 54.2g

Strawberry and Cream Cupcakes

Total Time Taken: 1 ½ hours
Yield: 12 Servings

Ingredients:

- ½ cup butter, softened
- ½ teaspoon salt
- 1 ½ cups all-purpose flour
- 1 ½ cups heavy cream, whipped
- 1 ½ teaspoons baking powder
- 1 cup fresh strawberries, sliced
- 1 teaspoon vanilla extract
- 2/3 cup white sugar

- 3 eggs

Directions:
1. Mix the butter and sugar in a container until fluffy and pale.
2. Put in the eggs, one at a time, then mix in the vanilla.
3. Fold in the flour, salt and baking powder then put in the strawberries.
4. Spoon the batter into 12 muffin cups covered with muffin papers and preheat your oven and bake at 350F for about twenty minutes or until a golden-brown colour is achieved and it rises significantly.
5. Let cool down then put whipped cream on top of each cupcake.

The cupcakes taste best chilled.

Nutritional Content of One Serving:
Calories: 239 Fat: 14.5g Protein: 3.5g Carbohydrates: 24.8g

Strawberry Chia Seed Muffins

Total Time Taken: 1 hour
Yield: 12 Servings
Ingredients:
- ½ teaspoon salt
- 1 ¾ cups all-purpose flour
- 1 cup plain yogurt
- 1 cup strawberries, sliced
- 1/3 cup canola oil
- 2 eggs
- 2 tablespoons chia seeds
- 2 teaspoons baking powder
- 4 tablespoons milk

Directions:
1. Mix the dry ingredients in a container.
2. Put in the oil, yogurt, eggs and milk and stir for a few seconds to mix.
3. Fold in the strawberries then spoon the batter in 12 muffin cups covered with muffin papers.
4. Preheat your oven and bake the muffins at 350F for a couple of minutes or until it rises significantly and starts to appear golden-brown.
5. Let the muffins cool to room temperature before you serve.

Nutritional Content of One Serving:
Calories: 178 Fat: 9.0g Protein: 5.3g Carbohydrates: 18.7g

Strawberry Matcha Muffins

Total Time Taken: 1 hour
Yield: 12 Servings
Ingredients:
- 2 eggs
- 2 cups all-purpose flour
- 1 teaspoon baking powder

- 1 tablespoon matcha powder
- 1 cup white sugar
- 1 cup strawberries, sliced
- 1 cup milk
- ½ teaspoon baking soda
- ½ cup butter, melted
- ¼ teaspoon salt

Directions:

1. Mix the flour, matcha powder, baking powder, baking soda and salt in a container.
2. Stir in the butter, eggs, milk and sugar and give it a quick whisk.
3. Fold in the strawberries then spoon the batter in a muffin tin lined using muffin papers of your choice.
4. Pre-heat the oven and bake at 350F for about twenty minutes or until a toothpick inserted into them comes out dry.
5. Serve the muffins chilled or store them in an airtight container.

Nutritional Content of One Serving:

Calories: 233 Fat: 9.1g Protein: 3.9g Carbohydrates: 35.2g

Strawberry Muffins

Total Time Taken: 1 hour
Yield: 12 Servings
Ingredients:

- ½ cup canola oil
- ½ cup milk
- ½ teaspoon salt
- ¾ cup white sugar
- ¾ cup whole wheat flour
- 1 ½ cups strawberries, sliced
- 1 cup all-purpose flour
- 1 teaspoon baking soda
- 2 eggs

Directions:

1. Mix the flours, baking soda and salt in a container.
2. Put in the canola oil, sugar, eggs and mix and stir for a few seconds to mix.
3. Fold in the strawberries then spoon the batter in 12 muffin cups covered with muffin papers.
4. Preheat your oven and bake the muffins at 350F for about twenty minutes or until a golden-brown colour is achieved and it rises significantly.
5. *Let cool down before you serve.*

Nutritional Content of One Serving:

Calories: 215 Fat: 10.3g Protein: 3.3g Carbohydrates: 28.3g

Streusel Banana Muffins

Total Time Taken: 1 ¼ hours
Yield: 12 Servings
Ingredients:

Muffins:
- 2 tablespoons wheat bran
- 2 eggs
- 2 bananas, mashed
- 1 teaspoon vanilla extract
- 1 teaspoon baking soda
- 1 ¾ cups all-purpose flour
- ½ teaspoon cinnamon powder
- ½ cup buttermilk
- ¼ teaspoon salt

Streusel:
- 2 tablespoons dark brown sugar
- 1 cup all-purpose flour
- ½ cup butter, chilled
- ¼ teaspoon salt

Directions:
1. For the muffins, combine the bananas, eggs and buttermilk in a container.
2. Stir in the flour, wheat bran, baking soda, salt and cinnamon and stir for a few seconds to mix.
3. Spoon the batter in a muffin tin covered with muffin papers.
4. For the streusel, combine all the ingredients in a container until grainy.
5. Top each muffin with the streusel and preheat your oven and bake at 350F for about twenty minutes or until a golden-brown colour is achieved and it rises significantly.

These muffins taste best chilled.

Nutritional Content of One Serving:
Calories: 212 Fat: 8.9g Protein: 4.6g Carbohydrates: 28.8g

Streusel Cranberry Muffins

Total Time Taken: 1 hour
Yield: 12 Servings
Ingredients:

Muffins:
- ¼ teaspoon salt
- ½ cup butter, melted
- ½ cup milk
- 1 ½ cups all-purpose flour
- 1 ½ teaspoons baking powder
- 1 cup fresh cranberries
- 1 cup ground pecans

- 1 cup white sugar
- 1 teaspoon vanilla extract
- 2 eggs

Streusel:
- ¼ cup butter, chilled
- ½ cup whole wheat flour
- 2 tablespoons brown sugar

Directions:
1. For the muffins, combine the butter, eggs, milk, sugar and vanilla in a container.
2. Stir in the flour, salt, pecans and baking powder then fold in the cranberries.
3. Spoon the batter in a muffin tin covered with muffin papers.
4. For the streusel, combine all the ingredients in a container until grainy.
5. Top each muffin with streusel and preheat your oven and bake at 350F for about twenty minutes or until a golden-brown colour is achieved and it rises significantly.

These muffins taste best chilled.

Nutritional Content of One Serving:
Calories: 276 Fat: 13.5g Protein: 3.7g Carbohydrates: 36.0g

Sugarless Muffins

Total Time Taken: 1 hour
Yield: 12 Servings
Ingredients:
- 3 bananas, mashed
- 2 eggs
- 1 teaspoon baking soda
- 1 ½ cups all-purpose flour
- ½ cup walnuts, chopped
- ½ cup applesauce
- ¼ teaspoon salt

Directions:
1. Mix the eggs, bananas and applesauce in a container.
2. Put in the flour, salt and baking soda then mix in the walnuts.
3. Spoon the batter in a muffin tin lined using muffin papers of your choice and preheat your oven and bake at 350F for about twenty minutes.

These muffins taste best chilled.

Nutritional Content of One Serving:
Calories: 130 Fat: 4.1g Protein: 4.1g Carbohydrates: 20.4g

Sugary Blueberry Muffins

Total Time Taken: 1 hour
Yield: 12 Servings
Ingredients:
- ¼ cup milk
- ¼ teaspoon salt
- ½ cup butter, melted
- ½ cup Demerara sugar
- ½ cup white sugar
- 1 ½ cups blueberries
- 1 teaspoon vanilla extract
- 2 cups all-purpose flour
- 2 eggs
- 2 teaspoons baking powder

Directions:
1. Mix the butter and sugar in a container. Put in the eggs and mix thoroughly then mix in the milk and vanilla.
2. Fold in the flour, baking powder and salt then put in the blueberries.
3. Spoon the batter in a muffin tin covered with muffin papers.
4. Top each muffin with Demerara sugar and preheat your oven and bake at 350F for about twenty minutes or until it rises significantly and starts to appear golden-brown.
5. *Let cool down before you serve.*

Nutritional Content of One Serving:
Calories: 223 Fat: 8.8g Protein: 3.5g Carbohydrates: 33.5g

Sugary Pumpkin Muffins

Total Time Taken: 1 hour
Yield: 12 Servings
Ingredients:
- 2 teaspoons baking powder
- 2 eggs
- 2 cups all-purpose flour
- 1 teaspoon ground ginger
- 1 teaspoon cinnamon powder
- ¾ cup light brown sugar
- ¾ cup butter, softened
- ½ teaspoon salt
- ½ cup white sugar
- ½ cup pumpkin puree
- ¼ cup buttermilk

Directions:
1. Mix the butter and brown sugar in a container until pale and light.
2. Put in the eggs, buttermilk and pumpkin puree and mix thoroughly.

3. Fold in the flour, salt, baking powder and ginger then spoon the batter in a muffin tin lined using muffin papers of your choice.
4. Mix the sugar and cinnamon in a container. Top each muffin with the cinnamon sugar and preheat your oven and bake at 350F for about twenty minutes or until it rises significantly and starts to appear golden-brown.

These muffins taste best chilled.

Nutritional Content of One Serving:

Calories: 261 Fat: 12.5g Protein: 3.5g Carbohydrates: 34.8g

Sultana Bran Muffins

Total Time Taken: 1 hour
Yield: 12 Servings
Ingredients:

- ¼ cup olive oil
- ¼ cup shredded coconut
- ½ cup sultanas
- ½ teaspoon cinnamon powder
- ½ teaspoon salt
- ¾ cup plain yogurt
- ¾ cup wheat bran
- 1 ¼ cups all-purpose flour
- 1 egg
- 1 teaspoon vanilla extract
- 2 bananas, mashed
- 2 teaspoons baking powder

Directions:

1. Mix the wheat bran, flour, baking powder, coconut, cinnamon and salt in a container.
2. Stir in the bananas, egg, yogurt, olive oil and vanilla.
3. Fold in the sultanas then spoon the batter in a muffin tin covered with muffin papers.
4. Pre-heat the oven and bake at 350F for about twenty minutes or until it rises significantly and starts to appear golden-brown.

These muffins taste best chilled.

Nutritional Content of One Serving:

Calories: 137 Fat: 5.7g Protein: 3.5g Carbohydrates: 19.7g

Sweet Potato Cinnamon Cupcakes

Total Time Taken: 1 ½ hours
Yield: 16 Servings
Ingredients:

Cupcakes:

- ¼ teaspoon salt
- ½ cup crushed pineapple

- ½ teaspoon baking powder
- ½ teaspoon baking soda
- ½ teaspoon ground ginger
- 1 cup butter, softened
- 1 cup light brown sugar
- 1 teaspoon cinnamon powder
- 2 cups all-purpose flour
- 2 cups sweet potato puree

Frosting:
- 1 cup butter, softened
- 1 teaspoon cinnamon powder
- 2 cups powdered sugar, sifted

Directions:
1. To make the cupcakes, sift the flour, spices, baking soda, baking powder and salt in a container.
2. Mix the butter and sugar in a separate container until fluffy and creamy. Put in the sweet potato puree and pineapple then fold in the flour.
3. Spoon the batter in a muffin tin lined with paper liners.
4. Pre-heat the oven and bake at 350F for about twenty minutes or until a toothpick inserted into them comes out dry.
5. Let the cupcakes cool down.
6. To make the frosting, combine the butter in a container until creamy.
7. Put in the sugar, ½ cup at a time, and stir thoroughly until fluffy and pale.
8. Pipe the frosting on top of each cupcake and drizzle with cinnamon powder.

These cupcakes taste best when fresh.

Nutritional Content of One Serving:
Calories: 388 Fat: 23.3g Protein: 2.5g Carbohydrates: 44.0g

Sweet Potato Cupcakes

Total Time Taken: 1 ½ hours
Yield: 16 Servings
Ingredients:

Cupcakes:
- ½ cup mini marshmallows
- ½ teaspoon ground ginger
- ½ teaspoon salt
- 1 ½ cups sweet potato puree
- 1 cup butter, softened
- 1 cup white sugar
- 1 teaspoon cinnamon powder
- 1 teaspoon vanilla extract
- 2 cups all-purpose flour
- 2 teaspoons baking powder
- 3 eggs

Frosting:
- ½ cup butter, softened
- 1 cup cream cheese
- 2 cups powdered sugar

Directions:
1. To make the cupcakes, sift the flour, baking powder, salt, cinnamon and ginger in a container.
2. In a separate container, combine the butter and sugar until fluffy and pale.
3. Put in the eggs and mix thoroughly then mix in the pumpkin puree and vanilla.
4. Fold in the flour then spoon the batter in 12 muffin cups coated with baking muffin papers.
5. Preheat your oven and bake the cupcakes at 350F for about twenty minutes or until it rises significantly and becomes aromatic.
6. To make the frosting, combine all the ingredients in a container until pale and fluffy.
7. Spoon the frosting in a pastry bag and top the cupcakes with it.

Nutritional Content of One Serving:
Calories: 408 Fat: 23.4g Protein: 4.5g Carbohydrates: 47.1g

Sweet Potato Maple Muffins

Total Time Taken: 1 hour
Yield: 12 Servings
Ingredients:
- ¼ teaspoon salt
- ½ teaspoon all-spice powder
- ½ teaspoon cinnamon powder
- ½ teaspoon ground ginger
- 1 ½ teaspoons baking powder
- 1 cup light brown sugar
- 1 cup milk
- 1 cup sweet potato puree
- 1 teaspoon vanilla extract
- 2 cups all-purpose flour
- 2/3 cup canola oil
- 3 eggs

Directions:
1. Mix the flour, salt, baking powder, cinnamon, ginger and all-spice powder in a container.
2. Put in the remaining ingredients and mix thoroughly then pour the batter in a muffin tin covered with muffin papers.
3. Preheat your oven and bake the muffins at 350F for about twenty minutes or until a golden-brown colour is achieved and fragrant.
4. *Let cool down before you serve.*

Nutritional Content of One Serving:
Calories: 278 Fat: 13.9g Protein: 4.6g Carbohydrates: 34.2g

Sweet Potato Zucchini Muffins

Total Time Taken: 1 hour
Yield: 12 Servings
Ingredients:

- ¼ cup canola oil
- ¼ cup heavy cream
- ¼ cup light brown sugar
- ¼ teaspoon salt
- ½ teaspoon baking soda
- 1 cup grated zucchinis
- 1 cup sweet potato puree
- 1 teaspoon baking powder
- 1 teaspoon orange zest
- 2 cups all-purpose flour
- 2 eggs

Directions:

1. Mix the sweet potato puree, zucchinis, sugar, cream, eggs, oil and orange zest in a container.
2. Put in the dry ingredients and stir for a few seconds to mix using a spatula.
3. Spoon the batter in a muffin tin lined using muffin papers of your choice.
4. Pre-heat the oven and bake at 350F for about twenty minutes or until well risen and a toothpick inserted into the center of a muffin comes out clean.
5. Let cool in the pan before you serve.

Nutritional Content of One Serving:

Calories: 170 Fat: 6.5g Protein: 3.6g Carbohydrates: 24.5g

Sweet Raspberry Corn Muffins

Total Time Taken: 1 hour
Yield: 12 Servings
Ingredients:

- ¼ cup canola oil
- ¼ teaspoon salt
- ½ cup apricot jam
- ½ cup white sugar
- 1 ½ cups all-purpose flour
- 1 cup buttermilk
- 1 cup raspberries
- 1 cup yellow cornmeal
- 1 tablespoon orange zest
- 2 eggs
- 2 teaspoons baking powder

Directions:

1. Mix the flour, cornmeal, sugar, baking powder and salt in a container.
2. Stir in the buttermilk, apricot jam, oil, orange zest and eggs and mix thoroughly.

3. Fold in the raspberries then spoon the batter in a muffin tin coated with baking muffin papers.
4. Preheat your oven and bake the muffins at 350F for about twenty minutes or until it rises significantly and starts to appear golden-brown.
5. Let the muffins cool in the pan before you serve.

Nutritional Content of One Serving:

Calories: 223 Fat: 6.1g Protein: 4.3g Carbohydrates: 39.4g

The Ultimate Blueberry Muffins

Total Time Taken: 1 hour
Yield: 12 Servings
Ingredients:

- 2 eggs
- ½ cup canola oil
- 1 teaspoon lemon zest
- 1 teaspoon vanilla extract
- 2 cups all-purpose flour
- ½ teaspoon salt
- 2 teaspoons baking powder
- 1 cup sour cream
- 1 cup fresh blueberries
- 2/3 cup white sugar

Directions:

1. Mix the eggs and sugar in a container until fluffy and pale.
2. Put in the oil and vanilla and mix thoroughly.
3. Fold in the flour, salt and baking powder then put in the sour cream and mix for a minute on high speed.
4. Fold in the blueberries then spoon the batter in a muffin tin covered with muffin papers.
5. Preheat your oven and bake the muffins at 350F for about twenty minutes or until it rises significantly and seems golden.
6. Let them cool before you serve or storing.

Nutritional Content of One Serving:

Calories: 258 Fat: 14.1g Protein: 3.8g Carbohydrates: 30.1g

The Ultimate Vanilla Cupcakes

Total Time Taken: 1 ½ hours
Yield: 12 Servings
Ingredients:

Cupcakes:

- ½ teaspoon salt
- 1 cup buttermilk
- 1 tablespoon vanilla extract
- 2 cups all-purpose flour
- 2 eggs

- 2 teaspoons baking powder
- 2/3 cup butter, softened
- 2/3 cup white sugar

Frosting:
- ½ teaspoon salt
- 1 cup butter, softened
- 1 cup white sugar
- 1 teaspoon vanilla extract
- 4 egg whites

Directions:
1. To make the cupcakes, combine the flour, salt, baking powder and sugar in a container.
2. Put in the butter and stir until grainy.
3. In a container, mix the eggs, buttermilk and vanilla and mix thoroughly. Pour over the flour and mix for a minute on high speed.
4. Spoon the batter in a muffin tin lined with baking muffins papers.
5. Pre-heat the oven and bake at 350F for about twenty minutes or until it rises significantly and starts to appear golden-brown.
6. Let cool in the pan.
7. To make the frosting, combine the egg whites and sugar in a container and place over hot water bath. Keep on heat and stir until heated and the sugar has melted.
8. Turn off the heat and mix for about five to seven minutes until fluffy and thickened, shiny and firm.
9. Put in the butter, all at once, and stir thoroughly for a couple of minutes. It will curdle up at first then it will come back together.
10. Put in the vanilla and mix thoroughly.
11. Spoon the frosting in a pastry bag and top the cupcakes with it.

These are best enjoyed fresh.

Nutritional Content of One Serving:
Calories: 435 Fat: 26.7g Protein: 5.2g Carbohydrates: 45.4g

Turkish Delight Muffins

Total Time Taken: 1 hour
Yield: 12 Servings
Ingredients:
- ¼ teaspoon salt
- ½ cup canola oil
- ½ cup sour cream
- ½ cup white sugar
- 1 cup Turkish delight, diced
- 1 teaspoon baking powder
- 1 teaspoon vanilla extract
- 2 cups all-purpose flour
- 4 eggs

Directions:

1. Mix the eggs and sugar in a container until fluffy and light.
2. Put in the vanilla, oil and sour cream and mix thoroughly.
3. Fold in the flour, salt and baking powder then mix in the Turkish delight.
4. Spoon the batter in a muffin tin covered with muffin papers.
5. Pre-heat the oven and bake at 350F for about twenty minutes or until a golden-brown colour is achieved and it rises significantly.

These muffins taste best chilled.

Nutritional Content of One Serving:
Calories: 239 Fat: 13.0g Protein: 4.3g Carbohydrates: 27.0g

Vanilla Cupcakes With Chocolate Buttercream

Total Time Taken: 1 ½ hours
Yield: 14 Servings
Ingredients:

Cupcakes:
- 2 cups all-purpose flour
- ¼ teaspoon salt
- 2 teaspoons baking powder
- 1 cup butter, softened
- 2 eggs
- 1 cup milk
- 1 tablespoon vanilla extract
- 2/3 cup white sugar

Frosting:
- ½ cup white sugar
- 1 cup butter, softened
- 1 cup dark chocolate chips, melted
- 1 teaspoon vanilla extract
- 2 egg whites

Directions:
1. To make the cupcakes, combine the flour, sugar, salt and baking powder in a container. Put in the butter and stir until grainy.
2. Stir in the eggs, milk and vanilla and stir for a few seconds to mix.
3. Spoon the batter in a muffin tin covered with muffin papers and preheat your oven and bake at 350F for about twenty minutes or until a toothpick inserted into them comes out dry.
4. Let the cupcakes cool in the pan.
5. To make the frosting, combine the egg whites and sugar in a container. Place over a hot
6. water bath and keep over heat until the sugar has melted.
7. Turn off the heat and whip for about five to seven minutes until shiny and fluffy.
8. Put in the butter and mix for at least two minutes until fluffy and creamy.
9. Stir in the chocolate and mix briefly then pipe the buttercream over each cupcake.

These cupcakes taste best when fresh.

Nutritional Content of One Serving:
Calories: 424 Fat: 29.8g Protein: 4.6g Carbohydrates: 37.5g

Vanilla Cupcakes With Maple Frosting

Total Time Taken: 1 ½ hours
Yield: 10 Servings
Ingredients:

Cupcakes:
- ½ cup butter, softened
- ½ cup whole milk
- ½ teaspoon salt
- ¾ cup white sugar
- 1 ½ cups all-purpose flour
- 1 teaspoon baking powder
- 1 teaspoon vanilla extract
- 3 eggs

Frosting:
- 1 cup butter, softened
- 1 teaspoon vanilla extract
- 2 cups powdered sugar

Directions:
1. To make the cupcakes, combine the butter and sugar until fluffy and pale.
2. Put in the vanilla then mix in the eggs and mix thoroughly.
3. Fold in the flour, salt and baking powder, alternating it with the milk.
4. Spoon the batter in a muffin tin covered with muffin papers.
5. Pre-heat the oven and bake at 350F for about twenty minutes or until a toothpick inserted into them comes out dry.
6. To make the frosting, combine the butter in a container until fluffy. Put in the sugar and continue mixing until airy and pale.
7. Put in the vanilla then spoon the frosting in a pastry bag and top the cupcakes with it.

Nutritional Content of One Serving:
Calories: 491 Fat: 29.5g Protein: 4.3g Carbohydrates: 54.2g

Vegan Blueberries Muffins

Total Time Taken: 1 hour
Yield: 12 Servings
Ingredients:
- ¼ teaspoon salt
- ½ cup canola oil
- ½ cup soy yogurt
- ¾ cup light brown sugar

- 1 cup almond milk
- 1 cup blueberries
- 1 teaspoon vanilla extract
- 2 cups all-purpose flour
- 2 tablespoons ground flaxseeds
- 2 teaspoons baking powder

Directions:

1. Mix the flour, baking powder, salt and sugar in a container.
2. Stir in the flaxseeds then put in the canola oil, almond milk, soy yogurt and vanilla.
3. Fold in the blueberries then spoon the batter in a muffin tin covered with muffin papers.
4. Pre-heat the oven and bake at 350F for about twenty minutes or until a toothpick inserted into them comes out dry.

These muffins taste best chilled.

Nutritional Content of One Serving:

Calories: 259 Fat: 14.7g Protein: 3.3g Carbohydrates: 29.4g

Vegan Chocolate Muffins

Total Time Taken: 1 hour
Yield: 12 Servings
Ingredients:

- ¼ cup cocoa powder
- ½ cup almond flour
- ½ cup dark chocolate chips
- 1 ½ cups all-purpose flour
- 1 ½ teaspoons baking powder
- 1 cup coconut milk
- 1 cup coconut sugar
- 1 teaspoon vanilla extract
- 1/3 cup coconut oil, melted

Directions:

1. Mix the flours, cocoa powder, baking powder and sugar in a container.
2. Put in the rest of the ingredient and stir for a few seconds to mix.
3. Fold in the chocolate chips then spoon the batter in a muffin tin coated with baking muffin papers.
4. Pre-heat the oven and bake at 350F for about twenty minutes or until a toothpick inserted into the center of a muffin comes out clean.

These muffins taste best chilled.

Nutritional Content of One Serving:

Calories: 251 Fat: 13.1g Protein: 3.0g Carbohydrates: 33.9g

Vodka Cupcakes

Total Time Taken: 1 ½ hours

 Yield: 12 Servings

 Ingredients:

Cupcakes:

- ¼ cup vodka
- ¼ teaspoon salt
- ½ cup white sugar
- 1 cup heavy cream
- 1 teaspoon vanilla extract
- 2 cups all-purpose flour
- 2 eggs
- 2 teaspoons baking powder

Frosting:

- 1 cup butter, softened
- 1 tablespoon heavy cream
- 2 ½ cups powdered sugar

Topping:

- ¼ cup heavy cream
- ½ cup dark chocolate chips
- 2 tablespoons vodka

Directions:

1. To make the cupcakes, combine the cream, eggs, vodka, sugar and vanilla in a container.
2. Stir in the flour, baking powder and salt and stir swiftly to combine.
3. Spoon the batter in a muffin tin covered with muffin papers and preheat your oven and bake at 350F for about twenty minutes or until it rises significantly and starts to appear golden-brown.
4. Let cool down in the pan.
5. To make the frosting, combine the butter in a container until pale. Put in the sugar and mix on high speed until fluffy and light.
6. Stir in the cream and mix for a few more minutes.
7. Pipe the frosting over each cupcake.
8. For the topping, melt the chocolate and cream together in a heatproof container over a hot water bath.
9. Turn off the heat and put in the vodka. Let cool down then sprinkle it over the frosted cupcakes.

These cupcakes taste best when fresh.

Nutritional Content of One Serving:

Calories: 439 Fat: 22.7g Protein: 3.9g Carbohydrates: 53.3g

Walnut Banana Muffins

Total Time Taken: 1 hour
Yield: 12 Servings
Ingredients:

- ¼ cup butter, melted
- ½ cup light brown sugar
- ½ cup plain yogurt
- ½ cup walnuts, chopped
- ½ teaspoon salt
- 1 ½ teaspoons baking powder
- 1 cup all-purpose flour
- 1 cup ground walnuts
- 2 eggs
- 3 bananas, mashed

Directions:

1. Mix the bananas, sugar, eggs, yogurt and butter and mix thoroughly.
2. Fold in the flour, walnuts, salt and baking powder.
3. Fold in the walnuts then spoon the batter in a muffin tin covered with muffin papers and preheat your oven and bake at 350F for about twenty minutes or until it rises significantly and seems golden.

These muffins taste best chilled.

Nutritional Content of One Serving:

Calories: 236 Fat: 14.1g Protein: 6.7g Carbohydrates: 23.2g

White Chocolate Lime Cupcakes

Total Time Taken: 1 ½ hours
Yield: 12 Servings
Ingredients:

Cupcakes:

- 3 eggs
- 1 teaspoon vanilla extract
- 1 tablespoon lime zest
- 1 tablespoon lime juice
- ½ cup buttermilk
- 1 ½ cups all-purpose flour
- ¼ cup cornstarch
- ½ teaspoon salt
- 1 teaspoon baking soda
- ½ cup white chocolate chips
- 2/3 cup butter, softened
- 2/3 cup light brown sugar

Frosting:

- ½ cup butter, softened
- 1 cup cream cheese, softened
- 1 tablespoon lime zest
- 2 cups powdered sugar

Directions:
1. To make the cupcakes, combine the butter and sugar in a container until pale and fluffy.
2. Put in the eggs, one at a time, then mix in the vanilla, lime zest and juice and buttermilk.
3. Fold in the flour, cornstarch, salt and baking soda then put in the chocolate chips.
4. Spoon the batter in a muffin tin covered with muffin papers and preheat your oven and bake at 350F for about twenty minutes until it rises significantly and starts to appear golden-brown.
5. Let them cool in the pan.
6. To make the frosting, combine the cream cheese and butter in a container until pale.
7. Put in the sugar and stir thoroughly until airy and light.
8. Stir in the lime zest then spoon the frosting over each cupcake.

These cupcakes taste best when fresh.

Nutritional Content of One Serving:
Calories: 462 Fat: 28.3g Protein: 5.5g Carbohydrates: 48.0g

White Chocolate Pumpkin Cupcakes

Total Time Taken: 1 ½ hours
Yield: 14 Servings
Ingredients:

Cupcakes:
- ¼ cup canola oil
- ½ cup dark chocolate chips
- ½ cup light brown sugar
- ½ cup milk
- ½ teaspoon baking soda
- ½ teaspoon cinnamon powder
- ½ teaspoon ground cardamom
- ½ teaspoon ground ginger
- ½ teaspoon salt
- 1 cup pumpkin puree
- 1 teaspoon baking powder
- 1 teaspoon vanilla extract
- 2 cups all-purpose flour
- 2 eggs

Frosting:
- 1 cup heavy cream
- 1 teaspoon vanilla extract
- 2 cups white chocolate chips
- 2 tablespoons butter

Directions:

1. To make the cupcakes, combine the flour, baking powder, baking soda, spices and salt in a container.
2. Mix the eggs and sugar in a container until fluffy and pale.
3. Put in the milk, pumpkin puree, canola oil and vanilla and mix thoroughly.
4. Fold in the flour mixture then spoon the batter in a muffin tin covered with muffin papers.
5. Pre-heat the oven and bake at 350F for about twenty minutes or until the cupcakes pass the toothpick test.
6. Let them cool in the pan.
7. To make the frosting, bring the cream to a boil. Turn off the heat and mix in the chocolate. Stir until melted and smooth.
8. Put in the vanilla and butter and mix thoroughly.
9. Let cool completely then whip the cream until fluffy and pale.
   10. Top the cupcakes with the frosting and garnish with a dusting of cinnamon powder.

Nutritional Content of One Serving:

Calories: 336 Fat: 18.7g Protein: 5.1g Carbohydrates: 38.4g

White Chocolate Pumpkin Cupcakes

Total Time Taken: 1 ½ hours

Yield: 12 Servings

Ingredients:

Cupcakes:

- ¼ teaspoon ground cardamom
- ¼ teaspoon salt
- ½ cup butter, softened
- ½ cup buttermilk
- ½ teaspoon ground ginger
- 1 ½ cups all-purpose flour
- 1 cup pumpkin puree
- 1 teaspoon cinnamon powder
- 2 eggs
- 2 tablespoons canola oil
- 2/3 cup light brown sugar

Frosting:

- 1 cup heavy cream
- 2 cups white chocolate chips

Directions:

1. To make the cupcakes, combine the butter, oil and sugar in a container until fluffy and pale.
2. Put in the eggs and mix thoroughly then mix in the pumpkin puree and buttermilk.
3. Fold in the remaining ingredients then spoon the batter in a muffin tin covered with muffin papers.
4. Pre-heat the oven and bake at 350F for about twenty minutes or until it rises significantly and becomes aromatic.
5. Let cool in the pan completely.
6. To make the frosting, bring the cream to a boil in a saucepan. Turn off the heat and put in the chocolate. Stir until melted then let cool down.

7. Pipe the frosting over each cupcake and serve them fresh.

Nutritional Content of One Serving:

Calories: 385 Fat: 23.8g Protein: 5.1g Carbohydrates: 39.2g

Whole Wheat Banana Muffins

Total Time Taken: 1 hour
Yield: 12 Servings
Ingredients:

- ¼ cup canola oil
- ¼ teaspoon cinnamon powder
- ¼ teaspoon salt
- ½ cup light brown sugar
- 1 cup buttermilk
- 2 bananas, mashed
- 2 cups whole wheat flour
- 2 eggs
- 2 teaspoons baking powder

Directions:

1. Mix the dry ingredients in a container.
2. Put in the remaining ingredients, all at once, and stir for a few seconds to mix with a whisk.
3. Pour the batter in a muffin tin coated with baking muffin papers and preheat your oven and bake at 350F for about twenty minutes or until a toothpick inserted into them comes out dry.
4. *Let cool down before you serve.*

Nutritional Content of One Serving:

Calories: 176 Fat: 5.7g Protein: 4.0g Carbohydrates: 27.7g

Whole Wheat Strawberry Muffins

Total Time Taken: 1 hour
Yield: 12 Servings
Ingredients:

- 2 eggs
- 2 cups whole wheat flour
- 2 bananas, mashed
- 1 teaspoon vanilla extract
- 1 teaspoon baking soda
- 1 teaspoon baking powder
- 1 cup strawberries, sliced
- ½ cup light brown sugar
- ½ cup canola oil
- ½ cup applesauce

Directions:

1. Mix the eggs, applesauce, canola oil, bananas, sugar and vanilla in a container.
2. Put in the flour, baking soda and baking powder and stir swiftly to combine.

3. Fold in the strawberries then spoon the batter in a muffin tin coated with baking muffin papers.
4. Preheat your oven and bake the muffins at 350F for about twenty minutes or until a toothpick inserted into them comes out dry.

These muffins taste best chilled.

Nutritional Content of One Serving:
Calories: 217 Fat: 10.1g Protein: 3.4g Carbohydrates: 28.7g

Wholemeal Muffins

Total Time Taken: 1 hour
Yield: 12 Servings
Ingredients:
- ¼ cup canola oil
- ½ cup white sugar
- ½ cup whole wheat flour
- ½ teaspoon salt
- 1 ½ cups all-purpose flour
- 1 cup milk
- 1 egg
- 2 tablespoons chia seeds
- 2 tablespoons hemp seeds
- 2 teaspoons baking powder

Directions:
1. Mix the flour, wheat flour, baking powder, salt, chia seeds and hemp seeds.
2. Put in the sugar, egg, milk and canola oil and stir for a few seconds to mix.
3. Spoon the batter into a muffin tin covered with muffin papers and preheat your oven and bake at 350F for about twenty minutes or until a golden-brown colour is achieved and it rises significantly.

These muffins taste best chilled.

Nutritional Content of One Serving:
Calories: 182 Fat: 6.9g Protein: 4.2g Carbohydrates: 25.9g

Wholesome Blueberry Muffins

Total Time Taken: 1 hour
Yield: 12 Servings
Ingredients:
- ¼ cup wheat bran
- ½ cup butter, melted
- ½ cup milk
- ½ teaspoon salt
- 1 cup all-purpose flour
- 1 cup fresh blueberries
- 1 cup whole wheat flour
- 2 eggs

- 2 tablespoons orange marmalade
- 2 teaspoons baking powder

Directions:
1. Mix the flours, bran, baking powder and salt in a container.
2. Put in the butter, eggs, milk and marmalade then fold in blueberries.
3. Spoon the batter in a muffin tin covered with muffin papers and preheat your oven and bake at 350F for about twenty minutes or until it rises significantly and starts to appear golden-brown.

These muffins taste best chilled.

Nutritional Content of One Serving:
Calories: 213 Fat: 10.7g Protein: 4.5g Carbohydrates: 25.9g

Yogurt Blackberry Muffins

Total Time Taken: 1 hour
Yield: 12 Servings
Ingredients:
- ¼ teaspoon salt
- ½ cup butter, melted
- ½ cup heavy cream
- 1 cup blackberries
- 1 cup white sugar
- 1 teaspoon vanilla extract
- 2 cups all-purpose flour
- 2 egg whites
- 2 eggs
- 2 teaspoons baking powder

Directions:
1. Mix the flour, baking powder and salt in a container.
2. Whip the eggs, egg whites, vanilla and sugar until fluffy and pale.
3. Put in the butter and mix thoroughly then mix in the cream.
4. Fold in the flour then put in the blackberries.
5. Spoon the batter in a muffin tin covered with muffin papers.
6. Pre-heat the oven and bake at 350F for about twenty minutes or until it rises significantly and starts to appear golden-brown.
7. Let the muffins cool to room temperature before you serve.

Nutritional Content of One Serving:
Calories: 244 Fat: 10.5g Protein: 4.0g Carbohydrates: 34.4g

Yogurt Vanilla Berry Muffins

Total Time Taken: 1 hour
Yield: 12 Servings
Ingredients:
- ¼ cup canola oil

- ¼ teaspoon salt
- ½ teaspoon baking soda
- 1 ¾ cups all-purpose flour
- 1 cup Greek yogurt
- 1 cup mixed berries
- 1 tablespoon vanilla extract
- 1 teaspoon baking powder
- 2 eggs

Directions:
1. Mix the eggs, oil, yogurt and vanilla in a container.
2. Put in the flour, salt, baking powder and baking soda and stir for a few seconds to mix just until incorporated.
3. Fold in the berries then spoon the batter in a muffin tin covered with muffin papers.
4. Pre-heat the oven and bake at 350F for about twenty minutes or until a toothpick inserted into them comes out dry.
5. Let cool in the pan before you serve.

Nutritional Content of One Serving:
Calories: 140 Fat: 5.8g Protein: 4.6g Carbohydrates: 16.4g

Zesty Pistachio Muffins

Total Time Taken: 1 hour
Yield: 12 Servings
Ingredients:
- ¼ cup canola oil
- ¼ cup plain yogurt
- ¼ teaspoon salt
- 1 cup all-purpose flour
- 1 cup fresh raspberries
- 1 cup ground pistachio
- 1 cup white sugar
- 1 teaspoon baking powder
- 1 teaspoon vanilla extract
- 3 eggs

Directions:
1. Mix the eggs and sugar in a container until volume increases to twice what it was.
2. Put in the oil, vanilla and yogurt and mix thoroughly.
3. Fold in the remaining ingredients then spoon the batter in a muffin tin covered with muffin papers.
4. Preheat your oven and bake the muffins at 350F for about twenty minutes or until it rises significantly and starts to appear golden-brown.
5. Let cool in the pan before you serve.

Nutritional Content of One Serving:
Calories: 184 Fat: 6.7g Protein: 3.3g Carbohydrates: 28.8g

Zucchini Carrot Muffins

Total Time Taken: 1 hour
Yield: 12 Servings
Ingredients:

- ¼ cup maple syrup
- ¼ teaspoon salt
- ½ cup brown rice flour
- ½ cup canola oil
- ½ cup golden raisins
- ½ teaspoon cinnamon powder
- 1 ½ teaspoons baking powder
- 1 cup almond flour
- 1 cup grated carrots
- 1 cup grated zucchinis
- 1 egg

Directions:

1. Mix the flours, salt, baking powder and cinnamon in a container.
2. Stir in the canola oil, maple syrup and egg and stir for a few seconds to mix.
3. Fold in the carrots, zucchinis and raisins then spoon the batter in a muffin tin covered with muffin papers.
4. Pre-heat the oven and bake at 350F for about twenty minutes or until a toothpick inserted into them comes out dry.

These muffins taste best chilled.

Nutritional Content of One Serving:

Calories: 164 Fat: 10.8g Protein: 1.8g Carbohydrates: 16.3g

Zucchini Chocolate Muffins

Total Time Taken: 1 hour
Yield: 12 Servings
Ingredients:

- 1 teaspoon baking soda
- 1 egg
- 1 cup grated zucchinis
- 1 ½ cups all-purpose flour
- ¾ cup white sugar
- ½ teaspoon salt
- ½ teaspoon cinnamon powder
- ½ cup walnuts, chopped
- ½ cup cocoa powder
- ½ cup canola oil
- ¼ cup buttermilk

Directions:

1. Mix the flour, cocoa powder, sugar, baking soda, cinnamon and salt in a container.
2. Stir in the egg, canola oil, buttermilk and zucchinis then fold in the walnuts.
3. Pour the batter in a muffin tin lined using muffin papers of your choice and preheat your oven and bake at 350F for about twenty minutes or until it rises significantly and becomes aromatic.
4. Let the muffins cool in the pan before you serve.

Nutritional Content of One Serving:

Calories: 233 Fat: 13.2g Protein: 4.2g Carbohydrates: 27.5g

Anna Goldman is an American professional baker. Born and raised in Kentucky, Anna loved her mother's baking and gradually developed an affinity to it. She started baking with her mother's recipes, and eventually came up with recipes of her own. She had always wanted to write a book about baking, but never got the time to do so until she had to shut down her bakery temporarily due to the coronavirus. Every cloud has a silver lining!

Almond Vanilla Cupcakes

Total Time Taken: 1 ½ hours
Yield: 12 Servings
Ingredients:

Cupcakes:
- ¼ cup milk
- ½ cup butter, softened
- ½ cup white sugar
- ½ teaspoon salt
- 1 cup all-purpose flour
- 1 cup ground almonds
- 1 teaspoon baking powder
- 1 teaspoon lemon zest
- 1 teaspoon vanilla extract
- 2 eggs

Glaze:
- 1 cup powdered sugar
- 1 tablespoon butter, melted
- 1 teaspoon lemon zest

Directions:
1. To make the cupcakes, combine the butter, sugar and vanilla in a container until fluffy and pale.
2. Put in the eggs, one at a time, then mix in the lemon zest and put in the flour, almonds, salt and baking powder.
3. Stir in the milk and mix for a minute on high speed.
4. Spoon the batter in a muffin tin covered with muffin papers and preheat your oven and bake at 350F for about twenty minutes or until a golden-brown colour is achieved and it rises significantly.
5. Let the cupcakes cool in the pan.
6. For the glaze, combine all the ingredients in a container. Sprinkle the glaze over each cupcake and serve fresh.

Nutritional Content of One Serving:

Calories: 245 Fat: 13.5g Protein: 3.9g Carbohydrates: 28.6g

Almond Vanilla Cupcakes

Total Time Taken: 1 ½ hours
 Yield: 12 Servings
 Ingredients:

Cupcakes:
- ½ cup all-purpose flour
- ½ cup butter, softened
- ½ cup buttermilk
- ½ cup white sugar
- ½ teaspoon almond extract
- ½ teaspoon salt
- 1 ½ cups almond flour
- 1 teaspoon baking soda
- 1 teaspoon vanilla extract
- 2 eggs

Frosting:
- 1 cup butter, softened
- 1 tablespoon vanilla extract
- 2 cups powdered sugar

Directions:
1. To make the cupcakes, combine the flours, salt and baking soda in a container.
2. In a separate container, combine the butter, sugar and vanilla until fluffy and creamy.
3. Put in the eggs, one at a time, then mix in the buttermilk and almond extract.
4. Fold in the flour mixture then spoon the batter in a muffin tin covered with muffin papers.
5. Pre-heat the oven and bake at 350F for about twenty minutes or until a golden-brown colour is achieved.
6. Let them cool in the pan.
7. To make the frosting, combine the butter and sugar for five minutes until pale and fluffy.
8. Put in the vanilla and mix thoroughly.
9. Spoon the frosting in a pastry bag and top the cupcakes with it.

Nutritional Content of One Serving:

Calories: 371 Fat: 25.7g Protein: 2.8g Carbohydrates: 33.8g

Almond White Chocolate Cupcakes

Total Time Taken: 1 ½ hours
 Yield: 12 Servings
 Ingredients:

Cupcakes:
- ½ cup all-purpose flour
- ½ cup butter, softened
- ½ cup plain yogurt
- ½ teaspoon almond extract
- ½ teaspoon salt

- ¾ cup white sugar
- 1 ½ teaspoons baking powder
- 1 cup almond flour
- 1 teaspoon vanilla extract
- 3 eggs

Frosting:
- 1 cup heavy cream
- 2 cups white chocolate chips

Directions:
1. To make the cupcakes, combine the butter and sugar in a container until fluffy and pale.
2. Put in the vanilla, almond extract and eggs and mix thoroughly.
3. Stir in the yogurt and stir thoroughly until blended.
4. Fold in the flours, salt, baking powder and mix using a spatula.
5. Spoon the batter in a muffin tin covered with muffin papers and preheat your oven and bake at 350F for about twenty minutes or until it rises significantly and seems golden.
6. Let them cool in the pan.
7. To make the frosting, bring the cream to a boil then remove from the
8. heat and put in the chocolate. Stir until melted and smooth then let cool in your refrigerator for a few hours.
9. When chilled, whip the frosting until airy and fluffy. Spoon the frosting in a pastry bag and top the cupcakes with it.
    10. *Serve immediately.*

Nutritional Content of One Serving:

Calories: 359 Fat: 22.9g Protein: 5.0g Carbohydrates: 35.2g

Apple Cranberry Muffins

Total Time Taken: 1 hour
Yield: 12 Servings
Ingredients:
- ¼ teaspoon salt
- ½ cup butter, melted
- ½ cup dried cranberries
- ½ cup light brown sugar
- ½ cup milk
- ½ teaspoon cinnamon powder
- 1 ¾ cups all-purpose flour
- 1 egg
- 1 red apple, cored and diced
- 1 teaspoon baking soda
- 1 teaspoon vanilla extract

Directions:
1. Mix the flour, sugar, baking soda, salt and cinnamon in a container.
2. Stir in the butter, milk, egg and vanilla and stir for a few seconds to mix.

3. Fold in the apple and cranberries and spoon the batter in a muffin tin lined using muffin papers of your choice.
4. Preheat your oven and bake the muffins at 350F for about twenty minutes or until it rises significantly and seems golden.

These muffins taste best chilled.

Nutritional Content of One Serving:

Calories: 179 Fat: 8.4g Protein: 2.8g Carbohydrates: 22.9g

Apple Muffins

Total Time Taken: 1 hour
Yield: 12 Servings
Ingredients:
- ¼ cup canola oil
- ½ cup ground walnuts
- ½ cup plain yogurt
- ½ cup white sugar
- ½ cup whole wheat flour
- ½ teaspoon cinnamon powder
- ½ teaspoon salt
- 1 cup all-purpose flour
- 1 teaspoon baking soda
- 1 teaspoon vanilla extract
- 2 apples, peeled, cored and diced
- 2 eggs

Directions:
1. Mix the eggs and sugar until fluffy and pale.
2. Put in the vanilla, oil and yogurt and stir thoroughly until blended.
3. Fold in the flour mixture then put in the apples.
4. Spoon the batter in a muffin tin covered with muffin papers and preheat your oven and bake at 350F for about twenty minutes or until a golden-brown colour is achieved and it rises significantly.

These muffins taste best chilled.

Nutritional Content of One Serving:

Calories: 195 Fat: 8.7g Protein: 4.5g Carbohydrates: 25.8g

Apple Pie Caramel Cupcakes

Total Time Taken: 1 ½ hours
Yield: 14 Servings

Ingredients:
- ½ teaspoon baking soda
- ½ teaspoon ground ginger
- 1 ½ cups all-purpose flour
- 1 pinch salt

- 1 teaspoon baking powder
- 1 teaspoon vanilla extract
- 2 eggs
- 2/3 cup butter, softened
- 2/3 cup buttermilk
- 2/3 cup light brown sugar

Frosting:
- ½ teaspoon cinnamon powder
- 1 cup butter, softened
- 2 cups powdered sugar

Topping:
- ¼ cup light brown sugar
- 1 tablespoon lemon juice
- 2 apples, peeled, cored and diced

Directions:
1. To make the cupcakes, combine the butter and sugar in a container until creamy and fluffy.
2. Put in the eggs and vanilla and mix thoroughly then mix in the buttermilk.
3. Put in the flour, spices, baking powder, baking soda and salt then pour the batter in a muffin tin covered with muffin papers.
4. Pre-heat the oven and bake at 350F for about twenty minutes or until a toothpick inserted into them comes out dry.
5. To make the frosting, combine the butter and sugar in a container for five minutes until pale and airy. Put in the cinnamon and mix thoroughly.
6. Top each cupcake with the frosting.
7. For the topping, mix the ingredients in a saucepan and cook over low heat just until the apples are tender. Let cool down then top each cupcake with a spoonfuls of apple mixture.

These cupcakes taste best when fresh.

Nutritional Content of One Serving:
Calories: 374 Fat: 22.9g Protein: 2.9g Carbohydrates: 41.1g

Apple Puree Muffins

Total Time Taken: 1 hour
Yield: 12 Servings
Ingredients:
- 1 ½ cups all-purpose flour
- 1 teaspoon cinnamon powder
- ½ teaspoon ground ginger
- 1 teaspoon baking soda
- 2 eggs
- ½ cup apple puree
- ¼ cup peanut oil
- 1 teaspoon vanilla extract
- 2 apples, cored and diced

- ½ cup golden raisins
- 2/3 cup light brown sugar

Directions:
1. Mix the flour, sugar, cinnamon, ginger and baking soda in a container.
2. Put in the remaining ingredients and stir for a few seconds to mix.
3. Pour the batter in a muffin tin coated with baking muffin papers.
4. Preheat your oven and bake the muffins at 350F for about twenty minutes or until it is aromatic and appears golden brown.

These muffins taste best chilled.

Nutritional Content of One Serving:
Calories: 179 Fat: 5.5g Protein: 2.8g Carbohydrates: 30.4g

Apricot Orange Muffins

Total Time Taken: 1 hour
Yield: 12 Servings
Ingredients:
- ¼ cup wheat bran
- ¼ teaspoon orange juice
- ½ cup buttermilk
- ½ cup canola oil
- ½ cup light brown sugar
- ½ teaspoon salt
- 1 ½ cups all-purpose flour
- 1 ½ teaspoons baking powder
- 1 tablespoon orange zest
- 2 eggs
- 6 apricots, halved

Directions:
1. Mix the flour, wheat bran, salt and baking powder in a container.
2. Put in the eggs, sugar, buttermilk, orange zest and orange juice and stir for a few seconds to mix.
3. Spoon the batter in a muffin tin covered with muffin papers.
4. Top each muffin with one apricot half and preheat your oven and bake at 350F for about twenty minutes or until a golden-brown colour is achieved and it rises significantly.

These muffins taste best chilled.

Nutritional Content of One Serving:
Calories: 187 Fat: 10.2g Protein: 3.3g Carbohydrates: 21.5g

Apricot Rosemary Muffins

Total Time Taken: 1 hour
Yield: 12 Servings
Ingredients:
- ¼ cup milk

- ¼ teaspoon salt
- ½ cup dried apricots, chopped
- ½ cup ground almonds
- ½ cup honey
- ½ cup plain yogurt
- ½ cup rolled oats
- 1 ½ cups all-purpose flour
- 1 egg
- 1 teaspoon baking powder
- 1 teaspoon dried rosemary

Directions:
1. Mix the flour, salt, baking powder, oats, almonds and rosemary in a container.
2. Stir in the honey, yogurt, milk and egg and mix thoroughly then fold in the apricots.
3. Spoon the batter in a muffin pan coated with your favorite muffin papers and preheat your oven and bake at 350F for about twenty minutes or until it rises significantly and starts to appear golden-brown.

These muffins taste best chilled.

Nutritional Content of One Serving:
Calories: 155 Fat: 3.0g Protein: 4.2g Carbohydrates: 28.7g

Banana Buttermilk Muffins

Total Time Taken: 1 hour
Yield: 12 Servings
Ingredients:
- ¼ cup butter, melted
- ½ cup rolled oats
- ½ cup white sugar
- ½ teaspoon salt
- 1 ¾ cups all-purpose flour
- 1 cup buttermilk
- 1 egg
- 1 teaspoon baking powder
- 1 teaspoon baking soda
- 2 ripe bananas, mashed

Directions:
1. Mix the dry ingredients in a container and the wet ingredients in a separate container.
2. Pour the wet ingredients over the dry ones and stir swiftly to combine.
3. Spoon the batter in a muffin pan coated with muffin papers.
4. Preheat your oven and bake the muffins at 350F for about twenty minutes or until a golden-brown colour is achieved or until mildly golden-brown and it rises significantly.

These muffins taste best chilled.

Nutritional Content of One Serving:
Calories: 176 Fat: 4.8g Protein: 3.7g Carbohydrates: 30.2g

Banana Chia Muffins

Total Time Taken: 1 hour
Yield: 12 Servings
Ingredients:
- ¼ cup whole milk
- ½ cup canola oil
- ½ cup white sugar
- ½ teaspoon salt
- 1 cup buttermilk
- 2 bananas, mashed
- 2 cups all-purpose flour
- 2 eggs
- 2 teaspoons baking powder
- 3 tablespoons chia seeds

Directions:
1. Mix the flour, chia seeds, sugar, salt and baking powder in a container.
2. Put in the remaining ingredients and stir for a few seconds to mix.
3. Spoon the batter in a muffin tin covered with muffin papers and preheat your oven and bake at 350F for about twenty minutes or until a toothpick inserted into the center of a muffin comes out clean.
4. Let them cool in the pan before you serve.

Nutritional Content of One Serving:
Calories: 266 Fat: 12.8g Protein: 5.7g Carbohydrates: 33.0g

Banana Chocolate Chip Muffins

Total Time Taken: 1 hour
Yield: 12 Servings
Ingredients:
- ¼ cup milk
- ½ cup dark chocolate chips
- ½ cup white sugar
- ½ teaspoon salt
- 1 ½ cups all-purpose flour
- 1 egg
- 1 teaspoon baking soda
- 1/3 cup butter, melted
- 3 bananas, mashed

Directions:
1. Mix the bananas, sugar, egg, butter and milk in a container until creamy.
2. Put in the remaining ingredients and fold them in using a spatula.
3. Spoon the batter into 12 muffin cups covered with muffin papers.
4. Pre-heat the oven and bake at 350F for about twenty minutes.

These muffins taste best chilled.

Nutritional Content of One Serving:

Calories: 191 Fat: 7.2g Protein: 2.9g Carbohydrates: 30.6g

Banana Crunch Muffins

Total Time Taken: 1 hour
Yield: 12 Servings
Ingredients:

- ¼ teaspoon salt
- ½ cup canola oil
- ½ cup light brown sugar
- ½ cup milk
- ½ cup shredded coconut
- 1 ½ teaspoons baking powder
- 1 cup rolled oats
- 1 teaspoon vanilla extract
- 2 bananas, mashed
- 2 cups all-purpose flour
- 2 eggs

Directions:

1. Mix the bananas, sugar, eggs, milk, vanilla and oil in a container.
2. Stir in the flour, salt, baking powder and coconut and mix using a spatula.
3. Spoon the batter in a muffin tin covered with muffin papers and top each muffin with rolled oats.
4. Pre-heat the oven and bake at 350F for about twenty minutes or until it rises significantly and starts to appear golden-brown.

These muffins taste best chilled.

Nutritional Content of One Serving:

Calories: 251 Fat: 11.8g Protein: 4.6g Carbohydrates: 32.3g

Banana Honey Muffins

Total Time Taken: 1 hour
Yield: 12 Servings
Ingredients:

- ½ cup buttermilk
- ½ cup honey
- ½ cup rolled oats
- ½ teaspoon salt
- 1 ½ cups all-purpose flour
- 1 egg
- 1 teaspoon baking soda
- 1 teaspoon vanilla extract
- 2 ripe bananas, mashed

Directions:

1. Mix the bananas, honey, buttermilk, egg and vanilla in a container.
2. Put in the remaining ingredients and mix using a spatula.
3. Spoon the batter in a muffin tin covered with muffin papers and preheat your oven and bake at 350F for about twenty minutes or until it rises significantly and starts to appear golden-brown.

These muffins taste best chilled.

Nutritional Content of One Serving:

Calories: 141 Fat: 0.9g Protein: 3.1g Carbohydrates: 30.9g

Cinnamon Oatmeal Cookies

Total Time Taken: 1 ¼ hours
  Yield: 30 Servings

Ingredients:
- ¼ cup golden syrup
- 1 egg
- 2 cups rolled oats
- 1 teaspoon cinnamon powder
- ¼ teaspoon salt
- ½ teaspoon baking soda
- 2/3 cup butter
- 2/3 cup light brown sugar
- 2/3 cup all-purpose flour

Directions:
1. Mix the butter, sugar and syrup in a container until fluffy and creamy.
2. Put in the egg and mix thoroughly then fold in the remaining ingredients.
3. Drop spoonfuls of batter on a baking sheet coated with baking paper.
4. Preheat your oven and bake the cookies at 350F for about fifteen minutes or until a golden-brown colour is achieved on the edges.
5. Let the cookies cool down before you serve.

Nutritional Content of One Serving:

Calories: 89 Fat: 4.6g Protein: 1.2g Carbohydrates: 11.1g

Cinnamon Snap Cookies

Total Time Taken: 1 ¼ hours
  Yield: 30 Servings

Ingredients:
- ¼ cup cocoa powder
- ½ teaspoon ground cloves
- ½ teaspoon ground ginger
- ½ teaspoon salt
- 1 cup butter, softened
- 1 egg
- 1 teaspoon baking soda

- 1 teaspoon cinnamon powder
- 1 teaspoon vanilla extract
- 2 cups all-purpose flour
- 2 tablespoons golden syrup
- 2/3 cup white sugar

Directions:

1. Mix the butter, sugar, vanilla and golden syrup in a container until pale and creamy.
2. Put in the egg and mix thoroughly then put in the flour mixture.
3. Make small balls of dough and place the cookies on a baking sheet coated with baking paper.
4. Preheat your oven and bake the cookies at 350F for about fifteen minutes until it is aromatic and appears golden brown.
5. These cookies taste best chilled.

Nutritional Content of One Serving:

Calories: 109 Fat: 6.5g Protein: 1.2g Carbohydrates: 12.3g

Cinnamon Sugar Cookies

Total Time Taken: 1 ½ hours
Yield: 25 Servings

Ingredients:

- ¼ teaspoon salt
- ½ cup coconut oil, melted
- ½ cup light brown sugar
- 1 cup white sugar
- 1 teaspoon baking powder
- 1 teaspoon cinnamon powder
- 1 teaspoon vanilla extract
- 2 cups all-purpose flour
- 2 eggs

Directions:

1. Mix the brown sugar and cinnamon in a container and set aside for later.
2. Combine the eggs and sugar in a separate container and stir until volume increases to twice what it was.
3. Put in the coconut oil and vanilla and mix thoroughly.
4. Put in the flour, salt and baking powder and mix using a spatula.
5. Make small balls of dough and roll them through cinnamon sugar.
6. Preheat your oven and bake the cookies at 350F for about fifteen minutes or until a golden-brown colour is achieved and fragrant.
7. These cookies taste best chilled.

Nutritional Content of One Serving:

Calories: 121 Fat: 4.8g Protein: 1.5g Carbohydrates: 18.6g

Clove Sugar Cookies

Total Time Taken: 1 ¼ hours
Yield: 30 Servings

Ingredients:

- ¼ teaspoon salt
- ½ cup powdered sugar
- ½ teaspoon baking powder
- 1 cup butter, softened
- 1 cup ground hazelnuts
- 1 egg yolk
- 1 teaspoon ground whole cloves
- 1 teaspoon vanilla extract
- 2 cups all-purpose flour

Directions:

1. Mix the butter and sugar in a container until pale and fluffy.
2. Put in the vanilla and egg yolk and mix thoroughly.
3. Fold in the flour, hazelnuts, cloves, salt and baking powder.
4. Transfer the dough to a floured working surface then roll the dough into a slim sheet.
5. Cut into small cookies with a cookie cutter and place them on a baking tray coated with baking paper.
6. Preheat your oven and bake the cookies at 350F for about fifteen minutes or until a golden-brown colour is achieved and fragrant.
7. These cookies taste best chilled.

Nutritional Content of One Serving:

Calories: 115 Fat: 7.9g Protein: 1.5g Carbohydrates: 9.7g

Coconut Butter Cookies

Total Time Taken: 1 ¼ hours
Yield: 20 Servings

Ingredients:

- ¼ teaspoon salt
- ½ cup coconut butter, softened
- 1 cup shredded coconut
- 1 egg
- 1 teaspoon baking powder
- 1 teaspoon coconut extract
- 2 cups all-purpose flour
- 2 tablespoons coconut oil
- 2/3 cup white sugar

Directions:

1. Mix the coconut butter, coconut oil and sugar in a container until pale and creamy.
2. Put in the egg and coconut extract and mix thoroughly.
3. Stir in the flour, coconut, baking powder and salt then form small balls of dough.

4. Put the balls on baking trays coated with baking paper and preheat your oven and bake at 350F for about fifteen minutes or until a golden-brown colour is achieved,
5. When finished, transfer the cookies in a container and dust them with powdered sugar.
6. These cookies taste best chilled.

Nutritional Content of One Serving:

Calories: 100 Fat: 3.0g Protein: 1.7g Carbohydrates: 17.0g

Coconut Florentine Cookies

Total Time Taken: 1 ¼ hours
Yield: 25 Servings

Ingredients:
- ¼ cup honey
- ¼ teaspoon salt
- ½ cup light brown sugar
- 1 ½ cups sliced almonds
- 1 cup butter, softened
- 1 cup shredded coconut
- 4 tablespoons all-purpose flour

Directions:
1. Mix the butter, sugar and honey in a heatproof container over a hot water bath until smooth and melted.
2. Turn off the heat and put in the coconut, almonds, salt and flour.
3. Drop spoonfuls of batter on a baking tray coated with baking paper.
4. Spread the mixture slightly then preheat your oven and bake the cookies at 350F for about fifteen minutes or until a golden-brown colour is achieved and crisp.
5. Let the cookies cool down before you serve.

Nutritional Content of One Serving:

Calories: 135 Fat: 11.3g Protein: 1.5g Carbohydrates: 8.3g

Coconut Lime Butter Cookies

Total Time Taken: 1 ¼ hours
Yield: 30 Servings

Ingredients:
- ½ teaspoon baking powder
- ½ teaspoon salt
- 1 cup butter, softened
- 1 cup shredded coconut
- 1 cup white sugar
- 1 lime, zested and juiced
- 1 teaspoon coconut extract
- 2 cups all-purpose flour
- 2 egg yolks

Directions:
1. Mix the butter and sugar in a container until creamy and pale.
2. Put in the egg yolks, lime zest and lime juice, as well as the coconut extract.
3. Stir in the flour, salt, coconut and baking powder then transfer the dough on a floured working surface.
4. Roll the dough into a slim sheet then cut small cookies using a cookie cutter of your choice.
5. Put the cookies on a baking tray covered with parchment paper.
6. Preheat your oven and bake the cookies at 350F for about fifteen minutes or until a golden-brown colour is achieved on the edges.
7. These cookies taste best chilled.

Nutritional Content of One Serving:

Calories: 124 Fat: 7.4g Protein: 1.2g Carbohydrates: 13.8g

Coconut Macaroons

Total Time Taken: 1 ½ hours
Yield: 20 Servings

Ingredients:
- ¼ teaspoon salt
- ½ cup all-purpose flour
- 1 can sweetened condensed milk
- 1 teaspoon vanilla extract
- 4 cups shredded coconut

Directions:
1. Mix the coconut, salt and flour in a container.
2. Put in the milk and vanilla and mix thoroughly.
3. Drop spoonfuls of mixture on baking trays coated with baking paper.
4. Preheat your oven and bake the cookies at 350F for fifteen minutes or until crisp and golden brown.
5. These cookies taste best chilled.

Nutritional Content of One Serving:

Calories: 118 Fat: 6.7g Protein: 2.1g Carbohydrates: 13.2g

Coconut Shortbread Cookies

Total Time Taken: 2 hours
Yield: 20 Servings
Ingredients:
- ¼ teaspoon baking powder
- ¼ teaspoon salt
- ½ cup powdered sugar
- 1 cup butter, softened
- 1 cup shredded coconut
- 1 egg
- 1 teaspoon coconut extract
- 2 cups all-purpose flour

Directions:
1. Mix the butter, sugar and coconut extract in a container.
2. Stir in the egg and mix thoroughly then put in the flour, salt, coconut and baking powder.
3. Wrap the dough in a plastic wrap and store in the refrigerator for about half an hour.
4. Transfer the dough to a working surface and roll it into a slim sheet.
5. Cut the dough into small cookies with a cookie cutter of your choice.
6. Put the cookies in a baking tray coated with baking paper.
7. Pre-heat the oven and bake at 350F for about fifteen minutes or until a golden-brown colour is achieved on the edges.
8. Best served chilled.

Nutritional Content of One Serving:

Calories: 157 Fat: 10.9g Protein: 1.8g Carbohydrates: 13.2g

Coffee Gingersnap Cookies

Total Time Taken: 1 ¼ hours

Yield: 20 Servings

Ingredients:
- ¼ cup coconut oil
- ¼ teaspoon salt
- ½ cup butter, softened
- ½ teaspoon ground cardamom
- 1 cup light brown sugar
- 1 egg
- 1 teaspoon baking soda
- 1 teaspoon cinnamon powder
- 1 teaspoon ground ginger
- 1 teaspoon vanilla extract
- 2 cups all-purpose flour
- 2 teaspoons instant coffee

Directions:
1. Mix the butter, coconut oil and brown sugar in a container until fluffy and creamy.
2. Put in the egg and vanilla and mix thoroughly.
3. Fold in the remaining ingredients then drop spoonfuls of batter on a baking sheet coated with baking paper.
4. Pre-heat the oven and bake at 350F for fifteen minutes or until aromatic and crunchy.
5. These cookies taste best chilled.

Nutritional Content of One Serving:

Calories: 142 Fat: 7.7g Protein: 1.7g Carbohydrates: 16.8g

Coffee Shortbread Cookies

Total Time Taken: 1 hour
Yield: 20 Servings
Ingredients:
- ½ cup butter, softened
- ½ cup powdered sugar
- ½ teaspoon baking powder
- ½ teaspoon salt
- 1 egg
- 1 teaspoon vanilla extract
- 2 cups all-purpose flour
- 2 teaspoons instant coffee

Directions:
1. Mix the butter, sugar and vanilla and stir until smooth and fluffy.
2. Put in the egg and mix thoroughly then fold in the flour, salt, baking powder and coffee.
3. Put the dough on a floured working surface and roll it into a slim sheet.
4. Cut into small cookies using a cookie cutter of your choices and position the cookies on a baking sheet coated with baking paper.
5. Preheat your oven and bake the cookies at 350F for about fifteen minutes or until it is aromatic and appears golden-brown on the edges.
6. Serve Chilled or store them in an airtight container.

Nutritional Content of One Serving:

Calories: 102 Fat: 5.0g Protein: 1.6g Carbohydrates: 12.6g

Colorful Chocolate Cookies

Total Time Taken: 1 ¼ hors
Yield: 30 Servings

Ingredients:
- ½ cup cocoa powder
- ½ cup crushed candy cane cookies
- ½ cup M&M candies
- ½ teaspoon salt
- 1 cup butter, softened
- 1 cup light brown sugar
- 1 egg
- 1 teaspoon baking powder
- 1 teaspoon vanilla extract
- 2 cups all-purpose flour

Directions:
1. Mix the butter, sugar and vanilla and stir thoroughly until fluffy and pale.
2. Stir in the egg and mix thoroughly then put in the remaining ingredients.
3. Drop spoonfuls of batter on a baking tray coated with baking paper.
4. Pre-heat the oven and bake at 350F for about fifteen minutes.

5. Let the cookies cool in the pan before you serve.

Nutritional Content of One Serving:

Calories: 129 Fat: 7.4g Protein: 1.5g Carbohydrates: 14.8g

Confetti Cookies

Total Time Taken: 1 ¼ hours
Yield: 20 Servings

Ingredients:
- 1 teaspoon vanilla extract
- 1 egg
- 2 cups all-purpose flour
- 1 teaspoon baking powder
- ¼ teaspoon salt
- ½ cup colourful sprinkles
- 2/3 cup butter, softened
- 2/3 cup white sugar

Directions:
1. Mix the butter with sugar and vanilla in a container until creamy and fluffy.
2. Stir in the egg and mix thoroughly then fold in the remaining ingredients.
3. Drop in the sprinkles and mix using a spatula.
4. Drop spoonfuls of batter on a baking sheet coated with baking paper.
5. Pre-heat the oven and bake at 350F for about fifteen minutes or until a golden-brown colour is achieved on the edges.
6. These cookies taste best chilled.

Nutritional Content of One Serving:

Calories: 136 Fat: 6.7g Protein: 1.7g Carbohydrates: 17.5g

Cornflake Chocolate Chip Cookies

Total Time Taken: 1 hour
Yield: 20 Servings

Ingredients:
- ½ cup butter, softened
- ½ cup dark chocolate chips
- ½ teaspoon baking soda
- ¾ cup white sugar
- 1 ¼ cup all-purpose flour
- 1 cup cornflakes
- 1 egg
- 1 teaspoon vanilla extract
- 2/4 teaspoon salt

Directions:
1. Mix the butter, sugar and vanilla in a container until creamy and pale.
2. Put in the egg then mix in the flour, baking soda and salt.

3. Fold in the cornflakes and chocolate chips.
4. Drop spoonfuls of batter on a baking sheet coated with baking paper.
5. Preheat your oven and bake the cookies at 350F for about fifteen minutes or until a golden-brown colour is achieved on the edges.
6. *These cookies taste best chilled.*

Nutritional Content of One Serving:

Calories: 120 Fat: 5.7g Protein: 1.4g Carbohydrates: 16.7g

Cracked Sugar Cookies

Total Time Taken: 1 ¼ hours
Yield: 30 Servings

Ingredients:
- ½ teaspoon salt
- 1 cup butter, softened
- 1 cup powdered sugar
- 1 cup white sugar
- 1 teaspoon baking soda
- 1 teaspoon vanilla extract
- 2 ½ cups all-purpose flour
- 3 egg yolks

Directions:
1. Mix the butter and sugar in a container until creamy and fluffy.
2. Put in the egg yolks and mix thoroughly then mix in the vanilla.
3. Fold in the flour, baking soda and salt then form small balls of dough and roll them through powdered sugar.
4. Put the balls on a baking tray coated with baking paper.
5. Pre-heat the oven and bake at 350F for about fifteen minutes or until mildly golden brown.
6. These cookies taste best chilled, handling them with care.

Nutritional Content of One Serving:

Calories: 139 Fat: 6.7g Protein: 1.4g Carbohydrates: 18.7g

Cranberry Biscotti

Total Time Taken: 1 ½ hours
Yield: 20 Servings

Ingredients:
- ¼ teaspoon salt
- ½ cup butter, softened
- ½ cup white sugar
- ½ teaspoon baking soda
- 1 cup dried cranberries
- 1 egg
- 1 tablespoon lemon zest
- 2 cups all-purpose flour

Directions:

1. Mix the butter and sugar in a container until creamy and fluffy.
2. Put in the egg and lemon zest and mix thoroughly.
3. Stir in the flour, baking soda and salt then put in the cranberries.
4. Put the dough on a baking tray coated with baking paper. Shape the dough into a log and bake it in the preheated oven at 350F for fifteen minutes.
5. Remove the tray from the oven and allow it to cool down for about ten minutes. Cut the log into 1cm wide slices and place them back on the tray with the cut facing up.
6. Carry on baking for fifteen minutes or until a golden-brown colour is achieved and crisp.
7. Let cool before you serve or storing.

Nutritional Content of One Serving:

Calories: 111 Fat: 5.0g Protein: 1.6g Carbohydrates: 15.1g

Custard Powder Cookies

Total Time Taken: 1 ¼ hours
Yield: 20 Servings

Ingredients:

- ¼ cup whole milk
- ¼ teaspoon salt
- ½ cup butter, softened
- ½ cup vanilla custard powder
- ½ cup white sugar
- 1 ½ cups all-purpose flour
- 1 teaspoon baking powder
- 1 teaspoon vanilla extract

Directions:

1. Mix the butter and sugar in a container until creamy and fluffy.
2. Stir in the milk and vanilla then fold in the remaining ingredients.
3. Drop spoonfuls of batter on a baking sheet coated with baking paper.
4. Preheat your oven and bake the cookies at 350F for about fifteen minutes or until a golden-brown colour is achieved on the edges.
5. *These cookies taste best chilled.*

Nutritional Content of One Serving:

Calories: 115 Fat: 4.8g Protein: 1.1g Carbohydrates: 17.3g

Date Pecan Ginger Cookies

Total Time Taken: 1 ½ hours
Yield: 30 Servings

Ingredients:

- ¼ teaspoon salt
- ½ cup olive oil
- ½ cup whole wheat flour
- 1 cup all-purpose flour

- 1 cup dates, pitted and chopped
- 1 cup light brown sugar
- 1 cup pecans, chopped
- 1 egg
- 1 teaspoon baking powder
- 1 teaspoon grated ginger
- 1 teaspoon vanilla extract

Directions:
1. Mix the oil and sugar in a container until fluffy and pale.
2. Put in the vanilla and ginger and mix thoroughly then fold in the flours, baking powder and salt.
3. Stir in the dates and pecans then drop spoonfuls of batter on a baking sheet coated with baking paper.
4. Preheat your oven and bake the cookies at 350F for fifteen minutes or until a golden-brown colour is achieved on the edges.
5. *These cookies taste best chilled.*

Nutritional Content of One Serving:
Calories: 93 Fat: 3.9g Protein: 1.0g Carbohydrates: 14.2g

Double Chocolate Cookies

Total Time Taken: 1 ½ hours
Yield: 30 Servings

Ingredients:
- ¼ teaspoon salt
- ½ cup cocoa powder
- ½ cup mini chocolate chips
- ½ teaspoon baking powder
- 1 ½ cups all-purpose flour
- 1 cup white sugar
- 1 egg
- 1 teaspoon vanilla extract
- 2/3 cup butter, softened

Directions:
1. Mix the butter and sugar until fluffy and creamy.
2. Put in the egg and vanilla and mix thoroughly then fold in the remaining ingredients and mix thoroughly.
3. Cover the dough with plastic wrap and store in the refrigerator for about half an hour.
4. Transfer the dough to a floured working surface and roll it into a slim sheet.
5. Cut into small cookies using a cookie cutter of your choices and place them on a baking pan coated with baking paper.
6. Pre-heat the oven and bake at 350F for about fifteen minutes.
7. *These cookies taste best chilled.*

Nutritional Content of One Serving:
Calories: 93 Fat: 4.6g Protein: 1.2g Carbohydrates: 12.8g

Double Chocolate Espresso Cookies

Total Time Taken: 1 hour
Yield: 20 Servings
Ingredients:

- 2 eggs
- 1 teaspoon vanilla extract
- ¼ cup coconut oil, melted
- 1 teaspoon instant coffee
- 6 oz. dark chocolate
- ¼ cup butter
- 2 tablespoons all-purpose flour
- ¼ teaspoon salt
- 2/3 cup white sugar

Directions:

1. Mix the chocolate and butter in a heatproof container and place over a hot water bath. Melt them together until smooth and melted.
2. Mix the eggs and sugar in a container until fluffy and pale. Put in the vanilla and oil and stir lightly. Stir in the coffee.
3. Put in the melted chocolate and stir lightly then fold in the flour and salt.
4. Drop spoonfuls of batter on a baking tray coated with baking paper.
5. Pre-heat the oven and bake at 350F for about ten minutes or until set.
6. *These cookies taste best chilled.*

Nutritional Content of One Serving:

Calories: 124 Fat: 8.0g Protein: 1.3g Carbohydrates: 12.4g

Double Ginger Cookies

Total Time Taken: 1 ¼ hours
Yield: 20 Servings

Ingredients:

- ¼ cup candied ginger, chopped
- ¼ teaspoon salt
- ½ teaspoon baking soda
- ½ teaspoon cinnamon powder
- 1 teaspoon ground ginger
- 1 teaspoon vanilla extract
- 1/3 cup butter, softened
- 2 cups all-purpose flour
- 2 tablespoons golden syrup
- 2/3 cup light brown sugar

Directions:

1. Sift the flour, ginger, cinnamon, salt and baking soda in a container.
2. Mix the butter, sugar, vanilla and syrup in a container until fluffy and pale.
3. Fold in the flour then put in the candied ginger.

4. Drop spoonfuls of batter on a baking sheet coated with baking paper.
5. Pre-heat the oven and bake at 350F for about fifteen minutes or until it rises and looks golden brown.
6. *These cookies taste best chilled.*

Nutritional Content of One Serving:

Calories: 98 Fat: 3.2g Protein: 1.4g Carbohydrates: 16.1g

Dried Cranberry Oatmeal Cookies

Total Time Taken: 1 ¼ hours
Yield: 20 Servings

Ingredients:
- ¼ teaspoon salt
- ½ cup butter, softened, melted
- ½ cup dried cranberries
- ½ cup light brown sugar
- ½ teaspoon cinnamon powder
- ½ teaspoon ground ginger
- 1 cup all-purpose flour
- 1 cup rolled oats
- 1 teaspoon baking soda
- 4 tablespoons golden syrup

Directions:
1. Mix the oats, flour, baking soda, spices, salt and cranberries in a container.
2. Stir in the butter, golden syrup and sugar and mix thoroughly.
3. Make small balls for dough and place the balls on a baking sheet coated with baking paper.
4. Flatten the cookies slightly and preheat your oven and bake at 350F for fifteen minutes or until a golden-brown colour is achieved and fragrant.
5. *These cookies taste best chilled.*

Nutritional Content of One Serving:

Calories: 106 Fat: 4.9g Protein: 1.2g Carbohydrates: 14.5g

Dried Fruit Wholesome Cookies

Total Time Taken: 1 ¼ hours
Yield: 20 Servings

Ingredients:
- ¼ cup applesauce
- ¼ cup coconut oil, melted
- ¼ cup dried apricots, chopped
- ¼ cup dried cranberries
- ¼ cup golden raisins
- ¼ cup rolled oats
- ¼ teaspoon salt
- ½ teaspoon baking soda

- ½ teaspoon cinnamon powder
- 1 ¼ cups whole wheat flour
- 1 egg
- 1 teaspoon vanilla extract

Directions:

1. Mix the coconut oil, applesauce, egg and vanilla and mix thoroughly.
2. Stir in the flour, salt, baking soda and cinnamon then put in the oats and dried fruits.
3. Drop spoonfuls of batter on a baking tray coated with baking paper.
4. Preheat your oven and bake the cookies at 350F for about ten minutes or until a golden-brown colour is achieved and crisp on the edges.
5. *These cookies taste best chilled.*

Nutritional Content of One Serving:

Calories: 68 Fat: 3.1g Protein: 1.3g Carbohydrates: 8.8g

Dried Prune Oatmeal Cookies

Total Time Taken: 1 ¼ hours
Yield: 25 Servings

Ingredients:

- ¼ teaspoon salt
- ½ cup coconut oil, melted
- ½ cup maple syrup
- ½ teaspoon baking soda
- ¾ cup all-purpose flour
- 1 cup dried prunes, chopped
- 1 teaspoon lemon juice
- 1 teaspoon vanilla extract
- 2 cups rolled oats

Directions:

1. Mix the prunes, oats, flour, baking soda and salt in a container.
2. Put in the rest of the ingredients and mix using a spatula.
3. Make small balls of dough and arrange them on a baking sheet coated with baking paper.
4. Preheat your oven and bake the cookies at 350F for about fifteen minutes or until a golden-brown colour is achieved.
5. *These cookies taste best chilled.*

Nutritional Content of One Serving:

Calories: 109 Fat: 4.9g Protein: 1.4g Carbohydrates: 15.9g

Earl Grey Cookies

Total Time Taken: 1 ¼ hours
Yield: 20 Servings

Ingredients:

- ½ cup powdered sugar

- ½ teaspoon salt
- 1 cup butter, softened
- 1 egg
- 1 tablespoon loose Earl grey leaves
- 1 teaspoon baking powder
- 1 teaspoon vanilla extract
- 2 cups all-purpose flour

Directions:

1. Mix the butter and sugar in a container until fluffy and pale.
2. Put in the egg and vanilla and mix thoroughly.
3. Stir in the remaining ingredients and mix using a spatula.
4. Transfer the dough to a floured working surface and roll it into a slim sheet.
5. Cut into small cookies with your cookie cutters and place them on a baking tray coated with baking paper.
6. Pre-heat the oven and bake at 350F for about ten minutes or until a golden-brown colour is achieved on the edges.
7. *These cookies taste best chilled.*

Nutritional Content of One Serving:

Calories: 143 Fat: 9.6g Protein: 1.7g Carbohydrates: 12.7g

Eggless Cookies

Total Time Taken: 1 hour
Yield: 20 Servings
Ingredients:

- ¼ cup whole milk
- ¼ teaspoon salt
- ½ cup butter, melted
- ½ cup dried cranberries
- ½ cup light brown sugar
- ½ teaspoon baking soda
- 1 ½ cups all-purpose flour

Directions:

1. Mix the flour, salt, baking soda and sugar in a container.
2. Stir in the butter and milk and mix using a spatula.
3. Fold in the cranberries then drop spoonfuls of batter on a baking sheet coated with baking paper.
4. Pre-heat the oven and bake at 350F for about fifteen minutes or until a golden-brown colour is achieved on the edges.
5. *These cookies taste best chilled.*

Nutritional Content of One Serving:

Calories: 92 Fat: 4.8g Protein: 1.1g Carbohydrates: 11.1g

Fig and Almond Cookies

Total Time Taken: 1 ¼ hours
Yield: 20 Servings

Ingredients:
- ½ cup butter, softened
- ½ cup ground almonds
- ½ teaspoon baking soda
- ½ teaspoon salt
- 1 ½ cups dried figs, chopped
- 1 ¾ cups all-purpose flour
- 1 cup powdered sugar
- 1 egg
- 1 teaspoon vanilla extract

Directions:
1. Mix the butter, sugar and vanilla in a container until fluffy and pale.
2. Put in the egg and mix thoroughly then fold in the remaining ingredients.
3. Drop spoonfuls of batter on a baking tray coated with baking paper.
4. Pre-heat the oven and bake at 350F for about fifteen minutes or until a golden-brown colour is achieved on the edges and slightly crisp.
5. *These cookies taste best chilled.*

Nutritional Content of One Serving:

Calories: 159 Fat: 6.3g Protein: 2.5g Carbohydrates: 24.4g

Everything - But - The - Kitchen - Sink Cookies

Total Time Taken: 1 ¼ hours
Yield: 20 Servings

Ingredients:
- ¼ cup applesauce
- ¼ cup coconut oil, melted
- ¼ cup dark chocolate chips
- ¼ cup dried apricots, chopped
- ¼ cup dried cranberries
- ¼ cup shredded coconut
- ¼ teaspoon cinnamon powder
- ½ cup walnuts, chopped
- ½ teaspoon ground ginger
- ½ teaspoon salt
- 1 cup rolled oats
- 1 cup whole wheat flour
- 1 egg

- 1 teaspoon vanilla extract
- 2 tablespoons butter, softened

Directions:
1. Mix the coconut oil, butter, vanilla, egg and applesauce in a container.
2. Put in the flour, oats, spices and salt then fold in the walnuts, apricots, cranberries, apricots, chocolate chips and coconut.
3. Drop spoonfuls of batter on baking trays coated with baking paper.
4. Preheat your oven and bake the cookies at 350F for about fifteen minutes or until a golden-brown colour is achieved and crisp on the edges.
5. These cookies taste best chilled.

Nutritional Content of One Serving:

Calories: 109 Fat: 7.0g Protein: 2.4g Carbohydrates: 9.8g

Flourless Peanut Butter Cookies

Total Time Taken: 1 hour
Yield: 30 Servings
Ingredients:
- ½ teaspoon salt
- 1 cup light brown sugar
- 2 cups smooth peanut butter
- 2 eggs

Directions:
1. Combine all the ingredients in a container until the desired smoothness is achieved.
2. Drop spoonfuls of mixture on a baking sheet coated with baking paper.
3. Score the top of each cookie with a fork then preheat your oven and bake the cookies at 350F for about ten minutes.
4. *These cookies taste best chilled.*

Nutritional Content of One Serving:

Calories: 124 Fat: 9.0g Protein: 4.7g Carbohydrates: 8.1g

Four Ingredient Peanut Butter Cookies

Total Time Taken: 1 hour
Yield: 20 Servings
Ingredients:
- 1 cup rolled oats
- 1 cup smooth peanut butter
- 1 egg
- 2/3 cup light brown sugar

Directions:
1. Mix the peanut butter, egg and sugar in a container until creamy then put in the oats.
2. Drop spoonfuls of batter on a baking tray coated with baking paper.
3. Preheat your oven and bake the cookies at 350F for about fifteen minutes or until a golden-brown colour is achieved on the edges.

4. *These cookies taste best chilled.*

Nutritional Content of One Serving:

Calories: 113 Fat: 7.0g Protein: 4.1g Carbohydrates: 10.1g

Fresh Blueberry Cookies

Total Time Taken: 1 ½ hours
 Yield: 30 Servings

Ingredients:
- ¼ cup whole milk
- ½ teaspoon baking soda
- ½ teaspoon salt
- 1 cup butter, softened
- 1 cup fresh blueberries
- 1 cup powdered sugar
- 1 egg
- 1 tablespoon lemon zest
- 1 teaspoon vanilla extract
- 2 cups all-purpose flour

Directions:
1. Mix the butter, vanilla and sugar in a container until fluffy and light.
2. Put in the egg, milk and lemon zest and mix thoroughly.
3. Stir in the flour, salt and baking soda and mix using a spatula then fold in the blueberries.
4. Drop spoonfuls of batter on a baking tray covered with parchment paper.
5. Pre-heat the oven and bake at 350F for about thirteen minutes or until a golden-brown colour is achieved on the edges.
6. *These cookies taste best chilled.*

Nutritional Content of One Serving:

Calories: 107 Fat: 6.5g Protein: 1.2g Carbohydrates: 11.2g

Fruity Cookies

Total Time Taken: 1 ½ hours
 Yield: 30 Servings

Ingredients:
- 2 tablespoons molasses
- 2 tablespoons golden syrup
- 1 egg
- ¼ cup milk
- 2 cups all-purpose flour
- ¼ teaspoon salt
- 1 teaspoon baking soda
- ½ cup sultanas
- ½ cup dried cranberries
- ½ cup raisins

- ½ cup dried apricots, chopped
- ¼ cup Grand Marnier
- 2/3 cup butter, softened
- 2/3 cup white sugar

Directions:

1. Mix the fruits with Grand Marnier in a container and allow to soak up for about half an hour.
2. Mix the butter, sugar, molasses and golden syrup in a container until pale.
3. Put in the egg and milk and mix thoroughly.
4. Put in the dry ingredients then fold in the fruits.
5. Drop spoonfuls of batter on a baking sheet coated with baking paper and preheat your oven and bake the cookies at 350F for fifteen minutes.
6. Let the cookies cool down before you serve.

Nutritional Content of One Serving:

Calories: 111 Fat: 4.4g Protein: 1.3g Carbohydrates: 15.7g

Fudgy Chocolate Cookies

Total Time Taken: 1 ¼ hours
Yield: 30 Servings

Ingredients:

- ¼ teaspoon salt
- ½ cup butter
- ½ cup light brown sugar
- 1 ½ cups dark chocolate chips
- 1 teaspoon baking powder
- 1 teaspoon vanilla extract
- 2 eggs
- 2 tablespoons white sugar
- 2/3 cup all-purpose flour

Directions:

1. Melt the butter and chocolate in a heatproof container over a hot water bath.
2. Mix the eggs and sugars in a container until fluffy and pale.
3. Stir in the chocolate and mix using a spatula.
4. Fold in the flour, baking powder and salt then drop spoonfuls of batter in a baking sheet coated with baking paper.
5. Preheat your oven and bake the cookies at 350F for about thirteen minutes.
6. *These cookies taste best chilled.*

Nutritional Content of One Serving:

Calories: 82 Fat: 5.0g Protein: 1.1g Carbohydrates: 9.4g

German Chocolate Cookies

Total Time Taken: 1 ¼ hours
Yield: 30 Servings

Ingredients:
- ¼ cup cocoa powder
- ½ cup coconut flakes
- ½ cup dark chocolate chips
- ½ cup white sugar
- ½ teaspoon salt
- 1 cup butter, softened
- 1 cup light brown sugar
- 1 cup pecans, chopped
- 1 teaspoon baking soda
- 2 ¼ cups all-purpose flour
- 2 eggs

Directions:
1. Mix the butter and sugars in a container until pale and creamy.
2. Put in the eggs and mix thoroughly then fold in the flour, cocoa powder, baking soda and salt.
3. Fold in the chocolate chips, coconut flakes and pecans.
4. Drop spoonfuls of batter on baking trays coated with baking paper.
5. Preheat your oven and bake the cookies at 350F for about fifteen minutes or until risen.
6. *These cookies taste best chilled.*

Nutritional Content of One Serving:

Calories: 142 Fat: 7.9g Protein: 1.8g Carbohydrates: 17.2g

Ginger Almond Biscotti

Total Time Taken: 1 ¼ hours
Yield: 20 Servings

Ingredients:
- ¼ teaspoon baking soda
- ½ cup blanched almonds
- ½ cup butter, softened
- ½ teaspoon salt
- ¾ cup white sugar
- 1 teaspoon baking powder
- 1 teaspoon ground ginger
- 1 teaspoon vanilla extract
- 2 cups all-purpose flour
- 2 eggs
- 2 tablespoons dark brown sugar
- 2 tablespoons molasses

Directions:

1. Mix the sugars, molasses, eggs and butter in a container until creamy.
2. Put in the vanilla then fold in the remaining ingredients.
3. Transfer the dough to a baking tray covered with parchment paper and shape it into a log.
4. Preheat your oven and bake the log at 350F for fifteen minutes or until a golden-brown colour is achieved on the edges.
5. When finished, let cool down slightly then cut the log into thin slices and place them back on the baking tray with the cut facing up.
6. Preheat your oven and bake the cookies at 350F for another ten to fifteen minutes.
7. Serve the biscotti chilled.

Nutritional Content of One Serving:

Calories: 145 Fat: 6.4g Protein: 2.4g Carbohydrates: 20.2g

Ginger Butter Cookies

Total Time Taken: 1 ¼ hours
Yield: 20 Servings

Ingredients:
- ¼ teaspoon salt
- ½ cup butter, softened
- ½ teaspoon baking soda
- ½ teaspoon ground cardamom
- ¾ cup light brown sugar
- 1 ½ cups all-purpose flour
- 1 egg
- 1 teaspoon ground ginger
- 1 teaspoon vanilla extract

Directions:
1. Mix the butter and sugar until fluffy and pale. Put in the egg and vanilla and mix thoroughly.
2. Stir in the flour, ginger, cardamom, salt and baking soda.
3. Drop spoonfuls of batter on baking trays coated with baking paper.
4. Preheat your oven and bake the cookies at 350F for about fifteen minutes or until a golden-brown colour is achieved and crisp on the edges.
5. *These cookies taste best chilled.*

Nutritional Content of One Serving:

Calories: 100 Fat: 4.9g Protein: 1.3g Carbohydrates: 12.6g

Ginger Chocolate Oatmeal Cookies

Total Time Taken: 1 ¼ hours
Yield: 30 Servings

Ingredients:
- ¼ teaspoon salt
- ½ teaspoon baking soda
- ½ teaspoon cinnamon powder
- 1 cup all-purpose flour

- 1 cup light brown sugar
- 1 cup rolled oats
- 1 egg
- 1 teaspoon grated ginger
- 2 tablespoons cocoa powder
- 2/3 cup butter, softened

Directions:
1. Mix the butter and sugar until fluffy and creamy. Stir in the egg and mix thoroughly.
2. Put in the rest of the ingredients and mix using a spatula.
3. Drop spoonfuls of batter on a baking sheet coated with baking paper.
4. Pre-heat the oven and bake at 350F for fifteen minutes.
5. *These cookies taste best chilled.*

Nutritional Content of One Serving:
Calories: 83 Fat: 4.5g Protein: 1.1g Carbohydrates: 10.0g

Ginger Quinoa Cookies

Total Time Taken: 1 ¼ hours
Yield: 30 Servings

Ingredients:
- ¼ cup quinoa flakes
- ¼ cup quinoa flour
- ¼ teaspoon salt
- ½ cup almond flour
- ½ cup coconut oil, melted
- ½ cup light brown sugar
- ½ teaspoon baking soda
- ½ teaspoon cinnamon powder
- ½ teaspoon ground ginger
- 1 cup all-purpose flour
- 1 egg
- 2 tablespoons butter, softened
- 2 tablespoons molasses

Directions:
1. Mix the coconut oil and butter, molasses and sugar in a container until creamy and fluffy.
2. Put in the egg and mix thoroughly.
3. Stir in the remaining ingredients then drop spoonfuls of batter on a baking sheet coated with baking paper.
4. Preheat your oven and bake the cookies at 350F for about fifteen minutes or until a golden-brown colour is achieved on the edges.
5. These cookies taste best chilled.

Nutritional Content of One Serving:
Calories: 79 Fat: 5.0g Protein: 1.2g Carbohydrates: 7.6g

Gingerbread Cookies

Total Time Taken: 1 ¼ hours
Yield: 30 Servings

Ingredients:
- ¼ teaspoon salt
- ½ cup golden syrup
- ½ cup white sugar
- ½ teaspoon ground cardamom
- 1 cup butter, softened
- 1 egg
- 1 teaspoon baking soda
- 1 teaspoon cinnamon powder
- 1 teaspoon ground ginger
- 2 cups all-purpose flour
- 2 tablespoons dark molasses

Directions:
1. Mix the butter, golden syrup, sugar and molasses in a container until fluffy and pale.
2. Put in the egg and mix thoroughly then fold in the flour, spices, baking soda and salt.
3. Make small balls of dough and arrange them on a baking sheet coated with baking paper.
4. Pre-heat the oven and bake at 350F for fifteen minutes or until it is aromatic and appears golden.
5. *These cookies taste best chilled.*

Nutritional Content of One Serving:
Calories: 119 Fat: 6.4g Protein: 1.1g Carbohydrates: 15.0g

Gingerbread Cookies

Total Time Taken: 1 ¼ hours
Yield: 20 Servings

Ingredients:
- ¼ cup molasses
- ¼ teaspoon salt
- ½ cup butter, softened
- ½ cup ground almonds
- ½ cup light brown sugar
- ½ teaspoon baking soda
- ½ teaspoon cinnamon powder
- ½ teaspoon ground cloves
- ½ teaspoon ground ginger
- 1 egg
- 2 cups all-purpose flour

Directions:
1. Mix the butter, molasses and sugar in a container until pale and creamy.
2. Put in the egg and mix thoroughly then mix in the rest of the ingredients.
3. Make small balls of dough and place them on a baking tray coated with baking paper.

351

4. Preheat your oven and bake the cookies at 350F for about thirteen minutes or until aromatic, risen and golden.
5. *These cookies taste best chilled.*

Nutritional Content of One Serving:

Calories: 129 Fat: 6.2g Protein: 2.1g Carbohydrates: 16.8g

Gingersnap Cookies

Total Time Taken: 1 hour
Yield: 20 Servings
Ingredients:
- ¼ cup molasses
- ¼ teaspoon salt
- ½ teaspoon baking powder
- ½ teaspoon cinnamon powder
- ¾ cup canola oil
- ¾ cup light brown sugar
- 1 egg
- 1 teaspoon baking soda
- 1 teaspoon ground ginger
- 2 cups all-purpose flour

Directions:
1. Mix the oil, molasses and sugar in a container.
2. Put in the egg and stir until creamy and pale.
3. Fold in the remaining ingredients then form small balls and place them on baking trays coated with baking paper.
4. Preheat your oven and bake the cookies at 350F for about fifteen minutes or until crisp and fragrant.
5. *These cookies taste best chilled.*

Nutritional Content of One Serving:

Calories: 154 Fat: 8.5g Protein: 1.6g Carbohydrates: 18.1g

Gooey Chocolate Cherry Cookies

Total Time Taken: 1 hour
Yield: 20 Servings
Ingredients:
- ¼ cup white sugar
- ½ cup butter, melted
- ½ cup dark chocolate chips
- ½ cup glace cherries, halved
- ½ cup muscovado sugar
- 1 ½ cups all-purpose flour
- 1 egg
- 2 tablespoons cocoa powder

Directions:

1. Combine all the ingredients in a container using a spatula.
2. Drop spoonfuls of batter on a baking tray coated with baking paper.
3. Pre-heat the oven and bake at 350F for about ten minutes.
4. *These cookies taste best chilled.*

Nutritional Content of One Serving:

Calories: 128 Fat: 5.8g Protein: 1.7g Carbohydrates: 18.2g

Hazelnut Chocolate Chip Cookies

Total Time Taken: 1 ¼ hours
Yield: 30 Servings

Ingredients:

- ¼ cup sour cream
- ½ cup mini chocolate chip cookies
- ½ cup rolled oats, ground
- ½ teaspoon salt
- 1 cup butter, softened
- 1 cup ground hazelnuts
- 1 cup light brown sugar
- 1 egg
- 1 teaspoon baking powder
- 1 teaspoon vanilla extract
- 2 cups all-purpose flour

Directions:

1. Mix the butter and sugar in a container until creamy and fluffy.
2. Put in the egg and vanilla and sour cream and mix thoroughly the mix in the dry ingredients and chocolate chips.
3. Transfer the dough to a floured working surface and roll it into a slim sheet.
4. Cut into small cookies with your cookie cutters and place the cookies on baking trays coated with baking paper.
5. Preheat your oven and bake the cookies at 350F for about fifteen minutes or until a golden-brown colour is achieved on the edges.
6. *These cookies taste best chilled.*

Nutritional Content of One Serving:

Calories: 135 Fat: 8.6g Protein: 1.8g Carbohydrates: 13.1g

Healthy Banana Cookies

Total Time Taken: 1 hour
Yield: 25 Servings
Ingredients:
- ¼ cup coconut flakes
- ¼ cup coconut oil, melted
- ¼ cup dried cranberries
- ¼ cup dried mango, chopped

- 1 cup dates, pitted and chopped
- 2 cups rolled oats
- 4 ripe bananas, mashed

Directions:
1. Mix the bananas and oil then mix in the rest of the ingredients.
2. Drop spoonfuls of batter on baking trays coated with baking paper.
3. Pre-heat the oven and bake at 350F for about fifteen minutes or until a golden-brown colour is achieved.
4. *These cookies taste best chilled.*

Nutritional Content of One Serving:
Calories: 114 Fat: 3.0g Protein: 1.3g Carbohydrates: 21.8g

Honey Cornflake Cookies

Total Time Taken: 1 ¼ hours
Yield: 20 Servings

Ingredients:
- ¼ teaspoon salt
- ½ cup honey
- ½ cup light brown sugar
- 1 ¾ cups all-purpose flour
- 1 cup cornflakes
- 1 egg
- 1 teaspoon baking powder
- 1 teaspoon vanilla extract
- 2 tablespoons pine nuts
- 2/3 cup butter, softened

Directions:
1. Mix the butter, honey and sugar in a container.
2. Stir in the egg and vanilla and mix thoroughly then fold in the remaining ingredients.
3. Drop spoonfuls of batter on a baking sheet coated with baking paper.
4. Pre-heat the oven and bake at 350F for about fifteen minutes or until a golden-brown colour is achieved on the edges.
5. *These cookies taste best chilled.*

Nutritional Content of One Serving:
Calories: 148 Fat: 7.1g Protein: 1.7g Carbohydrates: 20.4g

Honey Lemon Cookies

Total Time Taken: 1 ¼ hours
Yield: 40 Servings

Ingredients:
- ¼ cup honey
- ½ teaspoon salt

- ¾ cup white sugar
- 1 cup butter, softened
- 1 egg
- 1 lemon, zested and juiced
- 1 teaspoon baking soda
- 3 cups all-purpose flour

Directions:

1. Sift the flour, baking soda and salt in a container.
2. In a separate container, combine the butter, sugar and honey and mix thoroughly.
3. Stir in the lemon zest and juice, as well as the egg.
4. Fold in the flour mixture then roll the dough into a slim sheet over a floured working surface.
5. Cut the cookies using a cookie cutter of your choices.
6. Put the cookies in the preheated oven at 350F for about fifteen minutes or until a golden-brown colour is achieved on the edges.
7. *These cookies taste best chilled.*

Nutritional Content of One Serving:

Calories: 97 Fat: 4.8g Protein: 1.2g Carbohydrates: 12.8g

Icing Decorated Cookies

Total Time Taken: 1 ¼ hours
Yield: 20 Servings
Ingredients:

Cookies:

- ¼ teaspoon salt
- ½ cup butter, softened
- ½ cup powdered sugar
- ½ teaspoon baking powder
- 1 ½ cups all-purpose flour
- 1 egg yolk

Icing:

- ¼ teaspoon vanilla extract
- 1 cup powdered sugar
- 1 egg white

Directions:

1. For the cookies, combine the butter and sugar in a container until fluffy and pale.
2. Put in the egg yolk and mix thoroughly then fold in the flour, salt and baking powder.
3. Transfer the dough to a floured working surface and roll the dough into slim sheet.
4. Cut into small cookies with a cookie cutter and arrange the cookies on a baking tray coated with baking paper.
5. Preheat your oven and bake the cookies at 350F for about ten minutes or until a golden-brown colour is achieved on the edges.
6. For the icing, combine the sugar, egg white and vanilla in a container.
7. Spoon the icing in a small piping bag and garnish the chilled cookies with it.

Nutritional Content of One Serving:

Calories: 114 Fat: 4.9g Protein: 1.3g Carbohydrates: 16.2g

Layered Chocolate Chip Cookies

Total Time Taken: 1 ¼ hours
Yield: 30 Servings

Ingredients:

- ¼ cup dark brown sugar
- ½ teaspoon salt
- ¾ cup light brown sugar
- 1 cup butter, softened
- 1 cup dark chocolate chips
- 1 teaspoon baking soda
- 1 teaspoon vanilla extract
- 2 ¼ cups all-purpose flour
- 2 eggs

Directions:

1. Mix the butter and sugars in a container until fluffy and pale.
2. Put in the eggs and mix thoroughly then fold in the remaining ingredients.
3. Drop spoonfuls of batter on baking trays covered with parchment paper.
4. Preheat your oven and bake the cookies at 350F for about thirteen minutes or until a golden-brown colour is achieved.
5. *These cookies taste best chilled.*

Nutritional Content of One Serving:

Calories: 130 Fat: 7.6g Protein: 1.7g Carbohydrates: 14.6g

Lemon Poppy Seed Cookies

Total Time Taken: 1 hour
Yield: 20 Servings
Ingredients:

- ¼ cup butter, softened
- ¼ cup coconut oil
- ¼ cup cornstarch
- ¼ teaspoon salt
- ½ teaspoon baking soda
- 1 cup all-purpose flour
- 1 egg
- 1 tablespoon lemon zest
- 2 tablespoons lemon juice
- 2 tablespoons poppy seeds
- 2/3 cup white sugar

Directions:

1. Mix the butter, coconut oil and sugar in a container until fluffy and pale.
2. Put in the egg, lemon zest and lemon juice and mix thoroughly.

3. Fold in the remaining ingredients and mix using a spatula.
4. Drop spoonfuls of batter on baking trays coated with baking paper.
5. Preheat your oven and bake the cookies at 350F for about fifteen minutes or until a golden-brown colour is achieved or until a golden-brown colour is achieved on the edges.
6. *These cookies taste best chilled.*

Nutritional Content of One Serving:

Calories: 106 Fat: 5.7g Protein: 1.1g Carbohydrates: 13.2g

Lemon Ricotta Cookies

Total Time Taken: 2 hours
Yield: 40 Servings
Ingredients:
- ¼ cup butter, softened
- ½ teaspoon salt
- 1 cup ricotta cheese
- 1 cup white sugar
- 1 tablespoon lemon zest
- 1 teaspoon baking powder
- 2 eggs
- 2 tablespoons lemon juice 2 ½ cups all-purpose flour

Directions:

1. Mix the cheese, sugar, eggs and butter in a container until creamy.
2. Put in the lemon zest and lemon juice then fold in the flour, salt and baking powder.
3. Drop spoonfuls of baking batter on a baking tray covered with parchment paper.
4. Preheat your oven and bake the cookies at 350F for about fifteen minutes or until a golden-brown colour is achieved on the edges.
5. *These cookies taste best chilled.*

Nutritional Content of One Serving:

Calories: 69 Fat: 1.9g Protein: 1.8g Carbohydrates: 11.4g

Lemony Lavender Cookies

Total Time Taken: 1 ¼ hours
Yield: 25 Servings

Ingredients:

- ½ cup butter, softened
- ½ cup white sugar
- ½ teaspoon baking soda
- ½ teaspoon salt
- 1 cup all-purpose flour
- 1 cup almond flour
- 1 egg
- 1 tablespoon lemon zest
- 1 teaspoon lavender buds

- 2 tablespoons honey

Directions:
1. Mix the butter, honey, egg, lemon zest, sugar and lavender in a container until pale and light.
2. Put in the rest of the ingredients and mix using a spatula.
3. Drop spoonfuls of batter on a baking tray coated with baking paper.
4. Preheat your oven and bake the cookies at 350F for about fifteen minutes or until a golden-brown colour is achieved on the edges.
5. *These cookies taste best chilled.*

Nutritional Content of One Serving:

Calories: 82 Fat: 4.5g Protein: 1.1g Carbohydrates: 9.9g

Lentil Cookies

Total Time Taken: 1 ¼ hours
Yield: 30 Servings

Ingredients:
- ¼ teaspoon salt
- ½ cup butter, melted
- ½ cup walnuts, chopped
- ½ teaspoon baking powder
- ½ teaspoon cinnamon powder
- ½ teaspoon ground ginger
- ¾ cup light brown sugar
- 1 ½ cups all-purpose flour
- 1 egg
- 1 teaspoon vanilla extract
- 4 oz. lentil, cooked and pureed

Directions:
1. Mix the lentil puree, butter, egg, vanilla and sugar in a container until creamy and light.
2. Put in the rest of the ingredients and mix thoroughly.
3. Make small balls of mixture and place them on a baking tray coated with baking paper.
4. Preheat your oven and bake the cookies at 350F for about fifteen minutes or until a golden-brown colour is achieved and fragrant.
5. *These cookies taste best chilled.*

Nutritional Content of One Serving:

Calories: 93 Fat: 4.5g Protein: 2.3g Carbohydrates: 10.9g

M&M Cookies

Total Time Taken: 1 ¼ hours
Yield: 30 Servings

Ingredients:
- 1 cup butter, softened
- 2/3 cup light brown sugar

- 2 eggs
- 2 cups all-purpose flour
- 1 teaspoon baking powder
- ¼ teaspoon salt
- 1 cup M&M candies

Directions:
1. Mix the butter and sugar in a container until creamy and fluffy.
2. Stir in the eggs, one at a time, then put in the flour, baking powder and salt.
3. Fold in the candies then drop spoonfuls of batter on a baking tray coated with baking paper.
4. Preheat your oven and bake the cookies at 350F for fifteen minutes or until a golden-brown colour is achieved on the edges.
5. *These cookies taste best chilled.*

Nutritional Content of One Serving:
Calories: 102 Fat: 6.5g Protein: 1.3g Carbohydrates: 9.8g

Macadamia Cookies

Total Time Taken: 1 ¼ hours
Yield: 20 Servings

Ingredients:
- ¼ cup golden syrup
- ¼ cup light brown sugar
- ½ cup butter, softened
- ½ cup shredded coconut
- ½ teaspoon salt
- 1 cup all-purpose flour
- 1 cup rolled oats
- 1 teaspoon baking powder
- 2/3 cup macadamia nuts, chopped

Directions:
1. Mix the oats, flour, baking powder, salt, coconut and macadamia nuts in a container.
2. Mix the butter and syrup and sugar in a container until creamy and pale.
3. Fold in the remaining ingredients then drop spoonfuls of batter on a baking sheet coated with baking paper.
4. Pre-heat the oven and bake at 350F for about fifteen minutes or until a golden-brown colour is achieved on the edges.
5. *These cookies taste best chilled.*

Nutritional Content of One Serving:
Calories: 137 Fat: 9.0g Protein: 1.7g Carbohydrates: 13.5g

Mango Crunch Cookies

Total Time Taken: 1 ¼ hours
Yield: 20 Servings

Ingredients:

- ¼ cup white sugar
- ¼ teaspoon salt
- ½ cup butter, softened
- ½ teaspoon baking soda
- 1 ½ cups all-purpose flour
- 1 cup dried mango, chopped
- 1 egg
- 1 teaspoon vanilla extract

Directions:

1. Mix the butter, sugar and egg in a container until creamy. Put in the vanilla and mix thoroughly then fold in the flour, salt and baking soda.
2. Put in the mango and mix using a spatula.
3. Drop spoonfuls of batter on a baking tray coated with baking paper.
4. Pre-heat the oven and bake at 350F for about fifteen minutes or until a golden-brown colour is achieved on the edges.
5. *These cookies taste best chilled.*

Nutritional Content of One Serving:

Calories: 95 Fat: 5.0g Protein: 1.4g Carbohydrates: 11.5g

Ginger Sweet Potato Cake

Total Time Taken: 1 ½ hours
Yield: 10 Servings

Ingredients:

- ½ teaspoon baking soda
- ½ teaspoon salt
- ¾ cup canola oil
- 1 3/4 cups all-purpose flour
- 1 cup light brown sugar
- 1 cup sweet potato puree
- 1 tablespoon orange zest
- 1 teaspoon baking powder
- 1 teaspoon cinnamon powder
- 1 teaspoon vanilla extract
- 4 eggs

Directions:

1. Mix the sweet potato puree with the orange zest, canola oil, eggs, brown sugar and vanilla in a container.
2. Fold in the remaining ingredients then spoon the batter in a 9-inch round cake pan coated with baking paper.

3. Preheat your oven and bake the cake for around forty minutes or until a toothpick comes out clean after being inserted into the center of the cake.
4. Let the cake cool in the pan and serve, sliced.

Nutritional Content of One Serving:

Calories: 332 Fat: 18.4g Protein: 5.0g Carbohydrates: 37.4g

Ginger Whole Orange Cake

Total Time Taken: 1 ¼ hours
Yield: 10 Servings
Ingredients:

Cake:

- ½ teaspoon salt
- 1 cup butter, softened
- 1 cup powdered sugar
- 1 cup white sugar
- 1 tablespoon orange juice
- 1 teaspoon grated ginger **Icing:**
- 1 teaspoon orange zest
- 1 whole orange
- 2 cups all-purpose flour
- 2 tablespoons dark brown sugar
- 2 teaspoons baking powder
- 4 eggs

Directions:

1. To prepare the cake, place the orange in a saucepan and cover it with water. Cook for about half an hour then drain well and place in a food processor. Pulse until the desired smoothness is achieved. Put in the ginger and mix thoroughly. Place aside.
2. Mix the butter with the sugars in a container until creamy and fluffy. Stir in the eggs, one at a time and mix thoroughly.
3. Fold in the flour, baking powder and salt, alternating it with the orange mixture.
4. Spoon the batter in a 9-inch round cake pan coated with baking paper and preheat your oven and bake at 350F for about forty minutes or until a toothpick comes out clean after being inserted into the center of the cake.
5. Let the cake cool then move it to a platter.
6. For the icing, combine all the ingredients in a container and sprinkle it over the chilled cake. Serve immediately.

Nutritional Content of One Serving:

Calories: 430 Fat: 21.1g Protein: 5.8g Carbohydrates: 56.2g

Gingerbread Chocolate Cake

Total Time Taken: 1 ¼ hours
Yield: 10 Servings

Ingredients:

- ½ cup butter, softened
- ½ cup cocoa powder
- ½ cup sour cream
- ½ teaspoon ground cloves
- ½ teaspoon ground ginger
- ½ teaspoon ground star anise
- ½ teaspoon salt
- 1 ½ cups white sugar
- 1 teaspoon cinnamon powder
- 1 teaspoon orange zest
- 2 cups all-purpose flour
- 2 teaspoons baking powder
- 3 eggs
- 4 oz. dark chocolate, melted

Directions:

1. Mix the butter with sugar until creamy. Put in the eggs, one at a time, then mix in the melted chocolate and sour cream.
2. Fold in the flour, cocoa powder, baking powder, salt and spices.
3. Spoon the batter in a 9-icnh round cake pan coated with baking paper.
4. Pre-heat the oven and bake at 350F for forty minutes or until it rises completely and is aromatic.
5. Let the cake cool in the pan and serve, sliced.

Nutritional Content of One Serving:

Calories: 402 Fat: 17.1g Protein: 6.4g Carbohydrates: 59.6g

Gingersnap Pumpkin Bundt Cake

Total Time Taken: 1 ¼ hours
Yield: 12 Servings

Ingredients:

- ¼ cup canola oil
- ½ cup butter, softened
- ½ teaspoon salt
- 1 ½ cups pumpkin puree
- 1 cup white sugar
- 1 teaspoon vanilla extract
- 2 cups all-purpose flour
- 2 tablespoons dark brown sugar
- 2 teaspoons baking powder
- 3 eggs
- 6 gingersnaps, crushed

Directions:

1. Mix the butter, oil and sugars in a container until light and creamy.
2. Stir in the eggs, one at a time, then put in the pumpkin and vanilla and mix thoroughly.
3. Fold in the flour, baking powder and salt then put in the crushed gingersnaps.
4. Spoon the batter in a greased Bundt cake pan and preheat your oven and bake at 350F for 45 minutes or until a toothpick comes out clean after being inserted into the center of the cake.
5. Let cool in the pan then move to a platter.

Nutritional Content of One Serving:

Calories: 350 Fat: 16.1g Protein: 5.0g Carbohydrates: 48.0g

Graham Cracker Cake

Total Time Taken: 1 ¼ hours
Yield: 10 Servings

Ingredients:

- ¼ cup dark brown sugar
- ½ cup heavy cream
- ½ teaspoon baking powder
- ½ teaspoon cinnamon powder
- ½ teaspoon salt
- ¾ cup butter, softened
- 1 cup graham cracker crumbs
- 1 cup white sugar
- 2 cups all-purpose flour
- 2 teaspoons baking powder
- 3 eggs

Directions:

1. Mix the graham cracker crumbs, flour, baking powder, baking soda, salt and cinnamon in a container.
2. In another container, combine the butter and sugars until creamy and light.
3. Stir in the eggs, one after another, and mix thoroughly then put in the cream.
4. Fold in the flour mixture then pour the batter in a 10-inch round cake pan coated with baking paper.
5. Bake for about forty-five minutes in the preheated oven at 350F or until a toothpick comes out clean after being inserted into the center of the cake.
6. Let the cake cool in the pan and serve, sliced.

Nutritional Content of One Serving:

Calories: 380 Fat: 18.4g Protein: 5.0g Carbohydrates: 50.4g

Graham Cracker Pumpkin Cake

Total Time Taken: 1 ¼ hours
Yield: 12 Servings

Ingredients:

- ¼ cup dark brown sugar
- ½ cup butter, softened

- ½ cup whole milk
- ½ teaspoon salt
- 1 ¼ cups pumpkin puree
- 1 ½ cups graham crackers
- 1 cup all-purpose flour
- 1 cup light brown sugar
- 2 teaspoons baking powder
- 4 eggs

Directions:

1. Mix the butter with the sugars in a container until creamy and fluffy.
2. Stir in the eggs, one at a time, then put in the pumpkin puree and milk.
3. Put in the rest of the ingredients and mix thoroughly using a spatula.
4. Pour the batter in a greased Bundt cake pan and preheat your oven and bake at 350F for forty minutes or until it rises significantly and starts to appear golden-brown.
5. Let the cake cool in the pan before you serve.

Nutritional Content of One Serving:

Calories: 244 Fat: 10.7g Protein: 4.4g Carbohydrates: 33.9g

Grand Marnier Infused Loaf Cake

Total Time Taken: 2 hours

Yield: 14 Servings

Ingredients:

- ¼ cup grand Marnier
- ½ cup butter, softened
- ½ cup whole milk
- ½ teaspoon baking soda
- ½ teaspoon salt
- 1 ½ cups white sugar
- 1 cup cream cheese
- 1 cup dried cranberries
- 1 teaspoon vanilla extract
- 2 teaspoons baking powder
- 3 cups all-purpose flour
- 4 eggs

Directions:

1. Mix the cranberries and Grand Marnier in a jar and allow to soak up for an hour.
2. Mix the flour with baking powder, baking soda and salt.
3. Mix the butter, cream cheese and sugar in a container until fluffy.
4. Stir in the eggs, one at a time, then put in the vanilla and milk.
5. Fold in the flour mixture and stir until incorporated.
6. Put in the cranberries.
7. Spoon the batter in a large loaf pan coated with baking paper.
8. Pre-heat the oven and bake at 350F for about fifty minutes or until a toothpick inserted in the center comes out clean.

9. Let the cake cool in the pan then serve, sliced.

Nutritional Content of One Serving:

Calories: 336 Fat: 14.1g Protein: 6.0g Carbohydrates: 43.9g

Grand Marnier Infused Loaf Cake

Total Time Taken: 2 hours
Yield: 14 Servings
Ingredients:
- ¼ cup grand Marnier
- ½ cup butter, softened
- ½ cup whole milk
- ½ teaspoon baking soda
- ½ teaspoon salt
- 1 ½ cups white sugar
- 1 cup cream cheese
- 1 cup dried cranberries
- 1 teaspoon vanilla extract
- 2 teaspoons baking powder
- 3 cups all-purpose flour
- 4 eggs

Directions:
1. Mix the cranberries and Grand Marnier in a jar and allow to soak up for an hour.
2. Mix the flour with baking powder, baking soda and salt.
3. Mix the butter, cream cheese and sugar in a container until fluffy.
4. Stir in the eggs, one at a time, then put in the vanilla and milk.
5. Fold in the flour mixture and stir until incorporated.
6. Put in the cranberries.
7. Spoon the batter in a large loaf pan coated with baking paper.
8. Pre-heat the oven and bake at 350F for about fifty minutes or until a toothpick inserted in the center comes out clean.
9. Let the cake cool in the pan then serve, sliced.

Nutritional Content of One Serving:

Calories: 336 Fat: 14.1g Protein: 6.0g Carbohydrates: 43.9g

Granny Smith Cake

Total Time Taken: 1 ½ hours
Yield: 12 Servings

Ingredients:
- ¼ teaspoon salt
- 1 ½ cups all-purpose flour
- 1 cup canola oil
- 1 cup white sugar
- 1 cup whole milk

- 1 tablespoon lemon zest
- 1 teaspoon cinnamon powder
- 2 eggs
- 2 teaspoons baking powder
- 3 Granny Smith apples, peeled and diced

Directions:
1. Sift the flour, baking powder, salt and cinnamon in a container.
2. In a separate container, combine the canola oil, eggs and sugar until fluffy and pale. Put in the milk and lemon zest and mix thoroughly.
3. Fold in the flour then mix in the apples.
4. Spoon the batter in a 9-inch round cake pan coated with baking paper.
5. Pre-heat the oven and bake at 350F for around forty minutes or until a toothpick comes out clean after being inserted into the center of the cake.
6. Serve chilled.

Nutritional Content of One Serving:
Calories: 328 Fat: 19.8g Protein: 3.3g Carbohydrates: 36.4g

Hazelnut Chocolate Cake

Total Time Taken: 1 hour
Yield: 10 Servings
Ingredients:
- ½ cup butter
- ½ teaspoon salt
- 1 cup ground hazelnuts
- 1 cup Nutella
- 6 eggs, separated
- 6 oz. dark chocolate chips

Directions:
1. Combine the chocolate chips and butter in a heatproof container and place over a hot water bath.
2. Melt them together until smooth then turn off heat and fold in the egg yolks, followed by the Nutella and ground hazelnuts.
3. Whip the egg whites with a pinch of salt until firm then fold them in the batter using a spatula.
4. Pour the batter in a 9-inch round cake pan coated with baking paper.
5. Pre-heat the oven and bake at 350F for about half an hour.
6. Let the cake cool in the pan and serve, sliced.

Nutritional Content of One Serving:
Calories: 326 Fat: 25.3g Protein: 6.5g Carbohydrates: 22.0g

Healthier Carrot Cake

Total Time Taken: 1 ½ hours
Yield: 10 Servings

Ingredients:
- ¼ cup orange juice

- ½ cup coconut oil, melted
- ½ cup grated apples
- ½ cup quinoa powder
- ½ cup raisins
- ½ cup rolled oats
- ½ teaspoon ground ginger
- ½ teaspoon salt
- 1 ½ cups grated carrots
- 1 cup low-fat yogurt cake
- 1 cup whole wheat flour
- 1 tablespoon orange zest
- 1 teaspoon cinnamon powder
- 2 teaspoons baking powder

Directions:

1. Mix the yogurt, orange juice, coconut oil, orange zest, carrots, apples and raisins.
2. Fold in the remaining ingredients and mix using a spatula.
3. Pour the batter in a 9-inch round cake pan coated with baking paper.
4. Pre-heat the oven and bake at 350F for about fifty minutes or until a toothpick inserted into the center of the cake comes out clean.
5. The cake tastes best chilled.

Nutritional Content of One Serving:

Calories: 215 Fat: 12.0g Protein: 2.9g Carbohydrates: 25.1g

Holiday Pound Cake

Total Time Taken: 1 ¼ hours
Yield: 16 Servings

Ingredients:

- ½ teaspoon salt
- 1 cup butter, softened
- 1 cup buttermilk
- 1 cup cream cheese
- 1 teaspoon lemon zest
- 1 teaspoon orange zest
- 1 teaspoon vanilla extract
- 2 cups white sugar
- 2 teaspoons baking powder
- 3 cups all-purpose flour
- 6 eggs

Directions:

1. Mix the butter and sugar in a container until pale and light. Stir in the cream cheese and mix thoroughly.
2. Put in the eggs, one after another, then mix in the flour, baking powder and salt, alternating it with buttermilk.

3. Fold in the citrus zest and vanilla extract then spoon the batter in a large loaf cake pan coated with baking paper.
4. Preheat your oven and bake the cake for about fifty minutes or until a toothpick inserted into the center of the cake comes out clean.
5. Let the cake cool in the pan and serve, sliced.

Nutritional Content of One Serving:

Calories: 363 Fat: 18.6g Protein: 6.2g Carbohydrates: 44.5g

Honey Fig Cake

Total Time Taken: 1 hour
Yield: 8 Servings
Ingredients:
- ½ cup butter, softened
- ½ cup honey
- ½ teaspoon salt
- 1 ½ cups all-purpose flour
- 1 teaspoon baking powder
- 1 teaspoon orange zest
- 1 teaspoon vanilla extract
- 1 whole egg
- 3 egg whites
- 6 fresh figs, quartered

Directions:
1. Mix the butter, honey, egg whites and egg in a container until creamy. Put in the vanilla and orange zest and mix thoroughly.
2. Fold in the flour, baking powder and salt then spoon the batter in a 9-inch round cake pan coated with baking paper.
3. Top the batter with fig slices and preheat your oven and bake at 350F for about forty minutes.
4. Let the cake cool in the pan and serve, sliced.

Nutritional Content of One Serving:

Calories: 304 Fat: 12.4g Protein: 5.1g Carbohydrates: 45.0g

Hot Chocolate Bundt Cake

Total Time Taken: 1 hour
Yield: 12 Servings
Ingredients:

Cake:
- ½ cup canola oil
- ½ teaspoon salt
- ¾ cup butter, softened
- ¾ cup cocoa powder
- 1 cup hot water
- 1 cup light brown sugar

- 1 teaspoon vanilla extract
- 2 cups all-purpose flour
- 2 teaspoons baking powder
- 3 eggs
- 4 oz. dark chocolate, melted

Glaze:
- ½ cup heavy cream
- 1 cup dark chocolate chips

Directions:
1. For the cake, combine the butter, oil and sugar in a container until creamy and light.
2. Stir in the eggs, vanilla and melted chocolate.
3. Sift the flour with cocoa powder, baking powder and salt and fold it in the butter mixture.
4. Progressively mix in the hot water then spoon the batter in a greased Bundt cake pan.
5. Pre-heat the oven and bake at 350F for about forty minutes or until a toothpick inserted into the center of the cake comes out clean.
6. When finished, take out of the pan on a platter.
7. For the glaze, bring the cream to the boiling point then mix in the chocolate. Stir until melted and smooth.
8. Sprinkle the glaze over the cake and serve chilled.

Nutritional Content of One Serving:

Calories: 448 Fat: 29.9g Protein: 6.1g Carbohydrates: 43.6g

Jam Studded Cake

Total Time Taken: 1 hour
Yield: 8 Servings
Ingredients: 5 eggs
- ¼ cup canola oil
- ¼ teaspoon salt
- ¾ cup white sugar
- 1 cup all-purpose flour
- 1 cup apricot jam
- 1 teaspoon baking powder
- 1 teaspoon orange zest
- 1 teaspoon vanilla extract

Directions:
1. Mix the eggs and sugar in a container until its volume increases to almost three times it was.
2. Stir in the oil, vanilla and orange zest then fold in the flour, baking powder and salt.
3. Spoon the batter in 1 9-inch round cake pan coated with baking paper.
4. Drop spoonfuls of apricot jam over the batter and preheat your oven and bake at 350F for around forty minutes or until a golden-brown colour is achieved and it rises significantly.
5. Let the cake cool in the pan and serve, sliced.

Nutritional Content of One Serving:

Calories: 326 Fat: 9.8g Protein: 5.4g Carbohydrates: 57.1g

Lemon Blueberry Bundt Cake

Total Time Taken: 1 ¼ hours
Yield: 10 Servings

Ingredients:

- ½ cup butter, softened
- ½ cup cream cheese
- ½ teaspoon salt
- 1 ½ teaspoons baking powder
- 1 cup fresh blueberries
- 1 cup plain yogurt
- 1 cup white sugar
- 1 tablespoon lemon zest
- 1 teaspoon vanilla extract
- 2 cups all-purpose flour
- 2 egg whites
- 2 eggs

Directions:

1. Mix the butter, cream cheese and sugar in a container until creamy.
2. Stir in the eggs, egg whites, lemon zest and vanilla.
3. Fold in the flour, baking powder and salt, alternating it with yogurt.
4. Put in the blueberries then spoon the batter in a greased Bundt cake pan.
5. Pre-heat the oven and bake at 350F for about forty minutes or until a toothpick inserted in the center comes out clean.
6. Let the cake cool in the pan and serve, sliced.

Nutritional Content of One Serving:

Calories: 332 Fat: 14.7g Protein: 6.9g Carbohydrates: 43.9g

Lemon Ginger Cake

Total Time Taken: 1 ¼ hours
Yield: 10 Servings

Ingredients:

- ¼ cup lemon juice
- ¼ teaspoon salt
- ½ teaspoon baking powder
- 1 ½ cups white sugar
- 1 cup butter, softened
- 1 cup sour cream
- 1 tablespoon lemon zest
- 1 teaspoon baking soda
- 1 teaspoon grated ginger
- 2 ½ cups all-purpose flour
- 4 eggs

Directions:
1. Sift the flour, baking soda, baking powder and salt.
2. Mix the butter and sugar in a container until creamy and fluffy.
3. Put in the eggs, one at a time, then mix in the lemon juice, lemon zest and ginger, as well as the sour cream.
4. Fold in the sifted flour then spoon the batter in a 9-inch round cake pan coated with baking paper.
5. Pre-heat the oven and bake at 350F for around forty minutes or until a toothpick comes out clean after being inserted into the center of the cake.
6. Let the cake cool in the pan and serve, sliced.

Nutritional Content of One Serving:
Calories: 466 Fat: 25.4g Protein: 6.4g Carbohydrates: 55.5g

Lemon Raspberry Pound Cake

Total Time Taken: 1 ¼ hours
Yield: 10 Servings
Ingredients:

Cake:
- ½ cup cream cheese
- ½ teaspoon salt
- 1 ½ cups fresh raspberries
- 1 cup butter, softened
- 1 cup white sugar
- 1 teaspoon baking powder
- 1 teaspoon baking soda
- 1 teaspoon lemon zest
- 1 teaspoon vanilla extract
- 2 ¼ cups all-purpose flour
- 2 tablespoons lemon juice
- 4 eggs

Glaze:
- ½ cup cream cheese
- 1 teaspoon lemon zest
- 2 tablespoons lemon juice
- 2 tablespoons powdered sugar

Directions:
1. For the cake, sift the flour, baking soda, baking powder and salt in a container.
2. In a separate container, combine the butter, cream cheese, sugar, vanilla and lemon zest until creamy.
3. Stir in the eggs, one at a time, then put in the lemon juice.
4. Fold in the flour, mixing using a spatula.
5. Put in the raspberries then spoon the batter in a loaf cake pan coated with baking paper.
6. Pre-heat the oven and bake at 350F for about forty minutes or until a toothpick inserted into the center of the cake comes out clean.
7. When the cake is finished cooking, move it to a platter.

8. For the glaze, combine all the ingredients in a container.
9. Sprinkle the glaze over the cake and serve it fresh.

Nutritional Content of One Serving:

Calories: 466 Fat: 28.7g Protein: 7.3g Carbohydrates: 46.5g

Lemon Ricotta Cake

Total Time Taken: 1 hour
Yield: 8 Servings
Ingredients:

- ¼ cup butter, melted
- ¼ teaspoon salt
- ½ cup almond flour
- ¾ cup white sugar
- 1 ¼ cups all-purpose flour
- 1 cup ricotta cheese
- 1 teaspoon baking powder
- 2 eggs
- 2 tablespoons lemon zest

Directions:

1. Mix the cheese, eggs, sugar, butter and lemon zest in a container.
2. Fold in the flours, baking powder and salt then spoon the batter in a 8-inch round cake pan coated with baking paper.
3. Pre-heat the oven and bake at 350F for around forty minutes or until a toothpick comes out clean after being inserted into the center of the cake.
4. *The cake tastes best chilled.*

Nutritional Content of One Serving:

Calories: 262 Fat: 10.4g Protein: 7.4g Carbohydrates: 36.3g

Lemon Sprinkle Cake

Total Time Taken: 1 ¼ hours
Yield: 10 Servings
Ingredients:

Cake:

- ½ cup butter, melted
- ½ cup sour cream
- 1 ½ cups all-purpose flour
- 1 cup white sugar
- 1 teaspoon baking powder
- 2 tablespoons lemon juice
- 2 tablespoons lemon zest
- 5 eggs

Icing:

- 1 cup powdered sugar

- 1 tablespoon lemon juice
- 1 teaspoon lemon zest

Directions:
1. For the cake, combine the eggs and sugar in a container until twofold in volume and fluffy.
2. Put in the melted butter and stir lightly. Stir in the sour cream, lemon zest and lemon juice.
3. Fold in the flour, baking powder and salt then pour the batter in a 9-inch round cake pan covered with parchment paper.
4. Pre-heat the oven and bake at 350F for around forty minutes or until a golden-brown colour is achieved and it rises significantly.
5. Let the cake cool in the pan then move to a platter.
6. For the icing, combine all the ingredients then sprinkle it over the cake.
7. *Serve immediately.*

Nutritional Content of One Serving:

Calories: 330 Fat: 14.0g Protein: 5.2g Carbohydrates: 47.5g

Lime Pound Cake

Total Time Taken: 1 ¼ hours
Yield: 12 Servings

Ingredients:
- ¼ cup canola oil
- ½ cup sour cream
- ½ teaspoon salt
- 1 ½ cups white sugar
- 1 cup butter, softened
- 1 lime, zested and juiced
- 1 teaspoon baking soda
- 2 cups all-purpose flour
- 4 eggs

Directions:
1. Mix the butter, oil and sugar in a container until pale and creamy.
2. Stir in the eggs and mix thoroughly then put in the lime zest and lime juice. Stir thoroughly to mix.
3. Fold in the dry ingredients then put in the sour cream.
4. Pulse using a mixer on high speed for a minute.
5. Spoon the batter in a loaf cake pan and preheat your oven and bake at 350F for about forty minutes or until it rises significantly and starts to appear golden-brown.
6. Let the cake cool in the pan and serve, sliced.

Nutritional Content of One Serving:

Calories: 389 Fat: 23.6g Protein: 4.5g Carbohydrates: 42.0g

Madeira Cake

Total Time Taken: 1 hour
Yield: 8 Servings
Ingredients:

- ¼ cup whole milk
- ¼ teaspoon salt
- ¾ cup butter, softened
- ¾ cup white sugar
- 3 eggs
- 1 ½ cups all-purpose flour
- 1 teaspoon baking powder
- 1 teaspoon lemon zest

Directions:

1. Mix the butter and sugar in a container until creamy and firm. Put in the eggs, one at a time, then fold in the flour, baking powder and salt, alternating it with milk.
2. Put in the lemon zest then spoon the batter in a 9-inch round cake pan coated with baking paper.
3. Preheat your oven and bake the cake for around forty minutes or until it rises significantly and starts to appear golden-brown.
4. Let the cake cool in the pan and serve, sliced.

Nutritional Content of One Serving:

Calories: 337 Fat: 19.4g Protein: 4.9g Carbohydrates: 37.5g

Mango Ice Box Cake

Total Time Taken: 1 hour
Yield: 8 Servings
Ingredients:

- ½ cup white sugar
- 1 tablespoon lemon juice
- 1/3 cup sweetened condensed milk
- 15 graham crackers
- 2 cups heavy cream, whipped
- 2 ripe mangos, peeled and cubed

Directions:

1. Mix the mangos, sugar and lemon juice in a saucepan and place over low heat. Cook for about ten minutes until softened. Let cool completely.
2. To finish the cake, take a loaf pan and line it using plastic wrap.
3. Mix the cream and sweetened condensed milk.
4. Layer the crackers with the mango mixture and cream in the readied pan.
5. Wrap securely and store in the refrigerator for minimum an hour.
6. *The cake tastes best chilled.*

Nutritional Content of One Serving:

Calories: 303 Fat: 14.9g Protein: 3.5g Carbohydrates: 40.5g

Maple Syrup Apple Cake

Total Time Taken: 1 ¼ hours
Yield: 10 Servings

Ingredients:
- ¼ cup butter, softened
- ½ cup walnuts, chopped
- ½ cup whole milk
- ½ teaspoon salt
- 1 cup maple syrup
- 1 teaspoon cinnamon powder
- 1 teaspoon ground ginger
- 2 cups all-purpose flour
- 2 red apples, peeled, cored and diced
- 2 teaspoons baking powder
- 4 eggs

Directions:
1. Mix the flour, baking powder, cinnamon, ginger and salt in a container.
1. In a separate container, combine the butter and maple syrup. Stir in the eggs and the milk then fold in the flour.
2. Put in the apples and walnuts then spoon the batter in a Bundt cake pan lined using butter.
3. Pre-heat the oven and bake at 350F for around forty minutes or until it rises significantly and starts to appear golden-brown.
4. Let the cake cool in the pan and serve, sliced.

Nutritional Content of One Serving:

Calories: 306 Fat: 10.8g Protein: 6.8g Carbohydrates: 47.1g

Marble Cake

Total Time Taken: 1 hour
Yield: 10 Servings

Ingredients:
- ¼ cup cocoa powder
- ¼ cup hot water
- ½ cup butter, softened
- ½ teaspoon baking soda
- ½ teaspoon salt
- 1 cup white sugar
- 1 cup whole milk
- 1 teaspoon vanilla extract
- 2 ½ cups all-purpose flour
- 2 teaspoon baking powder
- 3 eggs

Directions:
1. Mix the cocoa powder with hot water in a small container.

2. Mix the butter and sugar in a container until creamy and firm. Put in the eggs, one at a time, then mix in the vanilla and milk.
3. Fold in the flour, baking powder, baking soda and salt.
4. Divide the batter in half. Spoon one half in a loaf pan coated with baking paper.
5. Mix the half that is left over of batter with the cocoa mixture.
6. Spoon the cocoa batter over the white one and swirl it around with a toothpick.
7. Preheat your oven and bake the cake at 350F for around forty minutes or until a toothpick inserted in the center comes out clean.
8. Let the cake cool in the pan and serve, sliced.

Nutritional Content of One Serving:

Calories: 311 Fat: 11.9g Protein: 6.2g Carbohydrates: 46.8g

CPSIA information can be obtained
at www.ICGtesting.com
Printed in the USA
BVHW011145040122
625446BV00013B/302